399 **KANSAS Characters**

399 KANSAS Characters

By Dave Webb

Illustrated by Phillip R. Buntin

Introduction by Dr. Leo E. Oliva
Historical consultant to the
Kansas Heritage Center

Kansas Heritage Center

Dodge City, Kansas

Kansas Heritage Center, PO Box 1275,
Dodge City, KS 67801 (316) 227-1616

Library of Congress Cataloging-in-Publication Data

Webb, Dave, 1948-
   399 Kansas characters/by Dave Webb; illustrated by Phillip R. Buntin;
introduction by Leo E. Oliva.
       p.   cm.
   Includes index.
   Summary: Biographical sketches of people "important to an understanding
of Kansas history and society."
   ISBN 1-882404-02-5 (pbk.): $19.95
   1. Kansas—Biography.   2. Kansas—Miscellanea.   [1. Kansas—Biography.]
   I. Title.
CT235.W43   1992
920.0781—dc20   92-73654
                                                           CIP
                                                           AC

Printed by Spearville News, Incorporated, Spearville, Kansas

6988

To Betty Braddock

who dedicated 25 years to preserving
our state's heritage at the
Kansas Heritage Center

Introduction

Have you ever been ashamed of being from Kansas? Have you thought that everything important happened someplace else and that life must be better in other states? Have you believed that all the interesting people live elsewhere? If so, you are not alone, but you are wrong. Kansas has an illuminating and enchanting heritage despite the stereotypical view that it is the flat, gray, backwater, dull and barren place where Dorothy and Toto survived until they were swept to the Land of Oz by a tornado.

As Dorothy eventually learned upon her return to Kansas, however, and as every Kansan should know, the real characters are in Kansas. Kansas, which has had an image problem since explorers of European ancestry arrived on the scene and called it a desert fit only for American Indians, actually provides a remarkable variety of landscapes, historical experiences, and, most important of all, people. Individuals comprise the most consequential part of the rich Kansas heritage, and they demonstrate the fallacies of the many derogatory impressions that too many people have about the state.

To understand what Kansas means, we must look at its diverse mixture of people, including those who are famous and infamous, noteworthy and ordinary, colorful and drab, profound and humorous, congenial and contemptible, legendary and unrenowned, and complex and simple. It is important to keep in mind that not every Kansan has been a William Allen White, Amelia Earhart, Gordon Parks, Dwight David Eisenhower, or Nancy Landon Kassebaum. Such notables are only part of the story. All types of characters comprise the state's heritage, and they are chronicled here because they are essential parts of that history. The good, the bad, and the indifferent are included, for they were here and need to be comprehended. Until now, with the publication of this splendid volume, it has been difficult for students and general readers to locate the widely scattered information about so many Kansas characters.

Dave Webb has provided an extraordinary service by compiling this authoritative and well-written collection of biographical sketches, a project for which he is uniquely qualified. With 22 years of experience as a classroom teacher in several Kansas communities, nine summers as a member of the staff of the Kansas Heritage Center, author of numerous excellent publications about Kansas printed by the Heritage Center, and presently its assistant director, Webb demonstrates distinctive talents of diligent research and inspiring communication. He is a tenacious seeker of truthfulness and a painstaking writer who narrates interesting stories without being excessively pedantic. The result is as pleasurable to read as it is informative.

The subjects for this book were obviously chosen from among thousands of possibilities. The primary consideration has been a Kansas connection, and the basic prerequisites have been either that the person was born in Kansas or lived in Kansas at some time. The author has attempted to include a cross section of natives and sojourners from many facets of life, and all individuals are important to an understanding of Kansas history and society.

This is an introduction to Kansas characters, not the sum total of all who deserve attention nor the final word on any of those included. As you read about these personalities you will want to learn more about many of them, and you should think of additional Kansans who can be added and, then gather details about them. If you live in Kansas, you and your family are part of this ongoing story. To know the characters of Kansas is to understand the true heritage of a remarkable state, a heritage that illuminates the past, defines much about the present, and points the way for the future. You will be proud to be a part of the Kansas saga. Perhaps your accomplishments, inspired by the stories related here, will be included in a subsequent edition about Kansas characters.

Dr. Leo E. Oliva

Preface

Fitting 399 Kansas characters into one volume has not been an easy task. This collection of biographical sketches developed out of *Kansas Characters*, a set of folders on fifteen Kansans I wrote for the Kansas Heritage Center in 1987. While gathering material for an expanded version, I watched the list of potential characters grow, enlarge—and then explode. Soon the question was not who to *include*, but who to *exclude*. Time and space finally forced me to limit this book to 399-plus people and animals. (Readers should note that the length of each story is not necessarily based on the amount of time a character spent in Kansas, nor should it be used to gauge a person's importance in our state's history.) Obviously, many interesting and influential characters with Kansas connections are missing from these pages.

Character sketches are listed numerically and are arranged alphabetically within chapters. Characters are indexed by boldface **guide numbers** and by page numbers. Bracketed numbers [**399**] in the text are cross references to numbered characters.

Towns and cities listed at the beginning of each sketch are the Kansas locations where an individual is known to have lived. With some exceptions, cities where a character attended college or served in the military are not listed if the location is also mentioned in the text. Topeka is not listed as the home of a state politician unless he or she lived there before or after holding office.

Other characters, with their names highlighted in bold, have Kansas connections, too. They are included within the numbered character sketches or at the ends of chapters. These other characters are indexed by page numbers only.

The eight chapters are an attempt to group the characters into categories—but Kansans, like their state, sometimes defy description. Were Carry Nation and John Brown crusaders or criminals? Was Arthur Capper a politician or businessman? Are John Cody and Don Coldsmith doctors or authors? Is Gordon Parks a composer or filmmaker or photojournalist? In most cases, characters will be found in the category by which they are best known. When in doubt, readers should consult the index.

This book would not have been possible without the generous support of my fellow staff members at the Kansas Heritage Center. Betty Braddock, retired director, helped edit the manuscript and gave valuable advice in selecting characters. Noel Ary, director, battled cantankerous copy machines to meet deadlines and was a constant source of support and encouragement. Librarian Jeanie Covalt—armed with her vertical file and card catalog—worked magic time after time in tracking down elusive facts. Barbara Vincent, secretary, funneled phone calls and correspondence to and from characters, libraries, historical societies and other sources. Thank you, Betty, Noel, Jeanie and Barb.

Phillip R. Buntin, chairman of the art department and instructor at Garden City High School, spent untold hours creating artwork for this book. Thanks, Phil, for being an artist-on-call and for sharing your time and wonderful talent.

I owe special thanks to the Heritage Center's historical consultant, Dr. Leo E. Oliva. A noted Kansas historian and former chairman of the history department at Fort Hays State University, Leo gave up time from his own writing projects and farming operation to read the manuscript. I sincerely appreciate his valuable suggestions. This book's accuracy has been greatly enhanced by the fact that he is always willing to share his knowledge of Kansas and Kansans.

The staff of the Kansas State Historical Society was also very helpful. Patricia Michaelis, Virgil Dean, Thomas Barr, Nancy Sherbert and personnel at the society's library deserve thanks for their research assistance. Others who contributed information are included in the source notes.

Researching and writing *399 Kansas Characters* has reinforced my belief that history is much more than dusty files full of forgotten facts. History is people—intriguing personalities—just waiting to introduce themselves to the interested reader.

Dave Webb

Source notes

Because the number of sources consulted in compiling this book runs into several thousand, a comprehensive bibliography has not been included.

For general Kansas history, these books were useful: Robert Richmond, *Kansas, Land of Contrasts* (1989); William Frank Zornow, *Kansas, A History of the Jayhawk State* (1957); John D. Bright, editor, *Kansas, The First Century* (1956); Louise Barry, *The Beginning of the West, 1540-1854* (1972); Daniel W. Wilder, *The Annals of Kansas, 1541-1885* (1886); Kirke Mechem, editor, *The Annals of Kansas, 1886-1925* (1956); Sondra Van Meter McCoy and Jan Hults, *1001 Kansas Place Names* (1989); Huber Self and Homer E. Socolofsky, *Historical Atlas of Kansas* (1988); Robert Baughman, *Kansas Post Offices* (1961); and William E. Connelley, *History of Kansas Newspapers* (1916).

In many cases, the information on individual characters is based on biographies and autobiographies from various publishers. Many characters were also found in issues of the Kansas State Historical Society's publications: *Kansas Historical Transactions* (1875-1880), *Kansas Historical Collections* (1881-1928), *Kansas Historical Quarterly* (1931-1977), and *Kansas History, A Journal of the Central Plains* (1978-1992). Other Kansas publications consulted were *Kanhistique*, *Kansas!* magazine and *KS* magazine. Most helpful were newspaper clippings and magazine articles from the libraries of the Kansas Heritage Center, Dodge City, and the Kansas State Historical Society, Topeka.

Biographical dictionaries were also consulted, including: Susan L. Stetler, editor, *Almanac of Famous People* (1989); *Webster's Biographical Dictionary* (1980); Howard R. Lamar, *The Reader's Encyclopedia of the American West* (1977); Charles Van Doren, editor, *Webster's American Biographies* (1974); and various editions of *Who's Who in America, Current Yearbook and Biography* and *Contemporary Authors*.

In addition to numerous county histories, Kansas characters were also found in these books: Homer E. Socolofsky, *Kansas Governors* (1990); David Dary, *True Tales of Old-Time Kansas* (1984) and *More True Tales of Old-Time Kansas* (1987); Nyle H. Miller and Joseph W. Snell, *Great Gunfighters of the Kansas Cowtowns, 1867-1886* (1963); D. Arie Delci, *El Camino Real, A Journal of Kansas Hispanic Profiles* (1990); Beccy Tanner, *Bear Grease, Builders and Bandits: The Men and Women of Wichita's Past* (1991); and Howard

Inglish, editor, *Larry Hatteberg's Kansas People, A Collection of Colorful Personalities from the Sunflower State* (1991).

These characters supplied additional information: Robert D. Ballard, Paul Bentrup, Abram Burnett IV, Don Carlton, Ellis "Skip" Cave, Paul Coker, John Cody, Lynn Dickey, Ed Dwight, Daniel Foley, Henry Harvey, William Stafford, Richard Taylor, Bradbury Thompson, Arthur Tonne, Jeanne Williams and Waldo Wedel. Friends and family members gave information on: Durrell Armstrong, Max Ary, Joe Bossi, Nolan Cromwell, John W. Dinsmoor, William Eckert, Jesse Harper, Stan Herd, Shirley Knight, Chip Lagerbom, Will Menninger, Franc Shor and Lyle Yost.

Government agencies and organizations: Kansas Supreme Court, Kansas Film Commission, Kansas Business Hall of Fame, Kansas All Sports Hall of Fame, Kansas National Educational Association, The International Group for Historic Aircraft Recovery and the offices of Senator Nancy Kassebaum and Representative Pat Roberts. Corporations: Beechcraft, Cessna Aircraft, Coleman Company, Dillons food stores, Duckwall-ALCO Stores, Hallmark Cards, H&R Block income tax services, Pizza Hut restaurants, Reuter Organ Company, Rubbermaid Corporation and White Castle hamburgers. County historical societies: Atchison, Clark, Cowley, Finney, Morton, Rawlins, Sherman, Smith and Wichita/Sedgwick, and Steve Jansen at the Watkins Museum, Lawrence. Public libraries: Beloit, Dodge City, Johnson County, Kiowa County, Lyons, Oberlin, Protection, Salina, Stockton and Wellington, as well as the Kansas State Library and KU Archives. Universities: Emporia State, Fort Hays State, Kansas, Kansas State, Pittsburg State and Wichita State. Newspapers: Libraries at the *Hutchinson News* and *Wichita Eagle*; staff of the Elkhart *Tri-State News*, *Kinsley Mercury* and *Lindsborg News-Record*; as well as Marion Boner of the *Independence Daily Reporter* and Bob Greer of the *Protection Press*. Other sources were Joe Collins; J.W. Irons; authors Thomas Fox Averill and Robert Smith Bader; and Larry Hatteberg, KAKE-TV.

Permission to reproduce copyrighted artwork was secured through Richard Crowson, the *Wichita Eagle*; Grace Darby, *The New Yorker* magazine; Hank Ketcham; Elizabeth Nolan, King Features Syndicate; the U.S. Postal Service; ESU; FHSU; K-State; KU; PSU; WSU and the corporations whose logos are included.

Contents

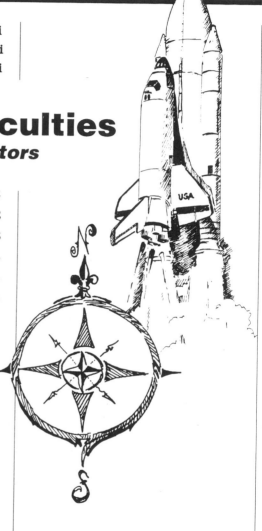

To the Stars through Difficulties
Explorers, Scientists, Adventurers and Aviators

Serving State & Nation
Soldiers and Politicians

U.S. 6c POSTAGE

DWIGHT D.
EISENHOWER

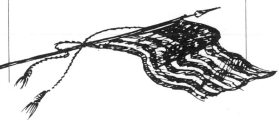

Movers & Shakers
Crusaders, Doctors and Educators

Dollars & Sense
Entrepreneurs and Inventors

Contents

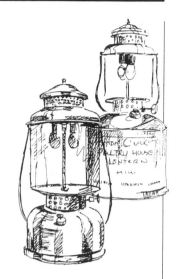

With Pen & Brush
Authors, Artists and Composers

Contents

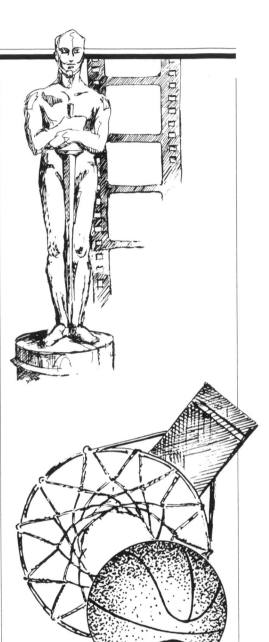

Fun & Games
Entertainers and Athletes

Contents

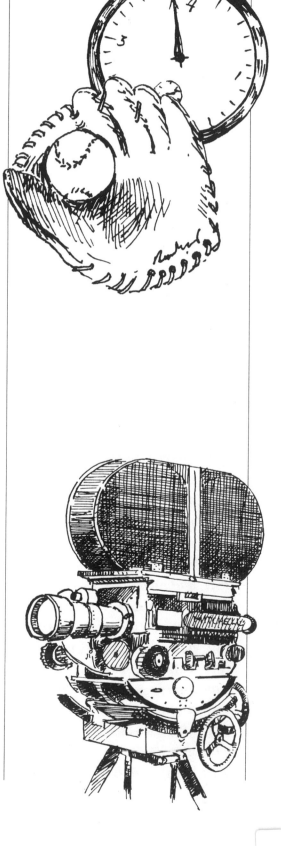

Wild & Woolly
Law Officers, Lawbreakers and Colorful Characters

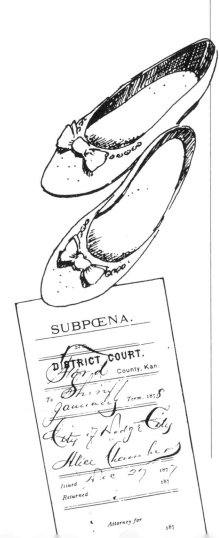

Fur & Feathers
Mammals, Birds and other Animals

To the Stars through Difficulties

Explorers, Scientists, Adventurers and Aviators

Runs Kansas' first space station

1 Max Ary

Space expert. Greensburg and Hutchinson. (Born 1950) Ary became interested in space when he worked at the Hutchinson planetarium during college. He had planned to earn a degree in biology, but by the time he graduated from Wichita State University, he had studied physics, chemistry and education. The 22-year-old Ary then used his talents to become the director of the Noble Planetarium in Fort Worth, Texas. There he met astronaut Alan Bean and worked part-time for NASA, the National Aeronautics and Space Administration.

Max returned to Kansas in 1976 to direct construction of a space museum at the Hutchinson planetarium. Today the Kansas Cosmosphere and Space Center is respected across the country and around the world. About 350,000 persons a year visit its galleries to see space artifacts from American and Soviet space missions.

Ary is the Cosmosphere's executive director. He has shared his knowledge on space as a consultant for the Smithsonian Institution, Paramount Pictures, NASA and even several astronauts. He has helped design space museums in foreign countries, including Japan and South Korea. He has also traveled to the former Soviet Union where he has friends in the Russian space program. ■

Flies across the state without wings

2 Francis X. Aubry

Santa Fe Trail trader. (1824-1854) Aubry set an amazing speed record on horseback across Kansas. As a 23-year-old Santa Fe trader, he decided he could make more money by hauling goods from Missouri to Santa Fe two or three times a year, instead of only once.

In late 1847, Francis rode from Santa Fe to Missouri to buy wagons, animals and supplies. By sending men and extra animals on ahead, he was able to make this first ride in just fourteen days, breaking the old record by ten and a half days.

He arrived back in Santa Fe with his first wagon train in late April. His second ride across Kansas in May was even quicker: eight days, ten hours. After he and his second caravan reached New Mexico in August, young Aubry made a third ride back to Missouri. It was the most unbelievable.

From September 12 to 17 he covered all 770 miles of the Santa Fe Trail—in only five days and sixteen hours! During that time, the "Skimmer of the Plains" claimed he ate only six meals and slept just two and a half hours. He traveled 600 miles through mud, ruined six horses, rode his favorite horse **Dolly** almost 200 miles in 26 hours—and still walked twenty miles! Aubry's record still stands. His third wagon train finally made it to Santa Fe that winter.

Aubry, who was born in Canada and came to the United States as a teenager, traveled the route of the Santa Fe Trail 27 times. He died at age 29 after being stabbed during an argument in a Santa Fe bar. ■

Solves deep mysteries

Undersea explorer, geologist, oceanographer, engineer and author. Wichita. (Born 1942)
Ballard's career has taken him to new heights—and depths. Since the early 1970s his undersea expeditions have discovered new marine life, unusual ocean geology and historic shipwrecks. Ballard's biggest find has been the *Titanic*—the "unsinkable" British passenger liner that rammed an iceberg and sank on its maiden voyage in 1912.

Loves the sea

Robert was born miles from the sea, in Wichita, on June 30, 1942. **William Ballard**, his grandfather, was marshal of Wichita and died in a gun battle there in 1920. Other Ballards arrived in Kansas just after the Civil War. But World War II took young Robert and his parents away from their home state.

In the mid 1940s they moved to southern California. His father was a test flight engineer and was transferred to a Mojave Desert test site during the war. Later, the elder Ballard became the U.S. Navy's representative at the Scripps Institution of Oceanography. This brought the family to a home near the Pacific Ocean where Robert spent most of his free time at the beach.

As a teenager, he was interested in scuba diving. Unlike his surfboarding friends he wanted to explore the world just below the ocean's surface. He also explored the world of books; his favorites were *20,000 Leagues Under the Sea*

and the true-life adventures of his idols, explorers Martin and Osa Johnson [**18-19**].

In 1965 Robert received a bachelor's degree in chemistry and geology at the University of California. He then spent a year studying marine geology at the University of Hawaii. To help pay his expenses, he worked at a marine park, training a pair of dolphins to dive through hoops.

During the Vietnam War, Robert was called into the U.S. Navy. He and his wife Marjorie moved to Massachusetts where he was assigned as a researcher at the Woods Hole Oceanographic Institution. Located on Cape Cod, it is one of the world's most important institutes for the study of the sea.

Titanic *dreams*

Ballard soon joined the Boston Sea Rovers, a group for those interested in underwater exploration. At club meetings he listened to the famous French ocean explorer Jacques Cousteau and other adventurers. At the same time, he began to dream about finding the world's greatest shipwreck, the *Titanic*.

When Ballard's Navy duty ended in 1969, he decided to stay at Woods Hole as a research associate in ocean engineering. Five years later he received his doctor's degree in marine geology and geophysics. At the same time, he was promoted to associate scientist, and later, assistant scientist. In 1983 he became a senior scientist.

Deep-sea designs

In 1973 Robert helped design a three-person submarine for the U.S. Navy. *Alvin*, as it is called, is capable of diving 13,000 feet deep—nearly two and one-half miles! In order to withstand the tremendous underwater pressure at that depth, *Alvin*'s hull is made of titanium, a very strong metal.

As he worked on the small sub, Ballard again thought of the *Titanic*. Titanium. . .*Titanic*. Suddenly he realized *Alvin* could dive deep enough to find the *Titanic*. At the time, however, few people were interested in such an expedition. So for twelve years he dreamed and planned. During that time, Ballard took part in a variety of other projects and deep-sea expeditions.

Undersea adventure

In 1973 and 1974 he made more than a dozen dives in *Alvin* to map the Mid-Atlantic ⇨

Ridge, an enormous underwater mountain range in the Atlantic Ocean. He and *Alvin*'s crew were guided by photographs taken by *Angus*—a remote-controlled underwater camera sled that he designed.

In the winter of 1975-76 he was chief scientist of a French-American expedition to the Cayman Trough, a 24,000-foot-deep gash in the sea floor south of Cuba. Ballard directed divers and marine geologists in *Alvin* and the Navy's bathyscaphe *Trieste*, a special submarine-like vehicle that can dive even deeper than *Alvin*. Expedition members made the first accurate map of the Cayman area. They also used *Alvin*'s mechanical arm to collect rock samples from the trough—the deepest layer of rock ever gathered from the seabed.

A year later Ballard joined an expedition to the Galapagos Rift in the Pacific Ocean west of Ecuador. Using the cameras on *Angus*, Ballard and his fellow scientists discovered several new species of marine life: giant clams, crabs and eight-foot red worms living in pockets of warm mineral water spouting from deep volcanic cracks.

In 1979 he found the spectacular black smokers. These underwater vents off the coast of Baja California shoot out hot liquids through chimneys of lava on the seafloor.

By the early 1980s, Robert had spent more time in the deep ocean than any other scientist. To further his research, he designed *Argo*, an unmanned diving vehicle. With money from the Office of Naval Research he then built the system. Loaded with powerful strobe lights, sonar scanners, computer-enhanced underwater cameras and a robot arm, *Argo* can dive to 20,000 feet.

Dreams into reality

When Ballard suggested to U.S. Navy officials that the *Titanic* search would be a fitting test for *Argo*, they agreed. His plans and dreams were taking shape at last.

In the summer of 1985 he gathered his equipment and a team of American and French marine scientists. On the French ship *Le Suroit* they headed for the *Titanic*'s last known position.

The weather in the North Atlantic is unpredictable much of the year, but the explorers felt

they could safely operate their sensitive gear for part of the summer. During six weeks in June and July, they crisscrossed the area, hoping to spot signs of the *Titanic* with a new French sonar device. They found nothing.

For the rest of the expedition, Ballard and his French partner, Jean-Louis Michel, moved to the American ship *Knorr*. They began the search again, this time towing the *Argo* and its cameras back and forth over the target area.

During the night of September 1, with less than a week of good weather left, they finally spotted something on the control room's video screen. Debris passed by, followed by images of something very large and round—a boiler from the *Titanic*'s engine room. Straight below—nearly two and one-half miles down—lay the wreck of the *Titanic*.

The expedition spent the next few days photographing the scene with cameras on the *Argo* and *Angus*. Although the wreck lay in two parts, much of the ship was still recognizable after decades at the bottom of the sea.

Ten months later, Ballard and his team returned to the wreck site. With help from the U.S. Navy he brought along *Alvin* and the Navy's newest self-propelled underwater robot, *Jason Junior*, or *JJ*. With the robot attached to *Alvin*, Dr. Ballard and two others dived to the *Titanic*—becoming the first humans in 74 years to see the ship. They found the stern, or rear portion, torn and mangled. But the bow, in Robert's words, was still "majestic."

Carefully, they set *Alvin* on the top deck and maneuvered *JJ* into the ship's lower levels. Through the robot's cameras and the windows of *Alvin* the explorers identified thousands of objects, many of them perfectly preserved. On one of their last dives, Ballard used *Alvin's* robot arm to place a plaque on the *Titanic's* stern. It honored the over 1,500 victims who died when the ship sank in 1912.

Using the hours of videotape and thousands of photographs they shot, Ballard and other experts then pieced together the last tragic minutes of the *Titanic*.

Expedition educator

Dr. Ballard is currently director of the Center for Marine Exploration at Woods Hole. He continues to travel the world making deep-sea expeditions, over 50 at last count.

In 1988 he discovered a sunken 1,600-year-old Roman sailing ship. The next year he explored the ancient wreck with his underwater robots—and shared the experience with thousands of children in television broadcasts from the Mediterranean Sea. It was the first live expedition broadcast sponsored by the JASON Foundation for Education, founded by Ballard.

He has also helped prepare television programs for PBS, TBS, the U.S. Navy, plus British, Japanese and German television networks. He has written four books and over 40 articles for scientific journals and magazines, including *National Geographic*. Although he lost valuable equipment in a 1991 barge accident, Dr. Ballard hopes someday to search the Great Lakes for sunken vessels from the War of 1812. He also wants to make live television broadcasts from the *Titanic*. ■

Trailblazing to Santa Fe

4 William Becknell

Santa Fe Trail trader. (About 1787-1856) Becknell created the Santa Fe Trail, the first major highway across Kansas. All he really wanted to do, however, was pay his bills.

In the fall of 1821, Becknell was living in Missouri. He was nearly broke and his creditors were angry. When they wanted to put him in prison, William decided to leave town. He told others he planned to catch wild horses, trap fur-bearing animals and trade with Indians. He hoped to earn enough money to pay off his debts. Today, some historians believe Becknell secretly planned to go to Santa Fe from the start.

With a few men and pack animals loaded with trade items, Becknell left Franklin, Missouri, and crossed Kansas. Mexican troops met the Missourians near the Rocky Mountains and invited them into Santa Fe. Mexicans had just won their freedom from Spain and they were eager to trade with Americans. Becknell quickly sold all his trade goods and returned to Missouri with silver coins, mules and blankets. Everyone, including his creditors, was impressed with his results. The Santa Fe trade had begun.

Becknell headed for Santa Fe again the next year, and on that trip he took the first wagons across Kansas. He avoided the steep mountain trails of his first trip by taking a shortcut that followed the Cimarron River toward New Mexico. Other traders took his lead, and for years this Cimarron Cutoff was the main route of the Santa Fe Trail.

For his work, Becknell was called the Father of the Santa Fe Trail. The trail helped put Kansas on the map. ■

Beaten by a girl

5 Napoleon Boone

First white boy born in Kansas. Present Jefferson County. (1828-1850) Napoleon, according to available records, was the first white boy born in Kansas. His August 22, 1828, birthday made him about two years younger than the state's first native-born white girl [23]. He was the twelfth and last child of ***Daniel M.*** and ***Sarah Boone***, and the grandson of frontiersman Daniel Boone. Baby Boone was born at the Kansa Indian Agency where his father was an agricultural advisor beginning about 1827. The Boone family moved to Missouri in the early 1830s. Napoleon died in California at the age of 21. ■

Lost in the Bermuda Triangle

6 Joe Bossi

U.S. Navy pilot. Arkansas City. (1924-1945) Bossi was the pilot of a training plane that disappeared off the coast of Florida during the night of December 5, 1945. His Avenger torpedo bomber and four others were manned by a group of fourteen pilots and student pilots based at Fort Lauderdale Naval Air Base.

After making a practice bombing run, Flight 19 ran into trouble. First, the lead plane's two compasses failed. Then heavy clouds confused the commanding pilot. As the mission continued, the men became disoriented in the darkness.

According to the pilots' radio conversations heard in the control tower, Bossi tried to convince the lost commander to turn west. The lieutenant refused, believing he was already west of Florida over the Gulf of Mexico. Bossi eventually pulled out of formation in hopes of reaching land. His last message was, "This is FT3. I'm ditching." By that time the commander's plane and the other three aircraft in the formation had already ditched into the ocean as well. Bossi and his crew were on the last plane to go down. None of the fliers or their planes was ever seen again. A rescue plane with a crew of thirteen also vanished.

The disappearance of the "Lost Squadron," as Flight 19 came to be called, helped create the myth of the Bermuda Triangle. Over the years, stories have grown as other planes and ships have been lost in the imaginary triangle connecting Bermuda, Puerto Rico and the southern tip of Florida.

Some feel the missing craft were taken into outer space by "flying saucers." Others believe they were pulled under the sea by forces from the lost continent of Atlantis. One theory says they vanished into another dimension. However, many people agree lost planes and ships are no more common in the Bermuda Triangle than anywhere else. During World War II, for example, the U.S. Navy lost more than 100 Avengers in the sea.

In 1991, high-tech explorers believed they had explained the mystery of Bossi's and Flight 19's disappearance. An underwater salvage company looking for old Spanish galleons discovered five Avengers just east of Fort Lauderdale. Markings on the planes, however, did not match those on the aircraft flown by Bossi and his friends. The newly-found Avengers had been lost in other missions.

Bossi, who grew up in Arkansas City, attended KU a short time before he joined the Navy at age eighteen. Joe loved to fly and spent three years training to be a pilot. Ironically, his plane wouldn't start on that fateful December night. The grounded Kansan needed one more flight to complete that part of his training, so he convinced his roommate to trade aircraft. In doing so, Bossi unknowingly flew off into history with the Lost Squadron. ■

Up in the air over helium

7 Hamilton Cady

Chemist and educator. Council Grove and Lawrence. (1874-1943) Cady was an assistant professor of chemistry at Kansas University when he heard of a problem in Dexter. The town had a new gas well, but the strange stuff refused to burn.

Cady analyzed samples of the gas in 1905 and discovered it was nearly two percent helium. Dexter's "gas" well was actually the best source of helium then known in North America. At that time, however, helium was mostly a novelty. Boys from Dexter, for instance, liked to fill buckets with the lighter-than-air gas and watch them float.

During World War I the U.S. government asked Dr. Cady to work on a secret project to find materials from which to make helium-filled observation balloons. He later helped set up a helium plant in Texas. ■

Travels the Kansas crossroads

Fur trader, scout, soldier and Indian agent. (1809-1868) Carson was a legend in the Old West. Although he never lived in Kansas, he had several adventures within the state, most along the Santa Fe Trail. He was born on his parents' farm in Kentucky, December 24, 1809. The family moved to Missouri a few years later.

Runaway on the trail

After his father died, fourteen-year-old Kit was apprenticed to a saddle maker in Franklin, Missouri. Young Carson liked his master, but he did not want to spend the rest of his life making saddles, so he ran away. Following the law, the kindly saddle maker advertised his apprentice's disappearance, but he offered a reward of just one cent for Carson's return.

By that time, seventeen-year-old Kit was in Kansas headed down the Santa Fe Trail. Working as a herder, he soon saw how dangerous the trail could be.

One of the men in their party accidentally shot himself in the arm. By the time the wagons had reached Walnut Creek near present Great Bend, the arm was badly infected. Young Kit watched while a volunteer cut off the injured limb with a razor and saw. To stop the bleeding, the "doctor" heated a large wagon bolt in the campfire, burned the open wound, and then covered it with tar from a wagon wheel! Amazingly, the victim recovered.

Carson spent the next several years trapping from the Rocky Mountains to California and into the Dakotas. In the early 1840s he met ***John C. Frémont*** who was preparing to explore the West. Frémont offered him $100 a month to be his guide. Although Carson led the explorer through the Rockies and into California and Oregon, it was Frémont who was given the nickname "Pathfinder."

Back on the Santa Fe Trail in 1843, Carson rescued a caravan of Mexican traders when he rode to New Mexico to get them a military escort. He traveled alone through dangerous Indian territory.

During the Mexican War, Carson guided troops from Santa Fe to California, and carried messages east to Washington, D.C. As he returned west, Carson helped chase Comanche raiders away from a wagon caravan camped at Pawnee Rock.

Targeted for death

Carson's adventurous life nearly ended on the Santa Fe Trail in 1851. He was camped just below Chouteau's Island in present Kearny County when a Cheyenne chief approached. The Indian had just been horsewhipped by an Army officer for no good reason; he decided to take out his anger on the next American he met. Carson was his target.

The quick-thinking Kit sent a runner to find a detachment of troops he knew was somewhere ahead. Carson warned the chief that the soldiers would hunt down any murdering Indians. The angry Cheyenne wasn't convinced, until Carson pointed out his runner's footprints alongside the tracks of the troops. The bluff worked. The chief changed his mind, little realizing Kit's "rescue squad" was actually days away.

In the Civil War Carson was a colonel of New Mexican volunteers. He battled Confederates in New Mexico, was sent on campaigns against Apache and Navaho Indians in Arizona, and fought Kiowas and Comanches at Adobe Walls, Texas. He established Camp Nichols on the Santa Fe Trail in 1865 and then commanded Fort Union, New Mexico, for a time.

Carson left the Army in 1867 and joined his family in southeastern Colorado. His wife died the next spring, after giving birth to their seventh child. Kit died at nearby Fort Lyon a month later, May 23, 1868. ∎

Makes magic peanuts

Agricultural scientist. Fort Scott, Olathe, Minneapolis and Beeler. (About 1864-1943)
Carver was born in Missouri, probably near the end of the Civil War. His parents were slaves, and while he was a baby, his father was killed in an accident. About the same time, Carver's mother Mary was bought by a German farm couple, Moses Carver and his wife. The Carvers hated slavery, however, so they gave Mary her freedom. They also let her and her children live with them. Because many slaves did not have last names, the Carvers gave infant George their name. They later chose Washington for his middle name because he was known for his honesty.

Kidnapped

One night, Confederate raiders kidnapped George and his mother. These bushwhackers sold blacks as slaves in the South. In hopes of finding Mary and her baby, the Carvers gave a neighbor a $300 horse to look for them. But all the searcher found was little George under a tree—cold, wet and nearly dead. His mother was never seen again.

George stayed with the Carvers until about age ten. At that time he began attending a school for black children in Neosho, Missouri. For the next several years, he went to school in various towns while he lived with different families.

Carver in Kansas

When he was about thirteen Carver came to Kansas to attend school at Fort Scott. With no friends or family nearby, he supported himself by doing laundry at the Wilder House. His room was a cot on the hotel's back porch.

After three years, he joined a railroad construction crew for a summer. He spent hot days roasting meat over open fires, washing dishes and carrying water buckets to laborers. Although the work was hard and George was small for his age, he enjoyed the chance to live in the great outdoors. That fall he cooked on a ranch and traveled into New Mexico for a short time. There he examined and sketched the fascinating desert plants.

Back in Kansas, George found work at a barbershop in Olathe. Soon he was taken in by kindly **"Aunt Lucy" Seymour**, an ex-slave from Virginia. Carver attended school, worked evenings and Saturdays in the barbershop, and helped Lucy with her laundry business. When she and her husband moved west to Minneapolis, George went along. He graduated from high school there in 1885.

The next year, Carver received a scholarship to attend Highland University in northeastern Kansas. However, when he arrived for classes and university officials discovered he was black, George was turned away. Their school was for whites only, the president said.

Discouraged, Carver went to work on a farm. When he heard others talking of homesteading in western Kansas, he went too. Soon he had a homesteader's claim in Ness County.

Curious about his new home, Carver observed and made sketches of the plants and animals in Ness County. He had had an interest in nature since childhood; as his interest grew friends began to call him the "Plant Doctor." Although he was happy with his new life, in the back of his mind he knew he must someday return to school. In 1888 that desire to learn took him away from Kansas.

College student

George moved to Indianola, Iowa, and entered Simpson College. Although few if any blacks had attended the church school, Carver was gladly accepted. As he studied he earned money by doing laundry for other students. Along with his ability in science, instructors discovered he had talent in art and music, and encouraged him to study those fields.

At the same time he was drawn to science classes. By 1891 George's professors convinced him he should be a scientist. Because they couldn't offer the courses he need, George transferred to the state agricultural college at Ames, Iowa.

There he continued his science studies, but he couldn't give up music and art. He took vocal

training to improve the unusual quality of his speaking voice. He sang so well in the college quartet that he was offered a scholarship to a Boston music school. He also painted and created remarkably lifelike illustrations of flowers and other plants. Several of his paintings were exhibited at the 1893 Chicago World's Fair.

When Carver earned his bachelor of science degree in 1894 he was made a member of the college staff, the first African-American on the faculty of Iowa State. For two years he worked as an assistant in the botany department while earning his master's degree.

During his years at Ames, he wrestled over his future. He knew wanted to work with plants—but as an artist or scientist? A letter from Alabama helped him decide.

300 peanut products

In 1896 Booker T. Washington asked him to become head of the agriculture department at Tuskegee Institute, a college he had founded for blacks. Carver, who wanted to give opportunities to young people like himself, knew he must answer Washington's call. He moved to Alabama.

Along with teaching, he worked to help poor Southern farmers. He studied different plants, looking for crops to plant on land worn out from growing cotton year after year. Not only did Carver find several crops that nourished the soil, but he invented new uses for them as well.

He made soybeans into plastic and sweet potatoes into cereal. From peanuts he made milk, cheese, coffee, paper, insulation, wallboard, shaving cream—and over 300 more by-

products! He also made wood shavings into synthetic marble, cotton into paving blocks, and weeds into foods and medicines. He worked with Henry Ford on a process to make rubber from goldenrod.

To share his discoveries, he held an annual farmer's conference at Tuskegee. He also sent his best pupils on the road with a wagon—and later a truck—full of demonstrations to improve farming. When he needed money to fund his programs, he took his musical talent on tour, giving concerts at the piano.

Honored scientist

In all, Dr. Carver wrote over 40 publications about his research with plants. Although he received many awards, he was always known for his humbleness. When Thomas Edison offered him a high-paying job in his research laboratory, Carver said he preferred to stay at Tuskegee. And, during the almost 50 years he worked at the school, he refused any raises in his yearly salary of $1,500.

George Washington Carver died at Tuskegee on January 5, 1943. After his death he was remembered by President Franklin D. Roosevelt and others as one of the world's most important scientists. ■

Speaks with a straight tongue

10 Jesse Chisholm

Indian trader and scout. Present Sedgwick County. (1805-1868) Chisholm, whose mother was a Cherokee Indian, claimed he could speak fourteen different Indian languages.

He grew up with the Cherokees in the Southeast and moved west with them in the 1830s—after gold was discovered on their Georgia homeland and the U.S. Army drove them to Oklahoma. At Fort Gibson, Jesse set up his own Indian trading post. At different times he also worked as an Army scout and interpreter.

During the Civil War, the Wichita Indians asked Chisholm to find them a place to settle. He led them to the junction of the Arkansas and Little Arkansas rivers in Kansas—the site of modern Wichita. He built a post nearby in 1863 and traded there for five years. Everyone knew him as a man they could trust; Indians called him "the man with a straight tongue." The trail Indians followed from Indian Territory to Chisholm's Kansas trading post became known as the Chisholm Trail. In the 1870s, Chisholm's name was also given to a cattle trail running between Texas and the Kansas railheads of Abilene [165] and Ellsworth. ∎

Wild golden goose chase

11 Francisco Vásquez de Coronado

Spanish explorer and provincial governor. (1510-1554) Coronado became governor of a Mexican province when he was 28. In 1540 he led an expedition of 300 Spanish soldiers and 1,000 Indians in a search for a land of riches Indians called the Seven Cities of Cíbola. The wealthy "cities" turned out to be a Zuñi Indian pueblo in New Mexico, but while Coronado was there he heard of Quivira, a land of amazing wealth farther east.

The Spaniard decided to find this land. Guided by The Turk, an Indian slave who said Quivira was his home, Coronado and a small party [124] headed east and north. They reached their goal in the summer of 1541. But they found no gold and jewels—just a Wichita Indian village in what is now central Kansas. Coronado was so angry that he had his men strangle the slave who had advertised Kansas.

The disappointed group returned to Mexico where Coronado was investigated for his failure to find gold. He was allowed to stay in office, but when he died, the explorer was still considered a failure.

Coronado, however, should be remembered, however, as the first non-Indian to visit and write about Kansas. The Spaniard liked what he saw in the future Sunflower State. It reminded him of his home in Spain. He thought Kansas would be a pleasant place in which to live. Some later explorers [22, 24] disagreed. ∎

Explores Arctic and more

Naturalist, explorer, educator and author. Ridgeway and Lawrence. (1857-1915) Dyche was a leader in wildlife conservation in Kansas.

Loves the outdoors

Lewis was born on March 20, 1857, in what is now Berkeley Springs, West Virginia. A short time later, his parents headed west to Kansas Territory. Near the Osage County community of Ridgeway—a ghost town today—they settled on 160 acres of land. Mrs. Dyche was ill from the effects of the long trip, so baby Lewis was cared for by women in a nearby camp of Sauk and Fox Indians. The Dyche family moved to a new farm near Auburn in 1866 when invading grasshoppers destroyed their crops.

As the oldest of twelve children, Lewis spent much of his time working. He helped plant and harvest corn, cared for livestock and worked in a sorghum mill. He enjoyed the outdoors and also trapped animals to sell the hides. On his hunting trips he visited nearby Indian camps to learn Native American ways. He ate their foods— roasted muskrats, turtles and snakes—and listened as Indian hunters talked about wildlife. As he sold his furs, he bought calves and eventually had his own herd of cattle.

Seeks an education

By the time he was sixteen, Lewis had gone to school only a few weeks. Realizing he needed an education, he sold his cows and used the money to enroll in the Kansas State Normal School in Emporia in the fall of 1874. After accepting the fact he would have to study grammar along with his beloved science, he learned quickly and was able to graduate in three years.

That fall, Dyche and a friend drove a covered wagon to Lawrence and enrolled at the University of Kansas. They camped at the bottom of Mount Oread, the hill on which the university's one building was located. Although there was only a five-dollar fee to attend the eleven-year-old school, living expenses kept many students away. Lewis and his friend saved money by living in their outdoor camp for a time.

Dyche had decided to attend KU after meeting its science professor, *Francis H. Snow*. Snow, at that time, offered a dollar to local boys who collected what proved to be new species of insects. Lewis impressed the professor almost immediately with his ability to gather specimens. The young man was an eager student in Snow's science classes, and he went along on the instructor's summer expeditions to western Kansas and the Southwest. On one such trip to New Mexico in 1881, Snow, Dyche and the ↻

rest of their group narrowly missed being attacked by a band of Apache warriors.

By 1882, Lewis was a junior at the university. (Like many other students with limited educations, he had spent his first few years taking "preparatory," or high school-level, courses.) At Snow's urging, he took an instructor's job and taught courses in zoology.

Taxidermist, naturalist, conservationalist

Two years later Dyche graduated from KU with two bachelor's degrees. He married **Ophelia Axtell** of Sterling that fall. The couple lived in Lawrence where Lewis continued teaching at the university. By then he had made it a goal to preserve specimens of mammals, reptiles and insects for future generations. With that in mind, he spent the summer of 1887 in Washington, D.C., training under the National Museum's chief taxidermist, William Temple Hornaday.

Dyche was soon a skillful taxidermist. In 1891 the U.S. Army asked him to preserve the remains of the old cavalry

horse, Comanche [**384**]—the only survivor found on the Little Bighorn battlefield after the defeat of George Armstrong Custer [**351**] and the U.S. 7th Cavalry. At the same time, he was preparing specimens for the Kansas exhibit at the World's Columbian Exposition in Chicago. By the time the 1893 event opened, Dyche and his assistants had set up an impressive display of 121 mammals, including Comanche. Up to 20,000 persons visited the exhibit each day. When the exposition closed, seven railroad cars were needed to ship the collection back to KU.

Dyche continued as a professor at the university, teaching during the school year and spending each summer collecting.

His 1894 trip was to Greenland. Although he was often seasick and his ship hit a reef and later sank, Lewis managed to return to Kansas with several hundred bird and mammal skins. The next summer he was part of an expedition sent by the American Museum of Natural History to pick up Admiral Robert E. Peary. The admiral, who finally reached the North Pole in 1909, had spent the winter of 1893-94 in northern Greenland after one of his unsuccessful pole expeditions

the previous summer. Dyche gathered skins of polar bears, walruses and other animals, and took many photographs.

Returning to America, Dyche made the most of his northern trip. He posed for photos wearing sealskins and shared his story with eager New York City reporters; Peary's men were sworn to secrecy so the admiral could publish his own story. At the same time Dyche announced plans for his own North Pole expedition. Back in Kansas, he toured the state giving lectures illustrated with lantern slides. The next summer he gathered specimens in Alaska. Although he never had enough funds to attempt his own North Pole trip, many believed he could have reached that goal before Peary.

In 1901 the state legislature voted to build a natural history museum at KU, a building Chancellor Snow and Professor Dyche had argued was needed for years. Dyche helped in planning the structure and then spent years installing exhibits. He never declared it completed.

In 1910 Dyche took on a new responsibility when Governor **Walter Stubbs** appointed him state fish and game warden. As perhaps the first qualified person to hold the job, Lewis worked to improve the fish and game department. Under his leadership, the state fish hatchery at Pratt was enlarged into one of biggest and most modern in the country. He wrote legislation that protected endangered species and set hunting seasons for most mammals and gamebirds. He also spoke of the need to conserve soil and water.

Dyche died in Topeka on January 20, 1915. Soon after his death, the museum he worked so hard to build at KU was renamed the Dyche Museum of Natural History. ■

Pioneer naturalist

Francis H. Snow, one of the first three faculty members at KU, has been called the pioneer naturalist of Kansas. He was born in 1840 and was educated in Massachusetts. Snow came to Kansas in 1866 to teach natural science and mathematics—although he was qualified to teach ancient languages and literature. He built an important collection of natural history specimens and became chancellor of KU in 1890. At the same time, he was state entomologist and did valuable research for farmers on how to kill chinch bugs. Snow resigned as chancellor in 1901 because of ill health, but he continued to take students on scientific expeditions to the Southwest. He died in 1908. ■

13 Amelia Earhart

First lady of flight

Aviator. Atchison. (1897-1937?) She was born in a quiet Kansas town and became the world's most famous female aviator. Decades after her disappearance in 1937, Amelia Earhart remains one of the best known Kansans.

Amelia was born in Atchison on July 24, 1897. Her mother, the former **Amy Otis**, grew up there and was staying with her parents when her daughter was born. **Edwin Earhart**, Amelia's father, was a graduate of the University of Kansas' law school. He was a railroad lawyer and traveled much of the time.

Because of that, Amelia and her younger sister **Muriel** stayed with their grandparents in Atchison during the school year and spent summers with their parents.

The Earharts encouraged their daughters to be curious and try new experiences. Dressed in bloomer-type gym suits, instead of dresses for proper young ladies, the girls brought home snakes, spiders and toads.

Millie and Pidge

"Millie" and "Pidge," as Amelia and her sister were nicknamed, also explored caves high in the banks of the Missouri River and tinkered with mechanical gadgets. Their parents sat with them on a shed roof to watch Halley's comet and once let them stay up late to see a lunar eclipse. The sisters were athletic, and enjoyed playing football and baseball with equipment their father gave them. They were good students as well, and the sandy-haired, gray-eyed Amelia was especially interested in math and science courses.

In 1908, her father began a new job in Iowa and the Earhart family moved to Des Moines. At the Iowa State Fair that summer, Amelia saw her first airplane. The future pilot wasn't impressed. She called it "a thing of rusty wire and wood and not at all interesting."

Family secret

In Iowa, Amelia's father began drinking heavily. He lost his job because of his alcoholism and did not find steady work for several years. Amelia was a teenager by then, and in four years she attended six high schools, all the time living ⇨

13

under the cloud of their family secret. One spring, the family was so short of money that Mrs. Earhart made new Easter dresses for the girls from old silk curtains. They prayed it wouldn't rain as they walked to church, afraid their dresses would leave a trail of green dye on the sidewalk.

Amelia graduated from Hyde Park High School in Chicago in 1916, but skipped the ceremony. She felt passing her courses was more important than a piece of paper proving it. She went off to college in Pennsylvania. During Christmas vacation in 1917 she visited Muriel, who was attending school in Toronto, Canada.

A little red plane

Amelia was deeply affected when she met Canadian soldiers who had been wounded in World War I. She left school and returned to Canada a few weeks later to take a job as a nurse's aide in a military hospital. She enjoyed her work, and "Sister Amelia" quickly became a favorite of the sick and wounded men.

One day, an officer from the Royal Flying Corps invited her to a nearby airfield. As she watched a stunt pilot doing loops and spins, her interest in flying began. She later wrote, "His little red airplane said something to me as it swished by."

Amelia's flying came later, however. She first returned to her college work, and began studying medicine at Columbia University in New York.

In 1920 she joined her parents in southern California where her father was having treatments for his alcoholism. On Christmas Day, he took her to an air show in Long Beach. She convinced him to pay ten dollars for her to have a ten-minute airplane ride over Hollywood. She knew immediately this first flight would not be her last. "I had to fly," she later recalled.

Expensive lessons

Her father didn't approve of the idea, for flying lessons cost $1,000, but Amelia hired Anita Snook as her flight instructor anyway. "Snooky," as she was known, was just a year older

than 24-year-old Earhart, but she was an experienced pilot. She gave lessons on credit while Amelia worked as a mail clerk and truck driver to pay for them.

The following June, after only ten hours of instruction, Earhart soloed in a small three-cylinder biplane. She liked it so much she bought a second-hand Kinner Canary aircraft for her own birthday present. She also purchased the standard pilot's gear: helmet, goggles and a leather jacket—but to make the new coat look properly old and wrinkled, she had to sleep in it. Within four months, the new pilot set her first "first." She flew her little wooden biplane at 14,000 feet and established a women's altitude record.

After her parents divorced in 1924, Amelia sold her plane and moved to Boston with her mother and sister. She was busy with physics classes at Harvard University and a job teaching English to foreign children. Flying was only a weekend hobby. That changed in the summer of 1928, a year after Charles Lindbergh [21] made

First flight

Amelia was nearly seven when her family visited the St. Louis World's Fair in 1904. She watched in wonder as the small cars sped around the elevated track of the roller coaster, and begged her parents for a ride. No, they answered. She would have to ride the safer Ferris wheel instead.

Back at home, Amelia convinced her sister and their friend Ralphie to help make a backyard roller coaster.

First they gathered materials: two-by-fours smuggled from the basement, a wooden packing crate and some nails given by a helpful uncle. The girls and their young carpenter friend then proceeded to build a 14-foot section of trackage down the roof of the toolshed. To complete their project, they hammered together a "trestle" ramp that extended out from the edge of the roof.

Amelia, of course, volunteered to be the first passenger. The girls lubricated

the runway with lard from the icebox. Then, with a shove from Muriel, Amelia zoomed down the track in a small wooden box.

Her ride was short. The box derailed as it hit the rickety trestle, wood splintered everywhere—and Millie was thrown out. Except for a bruised lip, she was unhurt. "Oh, Pidge," she jumped up shouting, "it's just like flying!"

Amelia Earhart had made her first flight.

the first solo flight across the Atlantic Ocean. George Putnam, a book publisher and explorer, invited Amelia to fly across the Atlantic—the first time a woman had done so.

Unhappy with Friendship

The plane was known as the *Friendship*. Earhart made the historic 20-hour, 40-minute flight, but only as a passenger. Two men piloted the plane. Even so, she was an instant celebrity.

London greeted "Lady Lindy" with parties and receptions; New York City gave her a ticker-tape parade. But the attention bothered Amelia. She felt she wasn't a true heroine. "I was just baggage, like a sack of potatoes. Someday I will do it alone."

Driven by that goal, she continued to practice her flying skills. She set more speed records and became the first woman to fly solo across North America and back. She successfully piloted an "autogiro," a craft that was part airplane and part helicopter, across the United States and back.

At the same time, she traveled the country on a speaking tour, worked as aviation editor of *Cosmopolitan* magazine, and became vice-president of an airline company. She also wrote a book about her experiences.

Alone over the Atlantic

In 1931, after he had proposed six times, she married George Putnam, her book's publisher. A year later, she told him she wanted to fly across the Atlantic a second time—by herself.

After careful planning and delays due to bad weather, Amelia took off from Newfoundland on the evening of May 20, 1932, the fifth anniversary of Lindbergh's flight. Fifteen hours, 39 minutes, and many problems later, she landed safely.

Earhart's flight set a new record time, but it could have ended tragically. As she flew at 12,000 feet, the altimeter, or altitude gauge, suddenly went out. Then she ran into a violent thunderstorm. Her big Lockheed Vega became covered with ice and began dropping rapidly through the clouds. With no way to measure her altitude, Amelia barely kept from splashing into the ocean. Next, a weld on the exhaust manifold broke. Flames shot from the crack and the plane began vibrating badly. And, in the last two hours of the trip, a fuel gauge leak filled her cockpit with sickening gasoline fumes. At the first sight of land, a cow pasture in Northern Ireland, Earhart landed her trouble-filled craft.

She had made it, only the second person to fly the Atlantic alone. This time she was a true heroine.

Earhart made more famous solo flights. In 1935 she claimed a $10,000 prize as the first to fly alone from Hawaii to the U.S. mainland. Ten pilots had died trying to make the dangerous 2,400-mile trip. Ten thousand cheering spectators greeted her when she completed the eighteen-hour flight. Four months later she flew nonstop from Mexico City to New Jersey in a little over fourteen hours.

Crowds were anxious to meet this daring young woman; she made 136 speeches within a few months.

One last flight

In February 1937 Earhart announced her plans to become the first pilot to fly around the globe along the equator. "I think I have just one more long flight in my system," she told reporters.

To begin her 29,000-mile journey, she and a three-man crew left Oakland, California, March 17, for the first leg of the trip, 2,400 miles to Hawaii. Their fifteen-hour flight set a record for an east-to-west crossing to Honolulu.

The takeoff from Hawaii two days later, however, was a disaster. Halfway down the wet runway a flat tire caused the plane to veer out of control. Amelia quickly shut off the ignition and prevented a fire. But one wing of her 10-E Electra was nearly torn off, and the craft had to be shipped back to California.

Lockheed rebuilt the plane in two months, but Earhart changed her plans. To take ⇨

advantage of better weather, she reversed her route to travel eastbound.

With her crew trimmed to only one, navigator Fred Noonan, she began the trip a second time, leaving Miami, Florida, on June 1. She flew south to Puerto Rico, then to Brazil and over the Atlantic.

By the middle of the month the pair had hopscotched over Africa and was headed to India. At each stop, Amelia checked her equipment, studied weather reports and rested. She greeted local officials, but had little time for sightseeing. Next they touched down in Australia and New Guinea. By June 30, they had covered 22,000 miles.

Next stop, Howland

On July 1, Earhart and Noonan began a 2,556-mile flight from New Guinea to a refueling stop on Howland Island, a narrow strip of sand in the Pacific near the equator. Three hours out, Amelia radioed Lae, New Guinea.

Their position, she said, was eight hundred miles over the Pacific, directly on course for Howland. But they never arrived.

The U.S. Coast Guard cutter *Itasca* waited near Howland to send a radio signal for her to follow. It is believed she flew within perhaps a hundred miles of the island, for several times during the night and early morning of July 2 the ship's radio picked up her faint signal. She calmly reported a heavy overcast and asked for a position, but the *Itasca*'s crewmen were unable to make her hear them.

Little did they know Earhart had left behind in Miami a trailing antenna that might have received their transmissions. She had replaced the antenna's weight with extra fuel. Her plane was also equipped with a radio directional finder, but at that time RDF was an experimental navigational tool. (On a 1935 flight from Los Angeles to Mexico City Amelia had tested an early model of inventor William Lear's [*163*] "Learoscope" RDF; he produced a much improved version in 1939.)

"Please take [a] bearing on us. . . I will make noise in [the] microphone," she called. Later the ship heard, "We must be on you but cannot see you. Gas is running low."

The cutter's radio operator tried again and again to reach her while the crew searched the sky. They saw nothing. At 8:45 a.m. the ship intercepted a faint transmission in her anxious voice: "We are circling but cannot hear you. . .position 157-337 . . .running north and south."

With that, Earhart, Noonan and their aircraft disappeared.

Mystery and myths

For the next three days, ship and shore radios heard faint distress calls in the area. At least 24 transmissions were intercepted, but the signals were very weak. At the same time, a commercial radio station in Honolulu transmitted special messages to Amelia. One asked her to respond with four Morse code dashes. After the broadcast, four dashes were heard in Hawaii and three other locations. Radio operators at Pan American Airways plotted the direction of the signals and determined they were coming from the area of Gardner Island, about 350 miles southeast of Howland. By that time a massive search operation was already underway. Planes and ships from the United States, England and other nations combed the waters and islands in that part of the Pacific.

After several days, three search planes from the *USS Colorado* flew over Gardner Island. The Navy pilots reported seeing signs of recent human activity on the island, but they circled the area repeatedly and found nothing more. They and their superiors assumed any humans on Gardner were native islanders. No one in the search operation realized Gardner was normally uninhabited.

At the end of two weeks, the ships and planes had covered 250,000 square miles of ocean and found nothing. At the time, many believed Earhart and Noonan flew off course, ran out of fuel, and crashed into the ocean. Others said it was possible the plane came down on or near a remote island. They felt the fliers probably died of thirst.

A few claimed Amelia was on a secret spying mission. Because the government marked her flight plans "confidential," they believed she was photographing military activity in the Pacific when she disappeared. They

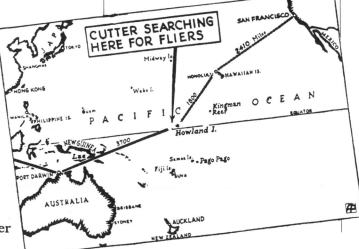

guessed she was captured by the Japanese in those tense years just before World War II. Actually, Earhart had asked that her plans be kept quiet so she might avoid large crowds of sightseers and reporters at each takeoff and landing.

Over the years, other stories surfaced to explain Amelia's disappearance. Several persons told of seeing an American couple held prisoner on the island of Saipan in the late 1930s. Others claimed Earhart and Noonan were jailed and executed as spies in Japan. A few U.S. ex-servicemen claimed they saw Earhart's plane and some of her belongings on an island Americans captured from the Japanese in the 1940s. Someone suggested the Japanese held Amelia several years and then secretly returned her to the United States where an embarrassed American government gave her a new identity! These stories and others fill several books.

Modern-day search

As years passed, the investigation continued. Based on information from local residents, unidentified graves on Saipan were dug up, but the remains could not be identified as Earhart's or Noonan's.

In the 1980s, an organization known as TIGHAR, The International Group for Historic Aircraft Recovery, began studying all the available data on Earhart's last flight. TIGHAR's members believed she disappeared near Gardner Island, now called Nikumaroro.

The fliers missed Howland, they said, because of a navigational error, or perhaps simply because they were tired. After a month of flying, the experts felt, both Earhart and Noonan were likely to have made mistakes.

When they discovered they were lost, TIGHAR decided, they flew on a north-south line, hoping to locate other islands in the area.

Nikumaroro is on the position line Amelia last reported. She could have crash-landed on a tidal flat that would have been exposed by low tides on the morning of July 2, 1937. A massive storm several days later might have washed the plane off the flat and over the edge of a coral reef into 2,000 feet of water. Before their plane was lost, according to the TIGHAR theory, the downed fliers sent the 24 signals heard by rescuers. Then, with no sources of fresh water—and in tropical temperatures reaching 120 degrees—they died of thirst and exposure.

Aluminum proof?

TIGHAR sent a seventeen-member team to the Pacific in 1989. Searchers and divers combed Nikumaroro and its surrounding waters. On land they found an aluminum box that was the first real evidence in the Earhart mystery. A serial number stamped on the box showed it was an aircraft navigator's map case manufactured in the 1930s. Experts believed the case came from Amelia's missing Lockheed. A photograph of the plane's interior shows a similar-sized box.

In 1991 TIGHAR returned to Nikumaroro to search the waters off the coral reef for the remains of Earhart's plane. The group included **LeRoy Knoll**, an amateur diver from Garden City. Knoll and other divers found nothing in the sea, but searchers on the island turned up some bits of evidence—including aircraft parts. The largest sec-

tion, a 23-by-19-inch piece of aluminum, was analyzed by its manufacturer, Alcoa. The company verified the metal was from a batch it made for Lockheed in the 1930s. Copper wire attached to the piece matched radio antenna wire from the same period.

The lab at the government's National Transportation Safety Board said the aluminum scraps could have come from a plane like Amelia's Lockheed 10-E Electra. Retired Lockheed engineers, however, disagreed.

Two other artifacts also pointed to Earhart. TIGHAR searchers found a metal medicine bottle cap identified by the Warner-Lambert Company as a cap used for a brand of stomach medicine it made in 1937. Amelia was known to have suffered from stomach problems.

A left shoe sole found on Nikumaroro was examined by the Biltrite Corporation. The footwear company found that it came from a woman's size nine Oxford style made as their Cat's Paw brand in the 1930s. The heel had been replaced. Amelia wore size nine shoes. Enlargements of photos taken of her on the 1937 trip showed her wearing that style of shoe, and experts said it appeared that her left shoe heel had recently been repaired.

When Richard Gillespie, TIGHAR's executive director, announced these findings in 1992, he said members of his organization would continue to search for her plane off the lonely shores of Nikumaroro. They were confident they had solved the Earhart disappearance. Others disagreed. More proof, they said, is needed to untangle the myth and mystery of Amelia Earhart. ∎

Out of this world Jayhawks

14 Joe Engle

Astronaut. Chapman. (Born 1932) In the 1960s, Engle was a U.S. Air Force test pilot. He flew the X-15 rocket plane six times faster than the speed of sound—about 4,000 miles per hour. These tests helped develop America's space shuttles.

Colonel Engle was scheduled to fly on Apollo 17 with Ron Evans [**15**], but NASA later decided to send a geologist instead. Joe's first mission was as pilot of the space shuttle *Columbia* on its second orbital flight in 1981, the first time a reusable spacecraft went back into space. Engle commanded another shuttle flight before he retired in 1986. ■

15 Ron Evans

Astronaut. St. Francis and Topeka. (1933-1990) Evans was the command module pilot on the Apollo 17 flight in 1972, America's last manned mission to the moon. For over 300 hours, Evans orbited the moon while two other astronauts landed a lunar module and explored the moon's surface in a lunar rover. Evans retired from the U.S. Navy and left the NASA program in the late 1970s. He was living in Arizona when he died. ■

16 Steve Hawley

Astronaut. Ottawa and Salina. (Born 1952) Hawley, who has doctor's degrees in

astronomy and astrophysics, made three space shuttle flights. He was on the first flight of the *Discovery* in 1984 when it put two communications satellites in orbit. Two years later, he flew on the *Columbia*. On a 1990 *Discovery* flight, Dr. Hawley was in charge of placing the Hubble Space Telescope into orbit.

That year Steve retired from active space flight and became a NASA administrator. He now lives in California. Hawley's former wife, Sally Ride, was the first American woman astronaut to fly in space. ■

First jet ace

17 James Jabara

U.S. Air Force pilot. Wichita. (1924-1966) During the Korean War, Jabara became the world's first jet ace—a combat pilot who has shot down five enemy aircraft. Piloting an F-86 Sabrejet at speeds up to 700 miles an hour, he flew 163 missions. By the war's end, James was a triple ace; he destroyed fifteen Soviet-built MiG-15 fighters.

Jabara moved to Wichita from Oklahoma at the age of nine. At seventeen he began his flying career by entering an officers' training school. Although his eyesight had been poor in high school, he ate twenty carrots a day for several years and passed the pilot's eye examination.

In World War II, the young Lebanese-American completed over 100 missions in Europe and shot down nine German planes. One encounter was so close that his plane collided with the enemy aircraft. Both pilots bailed out and, on the ground, Jabara and his German counterpart shook hands in salute to each other's courage.

Between wars, Colonel Jabara trained other pilots. In the mid 1960s, at age 43, he got into a "dogfight" as he delivered a jet to an air base in Vietnam. He told his commander he missed combat and asked for a 100-mission tour of duty in the war.

Ironically, Jabara and his daughter were killed in an automobile accident before he could begin his Vietnam assignment. The daring pilot was buried in Arlington National Cemetery. Jabara Airport in north Wichita was named for him in 1984. ■

Preserving the wild and exotic on film

Explorers, photographers and authors. Lincoln and Independence. (1884-1937) Chanute. (1894-1953) Martin Johnson was born in Rockford, Illinois, October 9, 1884. A year later, he and his family moved to Kansas, where his father ran a jewelry store in Lincoln.

As a boy, Johnson loved fishing and swimming in the nearby Saline River—but school was pure drudgery. By the time he reached sixth grade, his grades were so poor in all subjects (except geography) that he was held back. At first, he was so ashamed he ran away from home, but he returned to school to face his problems with help from his mother.

In 1895, Johnson's father moved his business and family to Independence. There he became a dealer for Eastman Kodak cameras and supplies, which sparked Martin's lifelong interest in photography. His father encouraged him to set up a darkroom and use materials from the store to develop film and print photographs.

Young Johnson took pictures of everything in sight, and when he saw posters that advertised a circus in Kansas City, he decided he wanted to photograph the wild animals. The thirteen-year-old packed his camera gear, slipped out his bedroom window in the night and climbed onto a northbound

Santa Fe freight train. Unfortunately, the train was headed to Topeka, and by the time he reached Kansas City the circus had moved on.

Penny photographer

Three years later, the young photographer loaded his equipment into a wagon and set out on a tour of eastern Kansas. He charged a penny apiece to take, develop and print photographs. However, without free supplies from his father, he soon spent more than he took in. He ran out of money in Chanute, where one of the photographs he made was of a three-year-old ⇨

boy dragged in by his sister, Osa Leighty. She was later to become Martin's wife.

Back in Independence, Johnson was expelled from school for faking photographs of several teachers embracing and kissing. Embarrassed, he bought a train ticket for Chicago and left home with $1.20 in his pocket. In Chicago, he worked at various jobs, and then headed to Europe—on a bet that he couldn't travel there and back using only the money he had on hand, $4.25. He won the bet, but didn't return to collect it until he was twenty. He then helped his father until adventure called again.

Off to see the world

In 1906, Johnson signed on as cook on the *Snark*, a boat belonging to the famous writer Jack London. Martin had convinced London that he could cook, which he could not. His secret was soon exposed, and when they made their first port in Honolulu, a real cook was hired. Johnson became engineer. For nineteen months, he worked onboard the *Snark*. During that time, he circled the globe and helped French movie cameramen film island people in the South Pacific.

He returned to the United States as a stowaway on a cattle boat, but Independence greeted him as a hero. Soon he had rented a local theater to show a copy of the Frenchmen's movie and some of the thousands of photographs he had taken himself.

After a shaky start—he forgot his talk and the projector operator broke some of his glass slides—the idea caught on. He took his show to neighboring towns and eventually opened

two more Snark theaters. They were among the first motion picture houses in Kansas.

One evening in the spring of 1910, sixteen-year-old Osa Leighty came to one of his shows. She had been born March 14, 1894, in nearby Chanute. In fact, she had spent all of her life there and had never traveled more than 30 miles from home. Except for their brief meeting at his photo studio years earlier, Osa knew nothing of this young adventurer from Kansas.

Horrible pictures

After they were introduced, she was even less impressed. Martin was conceited and his "cannibal pictures" were horrible, she said. The next day, however, he drove Osa to Coffeyville in his car, her first automobile ride. They dated for three weeks and then got married on the spur of the moment in Independence. On their honeymoon in Kansas City they decided to get married again—by a judge in Missouri—in case Osa's father tried to annul their Kansas wedding.

The young bride had hopes of building a home and raising a family in Kansas, but her husband disagreed. He wanted to tour with his lectures and films.

They began in Colorado, and eventually presented

programs in much of the United States, Canada and England. By 1912, they had saved $4,000 to pay for an expedition to the South Seas.

Exotic travels

For over twenty years, the Johnsons followed that pattern. They traveled to an exotic location and then put together lecture tours, films and books to finance their next expedition. One of their trips to the South Seas was nearly Osa's last. While visiting Chief Nagapate, a cannibal, he took a liking to her and made it plain he wanted Osa at his dinner table—as the main course! When their native guides deserted them and the chief's men captured Martin, their situation seemed hopeless. Fortunately a British gunboat arrived and Nagapate and his men quickly retreated.

The Johnsons traveled next to unexplored parts of Borneo where curious natives examined Osa's teeth, rubbed her skin and tugged at her long, golden hair. The explorers spent a year on the remote island, but their movies were disappointing. Downpours almost every day in the tropical jungles ruined much of their film.

In 1918 Martin joined the respected Explorers' Club of New York; Osa was given an honorary membership. On their expeditions, however, Osa's jobs were not just honorary. She was in charge of camp security and supplies, and also helped Martin with photography. Once she was standing guard as he filmed several rhinoceroses. When one of the rhinos suddenly charged her husband, Osa killed it. Martin didn't stop filming!

At home in Africa

The Johnsons sailed to Kenya in 1921 with tons of equipment. During the next fourteen years they photographed herds of wildlife on the Serengeti Plains, and were the first to film the pygmies of the Ituri Forest and olive baboons in what was then called the Belgian Congo. They also made the first sound motion picture in Africa, *Congorilla*, a film about mountain gorillas.

On one of their African safaris the Johnsons took 255 crates of supplies and $50,000 worth of photo equipment. They needed 235 porters, ten custom-built jeeps, plus various ox carts and mule wagons to carry all of it. With the help of George Eastman and the American Museum of Natural History they developed photographic techniques and set up a modern photo laboratory at Lake Paradise, a community they built in British East Africa.

In 1932 Osa and Martin received pilots' licenses and purchased two aircraft. They flew the entire length of the African continent the next year, taking the first aerial photographs of Africa's wildlife and becoming the first to fly over Mt. Kilimanjaro and Mt. Kenya.

Three years later the Johnsons decided to make another trip to Borneo. This two-year expedition was much more successful than their first. They became the first to fly over the interior of Borneo, and photographed much of the island's wildlife, including herds of elephants and water buffalo. Traveling up forbidden rivers by canoe, raft and houseboat, they managed to get film footage of the Tenggara headhunters. When their supplies of quinine medicine were destroyed, many in their party became ill with malaria.

Tragic flight

When it was completed, their film *Borneo* was an instant success. At that time, the Johnsons were at the height of their popularity. Together they had circled the globe six times, made eight feature movies, published nine books and many magazine articles, and traveled thousands of miles presenting lectures.

In January 1937, they began a nationwide tour to advertise their movie on Borneo. After lecturing to 9,000 school children in Salt Lake City, they boarded a flight to California.

Near San Fernando the plane ran into a thunderstorm and crashed into a mountainside. Martin was seriously injured, and died January 13. Osa suffered a concussion and a broken knee, but she finished the tour. From a wheelchair she gave over a thousand lectures.

She continued their work, producing four more motion pictures and writing another eight books, some for children. She married her lecture manager, Clark Getts, in 1939, but they were later divorced. In 1952 Osa was working on several projects, including a book, a script of a movie on Martin's life, and plans for a return visit to East Africa. That expedition never took place. She died of a heart attack in New York City, January 7, 1953, and was buried beside her husband in Chanute.

Both Osa and Martin Johnson are remembered for their important work in exploration and wildlife photography. Much of what they filmed and recorded is now gone. ∎

World-class airman

20 Harold Krier

Stunt pilot. Olpe, Ashland, Garden City, Dodge City and Rose Hill. (1922-1971) Krier flew on B-17s and B-26s in World War II—but as a crew member, not as the pilot. He learned to fly after the war and built his own experimental plane with his brother.

To support his new-found love of flying, Harold managed airports in several different towns. As a stunt pilot Krier won several national championships in aerobatic competitions in the 1950s and 1960s. He was also world Aerobatic Champion in 1968. Krier was known for several daring stunts, including flying upside and using his propeller to cut a ribbon stretched only fifteen feet above the ground.

Ironically, the skilled pilot was killed while he was flying a friend's test plane near Wichita. The plane went into a dive from which Krier couldn't recover. He bailed out, but his parachute failed to open properly. ■

Lone Eagle in Bird City

21 Charles Lindbergh

Aviator and inventor. Bird City. (1902-1974) Lindbergh, the first person to fly alone across the Atlantic Ocean, lived in Kansas for about a year. In the summer of 1922 he moved to Bird City and starred in a local air show. Known as The Daredevil, he made parachute jumps.

Just a few years later Charles became a living legend. On May 31, 1927, he and his plane, *The Spirit of St. Louis*, landed in Paris after making the first nonstop solo transatlantic flight.

Ironically, he could have made the trip in *"The Spirit of Wichita."* Lindbergh discussed his plans with his friend Marcellus Murdock [**228**] and asked Walter Beech's [**134**] Travel Air company to build a plane for the flight. Travel Air chose not to, perhaps afraid of bad publicity if Lindbergh failed.

After his successful flight, The Lone Eagle was greeted with praise and parades. On a cross-country tour, Lindbergh flew over Bird City. As he circled the town, hundreds saluted the former resident by spelling out WELCOME on the athletic field.

The aviator's triumph turned to tragedy in 1932 when his young son was kidnapped and murdered. To escape publicity, Lindbergh and his wife lived in England for a time. In 1936 he helped design the world's first artificial heart. He flew missions for the U.S. in World War II. ■

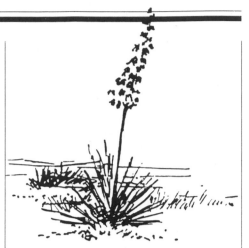

Explores the Kansas 'deserts'

22 Zebulon Pike

American explorer. (1779-1813) In 1806 Pike, a U.S. Army captain from New Jersey, explored what later became Kansas. Along with 22 men, he entered the southeastern part of the state and crossed Kansas on the way to a Pawnee village in present Nebraska.

At the village, Zebulon found a Spanish flag hanging on the chief's earthlodge. It had been given to the Indians by Spanish troops a few weeks earlier. Pike demanded that the foreign flag be taken down, and when the Pawnees did so, he gave them the Stars and Stripes to fly instead. Captain Pike then traveled south and followed the Arkansas River west.

In what is now Colorado, a mountain impressed him—it was later named Pike's Peak in his honor. Kansas, on the other hand, didn't seem to impress Pike at all. He wrote that the area would someday become as famous as the "sandy deserts of Africa." ■

It's a girl!

23 Lucia Pixley

First white child born in Kansas. Present Neosho County. (About 1826-?) When little Lucia was born in late 1826 or early 1827, her birth was the first one recorded in what is now Kansas. Her parents, Pastor **Benton Pixley** and his wife **Lucia**, were missionaries to the Osage Indians. In 1824 the Pixleys started the first Indian mission and school in Kansas, on the Neosho River near the present town of Shaw. It is not known when the younger Lucia died, but census records show she was living in Missouri in 1850. ∎

Worldly man

25 Franc Shor

Explorer, photographer and magazine journalist. Cimarron and Dodge City. (1914-1974) Shor attended Dodge City High School—where he graduated at the age of twelve! He later worked for newspapers in Chicago, New York, Denver and San Francisco. Franc eventually traveled and led expeditions around the world, often publishing reports and photographs in magazines like *Reader's Digest* and *National Geographic*. His journeys led to friendships with world leaders, including the Shah of Iran, China's Chang Kai Shek, and President Richard Nixon. Shor was an editor of *National Geographic* from 1953 until his death. ∎

A beastly place, he says

24 Thomas Say

Explorer and naturalist. (1787-1834) Say was the first important scientist to visit what later became Kansas. He arrived in 1819 on an expedition of the Missouri River area led Lieutenant Colonel Stephen Long. While Long's main party headed up the Missouri by steamboat, Say and a dozen others marched from Fort Osage, Missouri, to a Kansa Indian village near present Manhattan.

There the men were guests of **Little Chief**, who treated them to buffalo jerky, boiled corn and the Kansa Dog Dance. (An artist with Say made a sketch of the dance and published it in 1823, making it the oldest known printed picture of Kansas.) With Say, science apparently came first, for during their solemn meetings inside the chief's lodge, he couldn't resist capturing an unusual-looking beetle he spied nearby. The insect turned out to be a species previously undiscovered.

Say's notes contain interesting information about the Kansa tribe, but the naturalist from Pennsylvania did not say positive things about the future state of Kansas. Wading through tall prairie grasses wore him and his party out—along with their clothing and moccasins. They were bothered by blowflies, rattlesnakes and "excessive" heat. At one point they could find no game to eat except a black wolf.

These problems, plus a band of 140 Pawnee Indians that stole some their supplies and drove off their pack horses, convinced the explorers they had seen enough of Kansas. Thomas and his group quickly headed back east to Missouri.

Like Zebulon Pike [**22**], Say decided Kansas was a desert. He predicted the "desolate sands" of Kansas would never be more than "the unmolested haunt of the native hunter, the bison and the jackal." ∎

Pathfinder

26 Jedediah Smith

Explorer and fur trader. (1799-1831) Smith was born in New York and grew up in Pennsylvania and Ohio. As a teenager he worked as a clerk on a ship in Lake Erie.

Then, with a butcher's knife in his belt and a Bible in his bedroll, he headed for the West ➪

to seek his fortune as a trapper. Unlike most of the rough mountain men he joined, the young man openly followed his Christian faith. Jedediah did not use tobacco or liquor, he read his Bible regularly, and he often sang hymns on the trail. His friends respectfully called him "half grizzly and half preacher."

As he searched for new trapping territory, Smith became one of the West's most traveled pathfinders. He was the first white man to travel overland from the Rocky Mountains to California, part of the route that later became the Oregon-California Trail. Smith was also the first non-Indian to cross the Great Salt Lake Desert, and the first to lay out a trail from southern California to the Northwest.

Many times Smith faced danger and survived. In 1823 he was almost killed when a grizzly bear slashed away one eyebrow and nearly took off an ear. A companion sewed Smith's ear back in place and stitched up his other injuries. It took only ten days for the trailblazer to get back on the trail. Twice in the late 1820s Indians attacked parties he was leading, but he escaped alive. He and his companions survived the dangerous Great Salt Lake Desert by eating one of their horses.

Smith left the fur trade in 1830. After trying city life in St. Louis for a year, he decided to become a Santa Fe trader. On his first (or perhaps his second) trip down the Santa Fe Trail, his wagon train ran out of water in southwestern Kansas. Smith rode ahead to search for water holes along the Cimarron River and then disappeared.

According to stories told later by Indians, the young pathfinder was ambushed by Comanches looking for buffaloes. He approached the hunters peacefully, but when his horse jumped, they fired. Smith fought bravely but was overpowered. He died at a spring near the Cimarron River. ■

Studies human chemistry

27 Earl Sutherland

Scientist. Burlingame and Topeka. (1915-1974) Sutherland won the Nobel Prize for Medicine in 1971 for his research about human hormones. At the Vanderbilt University School of Medicine in Nashville, he discovered and identified the substance cyclic adenosine 3',5'-monophosphate, or cyclic AMP for short.

His work has helped explain the chemicals that regulate the body's functions. Some scientists have said Dr. Sutherland's findings are basic to understanding the chemistry of the human body.

Sutherland became interested in science as a boy, after reading about the French scientist Louis Pasteur. When the Depression of the 1930s wiped out his family's savings, Earl was able to attend Washburn University in Topeka on scholarships and assistantships. After serving as a U.S. Army doctor in World War II, he began his career in research. ■

Shoots camera in combat

28 Donald Thompson

Photographer. Topeka. (About 1884-19?) Thompson became interested in news reporting and photography after the Kansas River flooded Topeka in 1903. Several of his news accounts and photographs of the flood were published in the Topeka *Daily Capital*.

When World War I broke out, Donald traveled overseas. He managed to reach the action with his cameras, and even slipped behind enemy lines. His graphic photos and movie footage of the combat helped millions of Americans understand the horror of the war.

Later he toured the Far East, taking photographs and movies. During the 1920s and 1930s Thompson produced travel films in Hollywood. He was last heard from in Europe before the start of World War II. ■

Kansas farmboy has stars in his eyes

Astronomer. Burdett. (Born 1906) Tombaugh was born in Streator, Illinois, on February 4, 1906. When Clyde was ten, his father helped him build his own telescope from two small lenses and a wooden tube. It magnified objects only four times, but the future astronomer thought it was wonderful.

Clyde admired Sir William Herschel, an English astronomer who had discovered the planet Uranus. As Clyde read and reread Herschel's biography, he dreamed about building his own large telescope.

During World War I, the Tombaughs vacationed in Wisconsin. Twelve-year-old Clyde was eager to see the Yerkes telescope, the world's largest operating telescope at that time. Unfortunately the observatory was closed when the family arrived. Because of the wartime shortage of gasoline, they couldn't wait for it to open.

Enthusiasm builds

That disappointment only seemed to increase Clyde's enthusiasm for the stars. He haunted local libraries for books on astronomy, then saved his spending money to buy books of his own. After his father and uncle ordered a small telescope from the Sears Roebuck catalog in 1920, the young astronomer began making and recording his own observations of the heavens.

He told only a few friends about his hobby, and when he invited several neighbor boys to look through the new telescope, he was disappointed. They didn't share his enthusiasm. His father, however, was always eager to discuss astronomy with Clyde. This helped the teenager survive much of the teasing he got at school. His classmates thought he was strange for spending hours with a telescope, and often drew cartoons of him stargazing through big horn-rimmed glasses.

Off to Kansas

After World War I, the Tombaughs and their telescope moved to Kansas. Clyde stayed out of school one year to help his father plant their first wheat crop, then entered Burdett High School in the fall of 1923. His favorite subjects were geometry and trigonometry; he was fascinated with the thought of measuring unimaginable distances. He was also a pole vaulter on the school's track team—"to get nearer his beloved stars," someone said.

After graduation, Clyde stayed on the farm and spent time in the evenings on his hobby. In a small workshop he began making a larger telescope in 1926. He ordered two pieces of optical glass, and spent more than 100 hours carefully grinding two nine-inch mirrors.

He mounted the finished telescope on a frame built from an old cream separator. When his project was completed, he had spent only $36 to build a piece of equipment worth $1,000. ⬦

Clyde Tombaugh

During that time, Tombaugh began writing to the Lowell Observatory in Flagstaff, Arizona. Lowell officials were impressed with his interest in astronomy. They offered Clyde a position as assistant astronomer for $90 a month.

A real astronomer

When he arrived at the observatory in March 1929 they were photographing the skies in a search for "Planet X"—a small, slow-moving planet that astronomers believed was affecting the orbits of Uranus and Neptune.

Clyde ruined all the photos he made during his first few weeks, but he learned quickly. By the fall of 1929, he was working in the observatory's unheated dome on a bitterly cold mountaintop. Each night, he hunched over the telescope and exposed film until 2 or 3 a.m.

Blinking plates

After the plates were developed, he spent long hours at a "blink-microscope-comparator." This machine held two large photographs of the same part of the sky. As Clyde watched through its eyepiece, the comparator flashed back and forth between the two images. By comparing photos taken several days apart, he could locate any fast-moving objects because they blinked off and on, apparently changing positions. With as many as 2,000 star images on each square inch of the photographs, it was tedious work.

On the afternoon of February 18, 1930, Clyde was blinking photos exposed toward the star Delta. Suddenly, he spied a dim object popping in and out of the background. Nearby, a similar object flashed oppo-

sitely. The distance between the two images showed the object was traveling much slower than the hundreds of asteroids he had already noted.

He quickly took out other photographs taken during that period. With a hand magnifier he discovered the same moving object. Tombaugh excitedly told his supervisors, but they asked the 24-year-old to keep his discovery quiet until it could be carefully evaluated. Cloudy weather forced him to wait one night to rephotograph that same section of sky. When the new plates were developed, his small world appeared again. Astronomers agreed it was a small planet orbiting the sun.

Planet Pluto

For four long weeks, staff members at Lowell checked and rechecked the findings. Then on March 13, 1930, they announced that Clyde Tombaugh, a Kansas farmboy, had discovered a new planet. For his efforts, he received a raise— $10 per month.

Letters, telegrams, reporters and scientists poured in, along with ideas for the planet's name. Two months later the Lowell staff settled on *Pluto*, the god of outer darkness—not Mickey Mouse's dog, as some have said.

Most astronomers felt the little Pluto was too small to be the missing Planet X, so Clyde was told to search more plates. During the next several years, he examined about 90 million star images, saw evidence of

4,000 asteroids and counted over 29,000 galaxies. He found no other planets.

In 1931 the Royal Astronomical Society awarded him a medal for his discovery. A year later he took a leave of absence from the observatory to attend the University of Kansas. He earned a bachelor's degree in 1936 and moved back to Flagstaff with his new wife Patricia. He returned to KU in 1938 and spent a year completing his master's degree in astronomy.

During World War II, Clyde taught a U.S. Navy navigation program in Arizona, then spent a year on the faculty at UCLA in Los Angeles. The Tombaughs and their two children moved to New Mexico in 1947. There Clyde joined the staff of the White Sands Missile Range. He supervised a tracking system which was later used for the first American space satellites.

'Comet Clyde'

Tombaugh began teaching part time at New Mexico State University at Las Cruces in the 1950s. "Comet Clyde," as his students called him, soon caused the enrollment in astronomy classes to double. He became a full-time member of the NMSU staff in 1961, and made that school's astronomy department one of the best in the country. He remained at Las Cruces after he retired.

Over the years, Tombaugh has discovered several star clusters, a supercluster of galaxies, one comet and 775 asteroids. He has been a consultant to NASA, and has had an observatory and one of his "own" asteroids named after him. He still enjoys grinding his own telescope mirrors and often travels around the country lecturing on Pluto to raise funds for NMSU. ■

Digs into Kansas' past

Archaeologist. North Newton. (Born 1908) Wedel first became interested in archaeology as a boy. While he and a friend were playing on the campus of Bethel College in their hometown, they discovered an interesting-looking stone marker. Convinced it was a gravestone for one of Coronado's [11] soldiers, the pair of eager eleven-year-olds ran home to get their shovels.

Put it back, boys

The boys had dug an impressive hole around the stone and were just ready to pull it out of the ground when a member of the college faculty stopped them. The young archaeologists' Spanish tombstone was actually a surveyor's marker on the Bethel campus.

In the years following that accidental find, Wedel became one of the most respected archeologists in America. He was born September 10, 1908, in North Newton, and attended high school and two years of college at Bethel, where his father taught chemistry.

As a teenager, Waldo and a close friend eagerly read the historical writing of Paul Wellman [**254**]. They also enjoyed searching for Indian arrowheads and pottery pieces. But it was easier to uncover artifacts than it was to find books to identify them. And when they tried to locate an area university at which to study archaeology, the young men discovered there were no schools on the Plains that offered any courses on the subject. Together they attended the University of Arizona and both earned bachelor's degrees.

Emil Haury, Wedel's friend, later taught at the university and became one of Arizona's leading archaeologists. Over the years, books and articles written by Kansans Haury and Wedel have helped fill the information gap they faced in the 1920s. Wedel's *Prehistoric Man on the Great Plains* and *An Introduction to Kansas Archaeology* are today important reference books for archaeologists.

During college, Wedel spent several summers working on archeological digs. He received no pay, only free room and board. Although his room was often just a bedroll in a tent, he enjoyed the search for artifacts.

He earned a master's degree in sociology at the University of Nebraska. In 1936 he became the first person to receive a doctor's degree in anthropology with a specialty in archaeology from the University of California. While he completed his doctor's degree, Wedel worked at the Nebraska State Historical Society for several months. In August 1936 he joined the staff of the Smithsonian Institution in Washington, D.C. He spent 54 years working in the nation's capital.

During that time, Dr. Wedel held several positions at the Smithsonian's Natural History Museum: associate curator of archaeology, assistant curator of anthropology and curator of anthropology. He was also a senior scientist in archaeology.

Archaeologist emeritus

In 1976 he retired from active duty at the Smithsonian. He remained on the museum's staff until 1990 when he was named its archaeologist emeritus. Much of his work in the "nation's attic" involved research and writing about his fieldwork.

In digs over the years, Wedel identified several important prehistoric and historic sites, including the Pawnee village visited by Zebulon Pike [**22**] in 1806. He worked in most of the Plains states, as well as in his native Kansas.

After working in Rice County, Wedel decided it was the area that Coronado called Quivira in 1541. In 1978 he demonstrated an unusual calendar in a pasture near Lyons—an arrangement of Quiviran ceremonial fire pits. Wedel showed how these "council circles" line up to point toward the setting sun on the first day of summer and the rising sun on the first day of winter. He also said that a mysterious serpent design in a nearby field was made by Indians.

He and his wife Mildred, an ethnohistorian, retired to Colorado. ∎

Other Kansans aim at stars

James Ackert, born in Illinois in 1879, became a professor of zoology at Kansas State Agricultural College (later KSU) in 1918. For decades, he conducted research on insects. By the time of his death in 1969 the noted parasitologist's discoveries about controlling hookworms and other parasites were used worldwide. ■

Micky Axton, from Coffeyville, was a flight engineer and test pilot for the Boeing company in Wichita during World War II. One day in 1944 she was on a test flight of a new bomber, the B-29. When the pilot invited her to take the controls, she readily agreed. But on her way to becoming the first woman to fly a B-29, she climbed into the cockpit so quickly she nearly ripped her parachute. At a 1991 Wichita air show, Axton—then age 72—piloted the only B-29 still in flying condition. ■

Mark Carlton was a plant scientist from Concordia who did crop research for the United States Department of Agriculture until his death in 1925. While at the USDA he went to Russia to collect samples of hard winter wheat. Carlton used the seed to develop new wheat types that could be grown on the Great Plains. His studies included research on the ancestry of the wheat raised in Kansas by Mennonites [**96**] from Russia. ■

Mary Donoho is believed to have been the first Anglo woman to cross Kansas on the Santa Fe Trail. She, along with her husband, their small child, and 200 traders, traveled from Missouri to Santa Fe in 1833. After running a hotel there for four years, they returned to Missouri, making Mary perhaps the first white woman to travel the trail in both directions. She died in Texas in 1880. ■

Daniel H. Forbes, Jr., a native of Topeka, joined the U.S. Army Air Corps in 1942. His tour of duty included Europe, Africa, South America and Bikini Island in the Pacific Ocean. There he took part in the first tests of America's atomic bomb. Forbes was a test pilot in California when he died in the 1948 crash of a new aircraft. That same year the deactivated Topeka Army Air Base was reopened and named Forbes Air Force Base in his honor. The base was closed in 1949, but was again in operation from 1951 to 1973. It is now an airport called Forbes Field. ■

John C. Frémont, an American explorer who was called The Pathfinder—after Christopher "Kit" Carson [**8**] helped him find a path to the West—spent time in Kansas on four expeditions. In his accounts of those visits during the 1840s, he wrote of the good soil in what is now eastern Kansas and the plentiful buffalo grass on the western plains. Frémont's positive reports were some of the first to show Kansas was not part of the Great American Desert [**22, 24**]. ■

Antonio Gutierrez de Humaña was a Spanish explorer who entered Kansas in 1593 or 1594 without permission. Like Fran-cisco Vásquez de Coronado [**11**], Humaña hoped to find riches—but he found trouble instead. After visiting the Quivira Indians, Humaña killed his partner in a bloody quarrel. Ten days later one of their men and five Indian helpers deserted. Next, Indians set the tall prairie grass on fire, killing everyone in Humaña's party. Only the deserter lived to tell the tale of the explorer's ill-fated visit to Kansas. ■

Chip Lagerbom, born in 1964, has gone as far south as anyone can go on earth—to Antarctica, the frozen continent. During the Antarctic summer of 1990-91, the Lyons High School graduate lived in a tent in the Transantarctic Mountains. Lagerbom was a field assistant on a research expedition that studied the geology of glaciers. He dug soil and rock samples out of glacier ice and then hauled them back to camp. But he had no worries about getting back before dark, for during Antarctica's summer the sun shines day and night. Even in the sunshine, temperatures ranged from 30 degrees below zero to a "high" of 20 degrees above zero. Chip and the two other men at the camp had no showers for three months. Just brushing their teeth meant thawing glacier ice—and their toothpaste. ■

Elmer Verner McCollum was born in Fort Scott in 1879. He was a graduate and staff member of the University of Kansas before becoming a professor at the University of Wisconsin and then Johns Hopkins University in Maryland. A noted chemist and nutritionalist, McCollum discovered vitamins A, B, D and E between 1913 and 1922. Elmer also popularized the use of white rats in scientific experiments. He died in 1967. ■

Tom McConnell and his brothers **Fred** and **Edwin** grew up in Wichita and joined the U.S. Army together during World War II. All three trained as pilots in the Army Air Corps at Fort Riley and then in Arizona. They were also stationed together at air fields in New Mexico, Topeka, California and Guadalcanal Island in the Pacific.

Tom McConnell died in a 1943 plane crash while returning from a bombing mission over Japan. Fred made over 60 successful missions and returned to the United States. He was a military flying instructor at the Garden City air field when he was killed in a 1945 plane accident. Edwin left the military that same year and became a commercial pilot. In honor of the three brothers, Wichita Air Force Base was renamed McConnell Air Force Base in 1954. ■

Jacob Mohler was born in 1875 and grew up on a farm near Downs. In 1893 he left his studies at Washburn University to work as a clerk under his father, **Martin Mohler**, the Kansas secretary of agriculture. In 1950 Jacob retired after working at the Kansas State Board of Agriculture for 57 years—including 35 years as secretary. During his term, he encouraged Kansas farmers to raise a variety of crops and animals, or what is now known as diversified farming. Although he is sometimes given credit for the slogan "Kansas grows the best wheat in the world," Mohler said F.W. "Woody" Hockaday [**109**] originated the famous saying. ■

Benjamin Franklin Mudge was born in Maine in 1817 and raised in Massachusetts. He was a lawyer and then a chemist before he came to Kansas during the Civil War. Benjamin taught school in Wyandotte and in 1864 was appointed the first state geologist. From the late 1860s until 1874 he was a professor of natural science at Kansas State Agricultural College (KSU). Although he lost his job after an argument over the college's curriculum, Professor Mudge stayed in Kansas as a respected scientist in geology, zoology, archeology and paleontology. His fossil-gathering made him known nationwide.

On one search near Fort Wallace, with Senator Edmund G. Ross [**85**] along, he had to be protected from Indians by U.S. Army troops. Mudge died in 1879. One plant fossil he found, the *Sassafras mudgei*, was named for him. ■

Tod Peterson admired stunt pilot Harold Krier's [**20**] flying as a boy. Now a stunt pilot himself, Peterson lives in Ashland, once the home of Krier. The young stunt pilot has his own air show in which he flies Krier's restored planes. ■

Amedie Roulier, a retired farmer from Brewster, was one of Kansas' last living barnstormers. He sold his last plane in 1949 but kept his memories of aviation's "good old days." As a boy, he began working with an air show. In 1922 Roulier rode with barnstormer Charles Lindbergh [**21**] from Goodland to Bird City and back. Six years later he flew in a Beech [**134-135**] Staggerwing at a Wichita air show. The plane's pilot, he said, was a young flier named Amelia Earhart [**13**]. ■

David Schilling was born at Leavenworth in 1918 and graduated from high school at Kansas City. During World War II he flew 132 combat missions over Germany. He destroyed ten planes on the ground and 23 in the air—including five in one day. Colonel Schilling received numerous awards and later helped develop techniques used in mid-air refueling. He died in a car accident in 1956. The next year, Smoky Hill Air Force Base in Salina was renamed Schilling Air Force Base in his honor. The base was closed in 1965. ■

Charles H. Sternberg was born in New York in 1850 and came to Ellsworth at age seventeen. His interest in fossils led to a career in paleontology, and he eventually sold fossils to museums around the world. When asked how he could find fossils where others had already looked, he replied that the locations appeared in his dreams. In Wyoming in 1908 he made one of his most important finds—a fossilized trachodont, or duck-billed dinosaur. Helping on that expedition were his sons **George F.**, **Charles M.** and **Levi Sternberg** who followed in their father's fossil-finding footsteps. The elder Sternberg died in 1943. Today Fort Hays State University's Sternberg Museum contains many of the fossils he and his family discovered in Kansas.

George M. Sternberg, Charles H.'s older brother, was a noted bacteriologist. He discovered the organism that causes pneumonia and was later the surgeon general of the Army. He was born in 1838 and died in 1915. ■

Serving State
& Nation

Soldiers and Politicians

Doesn't spend a dime

31 Henry J. Allen

Governor, U.S. senator and newspaper publisher. Clay County, Burlingame, Salina and Wichita. (1868-1950)
Allen was a barber and a newspaper publisher who became a politician through his involvement in the Republican party. That party nominated Allen for governor in 1918 while he was out of the country with William Allen White [*256*], touring facilities for Kansas soldiers in World War I.

Henry stayed overseas until after the election, spent none of his own money on a campaign—and still won by nearly 55,000 votes! In fact, the new governor didn't know he had won the election until he read it in a Paris newspaper.

Allen was considered one of the best public speakers to serve as governor of Kansas, but few legislators seemed to listen to him. He unsuccessfully pushed for highway improvements, a state income tax and laws protecting workers. Governor Allen did establish a special court to settle labor disputes, but it did not last. During his first term he signed a law that required automobile owners to buy licenses for their vehicles.

As owner of the *Wichita Beacon*, he returned to Wichita after his second term. There the wealthy ex-governor built the state's first ten-story office building, even though many believed the Kansas winds would blow it over. Allen hired world-famous architect Frank Lloyd Wright to draw up plans for his home in Wichita, and it remains one of the few structures in Kansas designed by Wright.

Clyde Reed, governor from 1929 to 1931, appointed Allen to the U.S. Senate after Charles Curtis [*38*] became vice president. Allen ran for a full term in 1930 but he was not elected. ∎

First Kansan on high court

32 David Brewer

U.S. Supreme Court justice. Leavenworth. (1837-1910)
Only two Kansans [*92*] have served as justices on the U.S. Supreme Court. Brewer was the first. He was born in Turkey while his parents were missionaries there. In 1858 David came to Kansas to practice law.

He served as a local judge in the 1860s and took a seat on the Kansas Supreme Court in 1870. He was a federal circuit judge in Leavenworth when President Benjamin Harrison appointed him an associate justice on the high court in 1889. ∎

Changes the rules, and loses

33 Joseph Bristow

U.S. senator and newspaper publisher. Salina and Ottawa. (1861-1944) Bristow published newspapers in Salina and then Ottawa before he entered politics. One of his first political jobs was as the personal secretary to Governor *Edmund Morrill* in the 1890s.

After Morrill left office, President William McKinley appointed Bristow assistant postmaster general. In 1909 the Kansas Legislature elected him to the U.S. Senate. There Bristow pushed for reforms, or changes. One of his ideas was to change the U.S. Constitution and allow U.S. senators to be elected by the people of each state, instead of by state legislatures.

Bristow's proposal was passed by Congress, approved by two-thirds of the states, and went into effect as the seventeenth amendment to the Constitution in 1913. The next year Bristow ran for the Senate again, against challenger Charles Curtis [*38*]. For the first time, Kansans voted for their own senators— and Bristow lost!

During World War I, the former senator was chairman of the Kansas Public Utilities Commission. Through editorials in his Salina newspaper he crusaded against manufacturers and contractors. They were "robbing the people" by overcharging for munitions and other war materials, he said. ∎

Helps children across the state

Governor, U.S. senator, newspaper publisher and philanthropist. Garnett, Longton and Topeka. (1865-1951) Capper was born July 14, 1865, to Quaker parents. He grew up in Garnett, but the family also lived in Longton, and in New Jersey.

Arthur began his newspaper career as a ten-year-old salesman for the _Kansas City Times._ Two years later, his practical father gave him a small working printing press for Christmas. The young printer pleased his parents when he sold cards, tickets and handbills to neighbors and made a nice profit.

Devil of a guy

When he was thirteen, Arthur worked at the _Garnett Journal._ As the "printer's devil," his first task was inking the large hand press, which he had to reach by standing on a wooden cracker box. He also ran errands, set type, wrote news stories and was editor of his own column. His salary, one dollar a week.

After he graduated from Garnett High School in 1884, Capper left home to look for work as a printer. He traveled with only two possessions: a dollar and a watch that his mother had given him.

His journey ended in Topeka, where he found work at the _Daily Capital._ There he earned $25 a week arranging news stories and ads into finished pages. When Capper showed the editor a story he had written about a local politician, his boss promoted him to the job of reporter. The "promotion" was costly, however. A reporter's weekly salary was only $10!

Gets his feet wet

For several years Capper reported from the Shawnee County courthouse and the ⇨

Kansas statehouse. In 1891, he left Kansas for a time and worked for the *New York Tribune.* As one of his first assignments, the young country reporter watched a yacht race and wrote about it in a 600-word article. It was the first time Capper had even seen a yacht, but his surprised editor printed the story with no corrections.

His own boss

A year later Capper was a correspondent for the *Daily Capital* in Washington, D.C. Soon he returned to Topeka and married **Florence Crawford**, daughter of **Samuel Crawford**, Kansas governor in the 1860s. (As a member of the Florence town company in the 1870s, Crawford named that Marion County town in her honor.)

In 1893, the Cappers used $1,000 from Arthur's savings to make a down payment on their own newspaper, the weekly *North Topeka Mail.* Arthur was reporter, editor, advertising manager and pressman. Florence did the bookkeeping and addressed the papers. They hauled each week's mailing to the post office in a wheelbarrow.

The *Mail* was such a success that Capper was able to buy several other newspapers over the next few years. One of his purchases was his first employer, the *Daily Capital.* As Capper's business grew, his name and editorials became familiar around the state.

Close, close race

Republican leaders urged Capper to run for governor in 1912, which he did. However, he was defeated by **George Hodges** in the closest governor's race in Kansas history. Just 29 votes separated the two.

When Capper ran again two years later, he beat Democrat Hodges by over 47,000 votes and the Progressive candidate, Henry J. Allen [**31**], by an even wider margin. This election included two firsts: It was the first time women were able to vote for governor, and Capper was the first native-born Kansan elected to that office.

As governor, Capper always looked for ways to save the people's money. One of his first decisions was to live in his own home in Topeka, instead of in the state's executive mansion. During his two terms in office, he also changed the ways the state purchased materials and helped create a new state highway commission. At the same time, laws were passed allowing loans to rural people and pensions to widows with young children.

When America entered World War I, the Quaker governor put aside his religious beliefs in pacifism, or nonviolence. He made over 300 speeches, even though he was never known as a good public speaker. In each one he urged that the United States fight hard to win the war.

Senator Capper

In 1918, Capper ran for the U.S. Senate. He defeated three Republicans in the primary election, including former governor **Walter Stubbs** and former senator Joseph Bristow [**33**]. He beat his Democrat opponent that fall, and moved to Washington. There, in 1921, Capper organized senators and congressmen from farm states. The group, known as the farm bloc, worked for laws to help farmers.

Mrs. Capper died while her husband was serving in the Senate in 1926, but he stayed in Washington until he retired in 1949. Capper died in Topeka on December 19, 1951, at the age of 86. By that time, Capper Publications included ten newspapers and magazines with nearly five million readers, plus two radio stations.

A generous giver

Besides being one of Kansas' most recognized figures for many years, Capper was known across the nation as a generous philanthropist, or a person who

Happy birthday to Capper

During Capper's lifetime, thousands of children in the Topeka area enjoyed an extra holiday each year, July 14, his birthday.

For 43 years he filled a Topeka park with activities on that special day: carnival rides, entertainment, movies, races, contests, fireworks and even trolley and bus transportation to the event—all provided free. And, each guest was given

at least one free ice cream cone, passed out one year at the rate of 2,500 per hour!

The last Capper party was held in 1950. A crowd of about 20,000 persons jammed into Ripley Park to mark the senator's eighty-fifth birthday. The 1951 celebration had to be cancelled when the Kansas River caused a terrible flood in Topeka. Capper died later that year.

shares his wealth. He and his wife never had any children which is perhaps why he always supported causes for youth. About 1908, his newspapers first encouraged Kansas youngsters to join the Juvenile Flower Club. Free flower seeds were sent to members who agreed to share their flowers with patients in hospitals.

Then, when he was governor, Capper received a letter from a youngster saying, "Please help me buy a pig." Remembering a time in his own youth when a kindly man helped him, the governor loaned the boy money. He soon repeated the act for others.

Eventually Capper's name was on a long list of youth organizations: Boys' Pig Club, Girls' Poultry Club, Calf Club, Bee Club, Boys' Corn Club and Girls' Tomato Club. Up to ten children a year from each Kansas county could join the animal organizations, and buy livestock with money borrowed from Capper. After their animals were sold, members repaid the loans and kept any profits.

Each of those in the 1918 Pig Club earned about $150 after expenses were paid. By the 1920s, Capper had loaned over $100,000 to members of his clubs—and only $200 had not been returned. The senator was later a strong supporter of 4-H Clubs and other youth programs.

He established the Capper Foundation for handicapped children in 1920, after deciding that they needed more than candy at Christmas. In the mid 1950s, his estate gave funds for a new school and treatment center at the foundation. It still operates in Topeka and has provided help for thousands of children with special needs. In 1991, Capper—a politician, philanthropist and businessman—was inducted into the Kansas Business Hall of Fame. ∎

Milks cows

35 John Carlin

Governor. Smolan, Wichita and Topeka. (Born 1940) Before his election in 1979, Carlin was a dairy farmer and a member of the Kansas House of Representatives. During his two terms as governor, John was one of the state's most widely-traveled leaders as he tried to sell Kansas products in Europe and the Orient—in person. Carlin was divorced twice while in office, and was later married a third time. He ran for governor again in 1990, but like every other Kansas ex-governor who has tried to regain the office, he lost. Carlin was beaten in the primary election by state treasurer Joan Finney [**45**]. ∎

Wins 26 out of 26

36 Frank Carlson

Governor, U.S. senator and U.S. representative. Concordia. (1893-1987) Carlson was governor from 1947 to 1950. He was always popular with Kansas voters; they elected him in every one of the 26 elections he entered. This put Carlson in various elected offices almost continuously between 1929 and 1969. His 40 years of public service included terms in both houses in the U.S. Congress, something no other Kansas governor has done. Frank won his seat in the U.S. House of Representatives in 1934 by beating Kathryn O'Laughlin McCarthy [**72**]. Carlson resigned as governor after he was elected senator. He was one of several Republicans who convinced Dwight D. Eisenhower [**44**] to run for president. ∎

Slows war

37 Clark Clifford

U.S. secretary of defense. Fort Scott. (Born 1906) Clifford was born in Fort Scott and graduated from law school in St. Louis. He served in the U.S. Navy during World War II. After the war, he worked as a speech-writer and special counsel to President Harry S. Truman. One of Clark's assignments was to help write the law that created the Department of Defense in 1949.

In 1968, President Lyndon B. Johnson put Clifford in charge of the department he had helped create. As the secretary of defense, Clifford led a group of officials that persuaded Johnson to reduce America's role in the Vietnam War. ∎

Kansa becomes U.S. 'vice chief'

***U.S. senator and vice president. Topeka.
(1860-1939)*** Curtis was born near North Topeka, January 25, 1860, on land owned by his Indian grandmother. Because she was half French and half Kansa, Curtis was one-eighth Indian and a full member of the Kansa tribe.

His mother died in 1863, and when his father left to fight in the Civil War, three-year-old Charley lived with his Curtis grandparents in Topeka. Three years later, he rejoined his Indian grandmother and her family on the Kansa reservation near Council Grove.

Reservation life

He enjoyed Indian life: wearing the traditional clothing of the Kansa, learning marksmanship with a bow and arrow, and sleeping in a tipi. His mother taught him to swim the Indian way, by placing him in the Kansas River to splash about on his own.

Charley received some education at the mission school, but he spent most of his time with his pony Kate. He had learned riding skills early. His mother gave him his own horse when he was a year old and he could ride bareback by the age of three.

Raiding Cheyennes

In 1869, Cheyennes raided the Kansa reservation. Charley and several other boys were sent running down the creek to warn of the attack. Women and children took shelter in a barn

near the Indian agency. When the fighting was over, the chief asked English-speaking Charley to carry the news to Topeka.

With his pockets stuffed with buffalo meat, the young boy slipped away on foot at dusk. By traveling all night, he completed the 57-mile journey early the next afternoon.

Charley's Indian way of life ended after the raid; his Curtis grandparents felt he should leave the reservation and live in Topeka with them. The choice was a hard one for Charley to make, for he thought of himself

as an Indian. When they said he could bring his horse, he finally agreed to move.

At home in Topeka

Charley went off to school, where he stood out with his long black hair parted in the middle. Even though the nine-year-old could speak three languages—English, French and the language of the Kansa—he could not read. He studied hard, however, and soon reached the level of others his own age.

During his school years in Topeka, Charley helped support his grandparents. He sold fruit and peanuts on street corners, at Topeka's Union Pacific depot and at county fairs. He also shined shoes and was a newsboy, but another job made him famous.

'Indian Boy'

Charley used his horsemanship skills to become a jockey. After riding and winning in several races, he was known around the area as the "Indian Boy." He was hired to ride the famous racehorses of the time. Crowds loved his flashy Indian outfits, and admired the way he rode, hunched over Indian style. He used a rope running through the horse's mouth for reins.

One of Curtis' most exciting races was in 1872, but the excitement came from off the track. As he was waiting for the start of a quarter-mile race in Kansas City, the sound of gunshots was heard.

Word spread through the frightened crowd that the ticket window was being robbed. Everyone quickly scattered while the thieves made off with $6,000. Young Charley slipped off his racehorse and hid the valuable animal during the excitement.

When Curtis was fourteen, he was tempted to return to the Kansa reservation. His Grandmother Pappan, however, could see that his future was not with the tribe, and he sadly agreed.

He returned to racing for two years and earned $50 a month, plus ten percent of his winnings. At sixteen, however, his Grandmother Curtis convinced him to quit. He returned to school.

To support the two of them during his senior year, he drove a broken-down horse-drawn cab, or "hack," and carried passengers between Topeka's depots and hotels until midnight each night.

He graduated in 1879 as valedictorian of his class, and began studying law under a local attorney. In return, Curtis did janitor work around the law office. He became a lawyer in 1881 at the age of 21, and formed a partnership with another Topeka attorney.

Into politics

Just three years later he was elected county attorney. During his first month in office, Curtis enforced the prohibition law against selling liquor and closed 88 saloons in Shawnee County.

He returned to his law practice in 1889 and remained active in the Republican party. In 1892 Curtis ran for a seat in the U.S. House of Representatives. He won, and with his wife **Anna** and three children, moved to Washington, D.C.

"Our Charley," as Kansans called him, served in the House until 1907. Then he was appointed to a vacant seat in the U.S. Senate, making him the first native-born Kansan— and the first Native American— in the Senate. He remained there until early 1913. In those days, senators were chosen by the state legislatures, and he was not reelected by the Kansas lawmakers in their 1912 session. But when Curtis ran in the first popular election of senators in 1914, Kansans voted for him over Joseph Bristow [**33**]. Senator Curtis went back to work in Washington.

As a politician, he was not known for his long speeches. He did not sponsor many important bills. Instead, Curtis' strength was in convincing others to compromise, which helped make him a powerful Republican leader.

When that party met in Kansas City for its 1928 national convention, Curtis hoped to become the nominee for president. However, the delegates selected Herbert Hoover. Hoover then gave 68-year-old Curtis the vice-presidential spot in hopes of getting farmers' votes. The nomination was Curtis' reward for being a loyal Republican.

'Vice chief'

That fall, Hoover and Curtis were easily elected. Celebrations were held all over Kansas, and in neighboring Oklahoma, drums on the Kansa reservation beat out good news. A member of their tribe was "vice chief" of the nation. Sadly, Anna Curtis couldn't share in the joy. She had died in 1924. ✥

Not only was Curtis the first vice president from the Sunflower State, he was the first vice president of Indian ancestry—and the first to have an official automobile. Because he was a widower, his half-sister Dolly Gann served at events as his official hostess.

During the Great Depression voters turned down Hoover and Curtis' bid for a second term in 1932. It was the first and only election Curtis lost. He retired in Washington where he died February 8, 1936.

His body, along with a bow and arrow sent by a Kansa chief, was returned to Topeka. At Curtis' funeral in the Capitol, hundreds of people honored the Indian politician from Kansas. ■

Can't take no for an answer

39 Jonathan Davis

Governor. Bronson. _(1871-1943)_ Davis, a Democrat, was elected governor in 1922. His one term was stormy. He first upset the public when he forced the resignation of Dr. Samuel Crumbine [**101**], the respected secretary of the Kansas Board of Health. Next, Davis fired **_E.H. Lindley_**, the popular chancellor of the University of Kansas. And then, during his last hour in office, the controversial governor was arrested for selling paroles to convicts at the state penitentiary. He was later found innocent.

Although he served four terms in the Kansas House of Representatives and one term in the state senate, Davis spent most of his political career losing: He tried for the governorship in 1920, 1924, 1926, 1936, 1938, and lost. He tried for seats in the Kansas and U.S. legislatures in 1904, 1916, 1918, 1930, 1932, 1940, and lost.

In 1942 he ran for office one last time—in the lieutenant governor's race—and, yes, lost! ■

A family affair

40-41 George & Robert Docking

Governors. Clay Center, Topeka and Lawrence. (1904-1964) Lawrence and Arkansas City. (1925-1983) George Docking and his son Robert were the state's first father and son to both become governor. Both were also bankers.

The elder Docking was elected in 1956 and 1958, the first time a Democrat was reelected governor. He told voters he would limit state spending, and to prove it, he refused to live in Cedar Crest, which had just become the governor's mansion. He also promised to be more open than Fred Hall [**57**], the "secretive" governor before

him. True to his word, George Docking had a press conference with reporters every day.

Robert Docking entered the governor's office in 1967, just six years after his father left it. He was a popular leader, and during his administration the state's economy grew. In all, he was elected four times—the first governor in Kansas to serve third and fourth terms. (While Robert Docking was in office, the Kansas Constitution was changed. Under the old law, Kansas governors were elected to two-year terms, and could be reelected any number of times. Now the term of office is four years. A person can still become governor any number of times, but can serve only two terms in a row.)

Tom Docking, Robert's son and George's grandson, was lieutenant governor during John Carlin's [**35**] term. The younger Docking ran for governor himself in 1986. He lost to Republican Mike Hayden [**58**]. ■

Leads Republicans in the U.S. Senate

U.S. representative and U.S. senator. Russell. (Born 1923) Dole was born July 22, 1923, in Russell. His father ran a creamery and later managed a grain elevator. His mother was a seamstress who also sold sewing machines.

There was no money at the Dole house for extras like vacations and toys. Young Bobby, with his brother and two sisters, shared one bicycle and a pair of roller skates. One year the family lived in the basement of their small brick home and rented out the ground floor for extra income.

Bob had various odd jobs during his youth. He delivered copies of the *Russell Record*, helped at the elevator, washed cars and dug pipe trenches. He also worked at Dawson's Drugstore serving sodas and delivering prescriptions. He recalled, "I got a dollar a day for a full day and fifty cents for working nights, plus all the ice cream I wanted."

Tough athlete

In Russell High School, Bob was a tough competitor on the football, basketball and track teams. Basketball was his favorite, and the six-foot-two-inch senior was captain of his team. He also played basketball during the two years he attended the University of Kansas. Forrest "Phog" Allen [*264*] was his coach. Dole helped pay for his college tuition by working as a waiter and a milkman.

During World War II he left his premedical classes at KU to join the U.S. Army. He wanted to be a pilot in the Air Corps, but doctors discovered he was partially color blind, and he was sent to the infantry instead.

He quickly passed through officer's training school and was sent into combat in Italy. As a first lieutenant, he commanded a platoon of combat-trained skiers, although he himself had never skied.

Wounded in action

Dole was severely wounded in April 1945. He was leading an attack on a German gun position when a bullet shattered his right shoulder and broke his neck. Paralyzed, he lay for hours before medics found him. In the hospital, he first fought to stay alive—and then fought to use his arms and legs.

Doctors removed one of his kidneys, put him into a cast from his ears to his hips, and told him he might not walk again. After 39 months in hospitals in Italy, Africa and the United States, Dole's determination and physical therapy paid off; he began to walk once again.

He received a Bronze Star, a Purple Heart and the rank of captain for his ordeal. His right arm is still paralyzed.

Dole married ***Phyllis Holden*** soon after he left the hospital in 1948. At the same time, because of his handicap, he gave up his plans for a career in medicine and began studying law. While he learned to write with his left hand, his wife took notes and wrote out his examinations. ⇨

Young politician

Dole graduated with honors from Washburn University's law school in 1952. By that time he was already in politics. He had been elected to the Kansas House at age 27 and had served as a state representative during his last two years in law school. Several months after he graduated, he was elected to the first of four terms as county attorney in Russell County.

In 1960 Dole ran successfully for the U.S. House of Representatives, a seat he held for four terms. In the House, he voted against the spending programs of Presidents Kennedy and Johnson, but he was in favor of new civil rights laws. He supported most farm programs and served as a member of the Agriculture and the Government Operations committees.

When long-time Kansas senator Frank Carlson [36] retired in 1968, Dole was elected to the U.S. Senate. As a freshman lawmaker he defended President Nixon's unpopular decision to invade Cambodia during the Vietnam War. Some of Dole's critics called him Nixon's "hatchet-man," and the label lasted for several years.

National leader

Dole earned a national reputation when he was chosen to head the Republican National Committee in 1971, a job he held until 1973. During that period, Bob and Phyllis were divorced. She returned to Kansas and later married a banker. In 1975 he married Elizabeth Hanford, a member of the Federal Trade Commission.

President Gerald Ford selected Dole as his candidate for vice president in 1976. The senator traveled across the country speaking for their ticket, but some said his sarcastic comments during the campaign may have hurt Ford's chances for election.

Presidential tries

Dole ran for president himself in 1980, but withdrew after he didn't do well in several state primary elections. That November he was reelected to his third term in the Senate, and the following January he became chairman of the important Senate Finance Committee.

In 1984, Republican senators chose Dole to be the Senate Majority Leader. From this powerful post, he acted as a link between President Ronald Reagan and the Senate. When Republicans lost their majority in the Senate, Dole became the Minority Leader.

He ran for president again in 1988, and beat the other Republican candidates in the Iowa primary election—including George Bush. Polls predicted Dole would win in the important New Hampshire primary election, but Bush came out on top. Dole eventually dropped out of the campaign, and said later that his age would probably keep him out of any future presidential races. He continues his important job in the Senate.

Over the years, many say the senator from Kansas has changed his style. He has always been quick with his tongue, and for several years he was called "abrasive," a "political gunslinger," and a "hard-line conservative." Today his comments don't seem as sharp, and he is often described as being more moderate and agreeable, warm and witty.

Respected opinion

Dole's Senate position has often made him a spokesman for Presidents Reagan and Bush. He appears frequently on television to comment on situations in the United States and around the world. His wife Elizabeth has served as head of the U.S. Departments of Transportation and Labor. She became head of the American Red Cross in 1990. Some have said the Doles have more political power than any other couple in Washington. ∎

No dancing with wolves

43 John Dunbar

U.S. Army lieutenant, author and educator. Brown County and Topeka. (1841-1914) In the movie *Dances with Wolves*, a fictional U.S. Army lieutenant comes to Fort Hays, looking for the West. Michael Blake, author of the *Dances* novel and screenplay, borrowed the name John Dunbar for his character from a Civil War soldier who lived in Kansas, John Brown Dunbar.

The real Dunbar grew up in Nebraska and Brown County while his father was an Indian missionary. During the Civil War, Lieutenant Dunbar served in Louisiana and Virginia. In the 1870s he taught at Topeka's Washburn College. He was later a school official in the East. Dunbar wrote at least six books on Indians and history, including one about the Kansas visit of the French explorer *Étienne Véniard de Bourgmont*. So far as is known, Dunbar never danced with wolves. ∎

U.S. president, U.S. Army general and author. Abilene and Fort Leavenworth. (1890-1969) Although Dwight D. Eisenhower was born in the small Texas town of Denison, he was destined to become Kansas' best known citizen. His roots, in fact, went deep into the Sunflower State. In the 1870s, his Eisenhower grandparents moved from Pennsylvania to a farm near Abilene.

David Eisenhower, the future president's father, was then fourteen. Several years later he met and married ***Ida Stover***, a fellow student at Lane University in Lecompton. As a wedding gift from David's parents, they received $2,000 and a 160-acre farm. Instead of farming, David mortgaged the land and used the money to buy a general store in the small town of Hope near Abilene. Two years later, drought and hard times hit Kansas and their business went bankrupt. Humiliated and out of work, David moved his wife and two young sons to Texas. He took a mechanic's job with the Cotton Belt Railroad in Denison.

There, in a rented house, son David Dwight was born on October 14, 1890. While he was a baby, however, Ida reversed his names to Dwight David. She wanted to avoid having two Davids in the family.

Boy, oh boys

Before Dwight was a year old the Eisenhowers moved back to Kansas. David got a job as a mechanic at the Belle Star Creamery, a milk-processing plant in Abilene. Within several years he and Ida had a houseful of six boys. (A seventh son died as a baby.) Edgar, Dwight's next-older brother, was known as "Big Ike." Dwight was "Little Ike," and later, just "Ike."

Kansas' favorite son

When Ike was about eight, the family moved into a small, two-story house on the south side of Abilene—the "wrong side of the tracks." While the Eisenhowers were indeed poor, David and Ida provided a comfortable, loving home for their sons. The boys shared three rooms upstairs.

Mr. Eisenhower's salary barely paid for the family's clothing and medical care. At times, Ike and his brothers had to wear their mother's old high-button shoes to school. Except for buying supplies like fuel, coffee and salt, the Eisenhowers took care of their needs through what they raised in the garden and barn.

While David worked at the creamery twelve hours a day, six days a week, Ida ran the house, with help from her sons. ✐

Sharing the workload

The brothers took turns getting up before dawn to build a fire in the kitchen stove. Most of them learned to cook, too. Dwight, especially, enjoyed his time in the kitchen. After church school on Sundays he often helped fix dinner to give his mother a day off.

One Sunday he and a brother got into a fight while they were making a pie. Before the scuffle was over, boys and pie were all over the kitchen floor. When they heard their parents returning from church, the young chefs quickly scraped the mess into a pan and baked it. After Mrs. Eisenhower remarked about the tasty dessert, Dwight confessed.

While some brothers had cooking or cleaning duties in the house, the others fed the animals, gathered eggs and milked. During the spring and summer, the boys also helped in the garden. They knew if they didn't work they wouldn't eat. Their father allowed each boy to have his own piece of the garden, too. Dwight earned extra cash by raising and selling sweet corn for a penny or two an ear.

"Waste not, want not," the practical parents taught their sons. When Dwight accidentally shot one of the family's

chickens, he knew how upset his mother would be. To get rid of the evidence in the most practical way, he plucked, cleaned, cooked, ate it—and then buried the bones.

In his free time, Ike enjoyed sports, especially baseball and football. He also spent time with his friends and brothers hunting, fishing, swimming and camping at the Smoky Hill River.

In the spring of 1903, Dwight and Edgar nearly washed away. They and several friends were watching floodwaters rise along Abilene's Buckeye Street when a piece of wooden sidewalk floated by. The boys jumped on and began paddling their makeshift raft down the street. As they sang and played, they were unaware that the water was rushing toward the raging river.

A horseman spotted them, warned them to get off, and then herded them back home through waist-deep water. Ida met her sons at the door, whipped them with a maple switch and sent them to bed without supper. When David heard of their stunt, he made them clear the flood debris from their yard—and pump the mud and water out of their flooded cellar. The punishment took more than a week.

Sets his mind

The Eisenhower boys were close, but there were fights, too. Edgar once estimated he gave Dwight a hundred "lickings," but the younger brother's firey temper always brought him back for more.

Ike's mother called him "a little pouter." But sometimes his stubbornness paid off. As a young teenager, a cut on his knee became infected and he developed blood poisoning. For two weeks the family doctor warned that the boy would die unless his leg was amputated, but his worried parents said the decision was up to their son. Ike refused.

With Edgar promising not to allow the doctor to operate, Ike slipped in and out of con-

All six a success

After World War II, Ida Eisenhower was asked if she wasn't enormously proud of her famous son. "Which one?" she replied.

Perhaps her other five boys weren't really as famous as Dwight, but in different fields, each found success.

The youngest Eisenhower, Milton [103], was an educator and presidential advisor. *Roy* was a pharmacist, *Earl* worked in public relations and *Edgar* became a lawyer.

Arthur, the oldest, was a noted banker. Early in his career he roomed with a young Missourian named Harry S. Truman.

sciousness for several days. The family waited and prayed, and the swelling in his blackened leg gradually went down. By the time he recovered he had missed so much school he had to repeat the eighth grade.

Class historian

Dwight made average to above grades in most subjects, with ancient history being his favorite. For a time he was reading so many books on Greek and Roman history that his mother had to hide them to make sure he got his chores done.

When Henry J. Allen [31] spoke at Eisenhower's high school graduation ceremony in 1909, Ike had no real career plans. His school yearbook predicted he would be a history professor at Yale (and his brother Edgar would be elected president). He never expected to become a soldier.

Both Dwight and Edgar wanted to attend college, although Ike later admitted he was more interested in playing college football and baseball than in receiving a degree. Since their parents couldn't afford expenses for even one son, the two brothers agreed on a plan.

Edgar would enroll for a year, while Dwight would work to support him. The next year, Edgar would stay out of school and help Dwight. And so Ike took a night job at the creamery —84 hours per week. His wages of 26 cents an hour, plus money he earned shocking wheat and playing semi-pro baseball, helped him save nearly $300 for his brother's education.

Some nights at work, he was visited by a friend who hoped to get into the U.S. Naval Academy at Annapolis. As they talked, Ike had an idea. The military was a way to receive a free college education. Eisenhower wrote to Senator Joseph Bristow [33] and, with letters of recommendation from Abilene's important businessmen, he was allowed to take entrance exams for the Naval Academy and the U.S. Military Academy at West Point.

To prepare for the tough tests, Ike and his friend studied together six or more hours a day. He also returned to high school for a few months to take advanced courses in math and science. At the same time, he continued working at the creamery each night.

Young military man

Eisenhower passed both tests, and his score put him at the top of the list to go to Annapolis. When the Navy said he was a few months too old to meet its standards, he accepted a position at the U.S. Military Academy at West Point.

Dwight passed his final examination at St. Louis in the spring of 1911 and left Abilene early that June. Little did he realize he would return to Kansas only for short visits. Before he left, his mother told him joining the military was his own choice. But she was a strong pacifist, or one who doesn't believe in fighting wars. When he left for the depot, she said her goodbys at home; then she went to her room and cried.

Eisenhower arrived at West Point with five dollars in his pocket and a suitcase of belongings. As a freshman, or plebe, he accepted most of the harsh discipline given out by instructors and upperclassmen, but he broke his share of rules, too, and pulled some pranks.

One day an upperclassman ordered Ike and a friend to report to his room in full-dress coats, meaning their complete uniforms. When they appeared, they were wearing *only* their coats—nothing else. For that, Eisenhower had to spend hours standing with his body flat against the wall. For other demerits—being late for inspection, wearing unpolished shoes, smoking in his room—Dwight spent many Sunday afternoons marching on the parade ground.

His biggest interest at West Point was playing football. He was only on the second string his freshman year, but in his sophomore year he became a first-team halfback. Then a knee injury put the "Kansas Cyclone" on the sideline permanently. Ike was disappointed and thought of quitting the academy. Eventually his teammates elected him cheerleader. He also became a student coach.

When he graduated in June 1915, his injury nearly kept him from becoming an officer. For a time he considered going to Argentina to work as a cowboy. Physicians changed their minds, however, and Ike was made a second lieutenant in the infantry.

Newlywed soldier

During Eisenhower's first assignment, at Fort Sam Houston, Texas, he met Mamie Doud, a wealthy young girl visiting from Colorado. For him, it was love at first sight. A few months later Mamie accepted Ike's West Point ring. They were married in July 1916, at the Douds' home in Denver.

The same day he was promoted to first lieutenant. The newlyweds traveled by train to Abilene that night, and met the Eisenhower family at 4 a.m. the next morning. David greeted them while Ida prepared an early breakfast of fried chicken. ✿

When America was soon drawn into World War I, Ike wanted an assignment overseas. The Army had other plans. He spent most of the war training volunteers to drive a new weapon, the tank. Eventually he commanded the newly formed Tank Corps.

In the summer of 1919 Eisenhower took part in the first motorized transcontinental convoy. The "truck train" was a two-month trek of 81 military vehicles from Washington, D.C., to San Francisco. Most of the "roads" they followed were unpaved trails, either muddy or dusty. Forty years later, as president, Ike remembered the experience when he supported the Interstate Highway System.

In late 1920, the Eisenhowers' three-year-old son, Doud—nicknamed "Icky"—died of scarlet fever. That memory troubled Ike for years. Until his own death, he always sent Mamie flowers on Icky's birthday.

In 1922, several months before their second son, John, was born, Eisenhower was transferred to the Panama Canal Zone. There he was the executive officer to General Fox Conner. For three years Conner drilled him in military tactics. The general then helped Ike get

into the Army's Command and General Staff School at Fort Leavenworth.

More training

When he arrived at the Kansas post in 1925, Eisenhower was much more serious about his studies than he had been at West Point. On graduation day, out of 275 promising young officers in his class, he ranked first.

After a short assignment in Georgia, Ike was ordered to Washington. General John J. Pershing, Chief of Staff of the U.S. Army, wanted him to write a guide to the American World War I battlefields in France.

Pershing was pleased with Eisenhower's results, and sent him to the Army War College for further training.

Then, with Mamie and John, Ike spent fifteen months in Paris, studying the battlefields he had written about. He also became familiar with the French railroad and highway system, valuable knowledge that helped him during World War II.

From 1929 to 1935 the Eisenhowers lived in Washington while Dwight worked under Army Chief of Staff General Douglas MacArthur. When a newspaper offered him $20,000—five times his Army pay—to become a military writer, Ike was tempted to take the job; he was discouraged with desk work and wanted to command troops. He stayed on, however, and went to the Philippine Islands with General MacArthur in 1935.

The United States was about to give the Philippine colony its independence, and MacArthur and Eisenhower were to help the Filipinos organize their own army. During four years in the Pacific, Ike became a lieutenant colonel, his first promotion since 1920. He also took flying lessons, which later made him the first American president who could pilot a plane.

Eisenhower and his family left the Philippines in late 1939. By that time, Adolph Hitler's German troops had invaded Poland and World War II had begun. Although the United States was not directly involved, many realized America's days of peace were limited.

Back in the States, Ike enjoyed several short assignments in command of troops—"soldiering" as he called it. But in the summer of 1941 he returned to a desk as a planner in the Louisiana maneuvers, a large war

Poker face

A few weeks after they were married Ike took Mamie back to Abilene for a visit.

One afternoon, he went uptown to meet his old gang at their favorite cafe. As the hours passed, Mamie became angry and phoned Ike at the restaurant. He apologized, but said he was losing money playing poker. "Come home this minute!"

his new bride told him before she slammed the receiver down.

He didn't—until 2 a.m. when he left the game well ahead. She was waiting at the door. The fight that followed, they both said later, was their biggest, longest and most serious. The argument, however, gave them new respect for each other's strong will and brought them more deeply in love than ever.

game. Nearly 400,000 American troops took part. Eisenhower planned strategies for the 3rd Army, and it won easily.

In command of war

Three months later the Japanese attacked Pearl Harbor, pushing the United States into war. The Army's Chief of Staff, General George C. Marshall, quickly called Ike to Washington. By early 1942 Marshall and Eisenhower convinced top British commanders that the United States and Great Britain should combine their war efforts. After the plan was put into effect, Marshall decided Eisenhower should become supreme commander of the European Theater of Operations.

Ike arrived in England in late June 1942. Soon he launched Operation Torch, aimed at forcing the Axis powers—Germany and Italy—out of North Africa. The offensive began in November and by the spring of 1943 the Allies controlled African territory south of the Mediterranean Sea.

D-Day

In December 1943 President Franklin Roosevelt put Eisenhower in charge of World War II's most critical operation. Overlord, as it was called, was the Allies' plan to free Europe with an invasion across the English Channel into occupied France. But before Ike began the huge task of planning and carrying out Overlord, General Marshall insisted he take some time off. Early in January 1944 Eisenhower flew to the United States. His "vacation" consisted of meetings in Washington, a few precious days with Mamie, and a secret trip to Kansas for a brief family reunion.

Back in London, the Supreme Allied Commander took charge of 16,000 personnel at SHAEF, Supreme Headquarters Allied Expeditionary Force. D-Day, or the day of the invasion, was set for the first of May. By the end of January Eisenhower and his planners had moved the date to early June to allow more time to gather men and equipment. In all, 4,000 ships, 12,000 aircraft and 20,000 vehicles would be needed to move the 176,000 troops into place.

While General George Patton's troops and some fake equipment acted as a decoy at Dover, England, the real invasion force was assembled farther south along the English coast.

With everything in place, Eisenhower set the invasion in motion on the evening of June 3. Stormy weather, however, forced him to order the ships back to port about 4 a.m. on June 4.

That evening he visited paratroopers, including Kansans in the 105th Airborne, as they prepared to board their planes. A few hours later Ike gave the final go-ahead—although the weather was still bad. But the skies cleared and early on the morning of June 6, 1944, what he called the "Great Crusade" began.

Thousands were killed or injured on the beaches of France, but D-Day was a success. It was the beginning of the end for the German occupation of Europe.

Paris was liberated within a few weeks, the Allies captured their first German city that fall, and on May 7, 1945, Eisenhower accepted the surrender of Germany from its army's chief of staff.

Hero's homecoming

Ike—by then a five-star general—was a hero on two continents. He was cheered in Paris and was made a citizen of London. Back in the United States in June, he addressed a joint session of Congress, appeared in one of New York City's largest ticker-tape parades and then flew to Kansas City for a triumphant train ride to Abilene. His hometown of 5,000 swelled to perhaps 20,000 to welcome him home.

That fall, he was back in Washington as the Army Chief of Staff. In early 1948 he retired from the service. As a civilian for the first time in over three decades, he spent several months writing *Crusade in Europe*, a book about the war.

From the summer of 1948 through 1950, Eisenhower was president of Columbia University in New York City. Early the next year, President Harry Truman asked the popular retired general to go to Europe as the first military commander of the North Atlantic Treaty Organization. NATO, a group of nations that agreed to share in the defense of Western Europe, was an organization Ike strongly supported after the war. ↪

EISENHOWER • USA

6¢

'I like Ike'

Back at home, Democrats and Republicans alike felt Eisenhower should run for president. He had heard those suggestions before, and always said that he had no interest in the position; he was just a "Kansas farmer boy." But at the urging of top Republicans, including fellow Kansans Frank Carlson [*36*], Charles Harger [*207*] and *Harry Darby*, he began to change his mind. In early 1952 he agreed to run. When he returned from Europe that June, "I like Ike" was heard everywhere.

He was nominated a few weeks later at the Republican National Convention in Chicago—the first political convention broadcast live on television. The 61-year-old Eisenhower selected as his running mate a young senator from California, Richard Nixon.

In the weeks before the election, Ike and Mamie visited 45 states, most during a 50,000-mile trip on the "Look Ahead, Neighbor" train. At hundreds of towns and cities, they appeared on the platform of the rear car and spoke to crowds gathered along the tracks. Their rail journey was the last whistle-stop campaign for a presidential candidate. It was also a relief for Mamie. She hated to fly.

On Election Day 1952 Eisenhower defeated Adlai Stevenson, his Democratic opponent, in a landslide. The favorite son of the thirty-fourth state was elected the thirty-fourth president. (In 1956 Ike would beat Stevenson again by a wider margin—even after suffering a serious heart attack in the fall of 1955.)

Before his first inauguration, the president-elect visited Korea, scene of the two-year-old Korean War. Ike spent time on the front lines with American troops who were helping South Koreans fight the Communists of North Korea. There he drew his own conclusions about the best ways to end the conflict.

Mr. President

Six months after he was sworn in on January 20, 1953, the Korean War ended. During Eisenhower's eight years in office, however, Communism continued to threaten world peace. He supported SEATO, an organization of nations to defend Southeast Asia against Communist aggression. He allowed undercover action aimed at overthrowing Communist governments in Iran, Cuba, Guatemala and the Congo (Zaire).

At the same time, he tried to break the Cold War tension by meeting with Soviet premier Nikita Krushchev. The leaders did make some progress in two discussions about nuclear weapons, but just before their third meeting, the Soviets shot down an American U-2 spy plane deep in their territory. Not realizing they had captured the pilot, Eisenhower tried to cover up the truth in his statements to the public. Krushchev used this fact to embarrass the president at their meeting. Talks ended when Premier Krushchev and his advisors walked out.

At home, President Eisenhower signed a law creating the St. Lawrence Seaway, the important Canadian-American shipping lane from the Great Lakes to the Atlantic Ocean. He also supported creation of the Interstate Highway System—the first miles of which were built in Kansas, near Topeka.

In Eisenhower's first term, the Department of Health, Education and Welfare (now the Department of Health and Human Services) was established. After the Soviet Union launched *Sputnik*, its first satellite, the Eisenhower administration created NASA in 1958.

In the area of civil rights, President Eisenhower was opposed to the school desegregation decision of *Brown vs. Topeka Board of Education* [*94, 100*] because he felt states, not the federal government, should integrate schools. But when riots broke out in Little Rock, Arkansas, because black students were admitted into a white high school, Eisenhower sent 1,000 paratroopers to stop the violence.

At ease

In 1961, Ike and Mamie left public life and retired to a spacious farmhouse near Gettysburg, Pennsylvania. It was the only home they ever owned. He painted, followed politics and wrote three books: *At Ease: Stories I Tell to Friends* and *The White House Years*, a two-volume story of his presidency.

Eisenhower suffered a second heart attack in 1965. As his health failed, he spent much of his last year in Walter Reed Army Hospital in Washington, D.C. He died there on March 28, 1969. After funeral services in Washington, a special train carried his body back to Abilene for burial in the Place of Meditation at the Eisenhower Center. Nearby are his boyhood home, presidential library and museum.

Recent historians have called Dwight D. Eisenhower one of the ten greatest presidents in American history. ∎

Mrs. Governor and the first gentleman

Governor and state treasurer. Manhattan and Topeka. (Born 1925) First gentleman. Topeka. (Born 1931) Finney is the first woman governor of Kansas. She was born February 12, 1925, in Manhattan.

Although she is now a Democrat, Joan began her political career as a Republican. For sixteen years she worked for Senator Frank Carlson [**36**] in his Washington, D.C., and Topeka offices. The job put her in close touch with other important Republicans, Dwight D. Eisenhower [**44**] and Alf Landon [**67**].

A change in politics

When Carlson retired, Finney became the election commissioner for Shawnee County. She also worked as an assistant to the mayor of Topeka for a time. In 1972 she tried for a seat in the U.S. House of Representatives, but lost. Two years later, Governor Robert Docking [**41**] and other prominent Democrats urged her to join their party and run for the office of state treasurer. She accepted their invitation, won the election and held the treasurer's job for sixteen years.

Against the odds

Finney entered the governor's race in 1990 and traveled 28,000 miles, crisscrossing the state to meet voters. Even though political polls predicted she would lose by perhaps twenty percentage points, she beat the odds—and her primary election opponent, former Democratic governor John Carlin [**35**].

The win pitted her against Republican governor Mike Hayden [**58**] in the general election. Hayden's $2 million campaign spending, personal campaigning by President and Mrs. George Bush, and a predicted win in the political polls weren't enough to defeat Finney. She won the November 1990 election, fooling the polls once again.

When 65-year-old Finney and her lieutenant governor, former state senator **Jim Francisco**, were sworn in the following January, she became not only the first woman to run the state, but the oldest person to serve as governor of Kansas. And Finney is also perhaps the first harp player in the governor's office!

Wants populism

During her campaign Finney promised Kansas voters she would bring populism, or a "people's government" back to the state, much as Governor Lorenzo Lewelling [**70**], Governor **John Leedy**, and their supporters [**78, 89, 102, 112**] wanted to do in the 1890s.

Early in Finney's term, however, legislators didn't seem to agree with her brand of populism. The 1991 legislative ⇨

Courtesy **Richard Crowson**, *The Wichita Eagle*

session stretched into the longest on record as senators and representatives argued over her proposals. Four times she vetoed, or turned down, laws they had passed—only to have the lawmakers override, or kill, her veto. It was the first time since 1977 that the legislature had overruled a governor. In the 1992 session several of her proposals passed, including a new school funding plan.

Governor Finney's husband Spencer was born in Topeka on January 20, 1931. He was an auditor for the Kansas Department of Revenue and then spent 30 years working for the Santa Fe Railway. The Finneys were married in 1957 after they were introduced by Spencer's father, a friend of Senator Carlson.

As the state's "first gentleman," Spencer is in charge of the daily operation of Cedar Crest, the governor's mansion. He is also active in special causes. ■

Knows all the answers

47 Marlin Fitzwater

Presidential press secretary. Salina and Abilene. (Born 1942) Fitzwater, press secretary to Presidents Ronald Reagan and George Bush, grew up on a farm near Abilene. He became an award-winning public speaker in the sixth grade when he won a speech contest. Unfortunately, the young speechwriter came down with the mumps before he could claim his prize—a trip to Topeka.

Marlin got his prize job in Washington, D.C., after working as a speechwriter and public relations officer in several government offices, including the Environmental Protection Agency and U.S. Treasury Department. Fitzwater was the press secretary to Vice President George Bush when Ronald Reagan asked him to be his presidential press spokesman in 1987. The Kansan kept the job when Bush, his former boss, became president in 1989.

As White House press secretary, Fitzwater gave the president's official statements to the press and public. He also answered reporters' questions when the president was not available. Fitzwater made one of his most dramatic announcements in early 1991. His short sentence, "The liberation of Kuwait has begun," told listeners across the nation and around the world that the war in the Persian Gulf had started. ■

At the eye of the storm

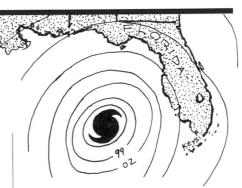

48 Neil Frank

Director of the National Hurricane Center and television meteorologist. Norton and Wellington. (Born 1930) Frank was a star player on the Wellington High School basketball team and went to Southwestern College in Winfield hoping to become a basketball coach.

Neil's plans were changed when he went into the military in 1953. While in the U.S. Air Force he studied meteorology. During a two-year assignment on the island of Okinawa he experienced his first hurricane.

After his discharge, Frank still hoped to be a coach. He enrolled at Florida State University, but his interest in weather eventually won out. He graduated with a doctor's degree in meteorology in 1961. That same year he was offered a job at the National Hurricane Center in Coral Gables, Florida. He was named deputy director of the center in 1973 and became its director a year later.

Dr. Frank was in charge of the NHC for over ten years. Along with other forecasters, he used reports from weather satellites, radar, pilot observations and other sources to predict the path of hurricanes. In hurricane season he often gave up-to-the-minute reports on network television and radio. During hurricane Elena in the fall of 1985, he did 140 live interviews in one weekend.

Frank still enjoys sharing his weather forecasts with the public, for now he is a television meteorologist in Houston. ■

49 Frederick Funston

Rough-and-ready Fred

Fearless Freddy

U.S. Army general. Iola. (1865-1917) Funston was born in Ohio on November 9, 1865. He came to Kansas three years later when his family moved to a homestead in Allen County near Iola.

Edward Funston, Frederick's father, became active in politics and served twenty years in the Kansas and U.S. Houses of Representatives. "Farmer Funston," as the congressman was called, was six feet, two inches in height, but his son stopped growing at only five feet, four. In his own way, however, the short Frederick towered over his tall father.

Fearless Freddy

At an early age the sandy-haired Freddy had a reputation for being fearless. Once, when he and several other ten-year-olds were raccoon hunting in the woods, a group of older boys heard about their plans and hid in the area. The teen-agers let out an outburst and all the young hunters ran, except Freddy. He raised his light rifle and calmly began firing in the direction of the sounds—which stopped immediately. The pranksters were not hurt, and Freddy's hunting trips were not interrupted again.

When he entered high school in Iola, he made the daily ten-mile round trip by horseback. He did his share of chores on the family farm and sometimes ⇨

Fred Funston

went to bed right after supper in order to begin studying at 4 a.m. the next morning. He read nearly every book he could find, and often used information he remembered to help his father write campaign speeches.

After his high school graduation in the 1880s, Funston applied for admission to the U.S. Military Academy at West Point, but he was turned down. Both his size and grade average were below the standards. He decided to teach at a rural school near Iola instead.

Tough teacher

He was about the same age—and smaller in size—than some of his pupils, but Frederick didn't mind. One morning the school bully began spitting tobacco juice on the floor. Instructor Funston told him to use the coal bucket as a spittoon, but the student refused. For good measure, he pulled out a pistol to scare the "new little teacher." A scuffle soon followed. The tobacco-spitter was trounced, sent on his way, and Frederick returned to his classes.

At the end of the year, Funston left teaching, took a long trip to Mexico, and then entered the University of Kansas in the fall of 1886. He worked to pay his own expenses, but his classwork suffered because his first concerns at college seemed to be friends and fun. He met William Allen White [256] while at Lawrence, and the two were close friends for years.

Frederick attended classes off and on for several semesters, but also took time for adventuresome work. He spent the summer of 1887 in western Kansas on a survey crew for the Santa Fe Railroad.

That fall, he was hired as a police reporter for a Kansas City newspaper. He shared a room with his friend White, who was also working in Kansas City. Funston later worked as a court reporter for an Arkansas newspaper. Then it was back to Kansas as a ticket collector for the railroad.

Desert heat to Arctic cold

In 1890 he left the university, without graduating, and joined a party of scientists on a trip to the Dakota Badlands. They were impressed with his work and hired him a year later to be a botanist on an expedition to Death Valley, California.

On that trip, Funston survived a 40-mile trek across the desert—in temperatures that hit 147 degrees. Once, on the side of a mountain, his horse lost its footing and began sliding toward a rocky gorge. Funston managed to grab a dangling shrub, but his animal fell 1,000 feet to its death.

Frederick helped open a new trail into Yosemite Valley and spent time with the Panamint Indians in California. He was next off to Alaska to study plant life. He traveled the snow-covered tundra by dogsled, crossing the Arctic circle to reach the Arctic Ocean. He spent the winter of 1893-94 alone on the banks of the Klondike River—at temperatures that reached 70 degrees below zero. The next spring he built his own boat and paddled 1,500 miles down the Yukon River to the sea.

That adventure was followed by a short stay in Central America where he tried to grow coffee. From there he went to New York City to represent the Santa Fe Railroad. While in

Pint-sized train conductor

During the months that Funston worked as a ticket collector for the Santa Fe Railroad, the young conductor met all kinds of characters on his runs between Kansas and New Mexico.

On one trip, a huge, drunken cowboy sprawled in the aisle and began shooting holes in the passenger car's ceiling.

The 23-year-old Funston (who weighed just over 100 pounds) burst in, kicked the revolver out of the man's hand, dragged him to the last car, and dumped him onto the rear platform. When the train stopped to let him off, the angry cowboy grabbed a rock and smashed a window. Frederick, his brown eyes blazing, then chased him a mile down the track.

Another cowpoke once got on the train with no ticket. He pulled out a pistol and told Frederick, "I ride on this."

Funston walked away saying quietly, "That's good, that's good," and soon reappeared with a rifle. He cocked the weapon, pointed it at the cowboy and said, "I came back to punch that ticket." The surprised man quickly paid his fare!

New York he heard a fiery speech about Cuba's fight for independence from Spain and decided to join the cause.

War hero

The young Kansan fought in the Cuban army for eighteen months, was wounded three times, and lost seventeen horses—some shot out from under him. Spanish forces eventually captured Funston and sentenced him to death, but he escaped by inventing a wild story and swallowing his passport. He returned to the front lines and became a lieutenant colonel before he became ill with malaria and had to go home in 1898.

That was just the beginning of Funston's exciting military career. In the Spanish-American War Kansas governor **William Stanley** made him colonel of a regiment of Kansas men. The force was sent to the Philippine Islands where Colonel Funston soon made a name for himself by capturing a notorious rebel leader named Emilio Aguinaldo.

With 100 Philippine soldiers, Funston and five officers marched through dense jungle to reach General Aguinaldo's fort. The Filipinos, pretending the Americans were their prisoners, took Funston and his men to Aguinaldo. Quickly, the Americans tied up the rebel leader and others in his group. Then, tightly surrounded by the native troops, Funston marched his captives away under the noses of a thousand of Aguinaldo's men.

Funston's brave action helped end years of fighting in the Philippines. He received the Congressional Medal of Honor and the rank of brigadier general for his heroism. At 34, he became

the youngest general in the U.S. Army; his name was a household word across the country.

After he returned to the United States, Funston married Eda Blankart. When San Francisco was struck by the disastrous earthquake of 1906, he was in charge of the Army's Department of California. General Funston immediately offered

troops and supplies. His firm control of the chaotic situation made him "the idol of millions."

Back in Kansas

The Funstons returned to Kansas where he commanded the Army's military college at Fort Leavenworth. In 1914, he took charge of American troops on the Texas-Mexico border.

President Woodrow Wilson appointed him major general that year, and for a time he was the commander of several future military leaders: Captain Douglas MacArthur, Lieutenant George Patton and Lieutenant Dwight D. Eisenhower [44].

Funston suffered a fatal heart attack during a banquet given in his honor at San Antonio, February 19, 1917. The 51-year-old Kansan was buried on a hill overlooking San Francisco. President Wilson praised Funston and the Army named Camp Funston, an important World War I training site near Fort Riley, in his honor. ∎

Greets the president at Congress' door

50 Ernest Garcia

Sergeant at arms of the U.S. Senate and presidential advisor. Garden City. (Born 1946) Garcia grew up in Garden City. He was nominated as the Senate's sergeant of arms by Senator Bob Dole [42] in 1985. In that job, Ernest was head of the Capitol police force and the building's tour guides. He was also in charge of daily operations

at the Senate. Perhaps best of all, it was his duty to greet the president and any foreign leaders as they visited the Capitol building. Garcia has also been an assistant to Senator Dole, a special assistant and advisor to President Ronald Reagan and deputy assistant secretary of defense. He is now a business executive in Washington, D.C. ∎

Air capital's chief fire fighter

51 Lawrence Garcia

Fire chief. St. John and Wichita. (Born 1936) Garcia grew up in St. John and served in the U.S. Marine Corps in the 1950s. After he left the military, he joined the Wichita fire department. He became its chief training instructor in 1980. In 1987 Lawrence was named the fire chief of Wichita where he is in charge of over 350 firemen. ■

Spying at the top

52 Robert Gates

Director of the Central Intelligence Agency and presidential advisor. Wichita. (Born 1944) Gates grew up in Wichita and first became interested in governmental spying, or intelligence gathering, when he was in college. After he completed his master's degree in history in 1966 Robert joined the CIA. Three years later he became an intelligence analyst, one who studies information about a country's foreign policy.

Gates received a doctor's degree in Russian and Soviet history in 1974. At the same time, he took a job with the National Security Council, the group that coordinates America's defense and foreign policy. The NSC's members include the president, vice president and other high officials.

Robert impressed those on the NSC, and he soon became a top aide at the CIA. In 1985 President Ronald Reagan named a new CIA director and Gates took the job of assistant director. He was later acting CIA director when the director died. Reagan nominated Gates for the director's position, but some accused the Kansan of taking part in a secret plan to sell weapons to Iran and give the profits to rebels in Nicaragua. Although Gates said he wasn't involved in the Iran-Contra scandal, he withdrew from the nomination.

Gates remained with the CIA and became President George Bush's deputy national security advisor in 1989. Two years later Bush again nominated Gates for the top CIA position. After weeks of hearings in the U.S. Senate, Gates finally got the job. ■

Governs two states and a pair of cities

53 John Geary

Territorial governor. Lecompton. (1819-1873) Geary had been a schoolteacher, store clerk, surveyor, lieutenant colonel in the Mexican War and the first mayor of San Francisco before President Franklin Pierce appointed him governor of Kansas Territory in 1856. The Bleeding Kansas fighting was at its height, and John worked hard to stop the battling between the proslavery and Free State forces.

Later that year he told President Pierce, "Peace now reigns in Kansas." But the trouble soon began again. When President James Buchanan took office in early 1857 he fired Geary. With threats against his life, the ex-governor packed up two guns and slipped out of Kansas during the night.

Geary went to Washington, D.C., and spoke openly about troubles in Kansas. He then returned to his home state of Pennsylvania. During the Civil War, he organized and commanded the 28th Pennsylvania Infantry. Geary became a brigadier general and was the military governor of Savannah, Georgia, for several months at the war's end.

Back at home again, Geary returned to politics and was elected governor of Pennsylvania in 1866. He died soon after his second term ended. Geary County was named in his honor in 1889. ■

High plains to the high seas

54 John Gingrich

U.S. Navy admiral. Dodge City. (1897-1960) Gingrich graduated from the U.S. Naval Academy in 1916 and retired from the Navy as an admiral in the 1950s. During World War II, he commanded the cruiser *USS Pittsburg*. In one battle with the Japanese, John led his ship through enemy fire to rescue a damaged American aircraft carrier.

Gingrich was later commander of the United Nations naval blockade of North Korea during the Korean War. Before he retired, he worked in Washington, D.C., as the U.S. Navy's deputy chief of operations. ■

Switch Glick?

55 George Glick

Governor. Atchison. (1827-1911) Glick was the first Democrat to be elected governor of Kansas. He served just one term, from 1883 to 1885. George, a lawyer and a rancher from Atchison, also helped organize the State Board of Agriculture and served as a member of it for 34 years.

In 1914, the state legislature chose Glick as one of two [63] Kansans to be honored in the U.S. Capitol's Statuary Hall. In the 1980s, several Republican lawmakers from Kansas wanted to switch Glick's statue for one of Dwight D. Eisenhower [44]. Democrats complained and the Capitol staff said no exchanges were allowed. The plan was dropped. Glick's statue still stands in the Capitol. ■

Treasurer of the United States in 1949—making her the first woman to serve in that office.

As treasurer, she acted as a banker for the government's funds. Georgia's signature appeared on all paper money issued during her term. Although she later admitted she was "not a brilliant mathematician," she handled the job capably.

Gray remarried in Washington, D.C., and left office when Dwight D. Eisenhower [44] became president in 1953. She and her husband moved to Richland where she was again the banker. She also ran a grocery store and other family businesses.

Ironically, just three years after she had carefully managed billions of U.S. dollars, the ex-treasurer was robbed. Thieves held her husband at gunpoint and forced her to open her bank and grocery store. The robbers gathered $2,000 in cash and left the Grays unhurt.

Georgia and her husband lived in Richland until the Clinton Reservoir covered the town with water in the 1960s. The Grays moved to Topeka where she built a new bank and was its president and chairman. ■

The first Mrs. Treasurer

56 Georgia Neese Clark Gray

U.S. treasurer. Richland and Topeka. (Born 1900) Gray was born in Richland and graduated from Washburn University.

She left Kansas during the 1920s and worked in New York as an actress in several Broadway plays. She earned almost $500 a week before the Great Depression closed many theaters in the 1930s. After an unsuccessful marriage ended,

Georgia moved to California and appeared in a few movies before returning to Kansas.

Back in her hometown, she worked in her father's bank and was its president after he died. At the same time, she became a national committeewoman in the Democratic party. Because of that position and her work in banking, President Harry Truman appointed Clark

Jumps into trouble

57 Fred Hall

Governor. Dodge City, Topeka, Wichita and Shawnee. (1916-1970) Hall was born and raised in Dodge City. He attended college in California and worked there and in Washington, D.C., before returning to Kansas during World War II. In 1954 Fred was elected governor, running against George Docking [**40**]. Their campaign was the first to use television to reach the voters.

Hall called himself a "do-something" governor, but the "something" he seemed to do best was cause controversy. He fired the director of the State Purchasing Agency and then refused to hear the man's appeal. He vetoed a controversial law about labor unions. And when Hall feuded with his fellow Republicans, the state Republican chairman refused to work as his campaign manager.

Hall lost his bid for a second term, but he had time for one more unpopular move—he resigned just a few days before his term was over. Hall had the new governor, his lieutenant governor John McCuish [**73**], appoint him as a justice on the Kansas Supreme Court.

People felt this "triple-jump" was an unfair move. When Hall left the court a year later to run for governor again, he lost. After his defeat, Hall returned to California. He practiced law and was active in the California Republican party until he came back to Kansas in the late 1960s. ■

Political biologist

58 Mike Hayden

Governor and assistant U.S. secretary of the interior. Atwood. (Born 1944) Hayden, a Vietnam War veteran, served seven terms in the Kansas House of Representatives. When Mike ran for governor in 1986, his biggest hurdle was beating six Republican opponents in the primary election. He won, however, and went on to defeat Democrat ***Tom Docking*** in the general election.

Hayden campaigned in favor of putting the death penalty back into law but after his election lawmakers refused to pass a capital punishment bill. He also promised improved highways, and the legislature approved a $2.65 billion, eight-year highway plan at the end of his term. Using his college degrees in biology and wildlife conservation, he worked to protect the state's ecology and underground water supply.

At election time in 1990, voters were unhappy with the increase in property taxes during Hayden's term, and they replaced him with Joan Finney [**45**]. In 1991 President George Bush asked the former governor to put his biology training to work in Washington, D.C. Bush nominated Hayden to be the assistant secretary of the interior for fish, wildlife and parks. In that position Hayden is in charge of the U.S. Fish and Wildlife Service, as well as the National Park Service. ■

Kansan gets northern exposure

59 Walter Hickel

Governor of Alaska and U.S. secretary of the interior. Claflin. (Born 1919) Hickel was an amateur boxer as a youth and won a Golden Gloves title in Kansas City in the late 1930s. About that same time, he left Kansas headed for Australia—but he ended up in Alaska instead.

Even though he arrived in the far North with only 37 cents in his pocket, 21-year-old Walter made a fortune in the construction business. He then entered into politics and was elected Alaska's governor in 1966. Richard Nixon appointed Hickel secretary of the interior in 1969, but the president later fired him. Nixon was upset when Hickel spoke out in favor of government policies to protect the environment.

Hickel returned to Alaska and was reelected governor of that state in 1990. ■

Watered down

60 Edward Hoch

Governor and newspaper publisher. Pawnee Rock, Florence and Marion. (1849-1925) Hoch came to Kansas in the early 1870s and became a newspaper publisher by accident: he received the *Marion Record* as the repayment of a debt.

In the 1890s Edward served two terms in the Kansas House of Representatives, and was a Republican leader during the "Legislative War" [**70**].

Hoch was governor from 1905 to 1909. As a Progressive Republican he supported reforms, or changes in government. During his term he worked for laws to allow voters to nominate candidates in a state primary election, and to improve Kansas' state hospitals, prisons and juvenile courts.

He also believed strongly in prohibition, or outlawing the sale of liquor. When the U.S. Navy asked Hoch and his daughter to help launch the battleship *Kansas* in 1905, he did not allow her to break the usual bottle of champagne over the ship's bow—she used a bottle of Kansas spring water instead. (The superstitious ship's captain wasn't satisfied. He later redid the job with champagne.)

After his term Hoch continued to publish his newspaper. For several years he was a popular speaker at Chautauquas, traveling tent programs featuring speeches and entertainment. ■

Yes, sir, ma'am!

61 Elizabeth Hoisington

U.S. Army general. Newton and Leavenworth. (Born 1918) Even before she became a soldier, Hoisington was no stranger to the military way of life. Her three brothers and father were in the U.S. armed forces. Her grandfather, Colonel **Perry Hoisington**, was known as the Father of the Kansas National Guard.

Elizabeth joined the U.S. Army in 1942. She attended several officer training schools, including the U.S. Command and General Staff College at Fort Leavenworth. During her military career, she was stationed at posts in the United States, Europe and the Far East. She served as director of the Women's Army Corps, or WACs, from 1966 until her retirement in 1971.

In 1970 Hoisington became the first woman in the U.S. Army to be promoted to the rank of brigadier general. ■

Don't give up Hope

62 Clifford Hope, Sr.

U.S. representative. Garden City. (1893-1970) Hope lived in Iowa and Oklahoma as a boy and moved to Finney County with his family in 1906. He received a law degree at Washburn University in 1917 and served in the U.S. Army during World War I.

After the war, the young lawyer spent six years in the Kansas House of Representatives before he was elected to the U.S. House of Representatives in 1927.

For the next 30 years Clifford was the representative from western Kansas. He spent his entire term serving on the House Agriculture Committee and was its chairman twice. In that position, Hope helped guide the nation's farm policies. He wrote important laws about marketing, farm credit, soil conservation and watershed protection—always keeping in mind the interests of farmers.

When Hope retired in 1957, he was called the best congressman Kansas ever had. As he closed his office in Washington, someone joked, "Oh, no. Now we're losing Hope!"

Back in Kansas, the former congressman continued to support agriculture. He became the founder and first president of Great Plains Wheat, Incorporated, an organization of wheat-growing states that encouraged the use of wheat all over the world. Before his death, Hope received several state and national awards. ■

Seals up the state

63 John J. Ingalls

U.S. senator. Atchison. (1833-1900) Ingalls came to Kansas in 1858. At Wyandotte the next year, he helped write the constitution that later became the framework of Kansas' government.

In 1861, John served on the legislative committee that designed the Kansas state seal. Legend has it that his first version included one silver star (Kansas) at the bottom of a cloud (Kansas' struggles to reach statehood) rising to join a constellation (one star for each of the states then in the Union). By the time the seal was adopted, Indians, buffaloes, covered wagons—plus a farmer, log cabin and a steamboat—had been added. His single star was gone.

According to some, Ingalls also suggested the Latin phrase *Ad astra per aspera*, "To the stars through difficulties," as the state motto. Others say the idea came from another legislator. When Ingalls was asked about the motto's origin a few

First in cabinet

64 William Jardine

U.S. secretary of agriculture, state treasurer and educator. Manhattan and Wichita. (1879-1955) Jardine grew up in Idaho where he worked as a cowboy. Although he didn't complete high school, he convinced Utah State College to admit him as a student. William graduated with honors and taught agronomy there for a year.

In 1906 Jardine took a job with the U.S. Department of Agriculture. Four years later, he was hired by Kansas State Agricultural College (later KSU) as a professor of agronomy. He advanced

years before his death, he said it didn't matter where it came from. (Kansans should be relieved their state motto wasn't based on his 1896 quote, "Kansas is the navel of the nation.")

By that time he had left the state senate and had served in the U.S. Senate for eighteen years. There he was known for his speaking ability; some said he could make words "sting like scorpions." When he argued against women's suffrage, or the right to vote, by saying "Women are women and their place is in the home," angry women helped him feel the sting himself.

Like many other Republicans, he lost his seat to a Populist [**78**] in the 1890s. Ingalls was one of two Kansans [**55**] whose statue was placed in the U.S. Capitol. Asa T. Soule [**172**] named the town of Ingalls after the senator in 1888. ∎

to dean of the division of agriculture and in 1918 he became the president of KSAC.

In 1925 President Calvin Coolidge appointed Jardine secretary of agriculture, making him the first Kansan in a president's cabinet. President Herbert Hoover later sent him to Egypt as the U.S. minister. When Jardine returned, Kansas government was in an uproar over the Finney [**358-359**] bond scandal. To help settle the situation, Governor Alf Landon [**67**] asked him to be state treasurer. From 1934 to 1949 Jardine was president of the University of Wichita (WSU). ∎

Heads NRA

65 Hugh Johnson

U.S. Army general and director of the National Recovery Administration. Fort Scott. (1882-1942) During World War I, Johnson was in charge of the selective service system that drafted men into the U.S. Army. He became a brigadier general in 1918. Hugh then worked in business for several years, but returned to government service in 1933 when President Franklin D. Roosevelt named him head of the National Recovery Administration. The NRA helped industries rebuild during the Great Depression. ∎

Still riding the political merry-go-round

U.S. senator. Topeka, Maize and Council Grove. (Born 1932) When Kassebaum was sworn into office in 1978, she became the first female senator from Kansas. She was also one of the first women elected to the Senate on her own, without first following her husband.

Nancy Jo

Nancy Landon was really born right in the middle of Kansas politics. On the day of her birth,

July 29, 1932, her father, Alf Landon [**67**], was campaigning for governor. That November he won the first of two terms.

Four years later, Nancy celebrated her fourth birthday the same week her father was nominated as the Republican candidate for president. As the Landon family toured the country on a campaign train that fall, newspapers and magazines everywhere were full of "Nancy Jo" photographs. Everyone

loved the bright, pretty four-year-old with a big white bow in her hair and a toy bunny in her arms.

Her father was defeated, but politics continued to be important in the Landon house. As he campaigned for other Republicans, she sometimes helped by passing out literature and tacking posters on telephone poles.

When a famous politician once visited their home, Nancy hid behind the drapes to listen in on the conversation. Many times, she went to sleep hearing political talk from her father's den coming through a floor vent into her upstairs bedroom.

The Landons' large white house just outside the Topeka city limits was a playground for Nancy and her friends.

When the big dining room was covered with tumbling mats, it became a gymnasium. The spacious backyard was a pet shop one summer, with animals kept in a chicken coop.

She attended public school in Topeka, then enrolled at the University of Kansas in Lawrence. Nancy always enjoyed reading, especially biographies. At college, she spent time nearly every night reading textbooks aloud to a friend who was blind. There, during her sophomore year, she also met *Philip Kassebaum*.

Studies politicians and diplomats

Nancy graduated from KU in 1954 with a bachelor's degree in political science. She and Philip then attended the University ⇨

of Michigan. They were married in 1955, and a year later she earned a master's degree in diplomatic history. When Philip set up a law practice in Wichita the couple moved to Maize.

For nearly twenty years, much of Nancy's life centered around her husband's career, their four children, and the family home. At the same time, she was vice president of Kassebaum Communications, a family business that operated two Wichita radio stations. She gained experience in public service as a member of the Kansas Governmental Ethics Commission and as president of the Maize school board.

In 1968, she attended the Republican National Convention to help her father and husband support Nelson Rockefeller for the presidential nomination. (Twelve years later Kassebaum appeared at the 1980 Republican National Convention—as its temporary chairperson.)

At work in Washington

The Kassebaums were legally separated in the 1970s. Nancy accepted a job on Kansas Senator James Pearson's staff, and with her three youngest children, then teenagers, she moved to Washington, D.C., for a year. In October 1977, Senator Pearson announced he would retire the following year. Several of Nancy's friends suggested that she run for the vacant seat.

She discussed the idea with all her family, including children, parents, in-laws and Philip. Everyone was enthusiastic. Everyone, that is, except her father. Landon was worried about her political chances against the seven other Repub-

licans trying for the nomination. He also felt Kansas wasn't yet ready for a woman senator.

When the August 1978 primary election was over and the votes were counted, Kassebaum had won the nomination with 7,000 more votes than her nearest rival. She immediately began her campaign for the November election: "A Fresh Face, A Trusted Kansas Name."

She told Kansans, "To be a good senator, you need to be willing to listen and able to work with people. You don't need to be a professional politician." They agreed. On Election Day she defeated her opponent, former U.S. representative Dr. Bill Roy, by over 85,000 votes.

Senator Nancy

Kansas' choice of its first woman senator made headlines across the country. Some writers and political cartoonists compared Nancy's trip to Washington with Dorothy's [**362**] journey in the *Wizard of Oz*, but it didn't seem to bother Senator Kassebaum. As she spoke before a crowd at one of her first appearances in the nation's capital, she joked, "Gee, Toto. I don't think we're in Kansas anymore."

Kassebaum has been an effective, fair-minded—and independent senator. She has served on several powerful Senate committees: Budget, Foreign Relations, Commerce, Science and Transportation. She is known for carefully studying bills and she rarely votes just because of politics.

Several times she has taken a stand against presidents of her own party. When President Ronald Reagan vetoed a bill in 1986 that would have put sanctions, or penalties, on

companies trading with South Africa, Kassebaum led the Senate in putting sanctions into effect anyway. She wanted the United States to show strong disapproval of South Africa's policies against blacks.

In 1989, Kassebaum felt President George Bush's friend, former Texas senator John Tower, was not a good choice to be the secretary of defense. She was the only Republican to vote against him, and he did not get the job. She has also supported laws to limit the purchase of handguns and semiautomatic weapons, when other Republicans have not.

Popular choice

Her work in Washington is respected by almost everyone. Republicans considered her a possible vice presidential candidate with George Bush in 1988. She has also been mentioned as a future candidate for president. Other senators respect her independence. At times, some have defended their own votes for unpopular laws by saying, "Well, Nancy voted for it."

Voters, too, have made their feelings plain about Senator Kassebaum. She was easily reelected in 1984. But her decision to run for a third term was a hard one to make.

When Kassebaum was first elected, she said she would serve no more than two six-year terms to avoid "Potomac fever," the "disease" politicians have when they think keeping their jobs in Washington is more important than representing voters. However, after much urging from voters, friends and family, she agreed to run again. In November 1990, Senator Kassebaum was reelected by a wide margin. ∎

Respected loser

Governor, oil company owner and presidential candidate. Independence and Topeka. (1887-1987)
Landon was born September 9, 1887, at his grandparents' home in West Middlesex, Pennsylvania. He grew up in Ohio, where his father was the superintendent of an oil refinery.

As a boy Alfred enjoyed raising birds. He caught pigeons in the schoolhouse attic and sold them for 25 cents a pair. He also raised chickens and exhibited them at poultry shows. One morning, he discovered Buddy, one of his prize hens, hadn't laid an egg. Convinced that she could—and should—he held her on the nest until she produced.

Young Alfred sometimes went with his father to the oil fields. Much of their talk was about politics. Mr. Landon enjoyed political rallies and debates.

Into politics early

At the turn of the century, thirteen-year-old Alfred traveled to West Virginia with his father to hear Theodore Roosevelt speak. In 1904, father and son went to St. Louis to listen to William Jennings Bryan at the Democratic National Convention. That was a busy year for Alfred. In June he graduated from Marietta Academy in his Ohio hometown. In September his family moved to Kansas when

his father took a job with the Kansas Natural Gas Company in Independence. A week later Landon enrolled at the University of Kansas in Lawrence.

"Fox," as he was nicknamed on campus, joined a fraternity and later became its popular—but serious-minded—president. He prohibited late evening visitors, outlawed gambling, supported Bible lessons, and cut ice cream from the menu to save money.

Drills for oil

Landon graduated from KU in 1908 with a law degree. But times were tough, and instead of trying to open his own law office, he took a bookkeeping job in an Independence bank. Within two years he was able to save enough from his $75 monthly salary to invest in some oil-drilling projects.

In 1911 he quit his bank job and became a full-time oil man. Alf, as he was then known, soon made a fair amount of money. He also became more active in politics. By 1914 he was the Progressive party chairman in Montgomery County.

In 1915 he married Margaret Fleming, a girl he met during summer vacations in the East. Their daughter, Peggy Anne, was born in 1917. Just a year later, Margaret died suddenly while they were visiting in Colorado. Alf was heartbroken. He arranged for the care of Peggy and joined the U.S. Army. In late October, he was sent to Virginia as a first lieutenant in the chemical warfare service. Three weeks later, World War I ended. He returned to Independence that December.

Before he enlisted, he had worked as the southeast Kansas chairman of Henry J. Allen's [31] campaign for ⇨

governor. After Allen was elected, he often called on Landon for advice. For a time in 1922 Alf was Allen's executive secretary.

At the age of 41, Landon was appointed chairman of the state Republican party—the youngest person to have that job. He managed the successful campaign that put **Clyde Reed** in the governor's office in 1928, and Reed's unsuccessful try for reelection in 1930. That same year he married **Theo Cobb**, daughter of a Topeka banker.

Governor Alf

In 1932 Landon decided to run for governor. Governor Harry Woodring [**95**] was a strong Democratic candidate for re-election, and the colorful Dr. John R. Brinkley [**342**] had followers across the state. Alf, however, believed he had ideas to help Kansas through the Great Depression. He was nominated at the Republicans' state convention, four days after Theo gave birth to their daughter, Nancy Jo [**66**].

The race was close, but that November Landon won with just over one-third of the votes. His inauguration in early 1933 was simple: no invitations, no parade, no seventeen-gun salute. The new governor felt hard economic times called for economy. He promised to cut the state's budget by 25 percent and came close to his goal.

During his first term, Landon lowered taxes and reorganized state government. He aided farmers who were in danger of losing their land and also began a water conservation program.

When the Finney [**358-359**] bond scandal was uncovered, the governor acted quickly. He asked state troops to guard the Capitol and called a special session of the legislature to investigate the situation. After the state treasurer resigned, he filled the vacancy with William Jardine [**64**], a respected Kansas educator and former U.S. secretary of agriculture.

In his second term he put into effect a cash basis law, meaning state agencies couldn't spend more money than was available.

Soon Landon was known around the nation. Led by Franklin D. Roosevelt, Democrats dominated most elections in the 1930s. Yet the Kansan went against the trend. He was one of a handful of Republican governors elected in 1932 and the only governor elected from his party in 1934.

Up against FDR

Because of this, many Republicans felt Landon was a logical choice to go against Roosevelt in the 1936 presidential election. As they gathered for their convention in Cleveland that summer, Alf stayed home, following the custom at that time. In his place were several "all-star" Kansas Republicans— Henry J. Allen [**31**], Arthur Capper [**34**], Clifford Hope, Sr. [**62**], William Allen White [**256**] and the former speaker of the Kansas House of Representatives, **John D.M. Hamilton**.

They had pushed his nomination for months and they were not disappointed. Their favorite son was nominated on the convention's first ballot. Frank

Knox, a Chicago newspaperman, was named Landon's running mate. Six weeks later, on July 23, Governor Landon formally accepted the nomination on the south steps of the Kansas Capitol. Perhaps the largest crowd in Topeka's history, 100,000 strong, cheered him on.

In the weeks that followed, Alf and his family made a whistle-stop campaign across the country on the "Sunflower Special." But the train ran out of steam in November; the popular Roosevelt was unbeatable. Landon received 16 million votes to Roosevelt's 27 million. The Kansan carried only two states—Maine and Vermont—meaning that in the all-important electoral college, he received just eight votes.

Elder statesman

Despite his loss, the progressive Landon supported many of Roosevelt's policies. In fact, FDR asked for Alf's advice several times. When Secretary of War Harry Woodring resigned in 1940, the president wanted his old opponent to be the second Kansan to fill the post. Landon agreed—if Roosevelt would not seek a third term. FDR refused.

Alf continued in the oil business and later bought several radio stations. He lived in Topeka for the rest of his long life. In time, he came to be known as the Grand Old Man of the Grand Old Party. Over the years he and Theo greeted a long line of important politicians at their Southern-style home. President Ronald Reagan visited there shortly before Landon's one-hundredth birthday. The noted Kansan died a few weeks later, on October 12, 1987.

Just east of the Capitol, the Alf M. Landon State Office Building bears his name. ■

Like nobody else

U.S. senator and antislavery supporter. Lawrence. (1814-1866) Lane was born in Lawrenceburgh, Indiana, June 22, 1814. During his colorful career he sat on both sides of the political fence. As a Democrat, he was Indiana's lieutenant governor and then its U.S. representative. When he voted for the Kansas-Nebraska Act in 1854, many believed he supported slavery.

But less than a year later, Jim had moved to Bleeding Kansas and joined the fight against slavery. And by 1859 he was a Republican.

Takes off talking

Lane's deep-set eyes and wild, black hair made him look "like nobody else." Winter or summer, he often wore the same outfit: overalls, a calfskin vest and a long bearskin overcoat. During his fiery speeches, his layers of clothing were like props for an actor. The longer he talked, the more outer garments he pulled off to wave at the audience.

To anyone who would listen, Lane preached against slavery. Slave-holding Missourians, he warned, were "wolves, snakes, devils." Kansans should vote to make their own territory free.

Man of action

But Lane did more than talk. With his rival, Charles Robinson [**82**], he led the Free State party, pushing to make Kansas a slave-free state. In 1856 he recruited 400 settlers from Northern states, including Edmund G. Ross [**85**], who later replaced Lane as a Kansas senator. Lane's Army of the North, as it was called, marched into Kansas on "Lane's Trail" through Iowa and Nebraska, avoiding a fight with proslavery Missourians. More often than not, however, Lane met his Missouri neighbors head-on in nighttime "jayhawking" [**387**] raids into that state.

In 1858 Lane got into a dispute with a Lawrence resident over some land. By the time the fight ended, the man was dead. Lane was charged with murder, but a jury later found him innocent.

His victim was a friend of Charles Robinson, which turned their long-running argument into a feud that soon dissolved the Free State party. Both then became Republicans and fought for control of that group. When Kansas became a state in 1861, Robinson was the first governor. The legislature—perhaps hoping to separate the feuding men—elected Lane one of the state's first two senators [**80**] and sent him off to Washington, D.C.

One day before he arrived, the Civil War broke out. Lane, thinking the South might attack the capital city, organized what he called the Frontier Guard. To protect President Abraham Lincoln—who Lane strongly supported—they set up camp in the East Room of the White House. After one night, however, the president "excused" them to the White House lawn.

A week later, extra Union troops arrived in Washington and Lane disbanded his group. Lincoln rewarded Lane with an officer's commission in the U.S. Army. When "General-Senator" Lane ➪

1st Kansas Colored

During the Civil War, thousands of escaped slaves found freedom in Kansas. In 1862 Lane organized hundreds of them into an all-black regiment. Under a white commander, the 1st Kansas Colored Volunteer Infantry began training at Fort Leavenworth that summer.

In the fall, part of the 1st Kansas marched into southeastern Missouri. On October 28, the men were surprised by 500 Confederates near the town of Butler. A sharp fight followed, but the 225 Kansans successfully drove off their attackers. Ten of the Kansas infantrymen were killed; twelve were injured. It was the first time in the Civil War that black troops had been in combat.

By the war's end, the 1st Kansas had fought in Arkansas and Oklahoma—and had seen more action than any other black regiment.

returned to Kansas to organize troops, his enemies pointed out that it was illegal to hold those two federal jobs at once. They no doubt hoped he would give up his Senate seat. Instead, he returned his U.S. Army commission, and accepted a position in the Kansas Militia.

He formed three units, the 3rd, 4th and 5th Kansas Regiments, or Lane's Brigade. In September 1861 he took command of these forces at Fort Scott. The bloody raid he then led against the Missouri town of Osceola earned him the nickname "Grim Chieftain." In part, William Quantrill's [373] raid on Lawrence in 1863 was in retaliation for the Osceola attack. Lane

hoped to use Indians in an even bigger military operation into Texas, but the Army stopped him and he returned to the Senate.

The senator was reelected in 1864, but by then many Kansans questioned his ideas. His critics called him insane, dishonest, vulgar and "utterly unreligious." They pointed out that he seemed to repent and join—or rejoin—the politically powerful Methodist Church just before every election. Lane died after committing suicide July 1, 1866. Some say he was worried over finances; others believe he was despondent over the death of Abraham Lincoln. Lane County and the town of Lane in Franklin County were named for him. ∎

Troubled agent

69 Jesse Leavenworth

U.S. Army colonel and Indian agent. Fort Larned. (1807-1885) Leavenworth came from a military background. His father, General ***Henry Leavenworth***, established Fort Leavenworth in 1827. Jesse graduated from West Point in 1830, but six years later he resigned, saying the Army wasn't for him. For over twenty years he was a civil engineer in Chicago.

During the Civil War he rejoined the Army as a colonel. Leavenworth commanded Fort Larned for a time in 1863, and was then put in charge of troops on the Santa Fe Trail. But with only one cavalry unit, he complained, it was impossible to guard hundreds of miles of the trail effectively. When he was

later appointed agent for the Kiowas and Comanches, he had a difficult time being effective in that job as well. In 1865 Army officers complained he was trying to make peace with the same Indians they planned to attack—and the Indians he was trying to help stole all of his horses. At the same time, others accused him of corruption.

In 1868 Leavenworth left his troubles in Kansas and returned to his family in Milwaukee. ∎

'Wartime' governor

70 Lorenzo Lewelling

Governor. Wichita. (1846-1900) Lewelling came to Kansas from Iowa in the late 1880s. He had been a carpenter, railroad worker, teacher, newspaperman and prison superintendent. In 1892 he was asked to give a welcoming speech at the Kansas Populist convention. Even with almost no political experience, he impressed the delegates. They nominated him and voters elected him that November.

Lorenzo was the first governor from the People's Party. There was no governor's mansion at that time, and to prove he could save the people's money, he lived in a dollar-a-day Topeka hotel.

Although he was a member of the peace-loving Quaker Church, Lewelling was best known for the legislative "war" early in his term. Republicans and Populists in the House of Representatives began arguing about who had a majority. The debate went on until Populists locked themselves inside the Capitol. That didn't sit well with Republicans who broke down the doors with a sledge hammer and took charge of the building. Lewelling then called out the state militia.

The disagreement eventually went to the Kansas Supreme Court which ruled in favor of the Republicans. But by that time the session was nearly over and very little was accomplished.

Lewelling returned to Wichita in 1895 and ran a dairy farm. ∎

Exoduster into office

71 Edward P. McCabe

State auditor. Nicodemus and Millbrook. (1850-1920)
McCabe was born in New York and came to Kansas in 1878. Although he arrived during the period of the "Exodusters" [*126*], Edward was not an ex-slave. He entered politics in Graham County and was elected its county clerk. In 1882 he ran for state auditor. When voters chose McCabe, it made him the first African-American to be elected to a state office in Kansas. He was also perhaps the first black to hold a major state office in any Northern state.

McCabe later moved to Oklahoma Territory where he founded several towns for ex-slaves and a black university. When residents discussed statehood for Oklahoma, he had a plan: It would become an all-black state—and he would become its governor. Others rejected his idea, but McCabe was later elected Oklahoma's deputy territorial auditor. ∎

First woman to Congress

72 Kathryn O'Loughlin McCarthy

U.S. representative. Hays. (1894-1952) McCarthy was the first Kansas woman elected to the U.S. Congress.

She graduated from Fort Hays State College and received a law degree from the University of Chicago. She got her first taste of politics when she served as clerk of a Kansas House of Representatives committee in 1920.

During the 1920s, McCarthy lived in Chicago. There she was a lawyer for several insurance companies, and later an executive in another insurance firm.

Always interested in reform, or change, she took a large cut in salary to become an attorney for a local legal aid office. In that office she used her legal skills to crusade for an eight-hour workday for women and for infant care.

When she returned to Kansas in 1930 she was elected to one term as a representative to the Kansas House. At that time, she was still single—and had to put up with teasing from other legislators when she and bachelor Governor Harry Woodring [*95*] went to a movie together.

When McCarthy took her seat in the U.S. House of Representatives in 1933, she was one of the few women in Congress. In those early years of the Depression, she supported the Democrats' New Deal and worked to get federal help for her district.

She ran for a second term but was beaten by a young Republican, Frank Carlson [*36*]. McCarthy, however, continued to work for others. When she saw how some black students were being discriminated against at Fort Hays State University, she paid their tuition and let them stay in her home. She also spoke out against the treatment of women in the state's prisons. ∎

Governs 264 hours, more or less

Rails against lawbreakers

73 John McCuish

Governor and newspaper publisher. Newton. (1906-1962) McCuish's time as governor is the shortest in Kansas history, January 3 to January 14, 1957—just eleven days. He was Fred Hall's [57] lieutenant governor, and came into office when Hall resigned just before the end of his term. As governor, John had little time to do anything, except appoint his ex-boss to the state supreme court, which was why Hall resigned in the first place. Not suprisingly, McCuish's unpopular action angered many. After running the state for less than 300 hours, he retired from politics and returned to Newton. ■

76 Vern Miller

Kansas attorney general. Wichita. (Born 1928) As the state's highest law officer in the early 1970s, Miller kept himself in the news. In the bright lights of television news cameras, Vern popped out of car trunks and pounded on doors as he led raids against drug dealers, gamblers and anyone selling liquor illegally.

He once climbed on an Amtrak passenger train and arrested lounge car hosts for serving alcoholic drinks to passengers as they sped across Kansas. Miller also ordered airlines to stop serving liquor in Kansas airspace on flights that took off or landed in the state.

Democrat Miller ran for governor in 1974 but lost a close race to the Republican candidate, *Robert Bennett*. ■

Ms. Justice

Mr. Mayor

74 Kay McFarland

Kansas Supreme Court justice. Coffeyville and Topeka. (Born 1935) McFarland was born in Coffeyville and grew up in Topeka. After she earned a law degree at Washburn University Kay practiced law for several years. In the 1960s she entered politics and was elected probate, then juvenile court judge. In 1973 Judge McFarland became the first woman elected district judge in the state. Four years later, she became the first woman justice on the Kansas Supreme Court when Governor *Robert Bennett* appointed her to the high court.

Before she became too busy with her judicial duties McFarland raised Tennessee walking horses and Irish wolfhounds. ■

75 Jim Martinez

Mayor. Hutchinson. (Born 1907) Martinez was born in Mexico and came to the United States as a teenager. He became an American citizen in 1943 and later started his own business in Hutchinson. When Martinez was elected to the Hutchinson city commission in 1969, he was the first Mexican-American in the state to win a seat in city government.

The next year, the commissioners elected him mayor, making him the first Mexican-American mayor in Kansas. Jim remained in city government until 1977.

Frances Calvillo Garcia, the first Hispanic woman mayor in the state, is also from Hutchinson. Garcia was elected to the city commission in 1985 and served as mayor of Hutchinson for two years. ■

OK father

77 David Payne

State legislator and soldier. Fort Leavenworth, Atchison, Wichita and Wellington. (1836-1884) Payne was born in Indiana and served in the U.S. Army during the Civil War. In the 1860s he was postmaster at the state's oldest post office, Fort Leavenworth, and a member of the Kansas Legislature. As a captain in the Kansas Cavalry he participated in the Washita Massacre [*341*].

After ranching near Wichita during the 1870s, David seemed anxious to leave Kansas. In 1883, he took over 500 homesteaders onto Indian land in Oklahoma—before the territory was opened to settlement. The Army jailed him for several days and escorted his illegal "sooners" back into Kansas. A year later, he led over 1,500 followers into the Cherokee Strip. Once again he was arrested and released.

Payne died unexpectedly that fall. Thousands attended his funeral and burial in Wellington. When Indian Territory was opened to white settlement five years later, he was called The Father of Oklahoma. ■

Marine top brass

79 Frank E. Petersen

U.S. Marine Corps general. Topeka. (Born 1932) When Petersen earned his pilot's wings in 1952, he was the first black pilot in the U.S. Marine Corps. He flew 64 combat missions in the Korean War, and received the Distinguished Flying Cross and six Air Medals.

During the Vietnam War Frank commanded a squadron of attack fighters and was awarded the Legion of Merit. In 1979 President Jimmy Carter named Petersen a brigadier general, making him the first African-American Marine general. ■

Beard and all

78 William A. Peffer

U.S. senator and newspaper journalist. Fredonia, Coffeyville, Topeka and Grenola. (1831-1912) Peffer came to Kansas after the Civil War and farmed in Wilson County. He also edited newspapers in Fredonia, Coffeyville and Topeka. For a time he was in charge of the *Kansas Farmer*, a paper that encouraged the growth of the populist movement.

It was Peffer's interest in agriculture, as well as his experience as an editor, teacher and lawyer, that helped push him to the front of the Populist party in the 1890s. Political cartoonists enjoyed drawing Peffer and his beard. It was so long it reached below his waist!

The Kansas Legislature chose him to replace John J. Ingalls [*63*] in the U.S. Senate in 1891. By that time, Populist legislators and voters were tired of Ingalls' "stuck-up" attitude, as Eugene "Ironquill" Ware [*252*]

Unknown cartoonist, *Puck* magazine

wrote. In Washington, new Senator Peffer tried hard to work for voters. He supported legislation that pushed for reform. Two of his ideas were workers' pensions and public works jobs to help the unemployed.

Peffer remained in the Senate for one term. By the time he was out of office, the Populist party had lost much of its strength. He continued his involvement in politics, and eventually rejoined the Republican party. ■

In a tight squeeze

80 Samuel Pomeroy

U.S. senator. Atchison. (1816-1891) Pomeroy, with James H. Lane [*68*], was one of Kansas' first two senators. When Lane formed his Frontier Guard to protect President Abraham Lincoln, Pomeroy joined. His uniform, however, had no belt —he was so fat none would fit!

Senator Pomeroy was in other tight squeezes, too. In 1861 some thought he helped himself to money and supplies meant for drought victims in Kansas. In 1873 Pomeroy was accused of paying a Kansas legislator $8,000 for the man's vote. (At that time, state ⟳

legislatures elected U.S. senators.) The bribery charge was never proved, but that—and questions about his 1867 election—caused Pomeroy to lose his Senate seat to John J. Ingalls [**63**].

Mark Twain wrote about the Pomeroy scandal in his novel *The Guilded Age.* Twain's fictional Senator Dilworthy represented the senator from Kansas. ∎

Governor in four capitals

81 Andrew Reeder

Territorial governor. Leavenworth, Shawnee Mission, Pawnee and Lecompton. (1807-1864) President Franklin Pierce appointed Reeder the first governor of Kansas Territory in 1854, a job Reeder hadn't even asked for. His term in office turned out to be a thirteen-month argument over whether Kansas should be a slave or free state. During that turbulent period, the territorial capital moved to four different locations.

Although some politicians believed Reeder supported slavery, he angered proslavery leaders in Kansas several times. When he called some Missourians "border ruffians"—perhaps the first time this nickname was used—one proslavery legislator, **John Stringfellow**, was especially upset. To prove to the governor just how rough ruffians could be, Dr. Stringfellow hit Reeder over the head with a chair and kicked him as he lay on the floor!

Proslavery politicians convinced President Pierce to fire Reeder in 1855, but the ex-governor decided to stay in Kansas. When Reeder's enemies charged him with treason he disguised himself as a wood-chopper and slipped out of the territory on a riverboat. Three Kansas post offices were named for Reeder, but they all were closed by the early 1900s. ∎

First governor and first first lady

82-83 Charles & Sarah Robinson

Governor and doctor. First lady. Lawrence. (1818-1894) (1827-1911) The Robinsons came from Massachusetts where Charles was a doctor, teacher and newspaper editor. In 1854 they led a group of settlers from the Massachusetts Emigrant Aid Company to Lawrence.

During the Bleeding Kansas period, Charles was active in the antislavery movement, first as a Free State party member and then as a Republican. Voters elected him Kansas' first governor in December 1859, but it wasn't until statehood was granted in January 1861 that his job became official.

During most of Robinson's two-year term he feuded with fellow Republican Senator James H. Lane [**68**]. Both wanted to control their party in Kansas. When Lane left Washington to lead "jayhawking" raids in the Civil War, Robinson appointed a new senator in his place. To retaliate, Lane tried to get Robinson removed from office. The governor was impeached, but legislators found him innocent at a trial. However, the incident happened so close to the Republican state convention that the party did not renominate him.

Robinson ran for governor again in 1882 as a National Labor Greenback candidate, and in 1890 as a Democrat. He lost both elections. (Ironically, Charles' participation in the 1882 election divided the votes and allowed George Glick [**55**] be elected the state's first Democratic governor.) In the late 1880s Robinson was superintendent of the Haskell Indian Institute. Robinson, a town in Brown County, was named for him.

The first governor and his wife donated the land in Lawrence where much of Kansas University now stands. Sarah Robinson met Charles in Massachusetts while he was practicing medicine. She also supported the antislavery cause and wrote a book about the evils of slavery. Sarah spent time in jail with her husband at Lecompton during "abolitionist trials" run by proslavery men.

In 1856 she saw for herself how dangerous the fight against slavery could be—Missouri border ruffians burned her home. The Robinsons built another house in Lawrence and remained there, because at the time Charles was elected, there was no official home for the governor in the state capital.

When Sarah had to entertain guests as the state's first "first lady," she borrowed houses in Topeka from legislators. ∎

Commands NATO

84 Bernard W. Rogers

U.S. Army general. Fairview. (Born 1921) Rogers attended Kansas State University, the U.S. Military Academy at West Point, and Oxford University in England. He served in the Korean and Vietnam wars and became the U.S. Army's chief of staff in 1976. Three years later, President Jimmy Carter put the four-star general in command of 4.1 million NATO (North American Treaty Organization) troops in Europe. ∎

Majority of one

85 Edmund G. Ross

U.S. senator and governor of New Mexico Territory. Topeka, Lawrence and Coffeyville. (1826-1907) Ross came to Kansas in 1856 leading one section of James Lane's [68] Army of the North. When he was chosen in 1866 to finish Lane's Senate term, few knew of the newspaper editor from Lawrence. Two years later Ross was known everywhere.

During Ross' term, the U.S. House of Representatives voted articles of impeachment against President Andrew Johnson.

Before the trial ended in the U.S. Senate, most senators revealed their voting plans. Ross chose to wait until all the evidence was heard. Thirty-six votes would declare the president guilty; Ross' undecided vote could be the crucial one.

As a Republican, he was expected to vote against the Democratic president. Pressure came at him from all sides: his fellow Kansas senator Samuel Pomeroy [80], other Republican politicians, telegrams and letters from hundreds of Kansans—even mysterious strangers who shadowed him around Washington. Still, Ross kept quiet.

On the day the official roll call vote was taken, each senator voted as expected. When Ross' name was called, the room became quiet. Not guilty, he said. After all the votes were counted, President Johnson was found innocent—by one vote.

It appeared Ross' vote made the difference. In reality, other senators probably would have voted with him, but his brave action made their votes unnecessary.

At any rate, Ross was the loser. Republicans refused to give him another term in the Senate. When he became a Democrat and ran for governor against John P. St. John [87] in 1880, he lost. Even the weather seemed to be against him. He tried running a newspaper in Coffeyville, and a tornado blew it away! He then moved to New Mexico where he was appointed territorial governor in 1885.

Eventually, many Kansans [346] admitted their senator's vote had been courageous. Ironically, in 1926 the U.S. Supreme Court overturned the law which Andrew Johnson had been accused of breaking. In a way, it proved Ross' vote years earlier had indeed been right. ∎

Fifty-year favorite

86 D.J. "Papa Joe" Saia

County official. Pittsburg. (1904-1990) As a fifteen-year-old coal miner in southeast Kansas, Saia helped organize local workers during a strike. As an adult, he continued to be active in labor unions and the Democratic party. His powerful Democratic friends included governors George and Robert Docking [**40-41**] and the Kennedy family of Massachusetts. Saia was known for giving out political rewards. Voters, in turn, rewarded "Papa Joe" by electing him to the Crawford County commission again and again—for 50 years. ■

Pushes prohibition with a capital *P*

87 John P. St. John

Governor and presidential candidate. Olathe. (1833-1916) During his campaign in 1878, St. John promised a state law for prohibition. Within two years, it was done. The Kansas constitution was changed to outlaw the sale of liquor, although it could still be sold in drugstores as medicine.

As governor, St. John helped "Exodusters" [**126**] who came to Kansas. He also held several "water banquets," at which guests were served no drinks stronger than water. St. John remained governor for four years; he beat Edmund G. Ross [**85**] in 1880, but lost to Democrat George Glick [**55**] in 1882. Two years later the national Prohibition party nominated St. John for president; he lost to Democrat Grover Cleveland. Through the years, St. John continued to push for prohibition in over 4,500 speeches he gave around the country.

While he was governor, the Stafford County town of St. John was named for him. The first town named St. John was in Decatur County, but unhappy residents changed its name. They didn't support his prohibition ideas. To the south, St. John County was renamed Logan County for the same reason. ■

Like father, like daughter

88 Suzanna Salter

Mayor. Argonia. (1860-1961) When Kansas women were given the right to vote in city elections in 1887, several Argonia men nominated Salter for mayor—as a joke.

They were angry that she and other women from the Women's Christian Temperance Union supported candidates who were against drinking. If just a few people voted for Salter, the men felt, it would embarrass her and the WCTU. But on election day it was the pranksters who

were embarrassed. Salter received two-thirds of the votes! Actually, the 27-year-old housewife and mother of four was more familiar with politics than many of the men in Argonia: Her father had been the town's first mayor and her father-in-law, *Melville J. Salter*, was a former Kansas lieutenant governor.

Salter's election made her not only the first woman mayor in Kansas, but the first woman mayor in the United States. ■

Runs with no socks

Truth Against the World

People's PARTY PICNIC!

AUGUST 18, 18

U.S. representative. Holton, Medicine Lodge and Wichita. (1842-1905) Simpson was born in the Canadian province of New Brunswick on March 31, 1842. His family moved to Michigan when he was a boy. Although he had few chances to go to school, he taught himself by reading nearly every book he found.

Sails Great Lakes

Before he was a teenager, Simpson signed on as a cabin boy on a Great Lakes ship. He progressed through the ranks and eventually became captain of a freighter. During a fierce storm, his ship was driven ashore, but Simpson reacted coolly and none of his men were lost.

Simpson left his maritime career in the late 1870s. With his wife and small daughter he came to Kansas and bought a farm near Holton. After his daughter died in a sawmill accident he and his wife moved to Medicine Lodge. There he bought a herd of cattle and was a successful rancher until his stock died in a blizzard in 1886.

In God he trusted, in Kansas he busted

By that time, Simpson was discouraged with the problems of agriculture. He had come to Kansas with $10,000; all he had left was a $10 pcr week job as the Medicine Lodge city marshal—with time off to dig sew-

ers for extra cash. In hopes of making his unhappy voice heard he ran for the Kansas Legislature. Voters turned him down twice, but he didn't give up.

When he saw the price of corn drop to ten cents a bushel in 1889—and farmers had to burn their record-breaking harvest as fuel—he entered the race for the U.S. Congress. By then Simpson had joined the Populists, a political party that wanted farmers and other "little people" to have a say in government.

'Sockless'

During his 1890 campaign, he earned the nickname "Sockless" Jerry. A reporter for the *Wichita Eagle*, making fun of Simpson's country "hick" image, wrote that the Populist candidate wore no socks.

Simpson, who could charm a crowd with his stories, turned the insult around. In a speech, he called his Republican opponent a wealthy prince who traveled in a private railroad car and wore silk stockings. "What does he know of the life and toil of such plowhandlers as we are?" Simpson cried. "I can't represent you in Congress in silk stockings, I can't afford to wear 'em!" ⟳

SOCKLESS SIMPSON

Voters liked his approach. They sent him more than 300 pairs of socks—and elected him to the U.S. House of Representatives three times. In Washington, Congressman Simpson was not the country bumpkin he sometimes pretended to be. He and Senator William Peffer [**78**] fought hard against Eastern bankers, railroads and programs they felt hurt farmers.

Simpson later worked for a livestock company in Wichita. He then moved to New Mexico and sold real estate. When he became seriously ill he had his wife put him on a train; he wanted to die in Kansas. She took him to a Wichita hospital where he died October 23, 1905. ■

Generally speaking

90 Lewis Walt

U.S. Marine general. Harveyville. (1913-1989) Walt, a native of Harveyville, joined the U.S. Marine Corps in the 1930s. During his tour of duty he had a variety of assignments in the United States and overseas during World War II, the Korean War and the Vietnam War. In 1968 he was promoted to the rank of general. For the next three years, General Walt was assistant commandant of the Marines. ■

91 Larry Welch

U.S. Air Force general. Liberal. (Born 1934) Welch grew up in Liberal and served in Washington, D.C., as the U.S. Air Force chief of staff in the late 1980s. In that job, the four-star general commanded all Air Force personnel and was one of the president's top military advisors. Earlier General Welch commanded the Strategic Air Command that guards North America against a surprise nuclear attack. He retired in 1990. ■

Dropout to high court

92 Charles E. Whittaker

U.S. Supreme Court justice. Troy. (1901-1973) Whittaker had to quit school at age sixteen when his mother died, but four years later he got into the University of Kansas City law school with help from a tutor. To pay for his tuition, he trapped animals and sold the furs.

He was a U.S. District Court judge in Missouri when President Dwight D. Eisenhower [**44**] appointed him to the U.S. Supreme Court in 1957. Whittaker was the second Kansan [**32**] on the high court. He served five years before bad health forced him to retire in 1962. ■

Beats FDR but loses

93 Wendell Willkie

Presidential candidate. Coffeyville. (1892-1944) Willkie was the Republican candidate for president in 1940. Like Alf Landon [**67**], the Republican candidate in the previous election, Willkie was a Kansan—for a short time, at least. He taught history at Coffeyville High School in 1913 and 1914.

Willkie grew up in Indiana. He enlisted in the U.S. Army during World War I and later went to law school. As president of a large power company in the 1930s, he fought a long legal battle with the government. During that time, he left the Democratic party in opposition to some of President Franklin D. Roosevelt's New Deal business policies. At the 1940 Republican convention, Willkie was an amateur politician and brand-new Republican, but hundreds of delegates chanted "We want Willkie" until he won the nomination.

Not surprisingly, Willkie and Landon both lost their presidential races to the popular Roosevelt. But Landon, the long-time Kansan, lost in 46 states—including his own. Willkie, a temporary Jayhawker, beat FDR in Kansas and ten other states. In all, he polled over 22 million votes. ■

WILL FOR PRESIDENT

Loses for a good cause

94 Paul Wilson

Assistant state attorney general. Quenemo, Ashland, Lyndon, Topeka and Lawrence. (Born 1913)
Wilson was a young assistant prosecutor for the Kansas attorney general when an important civil rights case, *Brown [100] vs. Topeka Board of Education*, went to the U.S. Supreme Court.

He had little experience, but Wilson tackled the case. (One of the first things he had to do was spend $40 on a dark-colored suit, the "dress code" for lawyers in the Supreme Court.) Wilson argued against opening Topeka's elementary schools to all races, even though many felt it was time to integrate schools everywhere.

When the Supreme Court announced its decision in 1954, Wilson had indeed lost. The nine justices ruled that an old Kansas law that allowed "separate but equal" elementary schools for different races was illegal. ■

SUPREME COURT OF THE UNITED STATES

Nos. 1, 2, 4 and 10.—October Term, 1953.

1	Oliver Brown, et al., Appellants, *v.* Board of Education of Topeka, Shawnee County, Kansas, et al.	On Appeal From the United States District Court for the District of Kansas.
2	Harry Briggs, Jr., et al., Appellants, *v.* R. W. Elliott, et al.	On Appeal From the United States District Court for the Eastern District of South Carolina.
4	Dorothy E. Davis, et al., Appellants, *v.* County School Board of Prince Edward County, Virginia, et al.	On Appeal From the United States District Court for the Eastern District of Virginia.
10	Francis B. Gebhart, et al., Petitioners, *v.* Ethel Louise Belton, et al.	On Writ of Certiorari to the Supreme Court of Delaware.

[May 17, 1954.]

Mr. Chief Justice Warren delivered the opinion of the Court.

These cases come to us from the States of Kansas, South Carolina, Virginia, and Delaware. They are premised on different facts and different local conditions,

Governor goes to war

95 Harry Woodring

Governor and U.S. secretary of war. Elk City, Neodesha and Topeka. (1887-1967)
Before he ran for governor, Woodring had not been involved in politics. Except for a short period of military service during World War I, he had led a quiet life as a bachelor bank cashier in Neodesha. He had, however, held state offices in the American Legion and the Kansas Bankers' Association.

Even with his lack of campaign experience, Woodring easily won the Democratic nomination for governor in 1930. He faced Republican ***Frank Haucke***, also a bachelor and former official in the American Legion. Their campaign that fall got off to a slow start. Both men spent nearly two weeks out of the state attending a Legion convention in Boston. Then Dr. John R. Brinkley [342] joined the race. Although it was too late for Brinkley's name to appear on the ballot, the infamous doctor campaigned as a write-in candidate. With his own radio station and a traveling troupe of entertainers, Brinkley had several campaign advantages over his opponents.

Woodring ignored Brinkley's challenge, but it nearly cost him the election. When the ballots were counted—it took nearly two weeks—Woodring had beaten Haucke by only 251 votes. Brinkley was in third place, but election judges had thrown out perhaps 60,000 of his write-in ballots saying they improperly marked. Haucke and the Republicans didn't challenge the close count, afraid Brinkley might be declared the winner in a recount. Woodring thus became governor.

During his term from 1931 to 1933 he dealt with many problems caused by the Depression. He led the state in making cost cuts by taking a ten percent cut in his $5,000 salary. With no wife in the governor's mansion, Woodring's unmarried sister served as his official hostess.

During the presidential election of 1932, Woodring was one of Franklin D. Roosevelt's strongest Kansas supporters. The governor hoped to be rewarded with a top cabinet post; FDR made him the assistant secretary of war instead. After the war secretary died in 1936, Woodring got the job, but he didn't agree with Roosevelt's pre-war plans. The president asked him to resign in 1940. ■

Others in government service

Henry Atkinson probably first visited Kansas in 1819 when he brought troops to Cantonment Martin, the first U.S. military post in what is now Kansas. (The camp, on an island in the Missouri River between present Atchison and Leavenworth, lasted only about a year.) At the time, General Atkinson was in charge of a fleet of steamboats that carried Lieutenant Colonel Stephen Long's expedition [**24**] up the Missouri River.

Atkinson was commander of the Army's Western Department when he died near St. Louis in 1842. In his honor, Fort Atkinson, one of the first military posts on the Santa Fe Trail, was named in his honor in 1851. Located just west of modern Dodge City, the lonely outpost was abandoned three years later. Its sod buildings were infested with mice and rats—even though a dozen cats were sent out from Fort Leavenworth on "rodent duty." Unlucky soldiers stationed at Fort Atkinson called it Fort Sod and Fort Sodom. ■

Thelma Boatman, a graduate of Washburn College in Topeka, practiced law with her husband in Norton. In 1932 she was one of the first women in the state to be elected county attorney. ■

Nellie Cline, a lawyer from Larned, appeared before the Kansas Supreme Court in the spring of 1918. In doing so, she became the first woman lawyer to argue a case in the state's highest court. ■

Henry Zarah Curtis was a major in the U.S. Army when he was killed in 1863. Curtis was one of 80 troops that died when William Quantrill [**373**] and his raiders attacked a Union force at Baxter Springs. A year later, Curtis' father, Major General **Samuel Curtis**, established a new fort on the Santa Fe Trail. In memory of his son, he named it Fort Zarah. The post was near the present town of Great Bend, not far from the junction of Walnut Creek and the Arkansas River. Fort Zarah was abandoned in 1869. ■

Grenville M. Dodge, a major general in the U.S. Army, was commander of the Army's Department of the Missouri when he ordered a new fort to be built on the Santa Fe Trail in the spring of 1865. According to some sources, the post was named Fort Dodge in his honor. Others say it was named for Colonel **Henry Dodge**, Grenville's uncle. Another name to add to the confusion is that of Colonel **Richard I. Dodge**. All three Dodges had Kansas connections:

Grenville led troops on a tough winter campaign in western Kansas in 1865. He later chose the route of the Union Pacific section of the transcontinental railroad. He died in Iowa in 1916.

Henry also fought Indians in Kansas and was commander at Fort Lea-

venworth before he became governor of Wisconsin. He was born in 1782 and died in 1867.

Richard, born in North Carolina in 1827, commanded Forts Hays and Dodge and was one of the founders of Dodge City. He died in 1895. ■

Paul F. Foster, born in Wichita in 1889, graduated from the U.S. Naval Academy in 1911. During a long career in the U.S. Navy he rose to the rank of vice admiral. Along the way Paul sank a German U-boat, rescued fourteen unconscious sailors from a burning gun turret, helped break the Japanese code used in World War II, and handled special assignments for President Franklin D. Roosevelt. As a result, Foster was the first to win the three highest honors a sailor can achieve: the Congressional Medal of Honor, the Distinguished Service Medal and the Navy Cross. Two years after his death in 1972, the Navy commissioned a new destroyer named in his honor, the USS Foster. ■

Gary Hart, born as Gary Hartpence at Ottawa in 1936, attended Yale University. There he graduated from the institution's divinity and law schools. While practicing law in Denver he became active in the Democratic party. That led to his job as national director of the Democratic presidential campaign in 1972. Two years later he was elected U.S. senator from Colorado, an office he held until 1987. In 1984 Hart ran for the presidency, but he failed to win enough Democratic delegates for the nomination. He tried again four years later, but he left the race after he was accused of having an extramarital affair.

Hart is one of several Kansans elected to the U.S. Congress from other states. Senator *Arlen Specter* was born in Russell in 1930. After serving as a public official in Philadelphia, he was elected one of Pennsylvania's senators in 1980. *Carl Hatch*, senator from New Mexico in the 1930s and 1940s, was born in Kirwin in 1889 and died in New Mexico in 1963. *John Rhodes*, born in Council Grove in 1916, ended a 30-year career as a representative from Arizona in 1983. From 1973 until 1981 Rhodes was Minority Leader of the U.S. House of Representatives. ∎

Elmer "Ted" Klassen was born in Hillsboro. At age seventeen he went to work as a messenger for the American Can Company in San Francisco. Forty years later Ted was the president of the billion-dollar company. When Congress reorganized the post office department into the U.S. Postal Service in 1972, Klassen begame the postmaster general of the United States. As he helped automate mail service, he caused controversy by cutting 33,000 postal workers from the payroll. Klassen, age 81, died in Florida in 1990. ∎

John W. Leedy was the second Populist governor [**70**] in Kansas—and the state's first chief executive to have an office with a bathtub! He was born in Ohio in 1849 and moved from Illinois to Coffey County in 1880. After losing his horse-breeding farm in the depression of the 1890s, John joined the Populist party. His 1896 campaign for governor included the unusual promise of allowing

voters to take a bath in his private bathtub. After he won, Governor Leedy kept his word. In his office he installed a large tub—big enough to hold his hefty 230-pound frame. It's not known how many taxpayers took him up on his bathing offer, but other state officials followed his lead and installed their own Capitol tubs, some of which remained in place until the 1930s.

After he left office in 1899 Leedy practiced law in Lawrence. He later lived in Washington and Alaska. He died in poverty in 1935 as a Canadian —the only Kansas ex-governor to become a foreign citizen. A year later the Kansas Legislature gave $1,000 to pay for his funeral and to mark his grave. ∎

Eva Rider became the first woman bailiff in the United States when District Judge *Granville Aikman* of El Dorado appointed her in 1912. Under the judge's direction, Eva installed an all-woman jury. After the ladies ordered that spitoons be removed from the jury box, they heard a case between a man who had bought land and a woman who had sold it. The man won. ∎

Bennet Riley, a major in the U.S. Army, led the first military escort of wagons across Kansas on the Santa Fe Trail in 1829. Because present southwestern Kansas was then part of Mexico, Major Riley was not allowed to accompany the traders as they crossed the Arkansas River onto foreign soil. He did, however, slip into Mexican territory long enough to frighten away Indians that attacked the wagon train. Fort Riley, still open in present Geary and Riley counties, was named in his honor in 1853. ∎

Roy Romer was born in Garden City in 1928. In 1987 he was elected governor of Colorado as a Democrat. In 1956, *George Brown*, another Kansan, was the first African-American elected to the Colorado state senate. After serving five terms, he was elected that state's first black lieutenant governor in 1974. Brown grew up in Lawrence and graduated from KU. ∎

Fred Seaton was born in 1909 in Washington, D.C., while his father worked for Senator Joseph Bristow [**33**]. After graduating from Kansas State Agricultural College (KSU), Fred was head of the Kansas Young Republicans. Seaton also helped with the presidential campaign of Dwight D. Eisenhower [**44**]. Ike later appointed him assistant secretary of defense, deputy assistant to the president and then secretary of the interior. As interior secretary he had an important role in bringing Alaska and Hawaii into the union. Seaton died in 1974. ∎

Leslie Short graduated from Plains High School in 1939 and joined the U.S. Navy shortly afterward. On December 7, 1941, he was on the battleship *USS Maryland* in Pearl Harbor when the Japanese launched their surprise attack. Leslie ran to one of the ship's large guns and fired several rounds that are believed to have shot down the first Japanese plane of the war. Short now shares his firsthand view of history with Kansas school children. ∎

Don W. Wilson, from Clay Center and Abilene, is the archivist of the United States. He began his career of taking care of public records and other documents at the Kansas State Historical Society in Topeka. ∎

Movers & Shakers

SUPREME COURT OF THE UNITED STATES

Nos. 1, 2, 4 AND 10.—OCTOBER TERM, 1953.

Oliver Brown, et al., Appellants,
v.
Board of Education of Topeka, Shawnee County, Kansas, et al.

On Appeal From the United States District Court for the District of Kansas.

Harry Tm

Crusaders, Doctors and Educators

MENNINGER CLINIC

First Kansas wheat queen?

96 Anna Barkman

Kansas pioneer. Hillsboro. (1866-About 1927) Barkman was born on a farm in Russia. In 1874, her Mennonite parents decided to move to Kansas with other members of their church [**170**]. According to some stories, eight-year-old Anna spent long winter evenings hand-picking two gallons—or about 250,000 grains—of her father's best wheat to use as seed in America. Mennonites in other families may have done the same thing.

The seed they selected may or may not have been the variety of hard winter wheat called Turkey Red. Historians still have questions about the beginnings of hard wheat in Kansas. Some say Mennonites like the Barkmans may have brought seed from soft wheat varieties—or perhaps even rye. There is little proof that hard red wheat was grown in the state until the early 1880s, although by the 1890s it was very popular [**179**].

However, one fact remains: Mennonite farmers helped make wheat the state's most important crop. Later, as the wife of a Kansas farmer, Anna Barkman Wohlgemuth was no doubt proud of her role—whatever it was—in the story of Kansas wheat. ∎

Sells Lincoln on whiskers

97 Grace Bedell

Presidential "advisor." Delphos. (1848-1936) Bedell was an eleven-year-old living in Westfield, New York, when Abraham Lincoln ran for president in 1860. The young girl liked the Republican candidate, but she worried about his "image."

Shortly before the election, she mailed Lincoln a letter suggesting that he grow a beard. "You would look a great deal better for your face is so thin," she wrote. "All the ladies like whiskers and they would tease their husbands to vote for you."

Lincoln wrote Grace back, thanking her for the advice. Soon, the beginnings of a beard were showing on his face. "Old Abe. . .is puttin' on (h)airs!" a newspaper joked. By the time he was inaugurated, his beard was complete—and he was America's first bearded president.

After Bedell was married she came to Kansas. She brought along her Lincoln letter and stored it in the vault of the Delphos bank where her husband worked. Grace Bedell Billings refused offers as high as $5,000 for her famous note. After she died, a television producer bought it for $20,000. ∎

Grandma doctor in a buggy

98 Mary Bennett

Pioneer doctor. Haviland and Nickerson. (1852-1935) Bennett and her husband were doctors in Ohio before they came to Kansas about the turn of the century. They set up a practice in Kiowa County where "Grandma Dr. Bennett" delivered over 1,500 babies. Many times, she drove her buggy many miles to bring a new baby into the world and then stayed to cook a meal for the rest of the new arrival's family.

On one trip, she was called to a one-room, dirt-floored shack. Inside, Dr. Bennett delivered a baby to a woman who had been deserted by her husband. When she found the new mother didn't have even a blanket, the doctor wrapped the newborn in paper and then went to town to gather food and clothing for them.

Mary once traveled twenty miles in a blizzard to treat a patient. She had to stop a dozen times to open and close wire gates—which froze to her fingers—plus tie and untie her horses to a fencepost at each stop. On another trip, her team ran away while she was getting out of the buggy. She dashed after it, jumped on the back of the buggy, climbed around to the front, stopped the runaway horses—and then went back over her trail to find her medical bag that had bounced out!

Bennett moved to Nickerson when she and her husband retired in 1911. After his death she returned to Haviland. ∎

One-woman whirlwind

Civil War nurse and veterans' supporter. Salina and Bunker Hill. (1817-1901)
Mary Ann Ball was born July 19, 1817, in Knox County, Ohio. Her mother died when Mary Ann was a baby, so she and an older sister were raised by their grandparents.

In 1847 Mary Ann married Robert Bickerdyke, a Cincinnati widower with four children. They eventually had four children of their own. The Bickerdykes moved to Galesburg, Illinois, where Robert died in 1859.

Home-grown nursing

As a young widow with a flock of young children to care for, Mary Ann worked as a laundress, housekeeper and home nurse. She cared for the sick using medicinal herbs and home remedies that she had learned from her grandmother and other farm women.

For a short time, Bickerdyke worked for Dr. Benjamin Woodward, a local physician. However, he joined the U.S. Army when the Civil War began and was sent to a government hospital in Cairo, Illinois.

Dr. Woodward soon wrote back to his church in Galesburg that conditions in the hospital were terrible. The congregation immediately collected $500 and Mary Ann agreed to deliver the church's gifts of clothing, medicine, soap and food. When she arrived at Fort Defiance on a June day in 1861, Bickerdyke took one look and decided to take action. Without being asked, she rolled up her sleeves and helped bathe soldiers who were lying on dirty straw pallets. From her supplies she gave them clean clothes.

She then began a clean-up campaign in the hospital. Her crew was young privates bribed with the promise of fried chicken. Together they freshened bedding, cleaned the mud floors and carried out piles of fly-covered waste. She went from tent to tent, doing her best to improve the terrible conditions.

'Mother' Bickerdyke

As she was leaving that night, a patient called out, "Good night, Mother"—and the nickname lasted the rest of her life.

The 44-year-old widow met with the commanding officer the next day and he gave her permission to remain in the camp. Not everyone, however, was glad to have Mary Ann around. She was somewhat large and overbearing; some called her "downright bossy." One surgeon complained that this "cyclone in calico" disrupted his hospital.

Bickerdyke spent the rest of that long, hot summer nursing the wounded in six Army hospital camps around Cairo. The next winter, General Ulysses S. Grant's forces moved up the Cumberland River. Mother Bickerdyke was there, waiting on a hospital ship.

She dressed wounds covered in frozen blood and mud, furnished fresh bedding, and warmed soldiers with cups of hot tea and broth. When the stretcher-bearers stopped bringing casualties on board each evening, she put on a heavy cloak and visited the tents, passing out dried apples and crackers. She also searched nearby battlefields for any wounded men overlooked in the darkness. ⇨

In all, Mother Bickerdyke cared for wounded soldiers on nineteen Civil War battlefields. On one of General Sterling Price's campaigns she set up a large laundry. In one day, her crew washed 600 towels, 2,300 pieces of clothing, plus 600 sheets and blankets. She followed General Grant to Vicksburg and General William Sherman on his march through Georgia.

'She outranks me'

A surgeon once complained to Sherman about her "insubordination." The general replied: "If it was Bickerdyke, I can't do anything for you. She outranks me." On that same march, she hauled a stove along and helped bake hundreds of loaves of bread each night for hungry troops.

The U.S. Sanitary Commission, an organization much like the later Red Cross, supported her. If supplies were low, she rounded up what was needed, often ignoring official orders. When she felt troops weren't getting enough milk and eggs, she took a steamboat up the Mississippi River to Illinois, and persuaded farmers to give her 200 milk cows and a thousand chickens. She also traveled to Northern cities, raising needed money.

At the close of the war, Mary Ann was still full of energy. Thousands of troops came to Washington, D.C., for a victory parade, and she was there with five boxcars of supplies. Grateful soldiers gave her an elegant outfit to wear as she watched the parade from a viewing stand, but Mother Bickerdyke had other ideas. In her faded calico dress and worn sunbonnet, she set up two tents near the parade route and handed out bread, tea and soft-boiled eggs.

In 1866 she left the Sanitary Commission and spent a year in Chicago at a homeless shelter. There she heard some of "her boys" from the Civil War talking about homesteading in Kansas. The state needed new settlers, but few ex-soldiers had the money to get there.

Off to Kansas

With her last Chicago paycheck, Bickerdyke traveled to Kansas. What she saw pleased her, so she went back to Illinois and straight into the office of a wealthy banker. She walked out with a $10,000 loan. Next, she visited the president of the Chicago, Burlington and Quincy Railroad. She convinced him to haul her boys to Kansas on CB&Q trains, free of charge.

Soon, 50 families had settled on claims near Salina. To get them started in farming, Mother Bickerdyke loaned them money to buy farm equipment. She also journeyed to Fort Riley and returned with extra Army wagons and teams from her friend General Sherman.

Instead of going home to Chicago, Bickerdyke stayed in Salina and opened a boarding house with money from the Union Pacific Railroad. The railroad named it the Pacific Hotel, but everyone else called it the Bickerdyke House. In two years, 250 families stopped at Mother Bickerdyke's on their way west. If they had no cash, that was no problem. She gave them rooms for nothing.

In 1869, Arapahos raided homesteads in northern Kansas. Mary Ann traveled to Washington and came back with tons of supplies. In Topeka, she persuaded the legislature to help settlers buy seed corn and potatoes.

Bickerdyke's good work went on, but the railroad was unhappy because she continually helped the needy—with profits from their hotel. When they hired a new hotel manager and fired Mary Ann, she was furious. She went to Washington, where the railroad was trying to get government aid. When she got through telling her story to legislators who were ex-Civil War officers, she still had no job— but the Union Pacific had no new government funds, either.

She then worked in the slums of New York City and Chicago. In 1874, she returned to Kansas just as swarms of grasshoppers ate all the crops. She hurried to Illinois, where she gathered donated food. Mother Bickerdyke made ten more trips to the East and Midwest that winter, collecting 200 carloads of clothing, food and grain for needy Kansas families.

Her health, however, suffered from all her traveling. To recover, she moved to California where she got pensions for her boys. When the U.S. Congress later voted to give Bickerdyke her own pension, it was only one-half what other Civil War veterans received. But she wasn't bitter. She looked at her first $25 monthly check and said, "It is so much. I can do a great deal of good with it."

Patron saint

In 1887 Mother Bickerdyke moved back to Kansas, and worked for two of her favorite causes, prohibition and voting rights for women. From her son's home in Bunker Hill, she also helped oversee a home in Ellsworth for veterans' widows and children.

Kansas honored its "patron saint" with a celebration on her eightieth birthday in 1897. She died at Bunker Hill, November 8, 1901, at the age of 84 and was buried beside her husband in Illinois. Civil War veterans and others across the country remembered Mary Ann Bickerdyke as the "one-woman whirlwind." ■

Caught in controversy

100 Linda Brown Buckner

Civil rights supporter and educator. Topeka. (Born 1943) When civil rights issues were being debated in the 1950s, a Topeka lawsuit became an important case in the U.S. Supreme Court.

Under an old Kansas law, larger cities in the state could have segregated, or separate, elementary schools for different races. At the same time, Kansas high schools were integrated—although black and white students often attended separate classes and played on separate athletic teams.

The Reverend **Oliver Brown** challenged the idea of segregated schools when he tried to enroll his six-year-old daughter Linda in Sumner Elementary School in 1950. Sumner at that time was an all-white school just four blocks from the Browns' Topeka home. The girl heard her father's voice grow louder and louder as he spoke in the school office. But the principal and the Topeka board of education turned them away, saying Linda would have to attend Monroe Elementary School, an all-black school in another part of the city.

The Browns and other parents from their neighborhood felt their children should not have to walk six blocks, cross dangerous railroad tracks and ride a bus for 30 minutes just to get to school. They signed petitions to have the policy changed, but the school board refused to act. Eventually the case went to court, with Oliver Brown's name first on the list of defendants.

When a panel of three Topeka judges ruled against the parents in 1951, they appealed. That sent the case to the U.S. Supreme Court. Similar lawsuits from three other states and the District of Columbia had also come before the high court, but the Kansas case was the first one chosen to be heard.

Charles Sheldon Scott, a young black lawyer from Topeka, was one of those who argued before the Supreme Court in favor of integrated schools. The nine justices agreed, and ruled in 1954 that "separate but equal" schools for different races were illegal. The State of Kansas, its young lawyer Paul Wilson [**94**], and the Topeka school board lost.

Brown vs. Topeka Board of Education was a landmark, or ground-breaking, case because it opened schools across the country to blacks. Some say it also helped African-Americans gain increased civil rights in other areas.

Linda Brown Buckner is now a teacher for the Head Start program in Topeka. Her sister, **Cheryl Brown Henderson**, is president of the Brown Foundation for Educational Equity, Excellence and Research, also in Topeka. The foundation helps minority students who want to become teachers. One of its organizers was Linda's mother, **Leola Brown Montgomery**. Sumner school, still in use, has been declared a national historic landmark. In 1992 Monroe school was designated a national historic site.

In 1979 some Topeka parents tried to reopen *Brown vs. Topeka Board of Education* because they felt local schools were not completely desegregated. Due to their efforts, the school district was ordered in 1989 to come up with a new plan for integrated schools. The district appealed. Some say another Supreme Court decision will have to settle the question. ■

Tireless crusader for good health

Doctor and public health official. Spearville, Dodge City and Topeka. (1862-1954) Samuel Krumbine was born in Venango County, Pennsylvania, on September 17, 1862.

His father was a soldier in the Civil War and died in a prison camp. While Samuel's mother worked, he and his sister lived with their grandmother. Then, as an eight-year old, Sammy went to a school for soldiers' orphans in Mercer, Pennsylvania.

There he picked up the nickname "Crummie." He eventually changed the spelling of his last name to match it.

During his school years Samuel decided to become a doctor. After he graduated at age sixteen he went to work at a drugstore in a nearby town. His employer, a physician and pharmacist, taught him well. Within three years, Crumbine was mixing prescriptions and helping with minor operations and house calls.

Gives away worthless cure

In the early 1880s, Crumbine moved to Ohio to study at a Cincinnati medical school. He was short of money, so to help pay his fees, he passed out samples of a patent medicine cure for tuberculosis. Crumbine was embarrassed by the worthless product, but the $25 he earned each week helped him continue his schooling.

He first came to Kansas in 1885 during a college vacation and worked at a Spearville drugstore. He continued the job for several summers, and eventually bought half of the business. After graduating at the top of his class in 1888 he returned to Spearville.

With $35, all the cash he had, he bought a buckskin pony and established his medical practice. His house calls often took him to Dodge City, and in August of the next year he moved there.

Dodge City's doc

Dressed in a Prince Albert coat with a six-shooter strapped to his hip, the spunky doctor was soon a familiar sight on Front Street. Crumbine was a short man (only five feet, six inches), but he expected patients of any size to follow his orders.

Once he was called to a cattle ranch 35 miles out of Dodge to treat the owner's broken leg. After a four-hour ride, Crumbine arrived, set the fractured bone, and started to return to town. The rancher insisted he stay until morning—and made his point by holding a gun on the doctor. Crumbine quickly agreed.

The next day the man paid Crumbine with a generous amount of cash, not the payment of eggs, butter, chickens or turkeys he often received.

On his birthday in 1890, the 28-year-old doctor married **Katherine Zuercher**, a girl he had met during medical school. She moved to Dodge City and soon they had two children. Accidents, epidemics and other medical emergencies, however, often kept him away from his family.

Crumbine traveled the countryside to treat patients in all kinds of weather. During one blizzard, he nearly froze to death when his horses fell into a snowbank. Another time he was seriously hurt as his carriage rolled off a steep bank into a creek.

He also took a wild ride on the Rock Island Railroad out of Dodge City. A railroader's wife was burned in an explosion and a special train hurriedly bounced and bumped the doctor over 28 miles of rickety track to Bucklin.

In fighting disease, Dr. Crumbine felt prevention was as important as treatment. When Fred Harvey [**154**] opened a new restaurant in Dodge City, the doctor convinced the local manager not to dip milk out of uncovered pails. Harvey then took Crumbine's advice and began serving milk in sealed glass bottles across his entire system of restaurants.

State's top doctor

Governor **William Stanley** appointed Crumbine to the Kansas State Board of Health in 1899. Later, he became the board's executive secretary and moved his family to Topeka.

This made Dr. Crumbine the state's first full-time public health officer. However, his new state health "department" had just two staff members, a budget of $3,000—and only one health law to enforce. Fortunately, he took office during a time when people were becoming interested in improving their health.

Dirty drinking water

In those days, people believed that flowing water purified itself every seven miles. Most cities and towns simply pumped their raw sewage into the nearest streams. To prove how dangerous this was, Dr. Crumbine and a professor from the University of Kansas spent two days floating down the Kansas River.

Between Topeka and Lawrence they took water samples every half mile. Not surprisingly, their test results showed the water was much too polluted to drink. Crumbine pushed for water and sewage laws and they were passed in 1907. ✍

A pair of new products

Dr. Crumbine's health campaigns helped popularize two ordinary household items.

Frank Rose, a Kansas schoolteacher in Weir City, heard of the doctor's crusade against flies and wanted his Boy Scout troop to be a part of it.

According to some stories, Rose made "fly bats" from wire screen cut into squares. He fastened the pieces to free yardsticks from a local drugstore. His scouts gave these early fly swatters away, and also convinced the local city council to pass the state's first ordinance spelling out the danger caused by flies.

After Dr. Crumbine outlawed public drinking cups in the state, an ex-Kansan living in New England visited Topeka. *Hugh Moore* showed Crumbine samples of a throwaway cup he had made from paper. The doctor was impressed and encouraged Moore to sell his invention in penny vending machines on railroad cars.

Later, this cup was the first product Moore manufactured in his new business—the Dixie Paper Cup Company.

That same year Governor Edward Hoch [**60**] signed the Kansas Pure Food and Drug Act.

Swat the fly

Crumbine also campaigned against the housefly. Through pamphlets, posters, cartoons and newspaper articles he warned the public about how "filthy flies" carried disease. He published directions on how to make flypaper, and urged people to cover food, use window screens and haul away animal manure.

Crumbine's most popular saying was first used in that crusade. While he was attending a Topeka baseball game one afternoon, the crowd cheered, "Sacrifice fly! Swat that ball!" An idea clicked in his head and he quickly jotted a slogan on the back of an envelope—"Swat the fly."

Children across Kansas helped the doctor in his battle against flies. Towns began paying a bounty for the dead insects; they were gathered by the basketload. Youngsters in Hutchinson collected 27 bushels! In some towns, kids could trade containers of dead flies for free movie tickets.

Common cups and towels

The "common" drinking cup was another disease carrier in those days. In schools, on trains, and in other public places, everyone used the same cup over and over.

Dr. Crumbine took cups from several trains and analyzed them. He found many kinds of bacteria, including tuberculosis. Because of his work, Kansas outlawed the public drinking cup in 1909. It was the first state to do so.

In his fight against tuberculosis the doctor helped establish a state sanitarium to treat victims of the disease. He convinced Kansas brick companies to stamp "Don't Spit on Sidewalk" into thousands of bricks that they made. When the special bricks were laid in sidewalks, streets and depot platforms around the state, they helped warn the public about another germ-spreading practice.

Crumbine also did away with the common towel hanging in public restrooms, schools and work places. Like the drinking cup, it was first banned in Kansas.

He also ordered that hotels change bedsheets each day, and warned people to "Bat the rat." He fought for laws that made weights and measures standard, regulations to help prevent sexually-transmitted diseases and better infant care.

Forced out of office

The popular Republican doctor worked for Kansans under six governors—until the stormy term of Democrat Jonathan Davis [**39**]. Davis became upset with Crumbine's frank state-ments about sexually-transmitted diseases. When Crumbine wouldn't back down, the governor appointed a new board of health and forced the doctor to resign in May 1923.

The public sided with Crumbine, but the doctor left Kansas for good. He moved to New York City and became general manager of the American Child Health Association. During the 1930s, President Herbert Hoover asked him to study health conditions in Puerto Rico for two years. He received many honors and was recognized around the world for his contributions to public health.

After his retirement, Crumbine spent his free time writing and doing research. He was 91 when he died in New York, on July 10, 1954.

Many health practices that we take for granted today were first encouraged by the doctor from Kansas. ∎

Little lady speaks her mind

102 Annie Diggs

Supporter of Populism and women's suffrage. Lawrence. (1853-1916) Diggs came to Kansas in 1873 to work in a Lawrence music store. Her job was to demonstrate pianos to customers, but she soon demonstrated a talent in politics instead. She first spoke out against alcohol and capital punishment. Next she wrote newspaper editorials that

Works for KSC and UNESCO

103 Milton Eisenhower

Educator and government official. Abilene and Manhattan. (1899-1985) Beginning in the 1920s, Eisenhower worked as an assistant to the secretary of agriculture under presidents Coolidge, Hoover and Roosevelt. During World War II he was president of Kansas State College (later Kansas State University).

In the early 1950s Eisenhower was the national chairman of UNESCO, the United Nations Educational, Scientific and Cultural Organization. With his leadership, Kansas was the first state to call a UNESCO conference and promote its work.

Before he retired in the early 1970s, Milton was the president of universities in Maryland and Pennsylvania. His opinions were valued, and he was often an advisor to all the presidents from Truman to Nixon, including his older brother Dwight [*44*]. ■

Sweeps her husband under the rug

104 Elizabeth Fisher

Antislavery supporter. Leavenworth, Lawrence, Ottawa, Atchison, Westmoreland and Topeka. (1826-1901) Fisher and her husband, a Methodist minister, worked for the antislavery cause during the Bleeding Kansas period. Because of this, William Quantrill [*373*] and his proslavery guerillas wanted to kill the Reverend ***Hugh Fisher*** during their attack on Lawrence in 1863.

Elizabeth, however, cleverly saved her husband's life. As Quantrill's raiders searched the Fishers' home, Elizabeth hid Hugh in the cellar. She managed to keep the outlaws from discovering him, but then, the raiders began to set fire to the house.

Thinking quickly, Elizabeth begged the men to let her save her carpet. They agreed. As she pulled the rug over the cellar's trapdoor, she signaled to her husband below. He crawled up through the hole in the floor, slipped under the wrinkled carpet, and crawled on his hands and knees as Elizabeth dragged the heavy rug outside—right under the noses of Quantrill's unsuspecting men! ■

---

supported women's voting rights and the Populist movement. Audiences loved Diggs when she gave a speech at a Populist convention in 1890. Soon "Little Annie"—she was not quite five feet tall and weighed just 90 pounds—was appearing at Populist rallies across Kansas and the Midwest.

Diggs often traveled with another Populist lecturer, Mary Elizabeth Lease [*112*]—but the two women were definitely not friends. They disagreed about several things, especially whether Populists should cooperate with Democrats. Diggs said yes; Lease, no. Their fight became public when Lease made a speech in Topeka and accused Diggs of not being loyal to the Populist cause.

When Lease finished, Diggs calmly pointed a finger at her and said, "Woman, you have lied." The crowd cheered. Democrats laughed and called it foolish "petticoat politics."

It was Annie, however, who had the last laugh. At the state Democratic convention in 1900, she convinced many delegates to join her and support Populist issues. ■

Kansas Book Lady

105 Ruth Gagliardo

Librarian and newspaper journalist. Topeka, Emporia, Lawrence and Wichita. **(1895-1980)** As a teenager in Topeka Gagliardo won several writing contests sponsored by Arthur Capper [**34**]. In the 1920s she worked as a reporter for William Allen White [**256**] at the *Emporia Gazette*. White asked her to write a column about new books, and in it she included titles for younger readers. It was the first newspaper column in America to review children's books.

In 1942 Ruth became the Kansas State Teachers Association's director of library services. During almost 25 years with the KSTA, Gagliardo started a variety of projects to help young Kansans enjoy books: reading fairs, radio programs and traveling libraries. The "Kansas Book Lady" also created the William

Allen White Children's Book Award in honor of her famous boss. Each year since 1952, Kansas readers in the fourth through eighth grades have chosen a favorite book in state-wide balloting. This award and several of Gagliardo's other projects have been patterns for children's reading programs in many states. ■

Travels for FDR

106 John A. Gregg

Educator and church official. Kansas City. **(1877-1953)** Gregg graduated from the University of Kansas and served as the president of black colleges in Florida, Ohio and South Africa. He was the first African-American to be president of Howard University in Washington, D.C.

During World War II Gregg was a personal representative for President Franklin D. Roosevelt. He traveled to Europe and the Pacific region to visit black troops and then reported to the president. From the 1930s until his death, he was also a bishop in the African Methodist Church. ■

Shares millions with his neighbors

107 Dane Hansen

Philanthropist and businessman. Logan. **(1883-1965)** Hansen spent all his life in Phillips County, managing various family businesses: a ranch, lumberyard, construction company and oil wells. He was a good friend of Dwight D. Eisenhower [**44**] and served on a presidential commission in the 1950s.

Hansen always said one can't make money before noon, so each day he stayed in bed until 10 or 11 a.m., went to his office at noon, and worked until 2 or 3 a.m. the next morning. Even though he became one of the largest independent oil operators in Kansas, Dane was still very concerned with the smallest details of his business. He once told the man in charge of his oil company to report each time a 2,000 foot-deep hole was drilled another six inches.

Hansen enjoyed sharing his wealth. The philanthropist supported many projects, and when he died he left $9 million to continue his giving. A foundation was created in his name that built an impressive museum in Logan. The foundation also gives away over half a million dollars each year in grants and scholarships to organizations and students in northwestern Kansas. Hansen was inducted into the Kansas Business Hall of Fame in 1990. ■

Country doc commutes to city

108 Arthur Hertzler

Pioneer doctor and author. Newton, Moundridge and Halstead. (1870-1946) Hertzler worked as a blacksmith before he went to medical school. He moved to Halstead to practice medicine, where he eventually built a clinic and hospital that is still respected around the state. For almost 40 years Dr. Hertzler taught at the University of Kansas School of Medicine in Kansas City during the week and drove home to work in his clinic each weekend.

Arthur always considered Halstead his hometown although he was often upset with some local group or individual. When the city council complained about his dog, Hertzler promised never to appear on Main Street again. For many years, he kept his word and slipped in and out of his favorite grocery story through a side door.

Hertzler wrote over twenty medical textbooks used by doctors across the country. His most popular book, however, was his autobiography, *The Horse and Buggy Doctor*. In it he described the joys and problems of practicing medicine during the frontier days of Kansas. Hertzler said that a well-equipped country doctor always carried a medical bag—plus a scoop shovel, wire cutters, hammer, lantern and a Colt revolver. ■

Puts Kansas on the map

109 F.W. "Woody" Hockaday

Businessman and public roads supporter. Caldwell and Wichita. (1884-1947) In the early days of automobiles, travelers often got lost as they followed unmarked roads and trails. Hockaday, owner of several auto supply stores, changed all that when he began nailing direction signs on fence posts and telephone poles in Kansas and nearby states.

His road signs were hard to miss. Each was marked with a bright red twelve-inch *H* and gave directions to nearby towns. Woody was one of the first Kansans to support a state system of numbered roads, and by 1917 he had spent $16,000 marking roads in Kansas.

A year later the Wichitan published one of the state's first road maps. Many Kansas highways still carry numbers that Hockaday assigned them. State highway 96, for example, was named after the telephone number of one of his auto supply shops. By the 1940s, crews working for him had marked 60,000 miles of roads in Kan-

sas, Oklahoma and northwest Texas. Hockaday also helped set up a national system to direct pilots by "air-marking" the tops of buildings.

He and his wife often traveled around the country speaking for world peace. At each stop they gave away small sacks of wheat from the Breadbasket of the World. Hockaday's enthusiasm, however, once got him in trouble. As President Franklin D. Roosevelt passed by in a parade, Hockaday ran into the street, jumped on the presidential car's running boards and tried to hand FDR a souvenir sack of Kansas wheat. Angry Secret Service agents nearly arrested him. ■

Brings first slaves

110 Thomas Johnson

Minister and Indian missionary. Present Johnson County. (1802-1865) In 1829 Johnson established the Shawnee Methodist Mission. There he set up a school and farm to help Indians. However, he also owned slaves and brought perhaps the first African-Americans into what is now Kansas. In the late 1850s the Reverend Johnson quit his mission work and moved to Westport, Missouri. He was assassinated during the Civil War because of his support for the Union. Johnson County was named for him. ■

In the business of buffalo

111 C.J. "Buffalo" Jones

Buffalo hunter and promoter. Garden City. (1844-1918)
Jones was a buffalo [*382*] hunter in Kansas during the 1860s.

A decade later, when buffaloes were nearly extinct, he captured a dozen of the animals, started his own herd and began selling buffaloes to zoos and parks. After a great blizzard struck western Kansas in 1886, Jones noticed that many of his buffaloes had survived the storm, when thousands of cattle had not. He then tried to crossbreed buffaloes and cattle into a tough new kind of livestock, "cattalo." His new breed was never a success. Modern breeders have tried a similar crossbreed, "beefalo."

Jones hunted with President Theodore Roosevelt. Starting in 1902, he worked at Yellowstone National Park to help build a buffalo herd there. The famous Western author Zane Grey featured Jones in one of his books, *The Last of the Plainsmen.* ∎

Mary Yellin'

112 Mary Elizabeth Lease

Lawyer and supporter of Populism. St. Paul, Kingman and Wichita. (1853-1933)
Lease came to Kansas as a fifteen-year-old and taught at the Osage Indian Mission in Neosho County.

By 1885 she was one of the few women lawyers in Kansas. Mary taught herself law at home, often studying from notes pinned above her washtub as she scrubbed.

In the 1890s Lease joined the Populist political cause as a traveling lecturer. With a deep, husky voice, she was an excellent public speaker. Her favorite topic was voting rights for women, but according to William Allen White [*256*] she "could recite the multiplication table and set a crowd hooting." In one speech, Lease supposedly told farmers to "raise less corn and more hell"—although she later claimed she didn't say it.

As Annie Diggs [*102*] discovered, Lease had a mind of her own. After the Populists stopped supporting women's suffrage, Lease dropped them. She joined the Republicans who had once nicknamed her "Mary Yellin'." She left Kansas in 1897. ∎

Lady lawyer

113 Lutie Lytle

Lawyer. Topeka. (About 1874-?) Lytle graduated from Topeka High School and went to work for a local black newspaper. In her job, she met lawyers and politicians and decided she, too, would be a lawyer. She taught school for two years to save money for law school, and then began her studies. Lutie graduated from a Tennessee law school in 1897. That same year she was granted a license to practice law in Kansas, making her the first African-American woman lawyer in the United States.

A year later Lytle was selected to teach law courses in the school from which she graduated. She was believed to be the only woman law instructor in the world at that time. It is not known when she died. ∎

Health care leader

114 Grace McNamara (Mother Mary Anne)

Nun, health care pioneer and educator. Wichita, Dodge City and Pittsburg. (1900-1991) McNamara grew up in St. Louis. She was a secretary for her father's plumbing business until, at age 27, she decided to become a nun.

When Grace entered the convent she took the name Sister Mary Anne. For nineteen years, she worked at Wichita Hospital (later St. Joseph Medical Center) and at hospitals in Dodge City and Pittsburg. In 1948 she became Mother Mary Anne when she was elected superior, or head, of the Sisters of St. Joseph.

With her background in health care, she helped found the University of Kansas School of Medicine in Wichita. Through her efforts, the Wichita order of the Sisters of St. Joseph established a 150-bed children's hospital and school in Japan.

Mother Mary Anne helped organize St. Mary of the Plains College in Dodge City, and she served as its first president from 1952 to 1954. She was also president and chief executive officer of St. Joseph Medical Center in Wichita from 1961 until 1983. ■

Music is his forte

115 Joseph Maddy

Music educator and author. Wellington. (1891-1966) Maddy organized the National High School Orchestra in the 1920s and later founded the National Music Camp and Arts Academy in Michigan. His textbooks for teaching music were adopted around the country. ■

Prints first Kansas book in Delaware

116 Jotham Meeker

Indian missionary and pioneer printer. Present Johnson and Franklin counties. (1804-1855) Meeker came to the Kansas area in the 1830s, bringing with him the future state's first printing press. He used it in 1834 when he published *Delaware Primer and First Book*, the first book printed in Kansas. He wrote the book for Delaware tribe members in their own language, using his own system of Indian spelling. Meeker also printed religious materials and an Indian newspaper, the *Shawnee Sun*—the first newspaper printed in Kansas. ■

Doctoring the spirit

117-118 Charles & Flora Menninger

Educators and mental health pioneers. Holton and Topeka. (1862-1953) Abilene, Clay Center, Holton and Topeka. (1863-1945) Charles Menninger came to Kansas in 1882 and taught at a small college in Holton. There he met and married one of his students, Flora Knisely. She was a teacher in Clay Center who had lived in Abilene as a girl.

The Menningers remained in Holton for two years. Together they ran a boardinghouse and taught school. Charles received a degree from a Chicago medical school in 1887 and had his own successful doctor's practice in Topeka by 1890. He received a second medical degree from the University of Kansas Medical School in 1908. Although Charles established the Menninger Clinic to specialize in internal medicine, he and his sons [119-120] later made it into one of America's leading psychiatric research and training centers.

Flo was known for her Bible study course. Unhappy with other Bible studies, she wrote her own. Nearly 200 persons enrolled when she first offered it in 1903. Over the next 45 years, she taught 2,500 others. Thousands more have completed her course since she died. ■

SIWINOWE

Kesibwi.

Care with 'Freud and friendliness'

Mental health pioneers and authors. Topeka. (1893-1990) (1899-1966) Along with their father, Dr. Charles Menninger [**117**], Doctors Karl and Will Menninger founded the Menninger Sanitarium in Topeka.

A group practice

The Menningers' famous clinic and and its treatment plan grew out of Charles' interest in group medicine, the idea that several doctors with different specialties could treat one patient.

He first heard of the new approach in 1908, and liked it. When he later combined it with Karl and Will's interest in mental illness, it proved to be an effective way of treating patients suffering from mental diseases.

Karl joined his father's practice in 1919, followed by the younger Will in 1925. A third son decided not to go into medicine. **Edwin Menninger** became a noted journalist.

In 1925, the Menningers opened their mental hospital in a vacant farmhouse on the edge of Topeka. In the small thirteen-bed facility, patients stayed in a family atmosphere, treated by doctors from several different medical areas. Therapy included physical exercise and a "mixture of Freud and friendliness."

The Menningers' success soon brought more patients and the need to expand. They eventually had nearly 40 buildings and over 400 acres in two Topeka locations. Since the early 1980s, the Menninger center has been located on a large campus just north of Topeka.

Research and teaching other physicians are important parts of the Menninger philosophy. Over the years, hundreds of psychiatric hospitals worldwide have adopted a treatment style similar to theirs. In 1941 the Menningers reorganized their sanitarium into the Menninger Foundation. Today many call it simply Menningers'.

Both of Charles' sons had strengths to add to the clinic, but differences in their personalities sometimes caused conflict. Karl loved change; Will loved stability. It was said the brothers sometimes worked together best by staying apart.

'Dr. Karl'

"Dr. Karl," born July 22, 1893, taught at Topeka's Washburn University in the 1930s. When he couldn't find a textbook for his class on mental health, he wrote his own—and soon became a best-selling author. In all he published fourteen books and came to be called the dean of American psychiatry. He advised the U.S. government and several states about mental health matters. He crusaded for improved psychiatric care and carried out his ideas with his own projects. He and his wife founded The Villages, a home in Topeka for troubled youth. He died in Topeka on July 18, 1990.

'Dr. Will'

"Dr. Will" was born October 15, 1899. He became medical director of the Menninger Foundation Psychiatric Hospital in 1930. During World War II, he was the chief psychiatrist for the U.S. Army. After his father died, Will was named president of the foundation. He gave speeches to 27 different state legislatures encouraging better mental health care. Before his death on September 6, 1966, he was president of several national psychiatric organizations.

Now four generations of the family have been part of the Menninger staff, including Karl's son **Robert** and Will's sons **Roy**, **Philip** and **Walter**. ∎

Takes 'medicine' out of Medicine Lodge

Temperance supporter. Medicine Lodge. (1846-1911) Nation was born in Kentucky, November 25, 1846, as Carrie Moore. (She later changed the spelling of her first name.)

The Moores were fairly wealthy, but Carry's father often had to spend money to humor his wife—she was mentally ill and believed she was Queen Victoria of England. Among other things, he bought her an elegant carriage and hired a coachman to drive it. Some historians, in fact, believe Carry's later behavior was partly due to her mother's mental illness.

Eight-year-old Carry and the rest of the family used the "Queen's coach" in 1854 when they left Kentucky to move to Missouri. The young girl was baptized in an icy stream shortly after arriving at her new home, and this religious experience stayed with her throughout her life.

Off to the West

When the Civil War began, the Moores joined a wagon train headed for Texas. They stayed there only a year, and then ⇨

moved to Kansas City. There teenaged Carry helped nurse wounded soldiers in a hospital. She also attended a school for ministers.

At the end of the war, Carry and her parents returned to their farm. Charles Gloyd, a young Army doctor, came to teach school nearby. He stayed in the Moore home and nineteen-year-old Carry soon fell in love with the Ohio man. Her parents warned her that he drank too much, but Carry and Charles were married late in 1867.

Unhappy marriage

Their marriage was an unhappy one. Carry soon learned the truth about her husband's alcoholism. He stayed out all night and she spent most of her time in tears. After several months, Mr. Moore took Carry back to the farm where she later gave birth to a daughter. Gloyd never saw his little girl, however. He died from the effects of alcoholism in the spring of 1870.

Throughout her life, Carry was always quick to aid those in need. After Charles' death, she and her child moved to Holden, Missouri, to care for his elderly mother.

To support her daughter and Mrs. Gloyd, Carry taught school. Her teaching ended four years later when a school board member gave the job to his niece. Never one to give up, Carry gave much thought and prayer to her problem. She decided another marriage was the best way to support her family.

David Nation, a lawyer and minister, seemed to be the answer. Like her first husband, Nation had been a captain in the Civil War. He was nineteen years older than Carry and although they had little in common, they were married in 1874.

Tough times in Texas

The wedding, however, did not end her financial problems. Mr. Nation left his job and moved

Carry, her daughter, Mrs. Gloyd and one of his daughters by another marriage to Texas. They bought a cotton farm, but the crop failed and most of their livestock died. Nation moved into a nearby town to establish a law practice and Carry tried to keep the farm running. Neither were very successful. Carry began managing a rundown hotel and her small income was enough to feed the family.

During this period, Carry became so involved in religion that others considered her almost crazy on the subject. For a time, she taught Sunday School in two local churches. When neither congregation would allow her to continue, she held her own services in the hotel.

At the same time, her husband was writing

Opinionated Carry

Carry Nation was never afraid to express her opinion to anyone—or at any time.

While her husband was a minister in Medicine Lodge, she sat near the front of the church at each service and sang vigorously. Sitting still for his sermon was another story. If he spoke longer than she felt was necessary, Carry would stand up and say, "That's enough for this time, David." He would obediently stop, and church was over for the day.

Once when she arrived at the Medicine Lodge depot after one of her trips, she prepared to board the local "omnibus" to ride uptown. Seeing a cigar dangling from the coach driver's mouth, she plucked it from his lips, threw it in a snow-drift and made a remark about the sins of smoking.

The driver answered by tossing her suitcases in the snow alongside the smoldering cigar. He then drove away, leaving Carry and her opinions out in the cold.

for a newspaper. After some unhappy readers tied him to a tree and whipped him, he and Carry decided to join his brother in Kansas. They moved to Medicine Lodge in 1890.

Mr. Nation tried preaching, but he soon quit the ministry to practice law. Carry spent most of her time working to help the poor and needy. In 1892, "Mother Nation" and the local Baptist minister's wife started a chapter of the WCTU, the Women's Christian Temperance Union. They worked to close saloons, or "joints" as they were called.

Even though saloons were against the law, Kansas law allowed drugstores to sell alcoholic drinks "for medicinal and scientific purposes." Many drugstores were actually bars where customers bought liquor by saying their doctor had ordered it for their health.

County cleanup

Carry and her temperance friend began complaining about Medicine Lodge's saloons in the summer of 1899, and managed to close down three of them. At a fourth joint, they used stronger tactics. Carry walked inside, rolled a barrel of beer into the street and smashed it with a sledge hammer in front of the astonished customers.

Next, Carry tackled saloons in the nearby town of Kiowa. There, she armed herself with bricks and rocks—and smashed liquor bottles, windows, lamps and other fixtures. In a year, Mrs. Nation managed to close all places in Barber County that sold alcohol illegally. Officials had to scratch their heads, however. Carry was doing their job of enforcing liquor laws—but she was also breaking laws at the same time.

The tall woman from Medicine Lodge first drew national attention in 1900 when she attacked the bar in Wichita's elegant Carey Hotel. With rocks and an iron rod, she managed to do over $2,000 worth of damage [**229**] before being arrested. Newspapers across the country printed stories of her raid. The WCTU and other groups praised her work.

'Hatchetizes' bars

Nation first used her famous hatchet in June 1901. From that time on, she and her weapon were symbols for prohibitionists everywhere. She "hatchetized" bars in other Kansas towns and paraded with her followers to gain support for new and stricter temperance laws.

She lectured against liquor in the United States and Canada and sold miniature hatchets to help finance her crusade. In all, Carry was arrested 30 times, but she was able to pay her fines and bail with money she earned on speaking tours. At first Mr. Nation supported his wife's ideas, but he divorced her in 1901 because she refused to stay at home.

In 1903, Nation officially changed the spelling of her first name from *Carrie* to *Carry*. She said it was her duty to "Carry A. Nation for Prohibition."

She moved to Guthrie, Oklahoma, in 1905 and published a monthly newspaper, *The Hatchet*. Still a tireless crusader, Carry took her campaign to Washington, D.C., and she even lectured in England against drinking tea.

Did what she could

When she returned from Europe, Nation moved to Arkansas. It was during a lecture there that she collapsed, saying, "I have done what I could." She died at a Leavenworth hospital five months later, on June 2, 1911. She was buried at Belton, Missouri.

Nation used money she earned to help others; one of her projects was a home for alcoholics' wives in Kansas City.

Although she was called everything from a "zealot" to a "crazy old woman," she still spoke out against what she called "evil" alcohol. Even her critics admitted she did more to enforce prohibition laws than anyone else.

In 1918 the WCTU erected a memorial in Carry's honor near Wichita's Union Station. Ironically, a beer truck backed into it in 1945, knocking it off its pedestal. The marker is now in a Wichita park. Nation's Medicine Lodge home is a museum. ∎

Pushes for women's rights

122 Clarina Nichols

Women's rights supporter, educator and newspaper journalist. Lawrence, Lane and Quindaro. (1810-1885)
Nichols was born in Vermont where she taught school and edited a newspaper owned by her second husband. In the early 1850s her editorials for women's rights earned her a national reputation.

Clarina visited Kansas Territory in 1854 and decided to join the antislavery cause. She and her family lived in Lawrence and the Douglas County ghost town of Lane. After her husband died, she moved her family to Wyandotte County in 1857. As associate editor of the Quindaro *Chindowan*, she crusaded for women's rights and the Free State party. Before the Wyandotte constitutional convention began in the summer of 1859, she traveled through Kansas Territory, lecturing and gather-

ing signatures on petitions. Her efforts paid off. When she presented her petitions to the convention, the delegates—all men—invited her to speak. And, although they would not allow her to vote, they assigned her a seat in the hall.

During debates, Clarina listened and knitted. Each time the meetings recessed, she met with delegates to discuss women's issues. With the help of delegate **William Hutchinson**,

another former Vermont resident, the final constitution included three parts written by Nichols. Two sections protected married women's rights in the custody of children and in selling property. A third let women enroll in the state university—which later made the University of Kansas the first state-run university in the world to allow women students. The delegates rejected Nichols' request for women's suffrage, or the right to vote. Instead, they gave women the right to vote only in school elections.

In the 1860s, Clarina's efforts helped pass laws benefitting women's rights in Ohio, Vermont, Wisconsin and Missouri. She left Kansas in 1871 and moved to California. ∎

Crusades for many causes

123 Katherine "Red Kate" O'Hare

Political crusader. Ada, Kansas City and Girard. (1876-1948) O'Hare was born as Katherine Richards on an Ottawa County farm. A drought in 1887 forced her family to move to Kansas City.

There young Kate began crusading early. By the time she was eighteen, she had done

missionary work for her church, a mission for the homeless and the Women's Christian Temperance Union.

After trying teaching, she became a machinist. At a union meeting she heard a fiery speech on socialism (the idea that the public should own all land and businesses). Fascinated, she

enrolled in a school for socialist organizers. Her new home was in Girard, the town where socialist publishers Emanuel and Marcet Haldeman-Julius [*205-206*] later lived.

In Girard she met and married **Frank O'Hare**. Together they toured the country, lecturing, organizing and writing for the Socialist party. As she gained popularity, she was elected to several high offices in the party. She was nominated, but not chosen, to be the Socialist candidate in the 1916 U.S. presidential election. Later that same year she was the first woman to run for the U.S. Senate. At that time, she was living in Missouri and writing for a socialist magazine in St. Louis.

In 1917 O'Hare was arrested in North Dakota while on a lecture tour. Officials accused her of urging young men to resist the military draft. The United States had just entered World War II, and many Americans were expressing their patriotism. In her highly-publicized trial, the judge was openly hostile. Newspapers labeled her "Red Kate"—after the Reds, a socialist group in the Russian Revolution.

Although she had spoken out only against America's reasons for entering the war, O'Hare was found guilty. She spent a

year in prison before President Woodrow Wilson commuted, or ended, her sentence. She then crusaded for better prison conditions and eventually was the assistant director of the state prison system in California.

Because she was later divorced and remarried, O'Hare is sometimes referred to as Kate Cunningham. ∎

First European to call Kansas home

124 Juan de Padilla

Priest and Indian missionary. Present Rice County. (About 1500-1543?)
Padilla was a Franciscan priest and chaplain for the Spanish explorer Coronado [**11**]. Traveling with Coronado's expedition, he visited what is now Kansas in 1541.

The next spring Father Padilla returned to the area as a missionary to the Indians. He and several assistants and servants were the first Europeans to settle in Kansas. They lived for a time, perhaps a year or more, among the Wichita Indians in a village along Cow Creek.

Unfortunately, the priest's stay in Kansas ended with his untimely death. According to his followers, their group was attacked by Indians when they tried to visit the "Guas," a neighboring tribe to the east. Everyone escaped except Father Padilla; his body was later found filled with arrows.

The time and place of the priest's death—as well as the reasons behind it—remain a

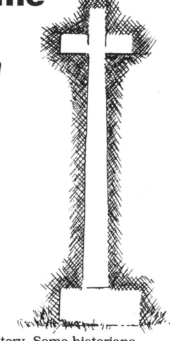

mystery. Some historians believe Padilla was killed by an enemy tribe of the Wichitas. Others suggest the Wichitas murdered him themselves, perhaps jealous that the missionary wanted to visit other tribes.

The brave priest is believed to be the first Christian martyr, or one who is willing to die for his faith, in what is now the United States. Memorials in Padilla's honor are located at Council Grove, Herington, and near Lyons. ∎

Educates his people

125 Henry Roe Cloud

Minister, educator and Indian leader. Wichita and Lawrence. (1884-1950)
Cloud, a Winnebago Indian, was born in Nebraska and later adopted by a family named Roe. He graduated from Yale University with a bachelor's degree in 1910, and received a theology degree three years later.

Henry was ordained as a Presbyterian minister, but he was best known for his work in Indian education. While still a student at Yale, he was one of the founders of the Society of American Indians. The SAI worked to give educational opportunities to young Native Americans. He also helped raise money for an Indian high school. In 1915 he used the funds to establish—in Wichita—one of the first all-Indian high schools in the country.

The school, later known as the American Indian Institute, operated until the mid 1930s. For several more years, the AII was a boarding place for Indian boys who attended high school and college in Wichita. Roe Cloud left it in 1931 to work for the Bureau of Indian Affairs.

Two years later, he was made superintendent of the Haskell Institute, an Indian high school in Lawrence. He was the first full-blood Indian to be in charge of such a school. He began courses in Indian history and art. When he died, Roe Cloud was superintendent of an Indian agency in Oregon. ∎

Sells sunny Kansas to ex-slaves

126 Benjamin "Pap" Singleton

Ex-slave supporter. Morris County. (1809-1892) Singleton was born into slavery in Tennessee. At age 37 he escaped, and made his way to Detroit. There he set up a secret boardinghouse for other escaped slaves. After the Civil War, he returned to Tennessee.

When he saw what the share-cropper system and the Ku Klux Klan were doing to ex-slaves, Benjamin began a crusade to improve their lives. Remembering John Brown [**344**] and the Bleeding Kansas struggle, he felt Kansas could be the "Promised Land" for blacks.

Singleton—sometimes called the Black Moses—spread hundreds of posters around the South telling ex-slaves about the advantages of "sunny Kansas." He also helped raise money for the new settlers. In 1873 he led a group of about 300 to Singleton's Colony in Cherokee County. Others came to Tennessee Town [**242**] in Topeka, Dunlap Colony near Emporia, and Wyandotte. He also supported the founding of Nicodemus, a black colony in Graham County started in 1877 by **W.R. Hill**, the founder of Hill City. (Nicodemus was never very large, but the community still survives. Ancestors of Lorenzo Fuller, Jr. [**286**] and Gale Sayers [**320**] came from there.)

The largest movement, or exodus, of ex-slaves was between 1879 and 1880; those who came were the Exodusters. Over 8,000 are believed to have come to Kansas from Tennessee alone. The governor during that time, John P. St. John [**87**], helped organize the Kansas Freedmen's Relief Association to help with the cause. Until his death, "Pap" Singleton was proud of his role as the Father of the Negro Exodus. ■

HO

FOR SUNNY KANSAS

FRIENDS AND FELLOW CITIZENS:

I have just returned from the Singleton Settlement, in Morris County, Kansas, where I left my people in one of the finest countries for a poor man in the World. I am prepared to answer any and all questions that may be asked. The Singleton Settlement is near Dunlap, Morris County, a new town just started on the Missouri, Kansas & Texas Railway. The surrounding country is fine rolling prairie. Plenty of stone and water, and wood on the streams. Plenty of coal within twenty-five miles.

I have this to say to all :

Now is the Time to Go to Kansas.

Land is cheap, and it is being taken up very fast. There is plenty for all at present.

BENJAMIN SINGLETON, President.

ALONZO D. DeFRANTZ, Secretary.
JOSEPH KEEBLE, Agent, Real Estate and Homestead Association.

For full information, address COLUMBUS M. JOHNSON, Topeka, Kansas.
General Agent.

Doctors still follow Dr. Still

127 Andrew Taylor Still

Doctor and founder of osteopathy. Present Douglas County. (1828-1917) Still came to Kansas in 1851 with Dr. **Abraham Still**, his missionary father. The younger Still treated Indians at the Wakarusa Mission and was elected to the territorial legislature in 1857.

After three of his children died of spinal meningitis in 1864, he developed a theory that diseases are caused by "osteopathic lesions," or problems in the body's joints. He believed that moving the joints could help the body heal itself.

In 1892 Dr. Still founded the American School of Osteopathy in Kirksville, Missouri. Today osteopathy is a recognized form of medicine in most states. Its doctors follow some, but not all, of Still's early beliefs. ■

Dr. Lucy doesn't give up

128 Lucy Hobbs Taylor

Pioneer dentist. Lawrence. (1833-1910) When she came to Kansas, Taylor was the state's only woman dentist. She had hoped to become a doctor, but could not find a medical school that would allow women to enroll.

Lucy then decided to go into dentistry and began studying with a dentist in Ohio. She learned how to pull teeth and make dentures during the daytime, and did sewing at night to pay her expenses. But, when she tried to enter a dental school, officials refused to let her attend because she was a woman.

Taylor, who felt she had enough experience to work as a dentist anyway, moved to Iowa. Dentists there liked her work and eventually forced the American Dentists Association to allow her and other women into dental schools. When Dr. Taylor graduated from a Chicago dental college she was the world's first fully-trained woman dentist.

She married another dentist and they moved to Kansas in 1867. At their clinic in Lawrence, "Dr. Lucy" was popular with her patients for over 40 years. ∎

Carries on Carry's crusade

129 Richard Taylor

Minister and temperance supporter. Enterprise, Salina, Concordia, Wichita and Berryton. (Born 1924) He doesn't carry a hatchet, but Taylor has been called a modern Carry Nation [*121*]. Since 1971 he has crusaded against the dangers of alcohol abuse.

Richard grew up on his parents' farm near Enterprise. He had an interest in machinery, and graduated at the top of his class from Northwestern University in Chicago with a degree in mechanical engineering. During World War II, he was a gunnery officer in the U.S. Navy. After the war he designed engines for railroad locomotives.

Taylor was asked to speak in several churches when there was a shortage of ministers, and he eventually attended a seminary. His ministry for the United Methodist Church included work at churches in Salina, Concordia and Wichita.

His crusade against alcohol began in earnest in the 1970s when some Kansans pushed for changes in the state constitution to allow the sale of liquor by the drink. The Reverend Taylor joined the fight as a member of the United Dry Forces. The organiziation, now called Kansans for Life at Its Best, lobbied legislators against the change. Taylor, whose voice box was damaged by cancer, led the debate against liquor. Although the constitution was eventually changed, the group continues its crusade. Taylor retired from the ministry in 1991, but he still travels widely speaking about the dangers of alcohol abuse. ∎

Leads early 'I do's'

130 Charles Van Quickenborne

Priest and Indian missionary. Present Leavenworth County. (1788-1837) Van Quickenborne was a Catholic priest who was born in Belgium. Charles joined the priesthood at age 27; two years later he was sent to the United States. In 1823, he and several other Jesuit priests in that religious order traveled to Missouri to open a school for Indians. His work with the Osages there eventually took him into Kansas.

In June 1830 Father Van Quickenborne married three couples along the Marmaton River, perhaps in present Bourbon County. These are believed to be the first recorded weddings in what is now Kansas. The three brides were Osages; one of the grooms was half Osage, the others were French. In 1836 Van Quickenborne helped set up a Kickapoo Catholic mission near Fort Leavenworth. He was then sent to a small church near St. Louis where he died unexpectedly. ∎

Terrorizes teachers

books to schools in Kansas and across the nation. In 1907 she formed her own publishing company.

First woman elected

In 1918 Wooster was elected state superintendent of public instruction, making her the first woman to win a state office in Kansas. As superintendent, Lizzie had high goals for education. She wanted more tax dollars to be spent for schools and more state aid for poor districts. She pushed for all rural schools to hold classes at least eight months a year. She also wanted better school libraries and a law to require school attendance until age sixteen.

No, no, no

Wooster also had a few other ideas. To teachers, she preached no dancing, no card playing, no smoking, no drinking, no

Educator and state superintendent of public instruction. Beloit, Salina and Topeka. (1868-1953)
Wooster was born in Ohio, July 24, 1868. In the early 1870s her family moved to Mitchell County. She attended high school in Beloit and began teaching when she was sixteen, earning $33 a month in a one-room school.

Lorraine eventually taught all grades from kindergarten through high school. She never married, believing, like many others in those days, that good "career teachers" should remain single. She wrote a textbook in 1894, and by the turn of the century she was selling her own reading, spelling and arithmetic cosmetics and no short skirts. As she toured the state, Lizzie often walked into classrooms and ordered instructors, "Lower that hemline," "Take off those silk stockings," or "Get that paint off your face."

Even in her own office, she was a tyrant. More than once her staff discovered her digging suspiciously through their wastebaskets. On a clerk's first day at work, she handed him a stack of material at 5 p.m. and told him to type it "immediately." He stayed three hours overtime to complete the job—but Lizzie ignored his finished work for several weeks.

In the 1920s, Wooster was chosen to head the national association of state school superintendents. In Kansas, however, she was headed for trouble. In 1922 she tried to fire several teachers in Cimarron after they had been seen at a dance. She also went after Cimarron's school superintendent because he smoked. The state attorney general, however, ruled that her anti-tobacco crusade was illegal.

No to Wooster

By that time, many people were tired of Wooster's "no" campaigns. She had also feuded with state legislators over several issues.

It was even said some men in Kansas government who didn't smoke used to puff on cigars just to blow smoke in her face.

Voters said no to Wooster in the 1922 election. And, when she ran for Kansas attorney general ten years later, she lost as well. In later years, her textbooks also lost out. Eventually she sold books just to Indian schools, with the support of her friend vice president Charles Curtis [*38*]. After he was out of office, she lost that market, too.

Wooster eventually became so poor she couldn't pay the rent. Her landlord evicted her, moving her furniture out into the street. She left Topeka in 1934 and moved to Chicago where she died on Independence Day 1953 at the age of 84. ∎

Pushes junior colleges

132 George Zook

Educator and U.S. commissioner of education. Fort Scott. (1885-1951) Zook grew up in Fort Scott and graduated from Kansas University in 1906. Most of his career was spent in education.

Before he received his doctor's degree at Cornell University, George taught history. He was then a professor at Pennsylvania State College. President Woodrow Wilson appointed him to an education committee in 1918. The next year he worked for the Treasury Department, and served as head of a division in the U.S. Bureau of Education.

After five years in Washington, D.C., Zook moved to Ohio to become president of the University of Ohio. He served on another presidential committee from 1929 to 1931, appointed by Herbert Hoover. In 1933 President Franklin D. Roosevelt appointed him U.S. commissioner of education. When he resigned a year later, Zook warned that the country should upgrade its educational system. Many of the 245,241 one-room rural schools then in use, he said, were "a disgrace to [America's] level of civilization."

Dr. Zook left government service to head the American Council on Education. One of his projects was junior colleges. While he didn't originate the idea of two-year colleges, he was a founder of the American Association of Junior Colleges that encouraged their growth. From the early 1920s until the 1940s, the number of JUCOs in the United States tripled.

Zook retired from the American Council on Education in 1950, after serving as chairman of President Harry Truman's commission on higher education. He was educational consultant to the Library of Congress until he died. ∎

Others making life better

Angela Bates is the great-granddaughter of a freed slave who left Kentucky in 1877 to come to Kansas. Along with other Exodusters [*126*], Bates' great-grandmother settled in Nicodemus. Although Angela was raised in California, she often visited Kansas in the summers. She became so caught up in the history of her ancestors' hometown that she moved to Hill City in 1990 to write educational materials on African-Americans. She has also led a crusade to preserve Nicodemus—the oldest all-black community west of the Mississippi River—and make it a national historic site. ∎

Paul Bentrup, born in Deerfield in 1917, is the first Kansan to be named an official Santa Fe Trail Ambassador by the Santa Fe Trail Association. Paul earned the 1987 honor the hard way—by trekking up and down the trail in Kansas and surrounding states. To generate interest in the historic route, he shares Santa Fe Trail stories, books and other materials with amateur historians, politicians, newspapermen and anyone else who will stand still. Always a fan of history, his interest in the trail was sparked in the 1950s when he inherited some Kearny County land that included a stretch of Santa Fe Trail ruts. Bentrup's "immersion" in Santa Fe Trail history has made him one of the trail's most diligent and determined researchers. ∎

August Bondi was born in Austria in 1833 and came to America when he was fifteen. Seven years later he followed newspaperman Horace Greeley's advice and went west to Kansas Territory. He settled first in Lane, and then helped found the Anderson County town of Greeley, named after the New York journalist. During the Bleeding Kansas period, August used his experiences as a Jewish freedom fighter in Europe to help abolitionist John Brown [*344*]. Bondi later lived in Salina where he owned several clothing stores and was postmaster. At the age of 63 he became a lawyer. He died in 1907. ∎

Kyle Carrico is an award-winning public speaker from Beloit. But the teenager has a disability most other public speakers don't have—he was born deaf. With the patient work of his parents and two brothers, Kyle uttered his first word when he was three years old. By labeling and color-coding objects all over their house, the family then helped him put words together into sentences.

Now a 4-H member, Kyle has entered public speaking contests around the state. In fact, he won top honors in the event at the 1991 Kansas State Fair at Hutchinson. His favorite topic as a speaker has been the need to increase the visibility of trains in order to prevent car-train collisions. Young Carrico lost a friend in a crossing mishap, and he later witnessed another such accident. Kyle's family and other concerned Kansans worked with Senator Nancy Kassebaum [*66*] as she introduced a bill requiring railroads to add extra lights to locomotives. The measure became law in 1992. The story of Kyle and his crusade as a public speaker has appeared in National Geographic's *World* magazine and *Reader's Digest*. ∎

Elmer Copley was born in Iowa in 1925. He studied music at colleges and universities in Illinois, Colorado, Iowa and at the important Julliard School of Music in New York City. Beginning in 1960, Dr. Copley was professor of music at Bethany College in Lindsborg for 29 years. All but three of those years he conducted the Bethany Oratorio Society's nationally-known performances of Handel's *Messiah*. Copley died in 1991. He was the father and first voice teacher of opera star Rebecca Copley [*279*]. ∎

Prudence Crandall founded New England's first school for African-American girls in Connecticut in 1833. But a mob soon vandalized it and the state general assembly passed laws against educating black people from out of state. Crandall was eventually arrested, tried and found guilty of breaking the "Black laws," but she appealed the verdict and won. (Arguments her attorneys used in the case were presented a century later before the U.S. Supreme Court in the *Brown* [*94, 100*] *vs. Topeka Board of Education* case against segregation.)

After the death of her husband, Crandall and her brother moved to Kansas in 1874. Until her death in 1890, she lived in Elk Falls. In Kansas, Prudence campaigned for equal rights for women, enjoyed visits from Exodusters [*126*] living in Kansas colonies, and gave shelter to needy strangers. In 1886 author Samuel Clemens (Mark Twain) convinced the state of Connecticut to apologize officially for Prudence's arrest fifty years earlier. ∎

Anna Ingleman was a teacher in Independence from 1908 until her retirement in 1946. Much of that time, "Miss Anna" taught English, speech and drama at the local high school. She also directed many plays at the school and in the community. Over the years her students included actress Vivian Vance [*330*], playwright William Inge [*215*] and television journalist Bill Kurtis [*219*]. ∎

Lawrence E. Lamb is a cardiologist, or heart specialist, who was born in Fredonia in 1926. He graduated from KU in 1949 and went on to earn his medical degree at the KU Medical Center. Dr. Lamb has taught at universities in Georgia, Texas and Switzerland. He has also been the head of departments at the hospitals of several U.S. Air Force bases. As chief of the Aerospace Medical Sciences Division at the U.S. Air Force School of Aerospace Medicine, he advised NASA during the Mercury space program. He has been a consultant to the President's Council on Physical Fitness and Sports. Dr. Lamb, who lives in Texas, began writing a nationally syndicated newspaper column in 1970. He has written numerous articles and books on everything from electrocardiography to arthritis to cooking. He has also appeared on *Health Talk*, a syndicated television series. ∎

Anne Laughlin was born near Effingham in the 1890s. After teaching for several years, she became active in politics. Like her cousin, Kathryn O'Loughlin McCarthy [*72*], Anne was a staunch Democrat. Her experience in education and support of Democratic candidates led to her appointment as Kansas director of the National Youth Administration by President Franklin D. Roosevelt. She later worked in Europe for United Nations organizations, including UNICEF. Long after reaching retirement age, Laughlin helped various youth and women's groups. She was living in Denver when she died in 1972. ∎

Isaac McCoy, a Baptist missionary to the Indians, was born in Pennsylvania in 1784. After working with tribes in Indiana and Michigan, he became convinced the only place Indians could survive in an expanding United States was in an all-Indian state in the West. Beginning in 1828, the Reverend McCoy helped place tribes in their new homes. For over ten years he toured and surveyed Indian lands, including those in northeastern Kansas. Under McCoy's leadership **Johnston Lykins** opened the Shawnee Baptist mission in 1831 where Jotham Meeker [*116*] later worked. McCoy died in 1846, two years before his followers built a mission for the Wea and Potawatomi tribes just west of present Topeka. ∎

Paul Ponziglione was born in Italy in 1818 and gave up his life as a nobleman to become a Catholic priest. When he was 30, he was sent to America. After he learned English, he came to Kansas in 1851 and was assigned to the Osage Mission where Father Charles Van Quickenborne [*130*] had been. He eventually learned the Osage language and wrote a prayer book for tribe members. In touring his large territory in southeastern Kansas, Father Ponziglione served Indians and white settlers of all faiths. He traveled by horseback or by wagon, on a circuit that took more than two weeks to cover.

In late 1872 or early 1873, the priest encountered Kate Bender [*338*] and her murdering family in Labette County. He arrived at their store one evening about sundown and was about to ask if he could spend the night. But two vicious dogs dashed toward him, and something told him to travel on. Soon afterward, the bodies of the Benders' victims were found. Ponziglione left Kansas in 1889 and went to an Arapaho mission in Wyoming. He died in 1900. ∎

Samuel N. Wood, an antislavery fighter with James H. Lane [*68*] and John Brown [*344*], also supported voting rights for women and blacks. Samuel was born in Ohio in 1825, farmed near Lawrence, "boomed" towns as editor of newspapers in Cottonwood Falls and Council Grove, was one of the first stockholders of the Atchison, Topeka and Santa Fe Railroad [*158*], and was also a lawyer, land agent, Civil War soldier and judge. He served several terms in the Kansas Legislature and was—at different times—a Republican, a Democrat and a Populist.

In 1886 Wood organized Woodsdale, a Stevens County town named for him. In a bitter county seat fight between citizens of his town and Hugoton, Wood was kidnapped, rescued, arrested for embezzlement, and finally murdered in 1891. Although his crusading often put him in conflict with others, throughout his life Wood remained a Quaker, a member of the peace-loving Society of Friends church. ∎

Dollars & Sense

Entrepreneurs and Inventors

Big on small hamburgers

Restaurant chain co-founder. St. Marys and Wichita. (1880-1963) Anderson was born at St. Marys, November 26, 1880. His business success began with a small restaurant —and a big idea that changed America's eating habits. In 1916 he borrowed $60, bought an old streetcar body and set it near a busy Wichita intersection. With some remodeling (and some borrowed meat) he had a little restaurant that sold just one food—hamburgers.

Savory sandwiches

Although hamburgers on buns had been sold since the 1904 world's fair in St. Louis, most of them were simply ground meat cooked dry. Anderson made his burgers juicy and appealing by flattening them into thin patties and searing them on both sides. Hungry customers liked his small, square "savory" sandwiches, and within four years, he owned three more hamburger stands in Wichita.

When the successful burger man tried to open a fourth diner on another street corner, however, he ran into trouble.

The owner of the property refused to give him a lease. He believed Anderson's busy hamburger stand was a front for bootlegging, or illegal liquor sales.

E.W. "Billy" Ingram, a Wichita real estate man, convinced the owner to rent the property to him. Anderson and Ingram then joined as partners and opened their restaurant at the location in 1921. As a sales gimmick, they built their diner of cement blocks, added small turrets and a tower, then painted the whole thing white.

First hamburger chain

That first White Castle was the beginning of a restaurant chain —the first chain of hamburger restaurants in the United States. Anderson was president of the operation, with Ingram as vice president.

During the 1920s they sold 24 million burgers— at five cents apiece, or six for a quarter. As profits mounted, the partners expanded the chain and provided benefits for their employees.

They also branched into other areas. In the late 1920s White Castle engineers patented a movable all-metal restaurant. Later, a new White Castle company sold the portable buildings. After Ingram designed a disposable paper cap for employees, they formed a paper products company.

By 1931 there were 116 White Castles in eleven states from Kansas to New York. That year the chain introduced a cardboard burger box and began a carry-out business. Kitchens were designed to turn out 2,000 hamburgers per hour. Employees were trained to follow strict sanitary and service standards. Posters reminded them to wash their hands, to wear trousers with no patches on the seat, and to "correct bad breath."

In 1933 Anderson sold his interest to Ingram, who became president in 1935, a year after the headquarters was moved from Wichita to Columbus, Ohio. Anderson remained in Kansas where he worked in the oil business and several other companies. He was also an active pilot, and for several years he managed the Swift airplane factory in Wichita that he had helped start in 1927.

Anderson died in Wichita, December 13, 1963. Today there are nine Kansas White Castles in the Kansas City area, and 247 more of the popular hamburger restaurants across the eastern United States. ■

White Castle

Aviation partners

Aircraft manufacturers and philanthropists. Arkansas City and Wichita. (1891-1950) Waverly, Paola and Wichita. (Born 1903) Walter Beech was born on a Tennessee farm January 30, 1891. His love of flying began when he designed and built a glider at the age of fourteen. Ten years later he made his first solo flight in Minnesota.

During World War I he was a flying instructor for the U.S. Army. Later Beech toured the Midwest as a barnstormer, or performing pilot. For a time he flew with a friend from Arkansas City. In 1921 he moved to Wichita and became a test pilot and salesman for the E.M. Laird Airplane Company, started by oilman *Jacob "Jake" Moellendick* and plane designer *E.M. "Matty" Laird*. When Laird split with Moellendick in 1923, Beech became manager of the company, renamed Swallow Aircraft.

The next year, Beech and Lloyd Stearman [*173*] left Swallow. They argued with Moellendick over building materials for new planes. Beech and Stearman felt welded steel tubing was the material of the future. Moellendick disagreed.

The two designers added a third partner, Clyde Cessna [*141*], and formed the Travel Air Manufacturing Company in 1925. Later that year Beech hired a secretary, Olive Mellor. She and Walter were married five years later.

In 1929, Beech merged Travel Air with the Curtiss-Wright company in St. Louis. Cessna and Stearman had already left Travel Air to start their own factories.

Staggerwings, spaceships and Starships

After living in New York City two years, the Beeches returned to Wichita and started the Beech Aircraft Corporation. They were able to sell their Staggerwing model through the 1930s, but times were hard. On weekends, Walter often gave $1 plane rides to raise cash to pay employees.

As America prepared for World War II, the Beeches geared up production. At the same time, Walter became ill and Olive ran the company for over a year. When war broke out, business mushroomed. Employment reached 10,000. The Beech plant produced 7,400 planes, many of them military trainers.

In post-war years, the Beeches built popular business aircraft. After Walter died November 29, 1950, Olive became president. Born in Waverly on September 25, 1903, she was no stranger to the business world. She had her own bank account at age seven and as an eleven-year-old she kept her family's financial records. During Olive's nearly twenty years in charge of Beechcraft, sales tripled. Beech products were used in NASA's Gemini, Apollo and space shuttle programs.

Olive retired in 1968 and then served on the company's board of directors. In 1980 she became the first woman to receive the Wright Brothers Memorial Trophy. She is also a member of the Aviation Hall of Fame and the Kansas Business Hall of Fame. Olive generously supports the arts, education and religion.

Beechcraft merged with Raytheon Company in 1980, but Beech planes are still made in Wichita —including the 21st-century Starship, a 400-mph jetfan. ■

His work is taxing

136 Henry Bloch

Income tax-preparation chain co-founder. Mission Hills. (Born 1922) Bloch and his brother Richard were born and raised in Kansas City, Missouri. After Henry served in the U.S. Air Force during World War II, the brothers went into business. They did bookkeeping and other recordkeeping for small businesses.

As an added service, they filled out clients' income tax forms free of charge. Soon others asked the brothers to complete their income tax paperwork, and by early 1955 they were computing taxes seven days a week and nearly every night. The Blochs then formed a new company, using their initials and a simplified spelling of their last name—H&R Block. In just a few weeks, they earned over $20,000 filling out customers' tax forms.

The next year, they opened offices in New York. In 1957 they added other offices in Missouri and Kansas. By the late 1960s, the H&R Block name appeared on over 3,200 tax preparation offices in the United States, Canada and Puerto Rico. In 1979 their company prepared more than one out of every nine income tax forms filed in the United States.

Henry has often appeared in his company's television commercials. He has lived in Mission Hills for many years. In 1992 he turned the operation of H&R Block over to his son. ■

Makes silk in Kansas

137 Ernest Valeton de Boissiere

Promoter. Silkville. (1810-1894) Boissiere was an ex-army engineer from France who came to America in 1869. He founded Silkville, a colony of French immigrants in Franklin County. Working together, the Frenchmen successfully produced silk for several years. In fact, some of their silk won first prize over foreign entries at the Philadelphia Centennial Exposition in 1876. Ernest's project ended in 1886 because merchants could buy cheaper silk from China and Japan. His French workers left him when they found they could make more money farming. Boissiere tried to run a dairy in his Silkville buildings, but it also failed to make money. ■

Flies high

138 Tom Braniff

Airline company executive. Salina. (1883-1954) Braniff was born in Salina and grew up in Kansas City, Missouri. His family then moved to Oklahoma City where he joined his father's insurance and real estate company. In 1927 Tom and several others bought a plane to use in their businesses. A year later he and his brother started an airline between Oklahoma City and Tulsa.

Although the Braniffs lost money at first, their business picked up in 1934 when they got a mail contract from the U.S. government. Soon they added other cities to their system: Kansas City, Chicago, St. Louis and Dallas. When Braniff died in a plane crash in 1954, Braniff Airlines was the sixth largest airline in the United States. The company went bankrupt in 1982, but the Braniff name has since been used by two other owners. ■

A fair deal

139 Emerson Carey

Salt company executive. McPherson and Hutchinson. (1863-1933) Carey was a wealthy businessman who owned several companies in Hutchinson, including the Carey Salt Company. Emerson also served several terms in the Kansas Legislature. In 1913 Senator Carey worked hard to make Hutchinson the permanent home of the Kansas State Fair. When his bill became law, Topeka and Wichita were unhappy. Each of those two larger towns had its own "state fair" and felt it should become the official fair for Kansas.

During World War I, Carey was the state fuel administrator. He was in charge of rationing coal, and set hours that Kansas businesses could be open. To save energy, he ordered cities and towns to shut off street lights. ■

Makes pizzas go everywhere

Restaurant chain co-founder. Wichita. (Born 1938) Carney was born in Wichita, April 26, 1938. While he and his older brother **Dan Carney** were attending Wichita State University in the late 1950s, they worked part-time in their parents' grocery store.

Homemade business

One day a fight broke out at a bar next door. The owner of that building told the Carneys she wanted to evict the manager and his noisy business. She suggested the brothers might open a small, quiet restaurant there instead. What should they serve? A popular new food called pizza.

With $600 borrowed from their mother, the Carney brothers, age 19 and 24, made plans for their new restaurant. While their family helped sew red and white-checked curtains for the dining area, the young men found an old oven for the kitchen. At first the oven didn't get very hot. But after they remodeled it, they found it not only baked pizza—it also melted the handles off the door!

The brothers named their restaurant Pizza Hut, because the letters fit perfectly on the sign used by the building's former occupant, the B&B Lounge.

From almost the day it opened in the summer of 1958, their little pizzeria was a success. Many of the Carneys' fellow WSU students were customers, and the restaurant soon made a name for itself across the campus. Within a few months the brothers were taking in more than a thousand dollars a week. They quickly replaced the baby bathtub in which they mixed the dough with larger bowls. Their original recipe of "a handful of this and a handful of that" turned into an exact formula.

After just over a year, the Carneys owned five Wichita Pizza Huts. In 1959 Topeka became the second Pizza Hut city. Then their small chain began to grow rapidly. More new outlets were opened in other towns in Kansas, Oklahoma and Texas.

Pizza worldwide

By 1970, there were Pizza Huts across the United States, Mexico, Canada and Australia. Several years later, the Carneys' giant company placed the world's largest order for cheese—one million pounds of Mozzarella.

Dan Carney left Pizza Hut in 1974 to try other business ventures, but kept his stock in the company. Three years later, he and Frank sold their restaurant chain to PepsiCo, Incorporated for $300 million.

Frank remained with Pizza Hut until 1980, the same year the company celebrated over $1 billion in sales, and the opening of restaurant number 4,000. He is now chairman of the Western Sizzlin' chain of steakhouses.

Today the Kansas business begun by the Carneys is the largest restaurant chain in the world. There are now more than 8,000 Pizza Huts in the United States and 64 foreign countries, including Russia. Wichita is the home of the company's international headquarters—and 24 Pizza Huts. ∎

Flying farmhand

THE COMET

Airplane manufacturer. Rago and Wichita. (1879-1954) Cessna was born in Hawthorne, Iowa, on December 5, 1879. He came to Kansas a year later and grew up on his father's Kingman County farm just east of Rago.

Genius with a wrench

As a boy, Clyde showed a talent for mechanics. "He took to tools when he was big enough to crawl," someone remembered. Mr. Cessna kept his son busy repairing machinery around the farm and lent his services to neighbors in need. He was paid no money for his repair-work and expected none; it was just one neighbor helping another.

Clyde married **Europa Dotzour** in 1905. The couple farmed in Kingman County until an implement dealer in nearby Harper heard about the "genius with a monkey wrench." The man offered Clyde a job and he accepted.

Cessna worked in the repair shop, but when the dealer began selling Overland automobiles, the young mechanic was soon as familiar with cars as he was with farm equipment. Alone in the shop one day, Clyde convinced a customer to buy an Overland so easily his employer made him a salesman.

When the car manufacturer heard of this amazing ability to sell others on the car, Clyde was put in charge of the company's agency in Enid, Oklahoma. He sold over 100 vehicles in his first year.

While living in Enid, Cessna drove to Oklahoma City to see an "air circus" put on by a group of traveling aviators.

The experience changed his life. He watched in fascination as the pilots assembled their aircraft before the show. One of the planes intrigued him—a French-designed monoplane. Although he was thrilled when he saw the three planes soaring like hawks, the most appealing part of the show was the money the flyers earned for their appearance. "Ten thousand dollars!" Clyde exclaimed. "Let somebody else sell Overlands."

Homemade aircraft

Cessna wanted to learn more about airplanes, so he journeyed to New York City in 1910. He began working for the Queens Aeroplane Company, but quickly decided he could build his own plane. He purchased an unassembled fuselage for $7,500 and shipped 800 pounds of parts back to Enid in the spring of 1911. On the way home, he stopped off in St. Louis and bought an 80-horsepower engine.

Cessna estimated he would have his aircraft assembled and ready for a demonstration flight in three weeks. Instead, it took months. In a rented Enid garage, the 31-year-old mechanic worked evenings and weekends on his project. From notes and sketches he had made at the air show, Clyde designed wings of spruce wood and covered them in Irish linen. Many nights that hot summer, a neighbor later remembered, Cessna kept the whole neighborhood awake as he started his plane's engine over and over.

When the completed machine was ready to fly, the would-be pilot towed it out to the Salt Plains along the Cimarron River. There, living with his family in a tent, Clyde spent the rest of 1911 making test flights and learning how to fly.

He finally made a successful flight—taking off, circling and landing in the same spot—near the end of the year.

Summer barnstormer

By that time, there were pilots making exhibitions almost everywhere, and the money they earned had dropped drastically. Clyde made his first public flights at the little town of Jet, Oklahoma, and was paid $300 for two appearances.

Without a job in Enid, Clyde, his wife and two children moved back to Rago and lived on their farm. At first there was no house on the site, so Clyde turned the barn's loft into living quarters. He used the ground floor for a workshop. After a winter's work on his plane, he was ready for exhibition flights. He named his rebuilt plane *Silver Wings*.

For a number of years, Clyde continued this cycle. He designed and constructed a new, improved plane each winter, and then spent the following summer farming and barnstorming.

He planned his flying appearances so that he could easily hop from one to the next, without having to take his plane apart, crate the pieces and ship them by train. In one busy season Cessna performed at 60 county fairs and other outdoor events across the region.

In one attention-getting stunt, he offered a five-dollar bill to anyone who could catch a football he dropped from his plane.

First aircraft in the aircraft capital

During the winter of 1916-17 it was Cessna who first built planes in Wichita, the future aircraft capital. With little cash to rent a building, Clyde moved his plane-building operation into the automobile manufacturing plant of **J.J. Jones**.

In return for the free space, the flyer advertised the Jones Light Six automobile in lettering painted on the wings of his Cessna Comet. He named his other Wichita-built plane the Cessna/Jones Six. After working in the city during the week Clyde flew home to Rago on weekends.

Cessna's skills in flying and building made him a valuable man in the new field of airplane building; Walter Beech [**134**] and Lloyd Stearman [**173**] asked him to become a part of the Wichita Travel Air Company in 1925. Investing $5,000 of his own, Cessna joined the firm. He served as its president for two years. ✿

Learning to take off and land—the hard way

Cessna faced many difficulties in getting his first homebuilt plane into the air. At first, the engine didn't have enough power to get the plane off the ground—it flopped the aircraft over on its nose and cracked the propeller.

Clyde made adjustments, and by late summer in 1911, he had made a short flight over Oklahoma's Salt Plains.

The next problem was learning how to turn and land his contraption. He was able to

stay in the air for nearly a mile, but he couldn't turn around. After touchdowns, he had to drag the plane back to the starting place with his car.

During one landing attempt, the plane turned sideways and smashed the wings into a useless heap. That October, Clyde was coming out of a perfect turn when his craft dropped straight to the ground. He wasn't seriously injured, but the plane looked like it had gone through a threshing machine.

Clyde's first twelve flights ended in twelve crashes, each doing about $100 worth of damage. Once he was thrown 100 feet after the plane smashed into a tree and upset in a creek. Another crackup left him in a hospital bed for ten days.

Cessna was discouraged, yet determined. After one crash, he threatened to fly the plane just once—and then burn it. When he made his first completely successful flight, that promise was forgotten.

During that time 65 Travel Airs were built, but Clyde wasn't satisfied. The craft was a biplane, and he was convinced a single-wing design could out-perform it. To prove his point, the stubborn Cessna rented a building where he spent evenings working on his own four-seat monoplane. Later, a plane of this design was the first commercial aircraft to fly from the U.S. mainland to Hawaii.

Winged arguments

Cessna continued to disagree with his partners over single-or double-winged planes and finally resigned from Travel Air in 1927. Later that year, Clyde formed his own aircraft company. He set out to build a cantilever-winged monoplane—a single-wing design with no supports or wires to hold the wings on the body. Cessna and six employees soon completed his first model. To prove his new design was strong, he piled sandbags on the wings and then climbed on top with his staff. The Cessna-designed wings held the 15,752-pound load.

Cessna manufactured the model AW, as it was called, during late 1928 and 1929. With a 110-horsepower engine it could reach speeds of 145 miles an hour and remain in the air for over seven hours.

Hard times, and a comeback

The success from this new model led Clyde into financial difficulties, however. In 1929, the Curtiss Flying Service contracted to take all the planes Cessna could produce. He borrowed thousands of dollars and expanded into five new buildings in east Wichita. When the stock market crashed later that year, the Curtiss company went bankrupt. Clyde was able to collect only a part of the money Curtiss owed him, and his own company was soon in trouble. The board of directors closed Cessna's plant in 1931 and rented the buildings to Beech Aircraft. Clyde returned to farming.

Three years later, Beech moved out and a new board of directors asked Clyde to return. With his nephews **Dwane** and **Dwight Wallace**, Cessna got the business running again.

Clyde sold his shares of the company to the Wallaces in 1936 and returned once more to farming. He kept busy raising wheat, selling grain augers, operating an earthmoving business and inventing farm machinery. He died November 20, 1954. During his burial services at a small cemetery in rural Kingman County, six jets from Wichita's McConnell Air Force Base flew over in salute.

Cessna was inducted into the Aviation Hall of Fame in 1978 and the Kansas Business Hall of Fame in 1992. His company is today one of the largest makers of small aircraft in the world.

Clyde's son, **Eldon Cessna**, designed and built planes of his own as a young man. Eldon later worked for Rockwell International, designing military aircraft and parts of the Apollo lunar module. He died in 1992. ∎

Builds bridges and gliders

142 Octave Chanute

Civil engineer and glider designer. Kansas City. (1832-1910) Chanute was born in Paris and came to the United States as a child. With no training, he became one of the best-known civil engineers in the nineteenth century.

Octave worked for railroads in the East, and came to Kansas City in 1867. There he designed and built the first bridge across the Missouri River—a feat many thought was impossible. He then built four railroad lines in Kansas. A Neosho County town on one of his lines was named Chanute in his honor. He later built several major bridges for the Atchison, Topeka and Santa Fe railroad [**158**], including one over the Mississippi River.

When he was nearly 60 Chanute developed an interest in aviation. He built and flew his own gliders, and later shared his designs and knowledge with Wilbur and Orville Wright. In fact, Chanute was one of the first to use the word *aviation*. ∎

Octave Chanute Aviation Pioneer

US Airmail 21c

Carried away with cars

Automobile manufacturer. Wamego and Ellis. (1875-1940) Chrysler, whose name now appears on thousands of automobiles, was born in Wamego, April 2, 1875. He got his start in business after his family moved to Ellis.

As a boy, he milked his family's cows and delivered the milk to customers around town. He charged a nickel a quart; his mother let him to keep a penny a quart as his pay. Teenaged Walter delivered groceries to help his family's income. He earned two cents an hour for a sixteen-hour workday.

After high school, Chrysler took a job with the Union Pacific Railroad. There he quickly showed talent as a mechanic in the Ellis shops. For the next eleven years, he worked for several railroads in the West.

Into Locomobiles

While working for an Iowa railroad, he advanced to superintendent of locomotives.

However, Chrysler soon shifted his mechanical interests from locomotives to automobiles. At an auto show in Chicago, he became so fascinated with a vehicle called the Locomobile that he borrowed nearly $5,000 to buy one of the expensive cars. But instead of driving it, Walter tore it apart and put it back together—again and again! He wanted to learn all he could about automobiles.

Chrysler at Buick

Chrysler next managed a locomotive factory in Pennsylvania. His continued interest in automobiles, however, soon led him to Detroit. He took charge of the Buick Motor Company's factory in 1912, became Buick's president just four years later—and increased production from 45 to 600 cars a day.

In 1920, after he got into an argument with the head of General Motors, he resigned. (But Chrysler could afford to quit his $500,000-a-year job; he was already a millionaire.)

The next year he became manager of the Maxwell Motor Corporation. When he introduced a new car in 1924—what he called the Chrysler—motorists liked its hydraulic brakes and improved engine design. They bought thousands. The Maxwell company, which had been $5 million in debt, suddenly made a $4 million profit.

Chrysler renamed it Chrysler Corporation, and added Dodge, DeSoto and Plymouth models. In 1930 he built the Chrysler Building in New York City. For a year, it was the world's tallest skyscraper [245]. Walter retired from his corporation in 1935. He died in Great Neck, New York, August 18, 1940. His Ellis home is now a museum. Chrysler was inducted into the Kansas Business Hall of Fame in 1991. ■

Has a brilliant idea

144 William Coleman

Manufacturer. Wichita. (1870-1957) In 1899 Coleman was a law student selling typewriters to pay for his college costs. One rainy night he noticed an extra-bright light in a small drugstore. He went inside to investigate, and found a lamp that burned a mixture of gasoline and compressed air.

The young salesman decided these lamps with their brilliant white light were much better products than his typewriters. He went to work for the lamp company, but discovered that sales were not as great as he had hoped. To improve the lamp, he redesigned it and began manufacturing his own version in a small building in Wichita.

In 1905 the lanterns lit one of the first night football games ever played. (It took place on the field of Wichita's Fairmount College, and the home team won.) By 1914, Coleman's lanterns were popular with farmers, campers and emergency workers. Through the years, he added more products: heaters, air conditioners and all types of camping equipment. Coleman is now a household word.

One of his most popular items was a "pocket stove." During World War II, American servicemen in Europe and Asia used over one million of Coleman's little stoves to warm themselves and heat up their cold rations.

After William's death, **Sheldon** and **Sheldon C. Coleman**, his son and grandson, managed the Wichita company. A New York investor took it over in 1989. In 1990 William Coleman was inducted into the Kansas Business Hall of Fame. ■

His work floats

146 Walter Dittmer

Parade float builder. Independence. (Born 1915) Dittmer is the founder of a unique company in Independence, Parade Specialties. He and his son **Jim Dittmer**, along with other family members and a staff of four, create parade floats.

Some of their customers are local businesses and organizations wanting entries for the town's annual "Neewollah" parade at Halloween. Larger corporations have hired the Dittmers to build floats for parades in southeastern Kansas, Oklahoma and Missouri.

Their small floats cost around $500, with large ones costing up to $25,000. Many are self-propelled, built on old vehicle frames. Some even include animation. It takes about 250 hours—plus yards and yards of plastic—to decorate their largest creations.

Walter built his first float in 1963 as a favor for a friend at the Sinclair Oil Company [*171*]. He hopes someday to have one of his creations in the Cotton Bowl Parade in Dallas. ■

Goes with groceries

145 Ray Dillon, Sr.

Grocery chain founder. Sterling and Hutchinson. (Born 1897) When Dillon first worked in his father's grocery store in Sterling, he was too short to see over the counter. After World War I, Ray, with his father and brother, **John** and **Clyde Dillon**, began building grocery stores around Kansas.

In the 1940s, the 24 Dillon stores became self-service supermarkets. Instead of clerks filling grocery orders, customers pushed carts around the store and selected items off shelves.

Today there are over 60 Dillon supermarkets and 200 Kwik Shops in Kansas and nearby states, plus other Dillon-owned supermarkets and convenience stores in western states. Kroger Corporation purchased the Dillon companies in the 1980s, but Dillon headquarters in Hutchinson still manages its own stores. Ray Dillon is now in the Kansas Business Hall of Fame. ■

110

Variety's his way of life

147 Alva L. Duckwall, Sr.

Variety store chain co-founder. Greenleaf and Abilene. (1877-1937) Duckwall first went into business in Greenleaf where he sold and repaired bicycles and sewing machines. In 1901 he sold his shop for $413 and borrowed that much more to buy a store in Abilene. *Wilbur Duckwall*, his brother, soon joined him, and they named their new firm "Duckwall Brothers Racket Store—A Little Bit of Everything." They felt there was a need for a store selling all kinds of small household items.

At first, business was slow. Alva's wife was the Racket Store's only clerk. By 1906, however, business had improved and Wilbur opened a second store in Salina. To advertise their venture, Alva traveled the countryside on Sunday afternoons with a big bucket of red paint in his buggy. With the permission of friendly farmers, he painted signs on their barns and gates: "There are others, but none like Duckwall Brothers."

By 1915 the Duckwall chain had nine stores, several operated by Alva's brothers and other relatives. At that time the family formed the A.L. Duckwall Five & Dime Store Company. Alva was its president. He remained with the company until his death. Today Duckwall-ALCO Stores, with its headquarters still in Abilene, operates 100 Duckwall Variety stores and ALCO Discount stores in Kansas and eleven other states. ∎

Makes tacos take off

148 Daniel Foley

Restaurant chain co-founder. Wichita. (Born 1932) Foley was born in Oklahoma and grew up in Wichita. He attended Wichita State University and worked at Boeing Aircraft for several years.

In the late 1950s he decided to go into business with his brother and cousin. His cousin had recently returned from California with an idea for a new type of restaurant, one selling Mexican food. The partners hoped the ethnic food would be as popular in Wichita as it was on the West Coast. They were right. In 1961 Foley and his brother *Robin Foley* officially formed the Taco Tico Company. They opened several more Mexican food restaurants in Wichita during the 1960s, and expanded to Dodge City in 1971.

By 1988, there were over 100 Taco Tico restaurants in Kansas and eight other Midwestern states. Foley sold his interests in the company at that time—and made a turnaround. After spending over twenty years in the restaurant business helping people put on weight, he became a partner in a chain of Nutri/System weight-loss centers. ∎

Giants in grain

149-150 Raymond & Olive Garvey

Grain company executives and philanthropists. Colby and Wichita. (1893-1959) Arkansas City and Wichita. (Born 1893) Raymond Garvey built a chain of elevators large enough to store over 200 million bushels—about half of one year's wheat crop in Kansas. After his death, his wife Olive continued to run their company, which also included oil wells and cattle ranches in several western states. Through the Garvey Foundation she contributed millions of dollars to schools, charities, the arts and other public projects in Wichita and across Kansas. ∎

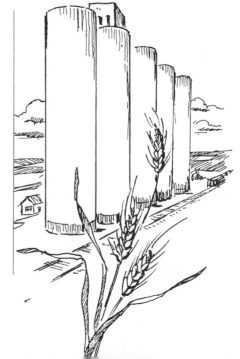

A cool idea

151 Henry Gott

Inventor and insulated water cooler manufacturer. Winfield. (1869-1953) Early in the twentieth century, oilfield workers had no way of keeping their drinking water cold on hot days. Gott, a hardware dealer, went to work on the problem and came up with an insulated water cooler made of metal.

In 1916 he began making his portable cooler in a small sheet metal shop in Winfield. Workers in the oilfields of Kansas, Oklahoma and Texas eagerly bought Gott's cooler. Although he didn't patent his invention, no one was able to match Gott's craftsmanship and quality. For years his Gottkool and Stakool brand coolers were among the most popular metal coolers made.

In 1942 Henry retired and sold his company to a Winfield family. They continued to make his coolers, although galvanized steel was difficult to obtain during World War II. By the early 1970s, the company's products were made of plastic. Gott's name was stamped on items sold in the United States, South America and Middle East.

Gott Corporation continued to expand and was purchased by the Rubbermaid company in 1985. It is now a division of the large corporation, with a one million-square foot plant in Winfield. Its 900 employees make personal and family-sized ice chests, thermal jugs, storage containers and modern plastic versions of Gott's insulated water cooler. The products are sold around the world. ■

Cattle baron in the Smoky Hills

152 George Grant

Promoter and rancher. Victoria. (1822-1878) Grant was a silk merchant from Scotland who made a small fortune in an unusual way. When a member of Britain's royal family died, he bought up all the black silk he could find and then sold it—at much higher prices—to funeral mourners.

Grant traveled in the United States in the early 1870s and decided to start a ranching colony along the Smoky Hill River. He bought over 30,000 acres from the Kansas Pacific Railroad at only two dollars an acre and established a town. In keeping with his British heritage, he named it Victoria, in honor of his queen. There George raised sheep, plus Durham, Galloway and Aberdeen Angus cattle. He was, in fact, the first rancher to import Angus bulls into the United States.

Most of the Englishmen in Grant's colony had moved away by the 1890s, but his success helped prove the Kansas prairies could support cattle and sheep. ■

Cares enough to live in Kansas

153 Donald Joyce Hall

Greeting card company executive. Mission Hills. (Born 1928) Hall is the chairman of Hallmark Cards, founded by his father, **Joyce Hall**, in 1913. The younger Hall graduated from college in 1950. He joined the U.S. Army and served in Japan before joining his father's card company in 1953.

As Hall moved up in the business, he was a vice president, then president, and eventually chief executive officer. After his father died in 1982, Donald became chairman of Hallmark's board of directors. He now owns one-third of the giant business—the largest greeting card company in the world. *Forbes Magazine* has estimated Hall's fortune at $755 million, making him the second richest person in Kansas [*162*]. He is a 1992 inductee into the Kansas Business Hall of Fame.

Although the Hallmark company's main offices are located in Kansas City, Missouri, the company operates plants in Topeka, Lawrence and Leavenworth. Hall and his family live in Mission Hills. His father lived in Leawood for many years. ■

Trains customers to expect the best

Restaurant chain founder. Leavenworth. (1835-1901)
Harvey was born in London June 27, 1835, and came to America when he was fifteen. Nine years later he opened a restaurant in St. Louis, but it went out of business when his partner ran off with their cash at the start of the Civil War.

Travelers tricked

Harvey eventually moved to Leavenworth and worked as a traveling freight agent for the Chicago, Burlington and Quincy Railroad. As he traveled about his territory by train, he was amazed at the poor eating conditions for rail passengers.

The menu was often the same —greasy stew and bitter coffee. Several times Harvey was the victim of a popular trick by dishonest trainmen and restaurant owners: Railroaders collected passengers' money before their train made a meal stop. Then—just as hungry passengers were served their food—the engineer whistled and began to pull away from the station.

Customers ran to catch the train, leaving uneaten food that the restaurant owner resold to unsuspecting travelers on the next train. Harvey soon got his fill of this treatment.

On the Atchison, Topeka and Santa Fe

Fred suggested that his company operate a clean, well-run restaurant in a depot. The CB&Q's managers laughed and sent him to a struggling new railroad, the Atchison, Topeka and Santa Fe [158]. Santa Fe officials liked Harvey's idea. In 1876, they invited him to Topeka where he opened the first Fred Harvey restaurant in the AT&SF depot. Because it offered good food, clean surroundings and polite service at reasonable prices, it was an immediate success.

Soon Harvey opened more eating houses. Eventually they grew into a chain of restaurants and hotels spaced every 100 miles along the Santa Fe's main line. At each Harvey House he insisted on using only the finest furnishings and table service, not to mention the highest quality food. To meet Harvey's tough standards, his company kept its own beef herd in western Kansas, operated its own dairies at Newton and other points, and shipped tank cars of fresh water to restaurants in desert areas.

The Harvey Girls

Perhaps the most popular part of his service was the "Harvey Girls." Harvey imported many of these waitresses from the East. He gave each a weekly salary of $17.50, plus room and board in the local Harvey House.

In their plain black uniforms with crisp, white collars and aprons, the Harvey Girls quickly became a symbol for the restaurant chain's respected reputation. They were trained to handle hungry crowds of train passengers quickly, efficiently and politely.

Before a train arrived, Harvey Girls had tables set and drinks ready to pour. As a train ⇨

Fred Harvey

pulled in, the restaurant manager rang a gong to signal the waitresses into action. Customers were quickly seated, served and eating with no complaints.

To make sure there was nothing to complain about, Harvey inspected all his restaurants and hotels personally, often by surprise. If he saw improperly set tables, he jerked the tablecloths away, flinging silverware and dishes onto the floor.

His high standards also meant that all male customers had to wear dinner jackets in his dining rooms. Each restaurant kept extra coats hanging near the door for men who tried to enter without one.

When the Santa Fe Railroad introduced dining cars in 1890, Harvey took charge of that service, too.

After his death on February 9, 1901, his family continued to operate the company. For many years, Fred Harvey's name meant the finest food and accommodations in the West. ■

Trader on the trail

155 Seth Hays

Merchant. Present Shawnee County and Council Grove. (1811-1873) Hays was a great-grandson of Daniel Boone and a cousin of Kit Carson [8]. He grew up in Missouri and came to Kansas in the mid 1840s. After working at a Kansa Indian trading post on Mission Creek, Hays helped set up another trading post for the tribe in 1847. The settlement—at the Santa Fe Trail crossing of the Neosho River—became Council Grove. For over twenty years, he was one of the town's leading citizens.

In 1857 he opened the Hays House, a hotel and tavern. Its restaurant is still open and is said to be the oldest continuously operated eating place west of the Mississippi River.

Three years later, Seth and a partner built a large store. Council Grove was the last chance for traders to buy supplies on their way to Santa Fe, and Hays made money "hand over hand." It was no wonder. During the busy year of 1860, he counted 2,667 wagons, 3,519 men and nearly 30,000 draft animals passing on the trail. After railroads ended the wagon train days of the Santa Fe Trail, Hays sold his store and opened a Council Grove saloon. When a local church group needed a meeting place, he kindly offered his drinking establishment. But before each Sunday service, he put the liquor away and covered the bar with canvas so worshippers would not be embarrassed.

Hays never married, but he adopted a daughter and raised her with the help of a slave, **Sarah Taylor**. When Kansas was admitted as a free state, Hays gave "Aunt Sallie" her freedom. She continued to take care of his home until she died. He buried her in his family plot in the Council Grove cemetery. ■

Stirs up sweet treats

156 Tom Henry

Candy maker. Hutchinson and Arkansas City. (1880-1963) Henry first made candy at the age of ten when he helped a candy maker after school. Two years later he sold his own candy on Denver street corners—until a policeman closed his business because he had no license. As an adult Tom worked at various locations in the Midwest and South. Then, in 1919, he moved to Arkansas City and opened a small candy factory. The next year he introduced his own candy bar, the Tom Henry. He later sold the recipe to a larger company where it became the "O'Henry" bar. When his business folded in 1931, Henry moved to Arkansas. His son, **Pat Henry**, opened a candy factory in Dexter in 1956. It is still run by the Henry family. They make nearly 70,000 pounds of candy each year. ■

Chemical genuis

157 Takeru Higuchi

Chemist and educator. Lawrence. (Born 1918) Higuchi was curious about chemistry as a child in California, partly because he began reading science fiction stories as a second grader. He earned a degree in chemistry from the University of California at Berkeley in 1939 and then completed a doctor's degree at the University of Wisconsin.

Takeru taught chemistry in Wisconsin until he moved to Kansas in 1967. At the University of Kansas, Professor Higuchi has set up a program in pharmaceutical, or drug, chemistry that is considered one of the best in the world. He has over 50 patents for chemical processes, including one that allows medicines to be released slowly into the bloodstream through a tiny hole in a pill's coating.

Dr. Higuchi has also been involved with private research laboratories that have shared their profits with KU. He has put over $1 million of his own earnings back into research and scholastic programs at the university. ∎

Gets a railroad on track

158 Cyrus K. Holliday

Railroad builder and state senator. Topeka. (1826-1900) In 1859 Holliday organized the Atchison, Topeka and Santa Fe Railroad and became its first president. But at that time his company wasn't much of a rail line. It owned no locomotives, no cars—not even track.

With years of work, however, Cyrus got his railroad rolling. Part of that time was spent convincing the U.S. Congress to give the AT&SF free land along its route in Kansas. The company later sold the land to new settlers [*170*].

Samuel Pomeroy [*80*] helped Holliday get the land grants, but the senator also tried to help himself. For several years, Pomeroy and his brothers-in-law took control of Holliday's railroad; Holliday later forced them out. Finally, in 1869, the AT&SF laid its first rails, a twenty-mile line between Topeka and Carbondale.

Three years later Holliday's railroad stretched across Kansas, following much of the Santa Fe Trail. In the 1880s the line was extended to California and Chicago. The Santa Fe Railroad became an important transportation link in the state.

During the Bleeding Kansas days Holliday supported the Free State cause and helped organize the Kansas Republican party—even though he was a Democrat. During the Civil War he was the adjutant general of the state.

He was a co-founder of Topeka and, as a member of the Kansas Legislature, he worked to make it the state capital. He donated land in the center of the city and helped design the Capitol building that was built there. The Johnson County town of Holliday was named for him. In 1989 he was named to the Kansas Business Hall of Fame.

For many years, Holliday's railroad was the largest in Kansas, with over 3,000 miles of track and hundreds of depots. Now the company operates from just a handful of Kansas depots and its trackage in the state has been trimmed by about half.

Through the 1960s, the Santa Fe *Super Chief* was one of the finest passenger trains in the West. Today, the government-owned Amtrak corporation operates Kansas' only interstate passenger train. It crosses the state on Holliday's AT&SF Railway. ∎

Makes a magic menthol medicine

Medicine manufacturer and philanthropist. Leavenworth and Wichita. (1848-1935)
Hyde was born in Massachusetts March 2, 1848. He came to Kansas as a teenager and worked in a Leavenworth bank.

Recovering a lost fortune

After Hyde moved to Wichita in 1872 he continued in the banking business and also sold real estate. By the late 1880s he had a fortune worth $100,000. Soon, however, the economy slumped and he lost everything.

With seven children to feed, Alexander could not afford to be without money for long.

Working with his brother-in-law **Clayton Smith** and a friend, **Walter Binkley**, Hyde raised $600 and began making Yucca brand soap. As their Wichita business grew, Hyde and his partners marketed new products: shaving soaps, "tooth soaps," flypaper, silver polish and Vest Pocket Cough Specific, a cough medicine made from menthol. At that time, the cooling remedy made from peppermint plants was hardly used in the United States, but it had long been a popular treatment in Japan.

In 1890 Hyde bought out his two partners. At the same time he began developing a new menthol product. He wanted an ointment mild enough to treat the nose or eyes, but strong enough to use on sore mus-

cles. After four years of experiments—with the help of doctors, druggists and chemists—Hyde's product appeared. He named it "Mentholatum," from the two main ingredients, menthol and petroleum jelly.

While he was testing the ointment, Hyde sold it door-to-door in Wichita. Soon his salesmen were promoting it to druggists across the area. Mentholatum seemed to sell itself, and as its popularity increased, so did the list of ailments it seemed to cure. Satisfied customers said it relieved not only muscle aches, cuts, burns, insect bites and cold sores, but headaches, toothaches, hay fever, bad breath, indigestion and varicose veins. One user claimed putting Mentholatum in his nose and throat brought back his hearing.

Sharing his success

Quickly the menthol ointment became Alexander's best-selling product. He eventually stopped making his soaps, and in 1906 he renamed his business the Mentholatum Company. By that time, the Hyde sons **Edward**, **Charles** and **Alexander** were involved in the expanding operation. They built a Spanish-style "Home of Mentholatum" building in Wichita in 1909.

Five years later they opened a plant in Canada, followed by one in Buffalo, New York, in 1919, and an overseas factory near London in 1923. In 1926, they sold more than twenty million 25-cent tins of their popular home remedy worldwide.

Hyde, then believed to be the richest man in Kansas [*162*], generously shared his wealth with others. The philanthropist gave away perhaps ninety percent of his profits to an impressive list of charities in Kansas and elsewhere. He and his wife **Ida Todd Hyde** contributed to YMCAs around the world and a wide range of other causes, from a small school for black youths in Mississippi to a prestigious college in Ohio, and from a mission for Mexican-Americans in Wichita to a playground for refugee children in Greece. Henry J. Allen [*31*] praised their work, saying they "invested in the happiness of others."

Hyde died in Wichita, January 10, 1935. His sons closed the Kansas factory in the 1940s and moved their headquarters to the New York plant. Hyde's Mentholatum, the "Little Nurse for Little Ills," is still manufactured there. ■

A pair of clever inventors

160 Jack Kilby

Inventor. Great Bend. (Born 1923) Kilby graduated from high school in Great Bend and later worked for the Texas Instruments electronics company.

In the late 1950s, he experimented with semiconductors, or materials that carry electricity at some times, and not at others. Jack used semiconductors to make integrated circuits, the groups of tiny electrical parts that make today's computers and other electrical devices smaller, more powerful and less expensive than earlier models.

Kilby is actually a co-inventor of the "monolithic integrated circuit"; another inventor produced a similar device at the same time. The two men worked on their projects separately, but they later met and became friends. Kilby also helped design Texas Instrument's first hand-held calculators. ■

161 Omar Knedlik

Inventor. Barnes, Belleville and Coffeyville. (1915-1989) Knedlik and his wife ran an ice cream parlor in Belleville after he came home from World War II. In 1957, they opened a Dairy Queen store in Coffeyville.

A few years later, Omar accidentally discovered a way to make frozen carbonated drinks. His soda fountain broke down and he put bottles of Coca-Cola into the freezer to cool. When he opened them, the Coke had changed from a liquid to a soft ice. Customers liked his cold drinks, so he began tinkering with a machine that would combine carbonated water, syrup and pressure into slush.

Knedlik's contraption worked. Today it is the technology used to make two popular brands of frozen drinks, Icee and Slurpee. Billions of Knedlik's slushy treats have been sold since he perfected his invention. ■

Billionaire Jayhawk

162 Charles Koch

Oil company executive. Wichita. (Born 1936) Koch attended a military academy and then earned two master's degrees in engineering from the Massachusetts Institute of Technology. In the early 1960s he went to work for one of his father's oil companies in Italy. When Wichita industrialist **Fred Koch** died in 1967, the 32-year-old Charles took charge of all of the family's businesses. Under his leadership, Koch Industries has grown into one of the largest privately-owned corporations in the United States. Much of Koch's business involves marketing oil and gas, but it also owns pipeline, chemical and cattle-ranching companies. Its headquarters are in Wichita.

Charles doesn't talk about his finances publicly, but he is often listed as the richest man in Kansas. In 1992 *Forbes Magazine* estimated the Wichitan and his brother **David Koch**, a Koch company executive living in New York City, each had fortunes worth about $1.25 billion. ■

Puts planes on autopilot

163 William Lear, Sr.

Inventor and aircraft manufacturer. Wichita. (1902-1978) Lear was born in Missouri where, as a teenager, he built his own battery charger. As William charged batteries for 25 cents apiece, he used the cash to help fund his curiosity.

Years later he sold several inventions to Motorola and RCA. Lear used that money to start two businesses of his own. After he sold those companies, he moved to Wichita in 1962. The next year he began manufacturing the Learjet, one of the first small jets for business or personal use. For a time, entertainers like Frank Sinatra, athletes such as Arnold Palmer, and other celebrities flocked to Kansas to take delivery of their own Learjets.

In 1967, when some of the glitter had faded from his aircraft business, Lear sold 65 percent of Learjet and used his earnings to buy an abandoned air base. He left Kansas and experimented in the Nevada desert with a low-pollution steam-powered automobile. At the time of his death, he was designing a new plane, the Learfan. Those inventions remain unbuilt—as does one of his ideas from the mid 1950s. Years before *Star Trek* fans first heard "Beam me up, Scotty," he envisioned a "teleporter" that would disintegrate passengers into electronic signals and zip them to their travel destinations in seconds.

For millions of realistic travelers, Lear's successful inventions have made life safe and enjoyable. He invented an improved radio direction-finder for aircraft [**13**], automatic pilot equipment, the automobile radio, and the eight-track cartridge and tape player.

Learjet still builds planes in Wichita, but it is now owned by a Canadian corporation. ∎

Birdman flies first

164 Alvin Longren

Aircraft manufacturer. Leonardville, Clay Center and Topeka. (1882-1950) Longren was a Topeka mechanic who was fascinated with all types of machinery: automobiles, motorcycles and especially airplanes. With help from his brother **E.K. Longren** and **William Janicke**, the mechanic decided to build his own plane.

The men began their project by making aircraft parts on the second floor of a rented building in Topeka. During the summer of 1911, they moved the pieces to a hayfield southeast of town. There, under a circus tent, they assembled their pusher-type biplane. The 39-foot long craft had a wingspan of 32 feet, a 60-horsepower, eight-cylinder engine, and a dollar watch for a fuel gauge—all held together with a half-mile of wire. As the plane took shape, the Longrens and Janicke took turns guarding it each night.

When the assembly was complete, Alvin flew the *Topeka I* on September 2, 1911—making the first successful flight of an airplane built in Kansas. Nine days later, he introduced his creation to the public with a flight over downtown Topeka. His aircraft was able to fly fifteen miles and reach an altitude of 1,000 feet. During the next three years, he was a popular barnstormer across the Midwest. Known as the Birdman, Longren gave thousands of Kansans their first glimpse of a plane in flight. He made 1,372 exhibition flights with only one serious accident. A gust of wind during a flight at Abilene slammed his plane to the ground and broke his leg in three places.

Alvin put much of his earnings from barnstorming into creating an airplane that he hoped would replace the automobile. With a molded fiber body and folding wings, Longren imagined one of his compact two-seat planes in everyone's garage.

Unfortunately, the public wasn't ready for personal air travel. Longren manufactured 21 of the planes in a Topeka factory before his company went broke in the 1920s. He then worked as a consultant for other aircraft manufacturers, including Clyde Cessna [**141**]. ∎

Beefs up the cow market

165 Joseph McCoy

Promoter and businessman. Abilene and Wichita. (1837-1915) McCoy was a cattleman from Illinois. When he heard that Texas was full of cattle after the Civil War he realized money could be made. The cattle were worth only $4 each in Texas, but hungry markets in the East would pay up to $40 per head.

Since there were no railroads in Texas—and the nearest tracks were in Kansas—Joseph built cattle pens and loading chutes in Abilene. He advertised his "cowtown" in Texas, and cattlemen drove their herds north. The northern section of the route they used, the Chisholm Trail [**10**], is sometimes called McCoy's Extension.

As cattlemen paid to use McCoy's pens, he quickly became rich. By 1871, over 1.6 million head of livestock had been shipped from the new cattle town. That same year, McCoy was elected Abilene's first mayor. There and in Wichita he eventually held a wide variety of jobs: grocer, real estate agent, fence salesman, Indian agent, cattle inspector, narcotics investigator and author. His *Historic Sketches of the Cattle Trade of the West and Southwest* is an important history of the cattle business. ■

Hatches helicopters

166 Rex Maneval

Inventor and helicopter builder. Centralia, Topeka and Frankfort. (1890-1974) Maneval wanted to be a mechanical engineer, but his parents sent him to school to be a banker instead. He worked at banks in his hometown and Topeka before managing a bank in Frankfort. In his spare time he continued to read about and tinker with machines.

In the early 1920s Rex invented an incubator to hatch chicks. He soon resigned from the bank and opened his own hatchery in Frankfort. It hatched 60,000 eggs in its first season. When Maneval increased production to 300,000 chicks a year, his was one of the largest hatcheries in Kansas.

After his wife and son died of accidental carbon monoxide poisoning in 1935, Maneval spent many lonely hours reading about aircraft. He became fascinated with helicopters and began designing one of his own.

Instead of the usual one large rotor and a smaller tail rotor, however, his helicopter used two large-sized rotors. He invented a special gearbox that allowed the two rotors to turn in opposite directions at the same time on the same shaft. Maneval completed his helicopter in 1941. He flew it several times—but always kept it fastened close to the ground with a heavy cable. He felt it vibrated too much to use safely in free flight. Although he tried several modifications, he never overcame the vibration problem.

He also worked on designs for a a high-speed passenger train and a plane that could use short runways.

Engineers have said that Maneval's helicopter was years ahead of its time. Modern helicopter builders have studied double-rotors similar to Maneval's designs for use in 400-mph "super copters." ■

Sells military planes

167 Glenn Martin

Aircraft manufacturer. Liberal and Salina. (1886-1955) Martin was born in Iowa but grew up in Liberal and Salina. He first showed a talent for aircraft manufacturing when he built and sold kites at the age of eight.

Glenn attended college in Salina for a short time, and then moved to California with his family in 1905. There Martin worked as a mechanic. He also rented an abandoned church where he spent three years building his own plane.

Soon he was a successful barnstorming pilot—and movie hero, after he appeared as a flier in a silent movie starring Mary Pickford. At the same time, he continued designing aircraft. In 1913 he sold the U.S. Army his tractor-propeller biplane design. He then opened his own California factory to build them. During World War I he designed a four-seat, twin-engine biplane that could carry a half-ton of bombs and five machine guns. The Army ordered several of them, but Martin made only nine before the war ended.

After the famous pilot Colonel Billy Mitchell used Martin's planes in 1921 to show the need for an American air force, the plane maker got more military contracts. During World War II, his aircraft company built important military planes, including the B-10, B-26 Marauder, B-51 and B-57 bombers.

His company also built space vehicles, including the Viking and Vanguard rockets that helped get America's space program off the ground in the 1950s. The Martin-Marietta Corporation still builds airplanes and spacecraft today. ∎

Blows and goes in a windwagon

168 Samuel Peppard

Windwagon builder. Oskaloosa. (1833-1916) Peppard came to Kansas Territory in 1856 and built a mill along a river in Jefferson County.

He ground grain and sawed lumber for a few years before gold was discovered in the mountains of western Kansas Territory—central Colorado today. Then the lure of striking it rich became strong.

In early 1860 the 27-year-old millwright and several of his friends began planning to go west. Their transportation was to be a homemade wind-powered wagon.

The idea was Samuel's, and while his buddies at first laughed at him, he convinced them a windwagon would be the fastest and cheapest way to reach the gold fields.

Their craft was finished by spring. On a test sailing near Oskaloosa, Peppard found it raced along so fast the ends of the wooden axles got hot. Unfortunately it also flew over a small hill, leaped 30 feet into the air, and landed with a crash.

Captain Peppard was unhurt, and the wagon was quickly repaired. A few days later, he and three friends set sail for western Kansas. The eight-foot body of the craft easily carried the men and their 400 pounds of supplies. With its two sails unfurled from the ten-foot mast, it was real prairie schooner.

The windsailors headed west on the Oregon Trail. At times they ran 30 mph, but they had to slow down to avoid overheating the ends of the axles.

One day they traveled 50 miles in three hours, passing 625 teams along the way. The teamsters had the last laugh, however, for there were many days that the windwagon was windless. Prairie breezes didn't always blow hard enough to move it.

On the fifth day out, a band of Indians approached. At first they apparently didn't see the dust-covered windwagon in the distance, but when Peppard lifted the sails, each rider raised up on his pony in surprise. As the wagon took off, so did the Indians, following close behind. The uneasy sailors felt sure they could outrun their pursuers—until the brake handle broke. Not wanting to sail without brakes, Peppard and his crew bailed out and each grabbed a wheel to stop their ship. As the Indians rode closer, the men quickly repaired the brake and sailed on. But

as it turned out, the Indians only wanted to race the strange contraption. They rode alongside for a mile or more until one rider on a gray mare finally outdistanced the windwagon when Samuel braked in a strong wind.

The windwagon rolled on toward Denver, but about 50 miles out of the city, its journey ended. A dust devil caught the sailors by surprise and swirled over them before they could lower the sails.

The wagon flew several feet in the air and landed hard on its back wheels. The damage was apparently so great that Peppard and his crew abandoned their ship by the side of the road. They traveled on to the gold fields with a wagon train.

Peppard found no gold, and returned to Kansas after serving in the 2nd Colorado Volunteers during the Civil War. He married, raised thirteen children, and built no more windwagons. ∎

Hopes crash with copter

169 William Purvis

Helicopter builder. Goodland. (1871-1944) Purvis and his machinist partner **Charles Wilson** worked for the Rock Island Railroad in Goodland when they designed and built a helicopter. It was, in fact, the first helicopter patented in the United States. But soon after they applied for that patent in March 1910, problems hovered over their project.

They had earlier demonstrated one of their working models on Thanksgiving Day 1909. The triangular-shaped craft was anchored to the ground, but using power from a belt on a steam engine, it successfully lifted a few feet into the air and landed. For a time things looked up. Eager witnesses rushed to purchase shares of stock in Purvis and Wilson's Goodland Aviation Company. The men quit their jobs with the railroad and spent all their time building a new, improved model.

However, at a second public demonstration in the summer of 1910, their hopes—and their 400-pound, two-engine craft—crashed. It refused to lift off at first, and then suddenly went up like a "crippled praying mantis," observers said. The light craft's twin seven-horsepower engines quickly tore it apart in the air.

After the failure, the builders began to repair their machine. Disappointed investors, ⇨

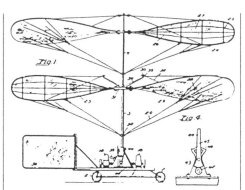

however, had their own ideas. They argued over new plans and insisted Purvis try their ideas. But he soon left town, followed by Wilson.

Townspeople also dropped the project—until 1976. As part of the American Bicentennial celebration, Goodland's High Plains Museum commissioned a modern-day machinist and inventor to build another Purvis-Wilson helicopter.

Harold Norton of Brewster used the men's original sketches and worked several years to complete a full-size replica of their machine. Like the original model, the new two-story helicopter doesn't fly, but visitors may push a button and watch its bamboo-covered blades turn.

Heavy metal

A.E. Hunt, a blacksmith in Jetmore, also built a helicopter-like craft in 1910. As strange as it looked, his two-motored "rotary aeroplane" could actually lift 400 pounds.

But there was only one problem: The flying machine was made of pipe and angle iron—and weighed more than three tons! Like the Purvis and Wilson aircraft, Hunt's invention didn't get off the ground. ∎

Mennonites' Moses

170 C.B. Schmidt

Promoter. Lawrence. (1843-About 1922) Schmidt was an implement salesman in Lawrence when the Santa Fe Railroad [**158**] hired him as a land agent in 1873. The railroad had been given thousands of acres of government land in central and western Kansas in return for building its tracks across the state.

It was Schmidt's job to attract new residents to the area, for what good were miles of new railroad track through uninhabited territory? The problem was, most American settlers were not interested in Kansas. Many still believed it was the "Great American Desert" [**22, 24**] and they didn't want to buy railroad land—especially when the government was giving away other land as homesteads.

At the same time, Mennonites had begun to leave Russia. They believed it was wrong to

fight as soldiers, which the Russian government expected each man to do. Schmidt, who was born in Germany and could speak the Mennonites' native language, encouraged some of them who had already come to America to move west to Kansas. He also worked to have the Kansas Legislature pass a law that excused the Mennonites from military service.

Schmidt found the Mennonites were eager customers, for when he showed a minister an area covered with grasshoppers, the man told him the land must indeed be good, or it wouldn't have attracted so many insects!

In 1874, the land agent brought 400 Mennonite families [**96**] from Russia to

central Kansas. He traveled to Russia early the next year and arranged a $56,000 land sale to about 6,500 Mennonites. When Schmidt had the Santa Fe charter a steamship to bring the immigrants to the United States, he was nicknamed "Moses of the Mennonites."

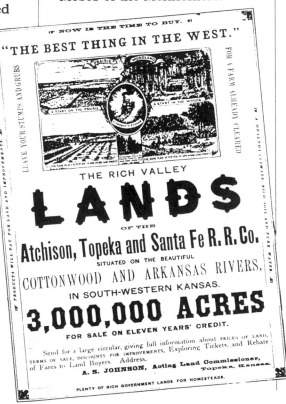

Once they were in Kansas, Schmidt and his boss at the Santa Fe, *Alexander Johnson* —son of missionary Thomas Johnson [*110*]—arranged for the Mennonites to live temporarily at the railroad's giant shop building in Topeka. Special trains then moved the families to their new lands.

The hard red winter wheat the Mennonites planted has helped make Kansas the Wheat State. But Mennonites from Russia are just one of a long list of immigrant groups that have come to Kansas. Since the first days of settlement, Germans, African-Americans, Czechs, Mexicans, Swedes, Scots, Irish, Italians, Austrians, Hungarians, Yugoslavians, Lebanese, Southeast Asians and others have helped create the state's culture and heritage. ■

Oil man in hot water

171 Harry Sinclair

Druggist and oil company executive. Independence. (1876-1956) Sinclair grew up working in his family's drugstore in Independence and was later president of the giant Sinclair Oil Company.

Harry decided to make the change from pharmaceuticals to oil after listening to oilmen's stories as they drank coffee in the drugstore. Using what he learned from his customers, Sinclair bought a few oil leases. Then with some skill—and luck—he made a million dollars by the age of 30.

In the 1920s, his company was involved in the "Teapot Dome" oil scandal. President Warren Harding's secretary of the interior accepted money from Sinclair's oil company for the right to drill in the Teapot Dome oil reserves in Wyoming.

The interior secretary went to prison, but Sinclair was found innocent of any criminal wrongdoing. He did, however, have to spend seven months in jail for not cooperating with the U.S. Senate's investigation of the affair. Sinclair also had to give up his oil lands in Wyoming. ■

Digs a dry canal

172 Asa T. Soule

Promoter. Dodge City. (1825-1890) Soule was a multimillionaire from New York who did a little of everything on his way to making a fortune. He was a farmer, a peach grower, a real estate agent, a banker, a hotel manager and a cough syrup salesman.

Much of his money was made from selling Hop Bitters, a patent medicine that was mostly alcohol. To advertise and promote his miracle medicine, Asa bought a baseball team and sponsored a rowing competition. After he was accused of rigging a race, he left the sporting world and went to western Kansas.

There, in 1883, he met two former New Yorkers living in Spearville. They convinced Soule to invest some of his millions in an irrigation canal that would carry water out of the Arkansas River. Farmers along the route were to pay from $1 to $1.50 per acre per year to use the water.

In 1884, Soule began digging the Eureka Canal. The waterway eventually ran from the town of Ingalls [*63*] to near Spearville, but it was used for only five years. The soil was so sandy that more water soaked in the canal than flowed along it. The shrewd Soule, however, lost little money in the deal, for

he sold all the Eureka stock to a group in London for $1.1 million in gold.

Before he left southwestern Kansas to return to New York, Soule also built a railroad and a Dodge City college that later became St. Mary of the Plains. During a fight over the Gray County seat, Soule hired several Dodge City "guns"— including *Jim Masterson*, brother of "Bat" [*368*]—to convince Cimarron residents to move the county seat to Soule's town of Ingalls. The plan failed. ■

Designs biplanes and swing-wings

Aircraft manufacturer. Wellsford, Harper and Wichita. (1898-1975) Stearman was born in Wellsford, October 26, 1898, and lived in Harper as a teenager.

Architect-airman

He attended Kansas State Agricultural College, planning to be an architect like his father. His plans were cut short by World War I. He joined the U.S. Navy in 1918 and trained as a pilot. Although the war ended before he flew in combat, Stearman remained fascinated with airplanes. He returned to Kansas and began working in Wichita for ***E.M. "Matty" Laird*** at his

aircraft company, where he was then building the Swallow, the first commercial airplane sold in the United States. Stearman began as a mechanic, but was soon promoted to foreman and then engineer.

Laird and his partner ***Jacob "Jake" Moellendick*** split in 1923 and Moellendick renamed the company Swallow Aircraft. Stearman became Swallow's chief engineer, working with Walter Beech [***134***], a test pilot and salesman.

A year later, the 25-year-old Stearman designed his first plane, the New Swallow. When Beech flew the craft in a national air show it was declared the nation's best-

performing commercial plane. Some features of Stearman's design were so advanced they were still included in biplanes manufactured through the early 1940s.

Famous partners

In 1925 Stearman and Beech left the Swallow company. They wanted to build aircraft made of welded steel tubing instead of wood, but Moellendick refused to allow it. The two asked Clyde Cessna [***141***] to join them in a new company, Travel Air Manufacturing. Part of the company's $100,000 capital came from another partner, wealthy Wichita businessman **Walter Innes, Jr.** Soon, Stearman had designed a biplane so popular they couldn't fill all the orders.

In the summer of 1926, Beech flew one of their Travel Airs in a two-week touring competition and won the event. When the contestants arrived in Wichita, however, tragedy struck.

Stearman took one of their planes up for a demonstration of stunt flying. As he was landing, the plane's propeller smashed through a spectator's automobile parked too close to the runway. **George Theis, Jr.**, prominent Wichita businessman and president of the Arkansas Valley Interurban Railway, was killed.

Stearman collapsed from shock in his cockpit and had to be carried from the plane. Two months later, he and his family left Kansas and moved to California.

His own company

There he did some stunt flying in movies. He also formed the Stearman Aircraft Company but within a year, he was nearly broke. Stearman found that his talent was at the drawing board, not in the financial office.

When several Kansas investors raised $60,000 to bring his struggling company to Wichita, he accepted. He merged Stearman Aircraft with the United Aircraft and Transport Corporation in 1929, and remained with the company for two more years. United Aircraft and Transport eventually became the Boeing Military Airplane Company. Using plans adapted from one of Stearman's designs, it built thousands of training planes in Wichita through World War II. One building at today's giant Boeing Wichita facility dates back to Stearman's company.

Rescues Lockheed

In 1931 Stearman left Wichita and moved back to California. Based on his reputation, he raised money to buy a bankrupt plane maker, Lockheed Aircraft. He became the first president of the reorganized corporation and designed several aircraft, including the Lockheed Electra model used by Amelia Earhart [**13**].

But once again, Lloyd enjoyed aircraft designing more than company management. When the pressures of his president's job became too great, he left

the company in 1935 to spend time designing. Twenty years later, however, Stearman amazed his old friends at Lockheed by asking for a job. Company officials quickly rehired their ex-president as a designer. At Lockheed's drawing board he designed swing-wings used on the F-111 fighter-bomber and worked on plans for vertical takeoff and landing craft. He even helped design spacecraft.

The aviation pioneer from Kansas died in Los Angeles on April 4, 1975. He saw the beginnings of manned flight above—and beyond—the earth. ■

Sticks his name on candy

174 Russell Stover

Candy maker. Alton and Mission Hills. (1888-1954)
Stover was born in a sod house near Alton and moved to Iowa with his father when his mother died. In 1910 he left college and became a candy salesman in Chicago. That job led him to Canada where he worked for another candy company.

When some customers complained that he had sold them some bad candy—and his boss refused to replace it—Russell quit and decided to make his own products. He was successful, until World War I began and several of his largest customers went bankrupt. He and his wife then returned to Iowa, where he worked as a superintendent in another candy factory. There a young man came to Stover one day with an idea for a chocolate-covered ice cream bar. Stover named the product Eskimo Pie and helped

develop the idea. He and his partner began selling the treats in 1921. Sales reached two million a day and then dropped off. But Stover had expected the numbers to keep rising and he had already signed a very expensive advertising contract. To keep from going bankrupt, he sold the Eskimo Pie patent for $25,000. With their share of the money the Stovers moved to Denver and began making "Mrs. Stover's Bungalow Candies." By the end of a year, they had opened five candy stores.

Their company grew, and in 1931 Stover moved the national headquarters to Kansas City, Missouri. When he died in 1954, Russell Stover Candies was manufacturing eleven million pounds of chocolates and other goodies a year. His wife sold the company in 1960 but the new buyer continued to use the Stover name. ■

Angry customer dials his own number

175 *Almon Strowger*

Inventor and mortician. Osage County, Rossville and Topeka. (1839-1902) Strowger taught school before he moved to Topeka in 1882 to operate a mortuary. He was frustrated there, according to some stories, because he believed a local telephone operator was in cahoots with his business rival. When Strowger wasn't called to handle the funeral of a friend, he was convinced the operator had directed the call to a competing undertaker instead.

After Strowger bought a mortuary in Kansas City, Missouri, in 1886, his telephone problems continued. He had trouble getting the operator, and sometimes days passed with no calls to his place of business. When Strowger stormed into the phone company office and complained, an executive agreed to look into his complaints.

It wasn't long before the telephone man discovered the angry undertaker's problem: when the wind blew through his business' open door, a metal sign hanging near his telephone was short-circuiting the line. But by that time the frustrated Strowger had begun working on a new telephone, one that didn't require connections made by an operator.

He showed his idea to the telephone executive who encouraged him to continue his work. With help from his nephew ***Walter Strowger***, a farmer and amateur scientist near El Dorado, Strowger eventually had a working model built by a Wichita jeweler. To finance the expensive proposition, Walter had to sell nearly everything he owned and get help from a wealthy El Dorado businessman, ***N.E. Frazier***.

By 1891 Almon, along with another partner, had gained a patent for his device. He had also moved to Chicago in hopes of locating backers to finance their telephone company. When they raised $50,000, the Strowger Automatic Telephone Exchange was formed and an engineer was hired.

A year later the company opened a telephone exchange in LaPorte, Indiana, outfitted with the new equipment. Chicago newspapers called the "girl-less, cuss-

less and wait-less" telephone a modern wonder. Seventy-five local subscribers agreed; today's telephone customers would not. To "dial" the number 62, for example, one had to punch the tens button six times, the ones button twice—and then turn a crank to ring the connecting phone.

The Strowger telephone also needed five connecting wires instead of two, more powerful batteries than the ordinary phone, and there was no way to stop incoming calls from interrupting calls in progress.

As other designers improved on Strowger's step-by-step telephone, however, it became the basis for more modern dial switching devices. When his health failed, the inventor sold the Strowger company in 1896 and retired to Florida.

Phone home

As Strowger's ideas were improved by others, more automatic telephones appeared. In Kansas, dial systems were used in Concordia, Stafford and Sterling about 1896 or soon after.

Unfortunately, the new technology didn't always work. In fact, some of the early dial telephones were replaced with old-style crank phones. Many small Kansas towns had operator-controlled telephones into the 1950s. ∎

Fun while it lasted

176 Francis J. S. "Ned" Turnly

Promoter. Runnymede. (18?-?) Turnly was an Irishman who wanted to teach wealthy young men from England the secrets of farming and ranching for a fee of $500 per year. In 1887 he bought land for his project near the small Harper County post office of Runnymede.

Ned's plans worked—for a few years. The young Englishmen arrived in Kansas with their parents' money, and the fun began. They held parties, polo, rugby and tennis matches, horse races and target practice. They even tried "foxhunts"—chasing rabbits and coyotes across the prairies. But when the British parents discovered their sons were spending more money than time learning about agriculture, they stopped the flow of funds.

That put an end to Turnly's colony. In 1892, he auctioned his belongings in Runnymede and returned to Ireland. When other residents moved away, the little town quickly disappeared. But as one of Turnly's young men wrote, "We had a good time while it lasted." ∎

Their photographs make news

177-178 Elmer & Bert Underwood

Photographers and photo news service founders. Ottawa. (1859-1947) (1862-1943) The Underwood brothers were born in Illinois and also lived in Iowa and Ohio. The family came to Kansas in 1877 while the boys were teenagers.

For three years Elmer took classes at Ottawa University while the younger Bert attended public school. Elmer then opened a printing office in Ottawa while Bert sold medical encyclopedias door-to-door in Cowley County. When he had covered the area with books, he began selling stereoscopic photographs and stereoscopes.

At that time the hand-held photograph viewers and sets of photo cards were very popular. A user clipped a rectangular card with a pair of almost identical photographs into the viewer, and then peered through its two lenses. Almost magically, the "stereo" photos appeared as a single three-dimensional image. Many families spent enjoyable evenings viewing illustrated plays, stories and travel photographs.

Bert sold the photographs and viewers so easily that Elmer decided to leave the printing office and join him. Soon they had exclusive rights from three major photographers to sell their stereoscopic photos in Kansas and Missouri. As the business grew, the photo publishers gave the brothers all the territory west of the Mississippi River.

By 1880, Elmer and Bert were officially the firm of Underwood and Underwood, headquartered in Ottawa. In 1884 they had a force of trained salesman on the road, and their selling territory extended across the United States. Soon the brothers enlarged their warehouse in Ottawa, and then built a supply depot in Baltimore, Maryland. As their business spread out of the country, they opened offices in Toronto, Canada and Liverpool, England in 1889.

Two years later they left Kansas and moved their national headquarters to New York City. At the same time, they began producing their own travel photos. ⇨

The Underwoods got into news photography in 1896 when Bert photographed combat action between Greeks and Turks fighting in Greece. He sent prints to Elmer, who was then in London. The *Illustrated London News* paid almost $300 to publish them, making Underwood and Underwood one of the first agencies in the world to supply news photos to newspapers and magazines.

By 1901 the brothers were producing 25,000 stereoscopic photographs a day and selling over 300,000 stereoscopes a year. They also established a very successful chain of portrait studios. Around 1904 they set up a separate company to fill the need for news photos. As publishers replaced woodcut and line-drawing illustrations with photographs, the Underwoods hired their own army of news photographers. They opened foreign branch offices in Paris, Bombay, Singapore, Shanghai, Manila and St. Petersburg. Underwood photographers covered wars, earthquakes, volcanic eruptions and shipwrecks, as well as presidential trips, royal coronations and discoveries in the Arctic and Antarctic regions.

Both brothers retired in 1925. Bert moved to Arizona, Elmer to Florida. In 1931 the Underwoods' company was reorganized into four divisions. For many years, their news photo division was said to have the largest collection of photograph negatives in the world. ∎

Grinds hard wheat

179 Bernhard Warkentin

Grain miller. Halstead and Newton. (1847-1908) Warkentin was born in southern Russia. He immigrated to the United States as a young man and, after living in Ohio, he moved to Kansas in the early 1870s. Bernhard built a grain mill at Halstead and helped bring perhaps 5,000 more Mennonites [*170*] to the area.

Warkentin is sometimes given credit for bringing the first hard, red wheat to Kansas. In reality, when he visited his native land in 1885 and brought back a car-load of Turkey Red seed to sell, the variety was probably already growing in the state. But Warkentin was the first to make it profitable to raise. He bought a mill in Newton and replaced its stone rollers with metal ones. (Before that time, Kansas mills were able to handle only soft kinds of wheat.) As he purchased farmers' hard wheat and ground it into high-quality flour, Warkentin demonstrated the advantages of the new seed.

Warkentin continued to promote Kansas wheat and became quite wealthy. Tragically, he was killed while he and his wife were traveling abroad. On a train trip between Turkey and Syria, another passenger's gun accidentally fired, and Bernhard was shot. He died later in a Beirut hospital. In 1989 Warkentine was inducted into the Kansas Business Hall of Fame. ∎

Sutler across the state

180 Theodore Weichselbaum

Trader and storekeeper. Leavenworth and Ogden. (1834-1914) Weichselbaum was born in Bavaria, now part of Germany. He came to the United States as a young man and worked as a peddler in New York City. Bavarian friends living in Ohio encouraged him to take his goods to the West. Theodore arrived in Kansas Territory in 1857 during the "Bleeding Kansas" period. For a time, he ran a store in turbulent Leavenworth. Eventually he moved to the small, quiet town of Ogden near Fort Riley.

Business there was good and by 1859 he had built his own stone building. The next year, he and a partner opened a sutler's store at Fort Larned. Like other post traders, Weichselbaum and his partner had a contract with the U.S. Army to operate a business at the fort. In return for an annual payment, the traders were allowed to be the only merchants at the post.

Weichselbaum was also a partner in sutler's stores at Forts Dodge, Harker and Wallace. He shipped goods in from the East on riverboats up the Missouri River and loaded his wagons at Leavenworth. But instead of pulling empty wagons back from the forts, he hauled thousands of buffalo [*382*] robes and sold them in Leavenworth for five or six dollars each. He also hired men to supply the Army with hay for its cavalry horses. During that period, 28-year-old Weichselbaum was married—to a woman he didn't know. His parents chose their son's bride and sent her from Europe to Kansas.

Theodore sold his interests in the sutler's stores in 1869 but continued in business at Ogden. During the 1870s he made and sold his own German beer. When the Kansas prohibition law against selling liquor went into effect in 1881 he closed his brewery, saying he lost $15,000. Weichselbaum kept his Riley County store open until after the turn of the century.

Samuel Weichselbaum worked in his brother Theodore's stores at Fort Larned and Fort Dodge. He was later one of the founders of Dodge City. ■

Makes hay balers while the sun shines

181 Lyle Yost

Farm equipment manufacturer. Hesston. (Born 1913) Yost founded the Hesston Corporation in 1947, with five employees working in a little quonset hut. He and a machinist friend designed the company's first product—an auger to unload grain from combines.

The corporation started small. The business manager was the pastor of Yost's church—and all he had for a desk chair was an orange crate. As sales increased, more products were added. Yost and his designers came up with over a hundred new devices, including straw choppers for combines, row-crop savers, and the first self-propelled hay cutter, or windrower. Hesston also built hay rakes and balers, sugar beet harvesters and potato harvesters.

By the mid 1970s the Hesston Corporation employed more than 3,500 workers in its Hesston plant and at other locations around the world. In 1975 it sold equipment worth over $200 million. However, sales dropped as the farm economy was hurt in the late 1970s.

In 1977 Yost sold his corporation to the Fiat Company in Italy. It was sold again in 1991 to an American manufacturer, Deutz-Allis. The Hesston plant still employs about 1,000 workers. It is operated in partnership with the J.I. Case Corporation, and is called Hay and Forage Industries. ■

HESSTON®

Their ideas make money

Durrell Armstrong, founder and owner of the Player Piano Company in Wichita, is one of just a handful of dealers in the United States who sells player piano rolls. He started his unusual business while still a high school student in the late 1940s. When he served in the Korean War, his parents filled orders in Wichita while Durrell handled his company's paperwork by mail in Korea. In the four decades since, his firm has shipped millions of music rolls to player piano owners around the world. ∎

Fred Bramlage, born in Junction City in 1910, served in the U.S. Navy before he became involved with a variety of successful businesses: banking, tire sales, real estate, oil and beverage bottling. Over the years he generously shared his wealth with a long list of organizations. Fred also headed the Kansas campaign of Dwight D. Eisenhower [*44*] for president and later worked to bring the Eisenhower Center to Abilene. In 1990 he was named to the Kansas Business Hall of Fame. KSU's Bramlage Basketball Coliseum is named in his honor. ∎

Earl C. Brookover, a Garden City cattleman, was a pioneer in the commercial feedlot industry. Early in the 1950s Earl demonstrated that feeder cattle could be raised economically in large pens while being fed a controlled diet. Brookover died in 1985, but thanks to his work and others in the cattle industry, Kansas is today a top producer of beef. More than six million cattle are fed in feedlots and on pastures around the state. The largest beef packing plant in the world is the IBP facility in Holcomb, just west of Brookover's hometown. ∎

Henry Call was a Topeka lawyer who in 1908 organized the Aerial Navigation Company of America at Girard. He funded his enterprise by selling ten million shares of stock—at a dime per share—to Socialists and other subscribers of *Appeal to Reason*, the Girard newspaper later purchased by Emanuel and Marcet Haldeman-Julius [*205-206*].

Although Henry operated what is believed to be first airplane factory in Kansas, he was not destined to join the ranks of Walter Beech [*134*], Clyde Cessna [*141*], Glenn Martin [*167*] and Lloyd Stearman [*173*]. His first aircraft looked like a "turkey gobbler with its wings clipped." Wind destroyed it in 1909, leaving Henry to haul away four wagonloads of junked aluminum and hundreds of yards of canvas. Fifteen planes later, he finally built a model that got off the ground—but it crashed after flying a quarter of a mile. A year later, in 1913, Call's company went bankrupt. ∎

Burton H. Campbell, an early-day cattleman, spent $90,000 and two years building a large home on the banks of the Little Arkansas River in Wichita. When it was completed in 1888, the impressive limestone mansion had 28 rooms—and a castle tower. Today Campbell's home, or Crumm Castle, as it is known, is the only castle-style home left from Wichita's 1880s boom days. ∎

Ellis "Skip" Cave grew up in Dodge City and graduated from KU in 1969. He then moved to Texas where he now works for Intervoice, a telecommunications company. Cave holds patents on fifteen inventions. In the early 1980s he invented an "OCR pricing wand" that reads the digits on price tags. Sears and other large retailers used the technology to automate records of their store inventories. Most of his recent inventions have to do with automatic dialing and other improvements in telephone communication—inventions that would no doubt amaze Almon Strowger [*175*]. ∎

Robert Eaton was born in Colorado in 1940 and grew up in Arkansas City. After earning a degree in mechanical engineering from KU in the early 1960s he was hired by General Motors. There he advanced to become a vice president, and then president of GM Europe in 1988. In 1992 the Chrysler [*143*] Corporation hired Eaton to replace the retiring Lee Iacocca as Chrysler's chief executive. ∎

D.R. "Cannonball" Green was born in Kentucky in 1839 and came to Kansas in the 1870s. After owning a livery stable in Kingman, he formed the Cannonball Stage Company based in Wichita. Pulled by thoroughbred horses, Green's Concord coaches traveled west and southwest to Kingman and Coldwater at "cannonball" speed. With a contract from his friend **Marshall Murdock** to carry the *Wichita Eagle* and government contracts to haul the U.S. mail, Green was soon making enough money to wear diamonds. His empire began to crumble when railroads built into the territory in the late 1880s. By 1893 he had moved on to Oklahoma where he tried politics. He died in California in 1922. Greensburg is named for him, and U.S. highway 54 west from Wichita is sometimes called the Cannonball Highway. ∎

Fred Koch got into business by starting an engineering company in 1925 with two partners. In the 1940s he established Koch Engineering Company and Koch Oil Company. Throughout his career Fred designed and built petroleum refineries around the world. After his death in 1967 his son Charles [162] became president of what is now called Koch Industries. Fred Koch was inducted into the Kansas Business Hall of Fame in 1992. ∎

Jacob "Jake" Moellendick was an oilman in El Dorado at the end of World War I. With extra money to spend, he decided an airplane would be a smart investment—it would allow him to move quickly from one oil field to another. But instead of buying just one plane, he ended up building dozens of them.

Jake convinced Chicago barnstormer **E.M. "Matty" Laird** and several friends to come to Kansas and design airplanes. Using Moellendick's money, they built Wichita's first commercial aircraft in 1920. It was named the Swallow when a bystander remarked during its maiden flight, "There she goes boys. . .just like a swallow." Laird left the company in 1923 and returned to Chicago. Oilman Moellendick stayed on, but he soon got into an argument with two of his employees. Walter Beech [134] and Lloyd Stearman [173] wanted to build modern planes of welded steel tubing; Jake said wood planes were making money, and overruled them. Both soon left and teamed up

with Clyde Cessna [141]. Today's skies are full of planes built by Beech, Cessna and Lockheed. How many of Moellendick's wooden Swallows still fly? ∎

Adolph C. Reuter enjoyed working with his hands as a small boy. When he decided he wanted to become a watchmaker, he literally camped on a jeweler's doorstep until the man hired him. A few years later he left his Ohio home to work for organ makers in Kentucky and then Illinois. There Adolph and several friends founded the Reuter Organ Company in 1917. Two years later they came to Kansas to install a large instrument in Lawrence. Local business owners encouraged them to stay, and they did. The Reuter company has remained in Lawrence ever since, and has built and installed fine organs all over the United States. From the 1930s into the 1960s, Adolph's son **Carl Reuter** was with the firm. ∎

T. Claude Ryan was born in 1898. At thirteen he saw an aircraft in flight for the first time as one flew over his hometown of Parsons. The experience led to a career in aircraft design and manufacturing. His family later

moved to California where Claude designed the first American high-wing monoplane. He also established the first year-round regularly scheduled passenger airline in the country. (Costs were so low that one passenger's $29.50 round trip

fare between Los Angeles and San Diego paid each day's operating expenses.) In 1926 Ryan built—in just three months—Charles Lindbergh's [21] record-setting plane, *The Spirit of St. Louis.* Two years later he founded Ryan Aeronautical Company, a major manufacturer of training planes, pilotless spy planes and other military aircraft. Ryan died in California in 1982. ∎

Tom Terning, from Valley Center, is a former employee of the Cessna Aircraft Company. Using old photographs—there were no blueprints available—he spent ten months building a replica of Clyde Cessna's [141] first plane, *Silver Wings.* Tom spent fifteen months testing the plane, but he luckily avoided having any accidents like the dozen crashes that grounded Clyde during his test flights. In late 1991, almost exactly 80 years after Cessna's first successful flight, Terning flew his wooden craft before a crowd at Wichita's McConnell Air Force Base. ∎

Ella B. Veazie was the first traveling sales agent for Alexander Hyde [159]. Beginning in 1896, she traveled across Kansas, Missouri and Nebraska, selling Hyde's Mentholatum, the "Little Nurse for Little Ills." After covering California, Oregon and Washington, she returned to the Midwest and attended the medical school run by Dr. Andrew T. Still [127]. Veazie then practiced osteopathy in Kansas City for a time, but eventually she went back on the road selling Mentholatum. When Hyde's company celebrated its fiftieth anniversary in 1939, Ella was a spry 88-year-old. Her only regret was that she was no longer a "traveling man." ∎

With Pen & Brush

Authors, Artists and Composers

Brings Kansas history to light

182 Louise Barry

Librarian, historian and soldier. Manhattan and Topeka. (1910-1974) Barry graduated from KSU and the University of Illinois. She joined the staff of the Kansas State Historical Society in 1936 as a librarian. Several years later she became head of the society's manuscript division.

Barry left Kansas temporarily during World War II and served in the Waves, the women's branch of the U.S. Navy. During her three years in the military, she became ill with a serious lung disease. She was hospitalized until 1947, and then returned to Topeka.

Because of her health problem, doctors said she could work just part-time, away from other workers. So, off and on for nearly 25 years, Louise did her work at the historical society only after the rest of the staff had gone home. During those lonely nights and evenings, she patiently indexed thousands of pages of the society's publications, researched the state's early history, and completed other historical projects.

Before her death, Barry wrote much about Kansas—over twenty articles and an impressive 1,296-page book, *The Beginning of the West*. Historians call Barry's labor of love the bible of early Kansas history. ∎

Draws 'Geech' in the dark

183 Jerry Bittle

Cartoonist. Wichita. (Born 1949) Bittle began drawing pictures as a young boy and got his first job as a professional artist at his hometown newspaper, the *Wichita Eagle-Beacon.* He left Kansas in 1975 and then worked as a political cartoonist for several years.

In the early 1980s Bittle created "Geech," a comic strip based on his memories of Wichita and Kansas. He sent his sketches to Universal Press Syndicate, a large distributor of cartoons. Even though its editors see several thousand new comic ideas a year, they liked "Geech" immediately. Jerry now has an eighteen-year contract with the syndicate—and millions of readers.

The cartoonist works out of his home in Texas. Because he feels he does his best drawing at night, he arranges his schedule to be able to work between midnight and 5 a.m.

Artie, a "Geech" character, sometimes wears a reminder of the strip's Kansas roots—a sweatshirt from Bittle's alma mater, Wichita State University. ∎

Keeper's artist

184 Blackbear Bosin

Artist. Wichita. (1921-1980) Bosin, a Kiowa-Comanche Indian, was given the Indian name *TsateKongia*, or Blackbear. As an artist in the 1930s, he sold paintings door-to-door for $1.50 each. He came to Kansas from Oklahoma in 1940 and worked as an illustrator for Boeing Aircraft.

Eventually he was known around the world for his Indian artwork. Blackbear's impressive sculpture, *Keeper of the Plains*, is a 44-foot steel Plains Indian at the junction of the Arkansas and Little Arkansas rivers in Wichita. Developers once suggested building a 300-foot replica of *Keeper* as a tourist attraction and symbol of the city. ∎

Legendary newslady

185 Mamie Alexander Boyd

Newspaper journalist. Humboldt, Welda, Phillipsburg and Mankato. (1876-1973) Boyd grew up in eastern Kansas. When it was time for her to go to college, she sold her favorite heifer calf for $17.50 and used part of the money to buy a new hat—and a train ticket to Manhattan.

At Kansas State Agricultural College (later Kansas State University), she met her future husband, **Frank Boyd**, a journalism student. They both worked in the college print shop, earning ten cents an hour. When Mamie later became ill with tuberculosis, Frank married her and nursed her back to health. Together they published newspapers in Phillipsburg, Mankato and other northwestern Kansas towns.

Over the years, Mamie became a Kansas legend in the newspaper business. She was a reporter, columnist and editor. She was active in community affairs and was elected president of several state organizations. Wherever she traveled, she proudly showed her Kansas heritage with a large sunflower pinned to her dress. She received numerous awards, including Kansan of the Year, Kansas Mother of the Year, and the William Allen White [**256**] Award for Journalistic Merit. KSU honored her with journalism awards, a dormitory named Boyd Hall, and a special seat at all football and basketball games.

At age 92 Boyd won first place in a statewide newspaper contest. Three years later she published her autobiography, *Rode a Heifer Calf through College.* She was still working for her family's newspaper chain when she died at the age of 96. ■

Writes of romance

186 Rebecca Brandewyne

Author. Wichita. (Born 1955) Brandewyne was born as Mary Wadsworth, but her legal name is now her pen name, Rebecca Brandewyne. Her family moved to Wichita when she was a baby and she later graduated from WSU with degrees in journalism and communication.

Before her first book was published in 1980, she edited a dental newsletter and was an executive secretary. Brandewyne has written over a dozen novels, mostly historical romances. She likes to create "tall dark heroes" like the characters she enjoyed reading about as a girl. Several of her books have been on national bestseller lists. ■

Pulitzer-winning poet

187 Gwendolyn Brooks

Poet. Topeka. (Born 1917) Brooks was born in Topeka and grew up in Chicago. She began writing poetry as a child, and had her first work published when she was thirteen.

When her second book, *Annie Allen*, won a Pulitzer Prize for poetry in 1950, Brooks was the first black woman to receive the award. For many years, she taught poetry and creative writing at universities in the Chicago area. After the death of world-famous poet Carl Sandburg in the 1960s, the state of Illinois made Brooks its poet laureate, or official state poet.

In the 1980s, Brooks was the first African-American woman chosen to be a poetry consultant to the Library of Congress. Gwendolyn now spends much of her time traveling the United States by train, speaking to college students about writing. To

encourage young poets and authors, she sponsors two literary contests each year.

In 1986 she was pleased to see one of her former students win the Pulitzer Prize for poetry. ■

Invisible character in 'Doonesbury' and 'Far Side'

188 Don Carlton

Artist. Fairway. (Born 1936) Carlton works as a finishing artist for cartoons. As an inker, he adds the final touches to comic strip panels before they are printed.

Since 1971, Carlton has produced the finished drawings for Garry Trudeau's popular cartoon "Doonesbury." Trudeau, who lives in New York, sends pencil sketches to Carlton over a fax machine. In the studio of his Kansas home, Carlton completes the drawings in ink, adds Trudeau's words above the characters' heads, and sends the finished work to Universal Press Syndicate in Kansas City, Missouri. From there, it is distributed to newspapers everywhere.

In 1991, Don began working on another well-known comic strip—"The Far Side." Carlton now adds shading to cartoonist Gary Larson's zany drawings. ∎

Hills' sage

189 Rolla Clymer

Newspaper journalist. Alton, Quenemo, Emporia, Olathe and El Dorado. (1888-1977) Clymer received numerous journalism awards and honors. He was often called the Sage of the Flint Hills for his essays about that section of Kansas. Rolla began his career working for William Allen White [**256**] in Emporia, and then edited newspapers in Olathe and El Dorado. Clymer was an active Republican and worked hard in Alf Landon's [**67**] campaigns for governor and president. ∎

Docs enjoy other arts

190 John Cody

Artist, author and doctor. Topeka, Larned and Hays. (Born 1925) Cody, who has a doctor's degree in psychiatry, came to Kansas in 1960 to train at the Menninger Clinic [**117, 119-120**] in Topeka. He was later a psychiatrist in Larned and Hays.

John's interest in art began at the age of five, when he was fascinated by a large moth and drew a sketch of it. He continued drawing and painting moths, took art classes in high school and college, and eventually worked as a medical and scientific illustrator for eleven years. His accurate watercolors of giant silk moths have earned him the nickname "The Audubon of Moths." In 1990 his work was displayed at the Smithsonian Institution in Washington, D.C. Dr. Cody has also written about a variety of subjects—from a biography of poet Emily Dickinson to a book illustrating human muscles. ∎

191 Don Coldsmith

Author and doctor. Iola and Emporia. (Born 1926) Coldsmith was a medic in World War II and returned to Kansas to work as a counselor, gunsmith, taxidermist and minister before he entered medical school. Don set up a practice in Emporia and enjoyed raising horses in his spare time.

His career as an author began in the late 1960s when he wrote a humorous article for a horse magazine. Soon "Horsin' Around" was a weekly column in several Kansas and Oklahoma newspapers. In the late 1970s, he wrote about his grandfather's adventures on the Santa Fe Trail. When publishers wouldn't buy the book, Coldsmith wrote a historical novel about sixteenth-century Kansas.

His starting point was an old Spanish bridle bit he found at an antique shop. Around it he wove the story of a lost Spanish soldier who lived with Indians and introduced the horse into the tribe's culture. *Trail of the Spanish Bit* was published in 1980 and became the first book in a twenty-volume series.

Although Dr. Coldsmith left his medical practice in 1988 to write full time, he is still staff physician at Emporia State University and teaches a writing course there. Coldsmith's popular "Spanish Bit Saga" has made him Kansas' most-published living author. ∎

Packs up his paint, pouts

192 John Steuart Curry

Artist. Dunavant. (1897-1946)
Born near a Jefferson County community that is now a ghost town, Curry studied art in Kansas City, Chicago and Paris. He worked as a magazine illustrator in New York City before a 1928 painting, *Baptism in Kansas*, brought him fame in the art world. Soon, his work was known internationally. Along with Thomas Hart Benton of Missouri and Grant Wood of Iowa, Curry became a leader in the art movement known as realistic regionalism.

At home in Kansas, however, the artist was almost unrecognized. Before 1937 he sold only one painting to a Kansan. Then a committee—including Governor **Walter Huxman** and newspapermen **Jack Harris**, **Paul Jones** and William Allen White [**256**]—asked Curry to paint murals on the second floor of the state Capitol. Suddenly fellow Kansans noticed his artwork, but not in the way he

had hoped. Many looked at his mural sketches and saw what they called mistakes: A farm woman's dress was too short and she was taller than a house. A cow's legs looked like stilts. A Hereford bull was too red. A skunk was walking with its tail straight behind instead of arched over its back. A pig's tail curled the wrong way while it ate. Curry tried to answer the criticism and even visited a hog pen to watch pigs' tails as they ate. But the arguments continued.

The project ended when Curry asked permission to remove pieces of marble from the statehouse walls. His work, he said, needed to flow continuously. But to his request, women's clubs said no. The state legislature said no. And as a result, Curry said no. The artist refused to paint the remaining scenes. Leaving his two completed two murals unsigned, he packed up his paintbrushes

and left the state. Curry returned to his home in Michigan where he died a few years later—of a broken heart, according to his widow.

In 1953 **David H. Overmeyer**, an artist from Topeka, added murals to the Capitol's first floor. By that time the Curry controversy had quieted, but the second-floor statehouse walls remained undecorated. Finally, nearly 40 years after Curry began the project, another Kansas artist, Lumen Winter [**260**], was chosen to finish it.

In 1992 the state senate honored Curry's Capitol murals with "belated, but sincere, appreciation." For the story of an artist whose most famous Kansas work is *Tragic Prelude*, it seems an ironic conclusion. Perhaps Curry's rifle-waving John Brown [**344**] would agree. ∎

Historical poet

193 Bruce Cutler

Poet. Wichita. (Born 1930)
Cutler was born in Illinois and came to Kansas in 1955 after working in Mexico and Central America. He taught at Kansas State University for several years and then moved to Wichita State University. During his 27 years at WSU, Cutler began the university's creative writing program.

Bruce has published eight books of poetry, most about Kansas and its history. In 1987, he retired from teaching and moved to Minnesota. ∎

Kansas storytellers

194 Kenneth Davis

Author. Salina and Manhattan. (Born 1912)
Davis grew up in Salina and attended Kansas State Agricultural College at Manhattan. In the 1940s, he wrote a biography of General Dwight D. Eisenhower [44] and worked for Eisenhower's brother Milton [103] at what was then called Kansas State College in Manhattan.

Davis has spent most of his working life as a writer. Even though he left Kansas in the 1950s, Kenneth has continued to write about his home state in essays and articles. Two of his novels were set in Kansas, and other books have featured Kansans. He has also written an important biography on President Franklin Roosevelt. ∎

195 Robert Day

Author. Merriam, Hays and Ludell. (Born 1941) Day grew up in the Kansas City suburb of Merriam, attended the University of Kansas and taught at Fort Hays State University.

Although he lived outside the state for many years, Robert returned to Kansas on regular visits and has used it as a setting for much of his writing. He now has a home in Ludell. Day is best known for *The Last Cattle Drive*, his 1977 novel about modern Kansas. Film producers once discussed making *Last Cattle Drive* into a movie—to be filmed, ironically, in Montana. ∎

Ex-pilot's career in art takes off

196 Ed Dwight

Sculptor. Kansas City. (Born 1933) Dwight and his sister were the first black students to attend Kansas City's Ward High School. In 1953 he joined the U.S. Air Force and ten years later he was the first African-American chosen to train as an astronaut.

Dwight entered a special test pilot training school in California but resigned from the Air Force in 1966. He was frustrated that he had not been given a mission in space. After leaving the military, he went to work for IBM as an engineer. His art career began accidentally when the company asked him to decorate a new building.

Ed couldn't find any pieces of art that he liked, so he created his own. Others liked his work, and today his bronze sculptures on Old West themes are known nationwide. Some of his sculptures of jazz musicians are in the collection of the Smithsonian Institution. He now lives in Colorado. ∎

Paints unpopular people

197 Jerome Fedeli

Artist. Kansas City. (18?-1902) While the state Capitol was being completed, Populist legislators hired Fedeli to decorate the inside of the building's dome. Using fresco, or paint on wet plaster, the Italian artist and six helpers spent three months painting elaborate murals.

But even before the paint had dried, Republican legislators began to criticize the artist's work. They were the most upset about his painting of sixteen women around the inside of the Capitol dome. Fedeli explained the mermaid-like women were Greek maidens linked together with garlands of flowers; the unhappy Republicans called them "nude telephone girls." Even after Jerome completed the project, the debates and arguments continued. Finally, in 1902, the Republican-controlled legislature ordered that the maidens be painted over. Artists from Chicago were brought in. They covered the ten-foot tall women with other designs—designs that cost $7,600, or nearly five times more than Fedeli had charged!

Ironically, the Italian-American was a Republican himself. He died shortly before his artwork was "corrected." Other decorations he painted in the Capitol remain, as well as examples of his work in Kansas City churches and other public buildings. ∎

Sculptors shaping the state in stone

198 Pete Felten, Jr.

Sculptor. Hays. (Born 1933) Felten was 24 years old when he discovered he was a sculptor. He says he began hammering on a stone for fun, and found a figure hiding inside. By that time, he had served in the U.S. Navy and spent a year at Fort Hays Kansas State College.

Using his newfound talent, Felten quit college and picked up a hammer and chisel. In four years he created over 150 works, most in his favorite medium, limestone. He now has pieces of sculpture across Kansas. Two of his largest creations are in his hometown. The *Monarch of the Plains*, a nineteen-ton sculpture of a buffalo bull, sits at the entrance of Historic Fort Hays. At the Fort Hays Experiment Station is a massive Angus bull he calls *Early Settler*.

In 1978 Pete beat out nineteen other artists, including Lumen Winter [**260**], for the honor of sculpting four famous Kansans. Today Felten's statues of Amelia Earhart [**13**], Arthur Capper [**34**], Dwight D. Eisenhower [**44**] and William Allen White [**256**] stand in the state Capitol rotunda. ■

199 Bernard "Poco" Frazier

Sculptor. Athol and Lawrence. (1906-1976) Frazier earned the nickname "Poco"—Spanish for *small*—as a student at the University of Kansas. He weighed just over 100 pounds and stood about five feet tall. After graduating, Frazier was an apprentice sculptor in Chicago for several years. He returned to Kansas and later taught sculpture at KU.

As his fame as an artist spread, Frazier was asked to produce pieces of artwork for hundreds of businesses, churches and public buildings in Kansas, Oklahoma and Missouri. His favorite subjects were Plains animals and people.

Some of his works were a challenge to complete. On the outside of the First United Methodist Church in Wichita, he created perhaps the largest —and heaviest—mosaic in the United States. The gigantic 72 by 24-foot scuptured design contains 70,000 clay tiles, each handmade and fired by the artist. It took three years for Frazier and his son to assemble the seven-ton project.

Several years later, the state government commissioned Frazier to sculpt large Spanish, French and American pioneers into the limestone walls of the Docking [**41**] State Office Building in Topeka. When workers inside complained that his hammering was too noisy, a judge agreed and ordered Poco to stop. The artist finished his project by working early in the morning and late at night.

He was also asked to design a statue for the top of the Capitol dome. Frazier suggested a fifteen-foot bronze model of the Roman goddess of grain. He planned to place the finished work atop the Capitol with a helicopter, but the idea was dropped—too expensive. Others felt it would have been too heavy.

Frazier's last project was a marble statue, *Justice*, for the Kansas Supreme Court Building. Just before he died, he finished a small version of the design and selected a block of marble in Italy. His son, **Malcolm Frazier**, completed the sculpture. ■

200 Robert Merrell Gage

Sculptor. Topeka. (1892-1981) Gage left his native Topeka to study sculpture in New York with the man who carved the faces of four presidents on Mount Rushmore, **Gutzon Borglum**. Borglum himself had earlier lived in Kansas when he studied art at St. Mary's College near Topeka.

Back in Kansas, Gage set up a studio in a barn behind his home. In it he created a well-known piece, the bronze statue of Abraham Lincoln that now stands on the Capitol grounds. Nearby is *Pioneer Mother Memorial*, also by Gage.

After he served in World War I, Robert taught at Washburn College and at the Kansas City Art Institute. In 1924 he left Kansas to teach at the University of Southern California. ■

Debuts in Kansas

201 William Gibson

Playwright. Topeka. (Born 1914) Gibson, one of America's best-known playwrights, began writing for the stage while he lived in the Sunflower State. A New Yorker, he had various odd jobs before he and his wife moved to Kansas in the early 1940s. She studied at the Menninger Clinic [*117, 119-120*] in Topeka.

There William joined a drama group. Working as stagehand, actor—and then as a writer, director and producer—he learned much about the theater. This, he later said, helped improve his writing. His first drama, *I Lay in Zion*, was written for a Topeka women's club. It was a success, even though the club voted to spend only $15 on the production—and the bill for typing Gibson's script was $14. He also directed the play, and had to be its star when his lead actor joined the military.

During Gibson's years in Topeka, the theater group presented two more of his plays. After he left Kansas in the late 1940s he wrote a novel. Then in 1957, his play, *The Miracle Worker*, appeared on CBS television. It told the story of Helen Keller and her teacher, Annie Sullivan. The story was so popular that he wrote two more versions, a stage play and a movie script. The play was produced on Broadway; the film won two Academy Awards. Gibson has written other plays, including *Two for the Seesaw* and a *Miracle Worker* sequel—plus many poems, short stories and magazine articles. ■

New Yorker

202 Jane Grant

Magazine co-founder and journalist. Girard. (1892-1972) Grant and her family moved to Girard in 1903. She graduated from high school there and then studied singing in New Jersey. She planned to teach voice in Girard, but moved to New York City instead. After writing for the *Saturday Evening Post*, Jane and her husband Harold Ross founded *The New Yorker* magazine [*378*] in 1925. She also started a women's rights group. ■

Flint Hills are hers

203 Zula Bennington "Peggy" Greene

Author. Bazaar and Topeka. (1895-1988) After an editor nicknamed her, Greene was "Peggy of the Flint Hills" for nearly 60 years. Readers of 25 different papers enjoyed her weekly columns about almost anything—her family, friends, interesting characters, animals, food, politics, the weather, current news. In the Depression of the 1930s, she and her husband left their farm and moved to Topeka. There Peggy helped start the Topeka Civic Theater, where William Gibson [*201*] later worked. For several years, she wrote scripts for a local radio station's soap opera, *The Coleman Family*, sponsored by the Coleman Company [*144*]. In the late 1970s, she played a small role in the ABC television movie *Mary White* [*256*]. ■

Strawberry Hill images

204 Mary Ann "Marijana" Grisnik

Artist. Kansas City. (Born 1936) Grisnik did not begin painting seriously until the 1970s. Her subject is the Strawberry Hill neighborhood, a section of Kansas City.

In the early 1900s, the area was settled by Croatians, immigrants from what was later part of Yugoslavia. Grisnik's grandparents were among those settlers. It is their heritage and customs she captures in her paintings. She signs each with her Croatian name, "Marijana."

When Grisnik started painting, she was afraid to show her art to others; she hid it under her bed and behind her couch. Now, Marijana has had exhibitions in Kansas, the Midwest and even in Europe. ■

205-206 Emanuel & Marcet Haldeman-Julius

Little book makers

Authors and publishers, Girard. (1889-1951) (1887-1941) Julius was born July 30, 1889. As a boy in Philadelphia, he once bought two ten-cent pamphlets at a bookshop. He enjoyed reading the little booklets and thought how wonderful it would be if everyone could afford the pleasure of owning books. Years later he made inexpensive books available to millions.

Socialism in Girard

After writing for newspapers in Chicago, Julius moved to Kansas in 1915. He worked for *Appeal to Reason*, a Girard newspaper that supported socialism, the belief that the public should own all land and businesses. A year later he married Marcet Haldeman. She was born in Girard, June 19, 1887, to **Henry Haldeman** and **Alice Addams Haldeman**, sister of the famous reformer Jane Addams. Marcet attended school in the East and was then an actress, but she returned to Girard to be president of her family's bank when her parents died.

Haldeman and Julius had very different backgrounds. She was Episcopalian; he was Jewish. She was a Kan-

sas Republican; he was a Socialist. Together, however, they believed in compromise. After their wedding, they combined their last names into Haldeman-Julius. They wanted to prove marriage was an equal partnership. Both were friends, by the way, of magazine journalist Jane Grant [**202**], also from Girard.

Pocket-sized reading

In 1919 the Haldeman-Juliuses purchased *Appeal to Reason* and its printing equipment. They continued the newspaper, and also made Emanuel's boyhood dream come true. They began publishing pocket-sized books with newsprint pages and cheap blue cardboard covers. The low-cost materials allowed them to sell their "Little Blue Books" at a nickel apiece. Their first titles were the ten-cent books Emanuel had bought years earlier, *The Ballad of Reading Gaol* and *Rubaiyat*.

In 1921, the couple wrote and published a novel, *Dust*. Using a cooperative approach, they composed the first draft together, made changes separately, and then combined their two versions into one. They later wrote short stories and another novel, but the Little Blue Books—over 6,000 different titles in all—were their most popular sellers.

Their small books were some of the first paperbacks ever published. Titles included reprints of classic stories, their own writing and how-to information—everything from *Alice in* ⇨

Opinions ahead of their time

The Haldeman-Juliuses were not afraid to express opinions. Some people called them radical "free-thinkers" and tried to censor their books.

However, many ideas the couple supported are no longer considered unusual:

voting rights for all, income tax, unemployment insurance, sex education, racial equality and child labor laws.

Some of Emanuel's most controversial writing was about religion. He strongly criticized organized churches.

A UNIVERSITY IN PRINT ★ ★ READ THE WORLD OVER — LITTLE BLUE BOOKS

Wonderland to *Facing Life Realistically* and *How to Tie All Kinds of Knots*. With sales of perhaps 500 million copies, the Haldeman-Juliuses were called the Henry Fords of publishing.

The couple legally separated in 1933 but lived in the same house until Marcet died February 13, 1941. A year later Emanuel married his secretary.

Several months after the multimillionaire publisher was found guilty of not paying income tax, he drowned in his backyard swimming pool, July 31, 1951. **Henry Haldeman-Julius** ran his parents' Little Blue Books business until the printing plant burned in 1978. ∎

Editor boosts Ike

207 *Charles Harger*

Newspaper journalist. Abilene. (1863-1955) Harger edited newspapers in Abilene and wrote for several national magazines. His writing appeared in the *Saturday Evening Post*, *Harpers* and *The Outlook*.

Although he could "take the hide off" his opponents with stinging editorials, Charles was also known for helping young journalists. One young journalism teacher at Fort Hays Kansas State College, Ben Hibbs [*209*], took Harger's advice and left teaching to begin writing full time.

Harger was a long-time friend of Dwight D. Eisenhower [*44*]. He helped in Ike's presidential campaigns and later worked hard to establish the Eisenhower Center in Abilene. ∎

Edits *Digest*

209 *Ben Hibbs*

Newspaper and magazine journalist. Fontana, Pretty Prairie, Kingman, Pratt, Hays, Goodland and Arkansas City. (1901-1975) Hibbs grew up in Reno and Kingman counties. When a local newspaper published his story of a fourth grade picnic, he decided to become a journalist. The ten-year-old liked seeing the words "by Benjamin Smith Hibbs" in print.

Outstanding in his field

208 *Stan Herd*

Artist. Protection, Dodge City and Lawrence. (Born 1950) Herd first gained attention in Kansas with his large outdoor historical murals. Now he is known across the nation for something even bigger—field art.

With the earth as his canvas and farm equipment as his brush, the self-taught artist produces artwork by the acre.

Since 1981 Herd has created field-sized versions of Kiowa chief Satanta [*374*], humorist Will Rogers, a vase of Kansas sunflowers, and a harvest still life. Most works have included growing crops to add color and texture. In 1991 he mowed and burned native grasses to make a field portrait of Lawrence teenager **Carole Cadue**—the daughter of Kickapoo tribal chairman **Steve Cadue**.

His portfolio also includes some eye-catching giant-sized ads—although he once poked fun at advertisers in his *Cola Wars*. In Kansas fields Stan has plowed and planted designs for the Kansas Wheat Commission, the KSN television network and a European liquor company that has used art by artists as famous as Andy Warhol. Another Herd design appeared in a music video.

In early 1992 General Motors asked Herd to cut a large Buick emblem in a wheatfield. He explained that Kansas wheat was months away from ripening. No problem, the company said. GM flew him south to work—all the way to a farm in Australia!

A lucky few have seen Herd's big creations from the air; millions more have viewed them on television and in magazines. ∎

After he graduated from Kansas University, Ben worked at several newspapers around the state and taught at Fort Hays Kansas State College. He left Kansas in 1929 to work for *Country Gentleman* magazine and later became its editor.

From 1942 to 1961 he edited the *Saturday Evening Post*, doubling its circulation. Before Hibbs retired he spent ten years as a senior editor for the *Reader's Digest*. ∎

His poetry is music

Poet and doctor. Gaylord. (1823-1909) Higley was born November 30, 1823, in Ohio. He came to Kansas after his first three wives had died and his marriage to a fourth was headed for divorce.

The doctor homesteaded in Smith County in 1871, where two years later he wrote a poem, probably in his home along Beaver Creek.

'My Western Home'

The six verses and chorus of "My Western Home," as it was called, gave the doctor's feelings about living on the prairie. Although no original copies survive, his poem was apparently printed in the *Smith County Pioneer* in 1873. A year later, the *Kirwin Chief* in neighboring Phillips County reprinted it.

About the same time, Higley's young neighbor, Daniel Kelley [**217**], set the poem to music. Nearly 75 years later, it was named the state song of Kansas—but first it was lost, found, and at the center of a lawsuit in a detective story.

In the 1880s and 1890s, Higley and Kelley's song was sung and enjoyed by many people. But as different singers repeated it, some of the words were changed. The first line in Higley's chorus —"A home, a home where the deer and antelope play"— became "Home, home on the range." It was under this title that a Texas college professor named John Lomax published the song in 1910.

At the turn of the century Lomax was interested in gathering folk music from the days of the Old West. During a visit to San Antonio he met a black singer who had worked as a cook on several cattle drives up the Chisholm Trail [**10, 165**]. Using an Edison recording machine, the professor recorded the old man singing several songs, including "Home on the Range." In a book of cowboy and frontier ballads he published, Professor Lomax called it an anonymous folksong. He had no way of knowing who wrote it.

Higley died in Shawnee, Oklahoma, May 10, 1911, so it is unlikely he had the chance to see Lomax's book and claim his work. Kelley couldn't have, either, for he died in Iowa in 1905.

FDR's favorite

For years, "Home on the Range" was just another cowboy song. That changed in 1933 when President Franklin Roosevelt supposedly said it was his favorite. Quickly, "Home" became popular. Since no author had copyrighted it, anyone could use the song without paying royalty fees. Many music companies sold printed copies and recordings of the song.

Then in 1934, a couple from Arizona sued radio networks, music companies, movie producers ⇨

and singers for half a million dollars. William and Mary Goodwin claimed they had registered the song in 1905 as "An Arizona Home." They wanted many years' worth of royalty payments for "their" song.

Detective work

The Goodwins' song was indeed copyrighted, but it was different from "Home on the Range" in several ways. To settle the argument, music publishers hired a New York attorney to investigate.

Samuel Moanfeldt soon uncovered Lomax's 1910 version of the song. He also received a letter from a Missouri woman who remembered singing "Home on the Range" in the 1880s. Moanfeldt traveled to Missouri and

Stolen songs

In 1949, Kansas historian Kirke Mechem [226], longtime secretary of the Kansas State Historical Society, revealed that other "songwriters" had claimed "Home on the Range."

In 1876 the Stockton *News* published "My Home in the West," a poem by a local woman. Only two words were different from Higley's poem.

In Dickinson County, neighbors remembered a "crazy old bachelor" who sang "Home Where the Buffalo Roam" in the 1880s. He said the song was his own. In 1882 a Colorado prospector claimed he wrote the words and music to the song. Another version called "Colorado Home" was supposedly written by a group of prospectors in 1885.

discovered many others who remembered the song from earlier times. He then went to Dodge City and found old-time Kansans who knew the song, too.

Soon the lawyer was led to Smith County by a letter from a lady whose mother had lived in Gaylord. There he met Daniel Kelley's brother-in-law. By memory, the 86-year-old man played his guitar and sang a version of "Home on the Range." It was the same version he had sung with Kelley's orchestra in 1874—the first time the song was performed in public, he said.

Moanfeldt's evidence proved the Goodwins had tried to claim rights to the song written many years earlier by Higley and Kelley. The lawsuit was dropped and the two Kansas men finally received credit for their work. Twelve years later, in 1947, the Kansas Legislature declared "Home on the Range" the official state song.

A Texas author?

The controversy about "Home on the Range's" authorship did not end when it became the Kansas state song. In 1974, CBS News broadcast an interview with a Texan named David Guion who claimed he had actually written the song.

Records did reveal a piece of music called "*Guion's* Home on the Range." But it could not have been the oldest "Home." Guion's version was copyrighted in 1930—over 50 years after Kansans first sang it, and twenty years after Professor Lomax recorded it. If that wasn't proof enough, how could the 80-year-old Texan have written a song that was then one hundred years old? Guion's words and music were so much like the original it was obvious he had simply published his own musical arrangement of the work first written by Kansans Higley and Kelley. ■

Sage of Potato Hill

211 Edgar Howe

Newspaper journalist and author. Atchison. (1853-1937) Howe founded and then edited the Atchison *Globe* for many years. As other editors reprinted his humorous comments, his reputation as an author grew.

Beginning in 1911 the Sage of Potato Hill, as he was known, published his own magazine. *E.W. Howe's Monthly* appeared until 1932. His articles also appeared in other national magazines, including the *Saturday Evening Post* and *Country Gentleman*. Howe published

many books, including his famous *The Story of a Country Town*, a novel about life in a small town.

Ed was always ready with a comment for any situation. When the Reverend Charles Sheldon [242] announced in 1900 that he would edit the *Topeka Daily Capital* for a week, Howe volunteered to take over the pastor's duties at Sheldon's Topeka church. Howe's son, ***Gene Howe***, followed his father as a writer and was a noted journalist in Texas and the Southwest. ■

Sculpts a fallen president

Sculptor. Leavenworth and Wyandotte. (1847-1914)
Ream was born in Wisconsin, September 24, 1847. She moved to Kansas Territory as a girl in 1854 after her father was hired by the surveyor-general in Leavenworth. The family also ran a hotel there, and later, one in Wyandotte. Her father's work eventually took him to Missouri, Iowa and Arkansas.

While she was attending a girls' school in Missouri, teachers encouraged her to develop her skills in art.

At the beginning of the Civil War, Ream and her family moved to Washington, D.C. When her father became unable to work, Vinnie—barely a teenager—got a job as a clerk in the post office. Her mother took in renters at their home.

Helping houseguests

Over the years, several congressmen stayed with the Reams. Other lawmakers often stopped to talk. When Vinnie told several visiting senators that she would like to sculpt President Abraham Lincoln, they at first laughed. When they saw an example of the seventeen-year-old's work, however, they changed their minds.

One of the legislators knew Lincoln and was able to arrange for Ream to visit the White House. During a five-month period in late 1864 and early 1865, she was allowed to work on a clay model in the president's office—about 30 minutes a day. Although she promised not to disturb him, Lincoln often shared his thoughts with the young artist. The Civil War was not going well. He was still grieving over the death of his son Willie. Ream modeled his sorrow in her clay.

On the afternoon of April 14, 1865, Lincoln posed for the girl one last time. A few hours later, he was dead from an assassin's bullet. Vinnie was heartbroken. Although her clay model was nearly completed, she did little more with her project until Congress decided to commission an official statue of Lincoln a year later. Sculptors from all over the country wanted the $10,000 job. In the end it was given to nineteen-year-old Ream.

Honored sculptor

Vinnie's request to sculpt the fallen president was perhaps accepted because of her visits to the White House. She was also supported by the congressmen staying in her family's boarding house, including a new senator from Kansas, Edmund G. Ross [**85**]. She was, at any rate, the first woman chosen for such an honor.

As she worked on her project in a basement room in the Capitol, trouble brewed upstairs. Lawmakers discussed the future of Lincoln's successor, ⇨

President Andrew Johnson. By the time Johnson was brought to trial by the Senate in 1868, Ream was in the middle of the controversy. Radical politicians believed Senator Ross planned to vote against impeaching the president. Some even visited the Ream home and tried to pressure Vinnie into helping change Ross' vote.

Political problems

After the final vote was taken, some of the same angry legislators ordered Ream's Capitol studio closed. They claimed senators who supported Johnson had planned their strategy in her basement room. It was not until Washington quieted down that she was allowed to finish her model. She and her parents then took the clay statue to Italy where craftsmen copied it in marble. The finished life-size Lincoln statue was dedicated in the rotunda of the U.S. Capitol in 1871—the same year the town of Vinita, Oklahoma, was named in Vinnie's honor.

A year later Ream received a $25,000 commission to sculpt Admiral David Farragut, a U.S. Navy hero from the Civil War. Although Ream's disappointed competitors criticized her once again, the admiral's widow supported the young girl and her work. In fact, before the statue was completed, Mrs. Farragut helped arrange Vinnie's marriage to Richard Hoxie, a young lieutenant in the U.S. Army.

In her later years, Vinnie Ream Hoxie taught sculpting to neighborhood children. She died November 14, 1914, and was buried in Arlington National Cemetery. Her impressive statue of Lincoln still stands in the Capitol rotunda. She is known to have completed over 50 other statues, including one of George Armstrong Custer [**351**]. ■

Dreams of racial freedom

213 *Langston Hughes*

Poet and author. Topeka and Lawrence. (1902-1967)
Hughes was born in Missouri, but because his parents were separated, he spent most of his boyhood living in Lawrence with his grandmother.

When he was six, he lived with his mother in Topeka for several months. Young Langston—like Gordon Parks [**231**]—learned firsthand about the unfair laws and customs of racial discrimination. When his mother tried to enroll him in the school closest to their apartment, the school board refused, saying blacks had to attend another school. She persisted and Hughes was finally allowed to go to the nearby school—where he often had to dodge rocks thrown by his white classmates.

At school in Lawrence the next year Langston and other blacks studied in a room apart from white students. He and his black friends could not buy ice cream in the corner drugstore. They could not attend movies at the local theater.

During his seventh grade year, Hughes was elected class poet; a decade later he published his first book of poems. By then

he had moved to Illinois with his mother and graduated from high school in Ohio. After dropping out of Columbia University in New York City he tried a variety of jobs: cook, waiter, doorman, farmer and sailor. He worked in Europe for a time and then returned to America and began writing. While working in a restaurant he left three of his poems at a table where the well-known poet Vachel Lindsay was dining. Lindsay was impressed with the young man's works and presented them in one of his own poetry readings. As Hughes' reputation as a poet grew, he won a scholarship to Lincoln University in Pennsylvania. After graduating in 1929 he published his only work set in Kansas, *Not Without Laughter*, a novel about a boy growing up in a small Kansas town.

In the early 1930s Hughes was a motion picture writer in Moscow and then a news correspondent in Madrid. At that time he was one of the few African-Americans able to support himself as a writer. He eventually completed twenty books, over half of them poetry. He also wrote short stories, essays, plays, song lyrics and an autobiography.

For many years, he lived in New York City's Harlem section. Although Hughes' work is full of the racial prejudice, discrimination and poverty faced by him and other African-Americans, he never lost sight of his dream:

I dream
A world where man
No other man will scorn;
Where love will bless the earth
And Peace its path adorn. ■

Reports from the front

**Newspaper journalist.
Bennington, Marysville,
Oketo and Junction City.
(1889-1967)** Hull was the first
woman in the United States to
become an accredited, or official, war reporter.

A beginning writer

She was born as Henrietta
Goodnough on a farm near
Bennington, December 31, 1889.
After her parents were divorced,
Henrietta lived with her mother
and stepfather in Marysville. At
school she was active on the
girls' basketball squad.

When she was fifteen her family
moved to Junction City. Her
high school teachers encouraged

her to
make
use
of her
writing
ability,
but she
was in a hurry to "be
somebody" and quit
school at sixteen. She
was apprenticed to a
cousin's husband as a
pharmacist in Oketo but
that soon ended.

Henrietta decided to go into
journalism after all. She felt a
career in newspaper reporting
would take her around the
world. When she applied for
work at the *Junction City Senti-
nel*, however, the editor hired
her as a typesetter—not as a
reporter.

Two weeks later, she got a
chance to try out her writing
skills. One of the regular
reporters could not go to a fire
and she was sent instead. The
editor realized how well she
could write and Henrietta was
officially a reporter.

At eighteen, she left Junction
City and worked for a time in
Colorado. In Denver she met
George Hull, nephew of the
city's mayor. He was twelve

years older than she, but they
were married in 1910. They
sailed for Hawaii two years
later and both worked for newspapers in Honolulu. Their marriage, however, did not work.
They separated in 1914 and
were later divorced.

She moved back to Denver
where she met and fell in love
with Harvey Deuell. The couple
drifted apart before they could
be married, with Henrietta
going to Minnesota. At the suggestion of an editor in Minneapolis, she shortened her pen
name. Henrietta Goodnough
Hull became Peggy Hull.

Society reporter
into combat

Until that time, most of her
newspaper writing had been for
the society columns or advertising pages. That changed in
1916 when she was working for
a paper in Cleveland, Ohio.

American troops under General
John J. Pershing were stationed on the Mexican border
to stop guerilla leader Pancho
Villa's raids into Texas and New
Mexico. Peggy was sent to cover
the story. She later wrote, "I
had always been idealistic
about the American Army and
when other girls were sighing
over love stories, I was stirred
by reading of the great military
campaigns. . . ."

In Texas the slender brown-
eyed blonde went along with
the troops on a drill. Even
though the march was difficult,
the five-foot, two-inch reporter
asked for no special treatment.
She wore an Army uniform,
carried her own equipment and
slept on her poncho unrolled ⇨

on the ground. That was just the beginning of her exciting career as a war correspondent.

Peggy was such a favorite of the troops that some of them helped her play a trick on Pershing. When word spread that the general had given up trying to capture Villa, newsreel cameramen were tipped off that the best photographs of the "retreat" could be taken at a certain spot. Soldiers hid the reporter nearby, and just as Pershing rode by, she appeared on her horse alongside him. The troops all cheered, the cameramen cranked their hand-powered cameras, and theater-goers around the world soon saw film footage of "American girl correspondent leading troops out of Mexico with General Pershing." The general was not amused.

Unfair treatment

Hull remained in Texas and worked for an El Paso paper. In 1917 she convinced the editor to send her to France to report on World War I. As a female correspondent, however, Peggy did not receive the same treatment as male reporters. Army officials felt they could not let a woman report from the front lines where the fighting was taking place.

She did, however, send American readers informative stories of life in war-torn France. With permission from General Pershing, Peggy spent six weeks at an artillery camp near the front. But male reporters were so jealous of her reports that they convinced Army officials to send her back to Paris.

Hull was restricted because she wasn't an official war correspondent. After she and several friends in Washington, D.C., pushed for the special designation, she received her war credentials in 1918. This made her the first woman accredited as a war reporter by the U.S. War Department. But her reward was an assignment in far-off, cold Siberia. She spent several months there writing news stories in miserable conditions, and then began working her way across Europe.

In 1922 she met an English sea captain, John Kinley, and they were soon married in Hong Kong. For over three years they lived on his ship and in Shanghai, but Peggy's second marriage was also unsuccessful. When she tried to return to the United States, she found that because of her marriage to a British citizen, her American citizenship had been taken away. She was furious, and began a successful fight to reclaim it.

Two more wars

Back in the United States, she met Harvey Deuell again in 1927. He was by then city editor of the *New York Daily News*, and they decided to marry. First, Peggy had to divorce Kinley in China.

She traveled there in 1932 and found herself in the middle of a conflict between Chinese and Japanese troops near Shanghai. Enjoying the excitement of the small war, she stayed to report for her future husband's paper. After her return in 1933, they were married and lived in a New York mansion until Deuell died six years later.

During World War II, 53-year-old Peggy returned to reporting. Once again she had to fight for war credentials. When the permission was granted, she covered fighting in the Pacific from the Marianas and Hawaiian Islands. During that war, as she had done earlier, the female reporter proved women could handle combat hazards as well as men. Even then, Peggy still suffered from discrimination. She was often assigned to small islands where male reporters thought no front page news was likely to happen.

After the war, Hull led a quiet life. The U.S. Navy presented her with a medal of commendation in 1946, and she later moved to California. She died in Monterey on June 15, 1967, and was buried beside Harvey Deuell in New Windsor, New York. ∎

Grounded by a wild flight

In 1918 Hull wrote about an exciting plane ride in France during the war: "The pilot brought out a little machine with one engine. It looked more like a mosquito than an airplane, and I had to be strapped in.

"I doubted the thing before we left the ground, and the higher we went the less I liked it. We flew back and forth over the target range and the French pilot kept nudging me and pointing below. I kept wishing he would mind the controls.

"[Suddenly] he stood the plane on one wing and began to spiral down—by the time I had caught my breath the earth was up here and the sky there. That was all I needed; I just toppled over unconscious." With that, the daring war reporter decided she could report just as well with both feet on the ground.

Setting: small-town Kansas

215 William Inge

Playwright. Independence, Wichita and Columbus. (1913-1973) Inge grew up in Independence and graduated from KU. Before he completed a master's degree in Tennessee, he was an announcer at radio station KFH in Wichita and a high school English, speech and drama teacher in Columbus.

In 1938 William moved to Missouri where he taught college-level English and drama. Five years later he moved to St. Louis. There he was a newspaper drama critic until he joined the faculty at Washington University for three years. His newspaper job put him in contact with several actors and writers. When he interviewed Tennessee Williams, the famous playwright encouraged Inge to write his own drama.

The Kansan took his advice and sent him a script in 1945. After Williams arranged to have it produced in Dallas, other local theater groups performed Inge's work. In 1950 his second play, *Come Back, Little Sheba,* became a Broadway

hit. Inge soon moved to New York City where he wrote a string of three more hit plays—*Picnic, Bus Stop* and *The Dark at the Top of the Stairs.* Each also became a successful movie.

The movie version of *Picnic* was made in Kansas in 1953, two years after the play won a Pulitzer Prize. Locations in and around Salina, Hutchinson, Halstead, Sterling and Nickerson represented Inge's fictional "Salinson," Kansas. It was the first major motion picture filmed in the state.

In the early 1960s Inge's screenplay for the movie *Splendor in the Grass* won an Academy Award. In addition to several more plays, he wrote two novels. In almost all of his writing, Inge used characters and settings from small-town Kansas. Although he often spoke of living again in his home state, he moved to Hollywood in 1963. He committed suicide there in 1973 after years of suffering from alcoholism and severe depression. ■

Pioneer writer

216 John Ise

Author and educator. Downs and Lawrence. (1885-1969) Ise enrolled in the University of Kansas in 1906, majoring in English and music. To pay his tuition, John played the piano at silent movies. After graduation he remained at KU and received a second degree, in law. Next he attended Harvard University and earned two degrees in economics. When he came back to Kansas, he joined the faculty at KU.

During the nearly 40 years he spent teaching, Dr. Ise was a popular professor and writer. His novel, *Sod and Stubble,* tells the story of his pioneer family and is considered one of the best books about early-day Kansas. An economics textbook he wrote was used across the country. Ise was also known for his strong statements about protecting the environment and the changes needed in education. ■

Tunes up state song

217 Daniel Kelley

Composer and carpenter. Gaylord. (1843-1905) Kelley came to Kansas in 1872 and worked as a carpenter in Smith County. In his spare time he played in a local dance orchestra.

In late 1873 or early 1874 the young musician composed a tune for a poem written by his neighbor, Brewster Higley [***210***]. Kelley and Higley's song became popular with local residents, and was often played and sung at dances and other gatherings. When the grasshopper invasion of 1874 destroyed crops in the area, the song we now call "Home on the Range" was a reminder of better times in Kansas. Kelley left the state in 1886 and moved to Iowa. ■

Oscar music

218 Gail Kubik

Composer. Coffeyville. (1914-1984) As a boy in Coffeyville, Kubik played the violin and enjoyed writing music. He was also interested in history.

Gail couldn't decide which area to go into until his mother entered one of his compositions in a state contest. It won first place; he chose a career in music. Kubik went on to publish over 60 musical works that won numerous awards. In 1951 his music for the cartoon movie *Gerald McBoing Boing* won an Academy Award. The next year he received a Pulitzer Prize for a symphonic piece.

Although he lived and worked in New York as an adult, Kubik kept his ties with his home state. He wrote pieces for special Kansas events and returned to conduct several concerts. ∎

Tops on TV

219 Bill Kurtis

Television journalist. Independence and Topeka. (Born 1940) Kurtis has been a national correspondent for CBS News and was a co-host of the *CBS Morning News* program for several years in the 1980s. He is now a television news anchor in Chicago. The young journalist began broadcasting at a radio station in his hometown of Independence. He earned a degree in journalism at Kansas University, but decided to go on to law school because he felt broadcasting wasn't challenging enough to be a career.

While Bill attended law school at Washburn University in Topeka, he worked part-time for television station WIBW. In the spring of 1966, he graduated from law school, passed the Kansas bar examination and was planning to join a law firm in Wichita—until Mother Nature changed his plans. He was on duty at the television station one evening when weather bulletins announced a tornado was heading for Topeka. The young reporter interrupted programming and warned thousands of residents to take cover. That experience, and his news stories on the deadly storm's damage to the capital city, convinced Kurtis to become a broadcaster after all. He has received several Emmy Awards for his reports on the Vietnam War and other topics. ∎

221 Jim Lehrer

Television journalist. Wichita and Independence. (Born 1934) Lehrer lived in Wichita and Independence until his father's small bus company went bankrupt. The family later moved to Texas where a high school teacher encouraged Lehrer to use his writing skills. Jim attended college in the mid 1950s and earned a journalism degree. After ten years working as a reporter, columnist and editor at Dallas newspapers, he began writing full time. He got into broadcasting with a part-time job at a Dallas public TV station.

Since 1975, Lehrer has been an anchorperson on PBS's award-winning newscast, *The McNeil-Lehrer News Hour*. He has written two books: *Viva Max*, also made into a movie, and *We Were Dreamers*, about his father's Kansas bus line. ∎

Draws life into art

220 Elizabeth "Grandma" Layton

Artist. Wellsville. (Born 1909) Layton is often called "Grandma" because she was in her sixties when she began drawing. A doctor suggested she try art as a therapy for depression. After taking just two drawing courses at Ottawa University, she began to produce works praised by critics.

She has had exhibitions of her pencil and crayon drawings in several Kansas galleries and art museums across the country, including the Smithsonian Institution. Through her art, Layton deals with current social issues—women's rights, AIDS, hunger, racism, censorship and problems of the elderly. ∎

Rescues Indian melodies

222 Thurlow Lieurance

Composer and Indian music expert. Neosho Falls, Chanute, Dodge City and Wichita. (1878-1961) Lieurance was born in Iowa and grew up in Neosho Falls. In the Spanish-American War, he was one of the youngest bandleaders in the U.S. Army. On the way to a post in Virginia, his unit—the 22nd Kansas Regiment —honored Kansas abolitionist John Brown [**344**] at Harper's Ferry. With Thurlow in the lead, the regimental band and troops marched around a monument to Brown, playing and singing "John Brown's Body."

After the war Thurlow taught at Chanute and Wichita University, and he also directed the Dodge City Cowboy Band for a time. He became interested in Indian music when his brother was in charge of the Crow Indian agency in Montana. Lieurance lived with tribe members, recording and studying their music. Although a wagon accident later disabled him, he continued his work. With help from the Smithsonian Institution in Washington, D.C., he preserved music of the Cheyennes, Taos and other Western tribes.

Lieurance wrote over 50 songs about Indians; the most popular was "By the Waters of Minnetonka." ∎

Sells shoes, then art

223 Roland "Kickapoo" Logan

Artist. Kickapoo, Leavenworth and Lawrence. (Born 1906) Logan, an artist born to Indian-Irish parents, received his nickname from his birthplace. After graduating from the University of Kansas, he worked as a trainer and coach at KU and at several universities in the East.

During World War II, he commanded a U.S. Navy ship in the South Pacific. After the war he moved to California where he manufactured athletic equipment and wrote a sports textbook.

Kickapoo had always enjoyed painting as a hobby, but he did not work at it full time until after he retired. His artwork is now recognized across the country. His favorite subjects are deserts, the sea, and farm scenes he remembers from his boyhood in Kansas. ∎

Popular novelist

224 Margaret Hill McCarter

Author and educator. Topeka. (1860-1938) McCarter was a former high school English teacher when she published her first novel, *The Price of the Prairie*, in 1910. For over twenty years her novels were widely read. She wove authentic Kansas settings and events into her stories of rugged pioneer days.

Margaret campaigned for years in favor of women's suffrage, or the right to vote. She made history in 1920 when she became the first woman to speak ⇨

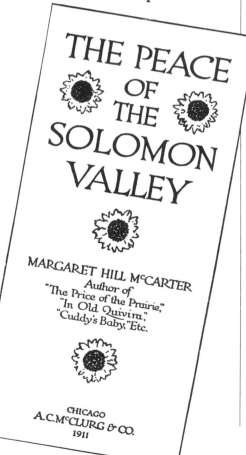

THE PEACE
OF
THE
SOLOMON
VALLEY

MARGARET HILL McCARTER
Author of
"The Price of the Prairie,"
"In Old Quivira,"
"Cuddy's Baby,"Etc.

CHICAGO
A.C.McCLURG & CO.
1911

before the Republican national convention. McCarter also made news that year when she registered to vote.

"Over 21," she answered when the clerk asked her age. Election officials, however, refused to give her a certificate. When Margaret asked for the Kansas attorney general's opinion, he agreed with her. "Over 21" was old enough to vote. From then on, voters have not been required to give their exact age when registering in Kansas. ∎

Historic writer

226 Kirke Mechem

Newspaper journalist and historian. Mankato, Topeka, Wichita and Lindsborg. (1889-1985) Mechem was born in Mankato and was a reporter for the *Topeka Daily Capital* and the *Wichita Eagle* before he served in World War I. Overseas during that time, he was editor of *The Jayhawkerinfrance*, a newspaper published by the 137th Infantry. Kirke later wrote many poems and short stories, as well as novels and plays. His play *John Brown* [**344**] received national attention in the late 1930s. Kansans remember him for his historical writing. During 30 years he spent with the Kansas State Historical Society, he was both secretary of the organization and editor of *Kansas Historical Quarterly*. Mechem retired in the 1960s and lived in Lindsborg. He died in California. ∎

Spoon feeds his readers

225 Edgar Lee Masters

Poet. Garnett. (1869-1950) Masters was born in Garnett and moved to Illinois with his family as a young boy. He later became a lawyer in Chicago, but had few clients. To fill his spare time, he began writing.

In 1898 Edgar published a book of poems, followed by several others. He had little luck selling his work until he wrote a series of free-verse poems for a St. Louis magazine in 1914. The collection, about persons in the fictional Illinois town of Spoon River, was published in book form a year later. *Spoon River Anthology* became very popular. It was eventually reprinted 70 times and translated into numerous foreign languages.

With his success as a poet, Masters gave up his law practice and moved to New York to write full time. In all, he produced a total of 53 books— including plays, novels, collections of poems, and biographies of Walt Whitman, Mark Twain, Vachel Lindsay and Abraham Lincoln. None of his later works, however, was as successful as his Spoon River poems. ∎

Honored moviemaker

227 Oscar Micheaux

Author and movie producer. Great Bend. (1884-1951) Micheaux lived in Great Bend as a child. After he left Kansas Oscar became an author and movie maker. In all, he produced 45 movies and wrote several novels.

When he made his novel *The Homesteader* into a silent movie in 1918, Micheaux became the first African-American to produce a full-length motion picture [**231**] with an all-black cast. In the 1940s, his book *The Case of Mrs. Wingate* was one of the first best-selling novels by a black author.

Today Micheaux is honored with a star on Hollywood's famous sidewalk, the Walk of Fame. ∎

'Air Capital' is his

228 Marcellus Murdock

Newspaper journalist. Wichita. (1883-1970) Murdock's first job was as a printer for the *Wichita Eagle*, founded by **Marshall Murdock**, his father. The younger Murdock was also a reporter and the paper's managing editor before he became its publisher in 1907. Under his leadership, the *Eagle* became the largest-selling newspaper in Kansas. Through his editorials, Murdock strongly supported the aircraft business in Wichita. It is believed he first coined the

city's nickname, The Air Capital of the World. In 1929, at the age of 45, Murdock wanted to take flying lessons, but Walter Beech [**134**] told him he was too old. That was all the encouragement the newspaper publisher needed—he took lessons and became an expert pilot. ∎

Paints nobly

229 John Noble

Artist. Wichita. (1874-1934) As a boy in Wichita, Noble loved to listen to frontier stories told by his neighbor, "Buffalo Bill" Mathewson [**369**]. He loved the West and made his first drawings of horses and cattle as a five-year-old.

John studied art for a few months as a teenager and then dropped out of school. He spent his young adulthood doing art-work for hotels and saloons across the Southwest. In Wichita he made newspaper sketches and worked for a photographer.

After the turn of the century, Noble traveled to Europe to do more studying and painting. In Paris he lived in an artists' colony and became friends with

several world-famous artists, Pablo Picasso, Gertrude Stein and Henri Matisse. He worked as a sailor and learned to paint the sea. Comparing it to his beloved prairies, he created several well-known seascapes, including *Toilers of the Sea*. In the 1920s he returned to America and produced works featuring frontier and prairie subjects.

Noble, who was always critical of his work, sometimes destroyed his own paintings. Once, while visiting in Wichita, he took a look at one of his early works and promptly set fire to it—as it hung on the wall!

When Carry Nation [**121**] attacked Wichita's Carey Hotel bar in 1900, she threw a rock at Noble's painting, *Cleopatra at the Bath*. But the artist wasn't upset. He called it bad art and said, "She may be terrible as a reformer, but Mrs. Nation has the makings of a great art critic." ∎

The secret behind V.I. Warshawski

230 Sara Paretsky

Author. Lawrence. (Born 1947) Paretsky is the author of a popular series of novels about Victoria Iphigenia Warshawski, a "tough-talking, but tender" private investigator.

Paretsky now lives in Chicago, but she grew up in Lawrence where she attended KU. As a child, Sara enjoyed writing poems and short stories. Writing was only her hobby, however, until New Year's Day 1979—just before she was about to complete a doctor's degree in history. Admitting to herself that she would rather be a mystery writer than an historian, she resolved to write a novel by the end of the year.

Dropping out of her history courses, Paretsky enrolled in a class on writing detective fiction. Her teacher was impressed with her work and helped get her first novel published in 1982.

At the time Paretsky was work-ing for an insurance company. When a national business magazine mentioned her successful novel, the chairman of her company became so jealous she decided to resign.

As a fulltime writer she has now published seven novels featuring Warshawski. In 1991 actress Kathleen Turner portrayed the detective in the movie *V.I. Warshawski*. Some critics, however, said the best version of the female private eye was still in Paretsky's books. ∎

Kansas' Renaissance man

Photographer, author, poet, composer and filmmaker. Fort Scott. (Born 1912) Parks, an internationally-known photographer, author, poet, composer and filmmaker, has been called a modern day Renaissance man. But unlike the Renaissance men of old, this multi-talented twentieth-century Kansan had to fight an army of racial barriers to achieve his creative success.

Miracle baby

Parks was born November 30, 1912, in Fort Scott, the last of fifteen children. His father,

Andrew Parks, was a day laborer and farmer. **Sarah Ross Parks**, his mother, worked as a maid.

According family stories, the Parks' youngest child barely made it into the world alive. At birth, the baby showed no signs of life until the doctor put him into a tub of cold water to stimulate his breathing and heartbeat. The grateful parents named their revived son in honor of the physician, Dr. Gordon.

Both Gordon's father and mother worked long and hard to provide for their children. They raised most of their food on land around their small home. As Parks later wrote, his family was terribly poor but he didn't realize it.

To the young boy, racial discrimination was a much bigger problem than poverty. Segregation, in those days, was a way of life for African-Americans in Fort Scott and many other Kansas communities. This separation of the races—in housing, businesses, schools, churches, and other public facilities—sometimes came from outdated laws and regulations. More often it grew out of feelings of prejudice, fear and unfounded hate.

Deadly racism

When he was nine, Gordon lost a favorite relative to racism. His older cousin Martin left Kansas to find work in the South. For several months the family heard little from the young man—until radio bulletins described him as one of the country's most-wanted criminals. He had killed two white co-workers after one called him a "dirty nigger" and spat in his face.

On a rainy night soon afterward, Martin slipped through a window into Gordon's bedroom. While Mrs. Parks prayed over her nephew and begged him to surrender, he gathered food from their icebox and disappeared into the night. Gordon could hardly believe what racial hate had done to the gentle cousin he once knew.

While young Parks experienced many ordinary boyhood pleasures, he also discovered "his place"—playing in the black neighborhood, attending the black school, and associating with black friends. Although

Gordon had a few white friends, even they were caught up in bigotry.

The summer Gordon was twelve his cousin Princetta, a fair-skinned girl with light red hair, came to visit from another city. As the two of them walked down the street, three white boys, thinking she was white, attacked Parks. They punched and kicked him to the ground before a white friend appeared and helped drive them away. The boy asked Gordon what had caused the attack and he explained.

"Idiots," his friend replied, "I knowed she was a nigger all the time."

Everything in black and white

At that point, racism began to eat away at Parks. He wondered why God had made some people black and others white. One troubling night he dreamed that he was white, but his skin was loose and flabby. He kept pulling and tugging, trying to make it fit. When he awoke from his nightmare, he realized he was stretching his long underwear—*white* long underwear. No one made black underwear for black boys.

As he searched for his identity, he saw everything in terms of black and white, and much of that was white. White angels and a white God at church; white heros in his school textbooks. It was his mother and handicapped brother who warned teenaged Gordon to put his emotions to work for—not against—himself.

"Fight with your brain," his brother told him. "It's got a lot more power than your fists."

Parks had to follow his brother's advice soon afterward. In 1928, his mother died

after literally working herself to death. Less than a week after her funeral, sixteen-year-old Gordon was living with his married sister in St. Paul, Minnesota.

Upside-down world

There he enrolled in high school, got a job clearing tables in a diner and joined a club for young black men. He was determined to make something of his life, but overnight his world turned upside-down. One evening shortly before Christmas, his drunken brother-in-law tossed Gordon and his small suitcase out in the snow.

A bitter wind was blowing, the thermometer read ten degrees below zero and with barely two dollars in his pocket, Parks had nowhere to go. He warmed himself in a nearby pool hall and then spent the night riding a trolley back and forth between St. Paul and Minneapolis.

After a week of working at the diner during the day and sleeping on trolleys at night, he had only eleven cents left. Early one morning, the conductor awakened him at the end of the trolley line. In the man's hand was a roll of bills he had collected from passengers. Gordon pulled out a knife, clicked open the blade and yelled, "Conductor!"

The man turned and answered calmly, "Yes?"

Shaking and embarrassed, Parks finally blurted out, "Would you like to buy this knife? I'm a little hungry."

The conductor told the young man to keep the knife and offered to give him a meal instead. Gordon, frightened and ashamed, refused the offer and ran away.

Although his sister secretly gave him food when possible, his situation went from bad to

worse. He lost his job at the diner when the owner was arrested. For a week he was a piano player in a house of prostitution—until he witnessed a murder and quickly left.

With enough money to stay in a boardinghouse, he found a room and returned to school. However, his grades dropped as he spent more time working than doing homework. Then he got into an argument with his landlady and once again found himself out in the cold. One morning on the way to school he was so hungry he killed a pigeon and roasted it over a small fire he built in an alley.

By spring, he had a job at a men's club. He had time to study and enough money to date. He met Sally Alvis and they soon made plans to be married.

But after the stock market collapsed in the fall of 1929, Parks again lost his job. He hopped a freight train to Chicago and found work as a janitor in a dirty, rundown hotel. When he tried to collect his wages, the drunken owner attacked him. They fought over the money, and Gordon knocked him unconscious. He left, taking only the money he was owed.

Music composed of trouble

Parks returned to St. Paul, where, by that time, his father and three of his sisters had moved. Having family nearby helped. He lived with one of his sisters, while he worked and attended school. In his busy schedule he also found time to participate in school activities, read, compose poems, sculpt, paint and write music.

Parks said later that music had been inside him since he was seven. As a child, he ⇨

didn't learn to read notes, but he often played the piano, trying to recreate the sounds he heard inside his head. As a teenager who had just broken up with his girlfriend, the music in his head echoed his feelings for her. His experimenting at the piano led to a love song for Sally, "No Love."

About the same time, the strain of Gordon's tough situation took its toll. He collapsed during a high school basketball game. Doctors said he was physically exhausted. They ordered him to quit school and his job for several months.

When Parks regained his strength he worked in the dining room of a St. Paul hotel. There he met several well-known musicians, and one agreed to play the young composer's song on a nationwide radio program. The broadcast of "No Love" brought Gordon and Sally back together, and got him a job traveling with an orchestra.

Unfortunately, the musical group made only a few stops before it broke up in New York City. Gordon was determined to stay in the city and become a composer, but times were hard during the Great Depression. All he received in New York was a word of encouragement from composer and music publisher W.C. Handy.

Parks left Harlem in the spring of 1933. He and a friend joined the Civilian Conservation Corps, a government work program for young men during the Depression. That fall, he married Sally in Minneapolis, and then returned to his CCC camp in upstate New York.

When he was discharged from the CCC the couple moved in with Sally's parents. Parks worked in a hotel dining room where he again met musicians and even had time to compose during slow afternoons. By the time Gordon, Jr. was born in 1934, several of Parks' songs had been played on radio broadcasts by the hotel's orchestra.

Powerful photography

Two years later he began working as a dining car waiter on the Northern Pacific Railway. On one trip he noticed a magazine article about migrant farm workers. As he studied the article's photos, he realized the powerful impact photographs could make.

During one of his layovers in Chicago, Parks watched newsreel reports of fighting between Japanese and Chinese forces. When he heard the photographer describe his experiences in shooting the dramatic film, Parks knew he wanted to go into photography. "Photography," he later wrote, "was the one way I could express myself about deprivation, about racial discrimination."

At the end of his run in Seattle, he bought a used camera for $12.50 at a pawnshop. After spending half an hour trying to load the film, he walked around the city taking pictures. On a wharf at Puget Sound he got so interested in photographing sea gulls that he fell into the water and nearly ruined his film.

Back home in Minneapolis, the film processor was so impressed with Gordon's photos that he asked the new photographer to set up a display in the store window. Soon some of Parks' work appeared in a St. Paul newspaper.

Parks continued taking pictures and studying about photography, but his read-

ing during free hours on the train angered the new head-waiter on the dining car. As the man loaded the "young uppity nigra" with more extra work to keep him away from his books, Gordon worked harder, and still found time each night to read. This angered the prejudiced supervisor so much he purposely bumped into Parks, causing him to spill bowls of hot soup. The men fought, and Parks lost his job a few days later.

About the same time, Sally divorced her husband. Unemployed and unmarried, Gordon lived with his sister in St. Paul. After several months he landed an unlikely job—a position on a semi-professional basketball team, similar to the later Harlem Globetrotters.

After a tour with the team, he met Sally at a party. Both agreed their divorce was a mistake and they remarried a week later. He again found railroad work, as a sleeping car porter on the Chicago-Northwestern.

Fashion photography

Meanwhile, a department store owner's wife arranged for him to photograph several stylish models. Parks quickly borrowed lights and other studio equipment. All

went well until 2 a.m. the following morning. In the darkroom, he discovered he had double-exposed every negative except one. Sally encouraged him to print the good negative, and the enlargement impressed the store owner and his wife. They wanted him to photograph more models.

With his photos on display in the store, he received more offers for free-lance work, but Sally had just given birth to their first daughter. Gordon was afraid to leave his good-paying job with the railroad.

That changed when a Chicago art center offered him an unpaid job and a rent-free darkroom. Gordon agreed with the understanding he could use the equipment for his own free-lance business. In Chicago, Gordon spent much of his time doing fashion photography, but he also shot portraits, landscapes and scenes around the city. In 1941 the art center exhibited some of his photographs. Based on his work, the Julius Rosenwald Fund offered him $200 a month to study photography for a year at a place of his choice.

Capital city prejudice

Parks chose to go to Washington, D.C. He wanted to study at the Farm Security Administration, the agency President Franklin D. Roosevelt had set up to help farmers stricken by the Great Depression and Dust Bowl. Some of the country's best photographers worked at the FSA and were responsible for the dramatic photographs of migrant farm workers Gordon had seen several years earlier.

On his first day in the nation's capital, Parks once again ran into racism. He was refused service at a lunch counter, ignored by white clerks in a department store, and turned away from a movie theater.

Gordon was anxious to document these injustices on film, but FSA director Roy Stryker locked the 29-year-old photographer's camera in a cabinet. First, he told Parks, put your feelings on paper. Next, Stryker had him study files of other FSA photographers' work and writing. The student photographer agreed their photos and written essays made a powerful combination.

'American Gothic'

One of Parks' first photographs for the FSA was equally powerful. He posed one of the office's black cleaning women with her broom and mop in front of an American flag. "American Gothic, Washington, D.C." remains one of Parks' best-known photos.

As impressive as his work was, Parks ran into opposition as the FSA's first black photographer. His friendship with white photographers upset other employees in the agency and some congressmen.

Before Parks' time in Washington was up, the FSA was shut down. Over the opposition of others, Stryker got Parks a position at the Office of War Information.

For two years, he covered a variety of OWI assignments. Then in 1943 he was assigned to document a squadron of black fighter pilots. Gordon spent several months with the men at their base in Michigan and by the time they were ordered overseas, he was considered a member of the squad. But he wasn't allowed to go with them—officials refused to send a black photographer on the mission.

He went to New York City, hoping to find work again as a fashion photographer. Editors at *Harper's Bazaar* magazine raved about his photographs, but told him their company was not allowed to hire blacks.

Thanks to his old friend Stryker, Parks landed a job with the Standard Oil Company. For three years he traveled for the oil company, documenting life in towns and cities in its territory. After Parks photographed the terrible situation of some Indians in Canada, he helped raise money to treat their sick children and educate a promising young Indian who hoped to return and help his people.

Photos for Life

Parks left Standard Oil in 1947, the same year he published his first book, *Flash Photography*. The next year he published another photo handbook. In 1949 he took a portfolio of his work to the offices of *Life* magazine. When he left, he had talked his way into an assignment—a photo story on a Harlem gang leader.

Although he knew no gang members, much less a gang leader, a friend in the police department helped Gordon meet Red Jackson, the tough teenaged leader of Harlem's Nomads gang. Within weeks, Parks had a graphic photo story on the violent gang leader, and the chance at a permanent position at *Life*. Parks refused the offer, until the magazine promised him an annual salary of $15,000. For the next twenty years, Parks' photos appeared in the high-quality publication.

He spent two years at *Life*'s Paris bureau and then returned to the United States to cover ⇨

the civil rights movement. When a white reporter refused to cover a story at a black Baptist church in Chicago, Parks not only took the photos, but wrote the story as well. By the early 1960s he was writing many of the articles that accompanied his photographs.

In 1962 the Harper & Row publishing company offered him $7,000 to write a book about his childhood memories. When it was published the next year, *The Learning Tree* told the story of Parks' youth in Kansas. Although written as a novel, it is autobiographical. Over the years, *The Learning Tree* has become an important work of black literature and is often used in high school literature courses.

Just before the book was finished, Parks married Elizabeth Campbell. He and Sally had been divorced a second time in 1957. In 1966 he published *A Choice of Weapons*, the first volume of his three-part autobiography.

In the movie world

In 1968 the Warner Brothers-Seven Arts company decided to film *The Learning Tree*; and asked Parks to direct it. As discussions with the studio continued, Parks became not only the first black director of a major motion picture, but the first black screenwriter and composer on a major film. He was also the movie's producer [**227**].

Parks hired more blacks for his cast and crew than most filmmakers generally did, and chose his hometown for the location of the filming. When some Fort Scott residents objected, director Parks and the mayor reminded them that the movie crew would spend perhaps $250,000 locally. Filming soon started. At the same time

the town held a special Gordon Parks Day, honoring the filmmaker in the same gymnasium where he had not been allowed to play basketball as a boy.

Some critics called *The Learning Tree* too nostalgic, but in 1989 it was one of 25 movies selected by the Library of Congress to go into its National Film Registry.

Shaft, the second movie Parks directed, was the first film about a black private detective. It was an immediate hit and MGM Studios quickly asked him to direct a sequel. For the 1972 *Shaft's Big Score*, Parks also wrote the theme song. Director Parks was proudest of his 1976 film, *Leadbelly*, but new executives at Paramount Pictures refused to promote it.

In 1973, Parks divorced his second wife and married Genevieve Young. Their marriage ended in 1977. Two years later Parks published the second part of his life's story, *To Smile in Autumn*; the third installment, *Voices in the Mirror*, was released in 1990. That same year he completed a ballet in tribute to Martin Luther King, Jr.

Parks continues to take photographs and has written thirteen books, including a collection of essays, a novel and poetry.

He is working on a variety of projects: a biography of a British painter, a movie about a black Russian poet that he hopes to film in Russia, an exhibit of his oil paintings, a sonata for his children, plus poetry and musical compositions.

Honored Kansan

Parks was honored in 1986 as Kansan of the Year, and was the first person to receive the state's Lifetime Achievement in the Arts Award. In 1988 President Ronald Reagan presented him with the National Medal of Arts. Universities around the country have given Parks over two dozen honorary doctor's degrees.

Wichita State University honored him in 1991 with its President's Medal—one of only four given in the university's history. Speaking in Wichita, Parks said, "This award means an awful lot. It's another step forward in my making peace with Kansas and Kansas making peace with me." ∎

Raising Cain

232
Nancy Pickard

Author. Fairway. (Born 1946) Pickard received a degree in journalism from the University of Missouri and worked as a reporter and editor before she started writing fiction. Nancy began her first book at the age of 35, and within six years she had produced six successful mystery novels. Each book in the series features Jenny Cain, who unwittingly gets involved in murder investigations.

Pickard lives near Kansas City and her husband manages a ranch in the Flint Hills. She used those locations as the setting of her 1990 Jenny Cain novel, *Bum Steer*. It was her first book set in Kansas. ∎

'With a pen he was a king'

233 Noble L. Prentis

Newspaper journalist and historian. Topeka, Lawrence, Junction City, Atchison and Newton. (1839-1900) Prentis was born in Illinois but lived with relatives in the Northeast after his parents died of cholera.

At the age of eighteen Noble became an apprentice to a printer and soon moved back to Illinois. There, at the beginning of the Civil War, Prentis and several friends decided to enlist in the U.S. Army.

At the recruiter's office, his six companions were accepted immediately—but Prentis was turned down because he didn't measure up to the Army's height standards. He was finally allowed to join after he convinced an officer he could fight for his country even if he wasn't "eight feet high."

After the war Prentis published newspapers in Missouri and Illinois. He later came to Kansas to help a friend run a newspaper in Topeka. From 1869 to 1890, he worked for and edited newspapers in several Kansas towns. He then joined the staff of the *Kansas City Star*.

He wrote several books and was best known for *History of Kansas*, a textbook used in Kansas schools for many years. When Prentis died an editor wrote, "On all practical matters he was as helpless as a child; with a pen he was a king." ∎

Composes himself

234
Carl Preyer

Composer. Baldwin and Lawrence. (1863-1947) Preyer came to Kansas from Germany in 1887 and taught at Baker University. He was later a professor of piano at the University of Kansas for many years. Preyer is known for the piano and violin pieces he composed. His piece for piano, "Concertstueck," was performed by the Chicago Symphony. ∎

His diary is history

235 Samuel J. Reader

Author. Topeka. (1836-1914) Reader kept a diary from the age of thirteen until almost the day he died. When he moved to Kansas Territory with his family in 1855, his diary's words and pencil sketches began to include accounts of the Bleeding Kansas conflict. During the Civil War, Samuel took his diary along when he joined the 2nd Kansas State Militia. In 1864 his unit was part of a force that tried to stop a Confederate invasion of Missouri. The 300 Kansans were greatly outnumbered by Major General Sterling Price's troops, and Reader was among 68 Union soldiers who were captured. After a three-day forced march toward southern Missouri, 28-year-old Reader managed to escape and found shelter with a Kansas farmer. He eventually turned himself over to a cavalry troop, using his diary to prove his identity. Years later, Reader added watercolor paintings to his fourteen-volume diary. Today it is an important record of early days in Kansas. ∎

Cartoonist's pen is mighty

236 Albert T. Reid

Cartoonist and composer. Concordia, Clyde, Lawrence, Salina, Topeka and Leavenworth. (1873-1958)
As a young man, Reid couldn't decide whether to become an artist or a musician, for he was talented in both areas. He wanted to follow his interests at Kansas University, but was unable to afford the tuition costs. Instead, Albert audited, or sat in on, a few classes at the university while he taught at a local business school. He also taught at Kansas Wesleyan University in Salina.

Reid then tried to get an artist's job at several newspapers, but he was unsuccessful and returned to his hometown of Clyde. He was working in a bank there in 1896 when publisher Arthur Capper [**34**] sponsored a contest for the best political cartoon by a Kansas artist. Reid was almost too discouraged to try, but at the urging of his brother, he entered—and won. For his cartoon of **John Leedy**, the Populist candidate for governor, the young artist received a $15 prize and a job at Capper's *Mail and Breeze*.

Reid eventually worked for newspapers in Kansas City, Chicago and New York. At the same time, he contributed cartoons to Capper's paper. Some of his work also appeared in national magazines like the *Saturday Evening Post*. Albert returned to Kansas in 1902 and soon started a daily newspaper in Leavenworth. For several years he was an active booster of Kansas. He also found time to compose several band numbers, one of which was played by the great bandmaster John Philip Sousa. Reid moved to New York in 1919 to take charge of publicity for the Republicans' national election campaign. He drew political cartoons until the mid 1930s and spent his retirement painting and teaching. ■

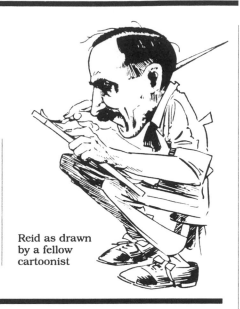

Reid as drawn by a fellow cartoonist

Paints a swath across Butler County

237 Frederic Remington

Artist and sculptor. Butler County. (1861-1909) Remington, who later became a world-famous Western artist, lived in Butler County during 1883 and early 1884. He had dropped out of his art classes at Yale University and traveled west in hopes of improving his health. Taking a friend's advice, he bought 160 acres south of Peabody.

The friend wanted Remington to go into the sheep business, but when the artist first saw "brown Kansas"—and discovered how sheep smelled—he holed up in the Peabody hotel.

Eventually the young New Yorker moved out to his ranch. Although he bought sheep, cattle and some horses, he was a "holiday" stockman. His hired hands did much of the work, while he cooked and helped with a few chores. Frederic spent most of his time having fun. On his favorite horse, Terra Cotta, he rode through the Flint Hills and practiced his roping skills on sunflowers. And he filled a sketchbook—plus the walls of his ranch house—with drawings of animals, neighbors, ranch scenes and Kansas landscapes.

Remington and several other bachelors also had time to get into trouble. The young men

celebrated Halloween by putting a cow inside a country church —and a buggy on the roof!

On Christmas Eve, they interrupted a local celebration by tossing paperwads. When authorities threw them out, they set fire to a box of straw outside the door. The crowd bailed out the windows—except for one large woman who got stuck halfway through. When the "gang" was brought to trial, the jury couldn't agree on a verdict. Remington paid the court costs and they were all freed. Soon he sold his land and left Kansas.

For a few months in 1884 Frederic ran a saloon in Kansas City. There he sold his first Western

sketches. Although he returned to New York and married, he continued to visit the West, riding with cowboys, living in Army barracks, and even hunting for a lost gold mine.

During his career, he used his experiences in Kansas and other parts of the West to help create bronze sculptures and more than 2,700 paintings and drawings of Indians, scouts, trappers, cowboys and soldiers. Today Remington's famous pieces of artwork and sculpture are considered some of the most accurate representations of the Old West. They are also some of the most valuable. ■

Broadcaster

239 Hughes Rudd

Television journalist. Wichita. (1921-1992) Rudd was born in Wichita and grew up in Texas. He attended the University of Missouri and served in World War II before working for the *Kansas City Star.* In 1959 he joined CBS News and reported from Europe, Asia, Africa and the anchor desk of the *CBS Morning News.* (He was the first of two Kansas-born newsmen [*219*] in that seat.) In 1979 he moved to ABC News; his reports appeared on *World News Tonight* and *20-20.* Although he covered serious news, Rudd was known for his humorous reports full of irony. He retired in 1986 and was living in France when he died. ■

Fine artist

238 Charles Rogers

Artist. Great Bend, Lindsborg and Ellsworth. (1911-1987) Rogers grew up wanting to be an artist, but when he graduated from high school during the Great Depression of the 1930s, he couldn't afford to go to college. For nearly six years Charles rode freight trains around the country, visiting art galleries and sketching each day, and sleeping on the ground at night. What he learned about art helped him win a scholarship to the National Academy of Art in New York.

Rogers later returned to Kansas and studied under Birger Sandzén [*241*] at Bethany College. When Sandzén retired, Rogers took his place. He is remembered for his paintings of Indians, Kansas landscapes and the Pacific Coast. ■

Writes in 'Runyonese'

240 Damon Runyon

Author and journalist. Manhattan, Clay Center and Wellington. (1884-1946) Runyon's father edited newspapers in several Kansas towns. At age fourteen young Damon ran away from home to serve in the Spanish-American War. When he returned, he wrote for newspapers in Denver and San Francisco. He covered the Mexican Revolution in 1912 and then World War I. By the 1930s he was living in New York and writing short stories about life along Broadway. He also wrote several movie scripts. Many of Runyon's characters spoke in a colorful city dialect that critics called "Runyonese." *Guys and Dolls,* perhaps his most famous story, later became a hit Broadway musical and a successful movie. ■

Paints his way into the heart of Kansas

Artist and educator. Lindsborg. (1871-1954)
Sandzén has been called the dean of Kansas artists. But today, outside of his adopted state, his work is often overlooked in the art world.

During his lifetime, however, Sandzén's paintings, drawings and prints were exhibited in the Library of Congress and in major art galleries across the United States, France, England

and his native Sweden. It was there in the town of Blidsberg that he was born, February 5, 1871.

Young at art

Sandzén grew up in a home where fine arts were important. His father, a Lutheran minister, played the violin and wrote poetry; his mother was an artist. Birger's own art talent appeared while he was very young. He watched his older brothers draw by tracing pictures out of books at the window, but he wasn't satisfied with that kind of drawing. He wanted to create art on his own.

Birger took informal art lessons for a time, and then his parents hired a drawing master, or expert, to instruct him. The teacher was strict, but in a fatherly way he taught ten-year-old Sandzén basic drawing techniques.

The young artist later enrolled at a nearby university where he was a student of French and aesthetics, the study of how people respond to beauty. The university had no art classes, however, so he left home to study with famous European artists Anders Zorn in Stockholm and Aman-Jean in Paris.

A challenge to visit Kansas

It was after Birger returned to Sweden that he decided to come to Kansas. He read a book by **Carl Aaron Swensson**, the president of Bethany College in Lindsborg. Dr. Swensson wrote of his struggles at the small Lutheran school on the Plains. He ended with a challenge to young Swedes: Come to Kansas and help at the college.

It was an offer 23-year-old Sandzén couldn't resist. He had enjoyed meeting American students while he studied in Paris, and he had been fascinated with American Indians since he was a boy. He wanted to visit the United States and experience the Plains for himself.

When he arrived in Lindsborg in the fall of 1894 he planned to stay only a year or two; he remained for the rest of his life.

Talent to spare

Young Sandzén was talented in many areas. In addition to his art abilities, he spoke six languages—Swedish, English, French, Spanish, German and Latin. He could lecture in art history and aesthetics. He had studied music and could play the piano. He also had interests in botany and geology. And his talents didn't go to waste at Bethany. He taught language and art history in the morning, painting and drawing in the afternoon—and for several years he held evening classes in his home. After his busy days ended at nine or ten each night, he relaxed by making charcoal drawings.

For many years he shared his musical talent by singing tenor solos with the Bethany Oratorio Society, known across the country for its Easter presentation of Handel's *Messiah*. He regularly wrote articles for Swedish-American newspapers. He also shared his knowledge about Chinese culture and Swedish archaeology.

Power in primary colors

In 1900 Sandzén married **Alfrida Leksell**, a pianist from McPherson and a former

Bethany student. By that time he was chairman of the college's art department. After work, in his studio at their home, he painted wildflowers, portraits, and his favorite subjects—powerful landscapes from Kansas and other western states.

Sandzén believed the most important element in art is order. That idea shows in each painting's careful composition, and in the way he kept colors separate from one other. Using wide brush strokes and bright shades of red, orange, yellow, blue, violet and green, he filled his canvases with towering rock formations, dramatic skies and silhouetted trees.

Some of his works were large—from four by five feet, up to six by eight. Birger generously donated many of them to schools and libraries around Kansas.

In addition to his oils and watercolors, Sandzén was known for his woodcuts and lithographs—ink prints made from designs carved in wood, stone or metal plates.

To gather new ideas and keep his work fresh, he taught and painted almost every summer at colleges and universities across the West. He also made sketches as he visited Mexico and Europe.

The rest of the time, along with his teaching duties, he traveled the Midwest, giving talks and art shows in libraries, schools, churches and rented halls. He had exhibits at major art galleries in Santa Fe, Chicago and Los Angeles.

After an important New York City exhibition in 1922, art critics raved: "Birger Sandzén has become the only painter of the great West who can fitly translate its forms and charm." "He surpasses all expectations of ▷

what such landscapes should be. . . ." "All the reports of [Birger Sandzén's art]. . .are more than justified."

The American-Scandinavian Foundation telegraphed the artist in Lindsborg, offering to send a plane to take him to the festivities in New York. "I am sorry. I have classes and cannot leave," he wired back.

Royal honors

Over the years, he gave a similar answer when many important schools and universities offered him prestigious positions. Each time the modest professor chose to remain in his beloved Lindsborg.

During his 52 years at Bethany, Sandzén received numerous awards and honors from organizations around the country. In 1940 the king of Sweden knighted the adopted Kansan in recognition of his artwork and his regard for his fellow man.

After Sandzén retired from teaching he continued painting and printmaking into his eighties. By the time he died on June 19, 1954, he had produced over 3,500 paintings, drawings, lithographs and woodcuts.

Sandzén's only child, **Margaret Sandzén Greenough**, studied art in New York and Paris, and still lives in Lindsborg. In the mid 1950s she and her husband **Charles Greenough**, a Bethany staff member, worked to establish the Birger Sandzén Memorial Art Gallery at the college.

She was honored for her efforts in 1991 when she received the Royal Order of the North Star by order of the Swedish king. Sweden's ambassador to the United States traveled to Lindsborg to give her the medallion. ■

Good news preacher makes his own headlines

242 Charles M. Sheldon

Author and minister. Topeka. (1857-1946) Sheldon came to Topeka in 1889 as a Congregationalist minister.

One of the Reverend Sheldon's biggest concerns was the needs of the poor. Several times he disguised himself in tattered clothing to see firsthand life on the "other side of the tracks."

What he saw in the Tennesseetown section of Topeka especially upset him—several thousand ex-slaves and their families living in almost unbelievable poverty. Determined to improve their lives, Pastor Sheldon started a variety of projects: a kindergarten, nursery, library, mothers' league, Sunday school, art and music classes, cleanup campaigns, plus free medical care and legal assistance. He later arranged for a graduate of his kindergarten, **Elisha Scott**, to attend law school at Washburn University. Scott became a leading Topeka attorney. His son, **Charles Sheldon Scott**, argued the winning side of *Brown vs. Topeka Board of Education* [**94, 100**] before the U.S. Supreme Court in 1953.

In 1897 Sheldon published a novel based on a series of popular sermons he had delivered. *In His Steps*, the story of modern characters who decide to live as Jesus would, quickly became a bestseller. It remains, in fact, perhaps the all-time bestselling book by a Kansas author. Because several versions were printed without a copyright, however, there is no way to know how many million copies have been sold.

The novel made Sheldon's name a household word. By the turn of the century he was one of the best-known Kansans in the United States.

Hold the phone

In 1901, Pastor Sheldon gave perhaps the first "broadcast" speech in Kansas history. Speaking by telephone from Topeka, he addressed a men's church group in Kansas City.

Seventy-five old-fashioned phone receivers decorated the banquet tables, and each of the listeners had to hold one to his ear in order to hear. According to news-paper accounts, the Kansas City men heard Sheldon in "perfect distinctness"—but holding the phones during the long speech was "somewhat tiresome."

At the height of his popularity, the Topeka minister decided that newspapers were "coarse and not uplifting." When he argued that readers deserved better, the *Topeka Daily Capital* gave him a chance to prove his point. For nearly a week in the spring of 1900, the *Capital* editor allowed Sheldon to edit the paper as he chose.

In doing so Sheldon made national headlines of his own. For six days the Reverend Editor Sheldon printed only news stories that he felt were positive. He cut out or downplayed what he felt were tragic and sensational articles. The temporary editor also refused to publish reports on the theater, politics and "brutal" sports.

At first, his experiment appeared to be a success. For nearly a week, the *Capital* sold over 360,000 copies a day, including editions printed in Chicago, New York City and London. Sheldon donated his $5,000 of the profit to charity.

But at the competing paper, the Topeka *State Journal*, circulation also increased. Thousands of Sheldon's readers bought the *Journal* to read what he had censored from the *Capital*. And within a year, the *Capital* was in financial trouble. Angry advertisers refused to support the newspaper because Sheldon had canceled their ads for theaters, patent medicines, tobacco and other "sinful" products. Arthur Capper [**34**] bought the *Capital* just before it went bankrupt.

While Sheldon didn't edit any more newspapers, he did publish several more books. He also continued to support various social reforms, including rights for women, the working class and minorities. He was also an important spokesman for the prohibition movement.

Other Charles M. Sheldon's gift tops them all

Interestingly, another *Charles M. Sheldon* worked in Topeka during the time the Reverend Sheldon ministered there. The other Sheldon was a Kansas City newspaper editor who was elected to the Kansas Senate in 1900.

In those days, the legislative session often ended with gift-giving—senators and representatives voting to present chairs, desks and other statehouse furniture to retiring members, staff and employees. To show the silliness of the costly custom, state senator

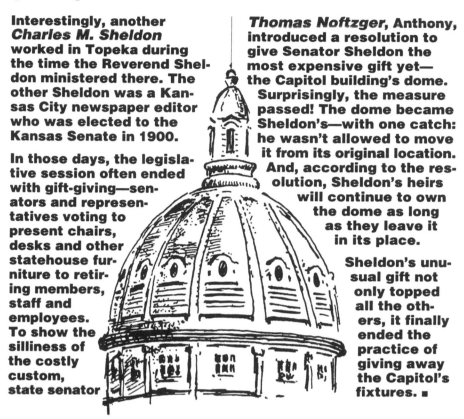

Thomas Noftzger, Anthony, introduced a resolution to give Senator Sheldon the most expensive gift yet—the Capitol building's dome. Surprisingly, the measure passed! The dome became Sheldon's—with one catch: he wasn't allowed to move it from its original location. And, according to the resolution, Sheldon's heirs will continue to own the dome as long as they leave it in its place.

Sheldon's unusual gift not only topped all the others, it finally ended the practice of giving away the Capitol's fixtures. ∎

Native American musician

243 Charles Skilton

Composer and educator. Lawrence. (1868-1941) Skilton was born in New England and studied music in Berlin and New York City before he came to Kansas in 1903. As a professor of organ and music theory at the University of Kansas, he taught his students that composers should write music about their own country. Working with Indian students, Professor Skilton composed music based on Native American melodies, legends and folklore. His Indian opera, *Blue Feather*, used Pueblo tribal music. It was produced on radio in 1930. He also composed orchestral music, cantatas and oratorios based on American folk stories and legends. In the 1940s some felt Skilton's music for the poem "The Call of Kansas" should become the state song. Legislators didn't agree [**210, 217**]. ∎

Homegrown poet

244
William Stafford

Poet. Hutchinson, Wichita and Liberal. (Born 1914)
Stafford was born in Hutchinson and graduated from high school in Liberal. He worked in sugar beet fields, on construction jobs and in an oil refinery while he attended junior college at Garden City and El Dorado. After William received his bachelor's degree at KU, he planned to stay in Kansas, but World War II took him away.

Based on his religious background, Stafford was a conscientious objector. Instead of going into combat in the military, he spent the war years with the U.S. Forest Service, the Soil Conservation Service and doing church work. Afterward he taught English in high schools and universities in the West.

Since the publication of his first title in 1947 he has written over 30 books, most of them poetry. His *Travelling Through the Dark* won the National Book Award in 1962. Critics have admired the "simple richness" of Stafford's work, and his ability to create a sense of place through poetry.

Like fellow Kansan Gwendolyn Brooks [**187**], Stafford has been a poetry consultant to the Library of Congress. Although he has lived in Oregon for over 40 years —he is that state's poet laureate, or official poet—Kansas is also important to him. He visits his home state as often as possible and includes it in his work. His most recent book, *The Kansas Poems of William Stafford*, was published in Topeka in 1991. ∎

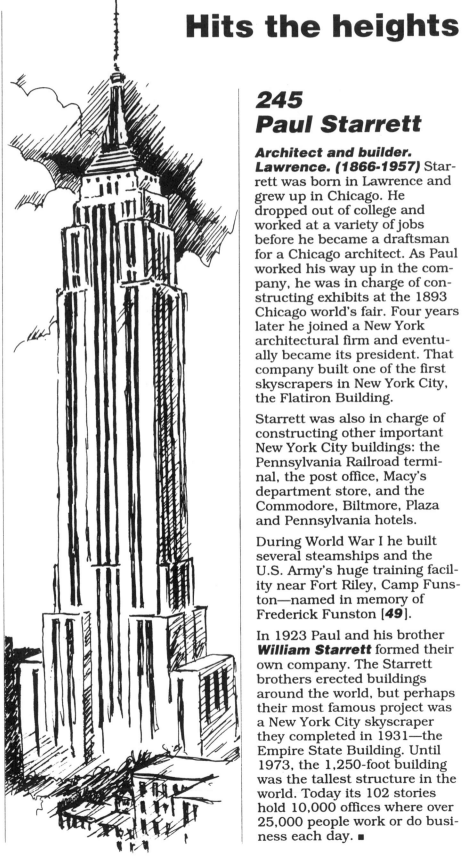

Hits the heights

245
Paul Starrett

Architect and builder. Lawrence. (1866-1957) Starrett was born in Lawrence and grew up in Chicago. He dropped out of college and worked at a variety of jobs before he became a draftsman for a Chicago architect. As Paul worked his way up in the company, he was in charge of constructing exhibits at the 1893 Chicago world's fair. Four years later he joined a New York architectural firm and eventually became its president. That company built one of the first skyscrapers in New York City, the Flatiron Building.

Starrett was also in charge of constructing other important New York City buildings: the Pennsylvania Railroad terminal, the post office, Macy's department store, and the Commodore, Biltmore, Plaza and Pennsylvania hotels.

During World War I he built several steamships and the U.S. Army's huge training facility near Fort Riley, Camp Funston—named in memory of Frederick Funston [**49**].

In 1923 Paul and his brother **William Starrett** formed their own company. The Starrett brothers erected buildings around the world, but perhaps their most famous project was a New York City skyscraper they completed in 1931—the Empire State Building. Until 1973, the 1,250-foot building was the tallest structure in the world. Today its 102 stories hold 10,000 offices where over 25,000 people work or do business each day. ∎

Millions of mysteries

246 Rex Stout

Author. Topeka. (1886-1975)
Stout enjoyed reading books as a child and had read more than 1,000 volumes in his father's library by the time he was ten. At the same time, his parents took him around the state giving demonstrations of his talents in math. Rex finished high school two years early, and then began a series of interesting jobs.

At age nineteen, he kept Theodore Roosevelt's financial accounts on the presidential yacht. He managed a hotel a few years later and published his first successful novel at age 26. He then owned a publishing company and ran a multi-million-dollar banking business. When he was in his late forties, Stout wrote a novel featuring a detective named Nero Wolfe and an assistant, Archie Goodwin. The author had left Kansas by that time, but he named his Archie character after a police chief he had known in Topeka.

Between the 1930s and 1970s, Stout featured his detective team in more than 70 mysteries. The Nero Wolfe series, plus over 50 other books he wrote, have sold more than 100 million copies. This makes Stout one of the most popular writers in the country. ∎

Keeps on talking

247 John Cameron Swayze

Radio and television journalist. Wichita, Atchison and Lawrence. (Born 1906)
During the 1940s and 1950s, Swayze was a popular broadcaster for NBC radio and television. He was born in Wichita and went to school in Atchison. John attended classes at the University of Kansas, but left college in hopes of becoming an actor in New York. When he couldn't find an acting job, he returned to Kansas.

Swayze soon found work at a Kansas City newspaper, and then anchored a local radio news show. Within a few years he was a reporter for NBC. His *News Caravan* was the first evening news program on network television.

After he left journalism, Swayze advertised H&R Block [*136*] income tax services, Orkin exterminators and Timex watches. Week after week, in front of live cameras, he put the durable timepieces through unusual tests. He demonstrated Timexes strapped on everything from a roaring powerboat motor's blades to an elephant's foot. Then, as cameras zoomed in on each dripping or dirty watch face, he would proudly conclude—most of the time—"Timex takes a licking and keeps on ticking!" ∎

He has designs on everything

248 Bradbury Thompson

Artist and designer. Topeka. (Born 1911) Thompson's love of art began as a boy. He spent hours and hours at the Topeka Public Library, enjoying books for both their stories and their design.

In junior high school, Bradbury got a chance to see his own work in print. He worked on the school newspaper staff and patiently lettered headlines with stencils to give the publication a professional look. In high school he used his talent to design two yearbooks. At the same time he worked as a draftsman for a construction firm. In his spare time the young artist visited a local printing office to learn all he could about typesetting and printing.

Thompson attended Topeka's Washburn University where he edited two prize-winning yearbooks. He also designed the version of the university's "Icabod" mascot that is still in use. After graduation, he worked as a book and magazine designer at Capper [*34*] Publications.

By 1938 Thompson realized his best chances for a career in graphic design lay outside of Topeka. So, with examples of his best work under his arm, he headed to New York City. There he showed his portfolio to art directors at several corporations, magazines and advertising agencies. After he ↻

returned home, Thompson had two job offers within two weeks. One was from the designer of *Vogue* and *Vanity Fair* magazines; the other was with an important advertising agency. Against the advice of others, he chose the ad agency job.

A year later, his advertising job led to a position with the Westvaco Corporation. There he designed and edited the company magazine; he still works as a consultant for the company.

During World War II, Bradbury worked for the Office of War Information at the U.S. State Department in Washington, D.C. He designed two OWI magazines, *Victory* and *USA*. After the war he returned to New York and spent fifteen years as the art director of *Mademoiselle* magazine.

In 1950 he and his wife moved to Connecticut where he set up his own studio in their oceanside home. Working as a consultant, he has designed or redesigned nearly 40 magazines, including *Art News, Business Week, Harvard Business Review* and *Progressive Architecture*. When the Smithsonian Institution began publishing its own magazine, *Smithsonian*, Thompson was asked to create the new publication's design.

He began teaching a class in graphic design at Yale University in 1956, and continues teaching there, using his own book, *Bradbury Thompson: The Art of Graphic Design*, as a text.

Thompson's most widely-circulated work has been for the U.S. Postal Service. In 1957 he was asked to design a postage stamp to commemorate the 1958 Brussels Universal and International Exhibition. In 1964 another of his designs was used on a stamp honoring American music. He was then invited to join the Citizen's Stamp Advisory Committee. This eighteen-member group meets every other month in Washington, and, along with the postmaster general, is responsible for the selection and design of all U.S. postage stamps.

Since joining the committee, Thompson has designed over 100 stamps—including most of the American Bicentennial stamps and every religious Christmas stamp issued since 1973. On some stamps, he uses his own artwork, on others he uses different artists' paintings with his own choices of lettering and design. ■

His sermons make people laugh

249 Arthur Tonne

Author and priest. Emporia, Little River, Pilsen and Marion. (Born 1904) Tonne was born in Michigan and became a Catholic priest as a young man. By the time he retired in 1991, Monsignor Tonne had delivered thousands of homilies, or short sermons. In almost all of them he tried to use humor, for, as he says, "Religion is a serious, but joyful, business."

When other priests asked him for copies of his sermons he put his suggestions into a book and published it in 1945. It sold 25,000 copies, and a second book was nearly as popular. Since then he has authored over 50 other books. Nine of those titles are from a series Tonne calls *Jokes Priests Can Tell*. Since 1953 he has compiled several thousand jokes and humorous stories that pastors can use to illustrate sermons.

After serving in Emporia and Little River, Tonne spent the last 38 years of his ministry at the St. Johns Catholic church in Pilsen. The audience for his jokes, however, has become much larger than the small Marion County congregation. In 1990 he appeared on the NBC television show *Late Night with David Letterman*. There an estimated six million viewers laughed with the Kansas priest as he told some of his favorite jokes. ■

Christmas USA

Independence Hall

U.S. 10¢

Bicentennial Era

Beetle's boss grows up in Kansas

250 Mort Walker

Cartoonist. El Dorado. (Born 1923) Walker was born in El Dorado and learned to love drawing from his parents. His father was an architect; his mother worked as a designer and illustrator.

Mort began selling cartoons at the age of twelve. In 1942 he got his first real job in the art world was as a designer at the Hallmark [153] company in Kansas City, Missouri. After his service in the U.S. Army in World War II, Walker moved to New York City and worked for the Dell Publishing Company. He also sold art to the *Saturday Evening Post* and *The New Yorker* [202] magazines.

In 1950, he created a comic strip about a young college student who wore his hat pulled down over his eyes. Editors at King Features Syndicate liked Walker's idea, but told him he should rename Spider, his main character.

The cartoonist was eager to sell his work so Spider quickly became Beetle Bailey. The first strip appeared on Mort's twenty-seventh birthday. After six months, however, only 25 newspapers carried the cartoon. Another change was made: Walker put Beetle in the U.S. Army and introduced new characters.

Walker based his new Sarge character after his own tough World War II sergeant. He patterned the young, over-eager Lieutenant Fuzz after himself.

The changed comic grew more popular and by 1960 it had become only the second strip to reach a circulation of 1,000 newspapers. That number has

Reprinted with special permission of King Features Syndicate

almost doubled today. "Beetle" is published in nearly 40 countries and is one of the top three comic strips.

In 1954, Walker started another strip with cartoonist Dik Browne. "Hi and Lois" is based on the adventures of Beetle's sister Lois and her family. Today "Beetle Bailey" and "Hi and Lois"—along with five other comics Walker draws with other partners—are enjoyed by over 150 million newspaper readers around the world each day. Walker has more comic strips in daily syndication than any other cartoonist now working.

He has also written over 100 books about his popular cartoon characters. His drawings have

been exhibited at several world's fairs, as well as in Europe and at the Metropolitan Museum of Art in New York City.

Walker, who now lives in Connecticut, has won many awards and honors for his artwork. He founded the Museum of Cartoon Art, which features work by cartoonists from around the world. ■

Prairie poet

251 May Williams Ward

Poet and artist. Osawatomie, Arkansas City, Spearville, Montezuma, Belpre and Wellington. (1882-1975) Williams and her family moved from Missouri to Osawatomie when she was seven. She later graduated from the University of Kansas and taught math in her hometown and Arkansas City. After her marriage in 1908, May lived in Kansas and Colorado towns while her husband managed and owned grain elevators. ⇨

Ward's professional writing career began in 1921 when _Life_ magazine paid $5 for her second-place entry in a Colorado poetry contest. Within five years she had sold over 300 poems to 35 magazines, including _Ladies Home Journal, Good Housekeeping_ and _Country Gentleman._

Over the next half century, Ward wrote numerous plays, short stories, radio programs and hundreds of poems. She edited a national poetry magazine and published seven books, including her autobiography and five volumes of poetry. Kansas was a favorite subject of her work. Her group of poems called "Dust Bowl" won the Poetry Society of America's first-place award in 1937. She had a national reputation, and was the friend of such famous poets as Sara Teasdale and Stephen Vincent Benét. Ward's friend William Allen White [**256**] said her prairie poetry "makes music" of Kansas. ∎

Writes with an iron quill

252 Eugene "Ironquill" Ware

**Poet and newspaper journalist. Fort Scott, Topeka, Kansas City and Cherokee County. (1841-1911)** Ware moved to Kansas after the Civil War and soon convinced his parents and brothers to come from Iowa to Fort Scott. There he worked for the _Fort Scott Monitor_ and studied law. After editing the paper for a year, he opened a law office in 1873.

At the same time Eugene began writing poetry. His first poems were rhyming advertisements for his family's harness shop, but the newspaper asked him to write more verse. As his poems circulated, people around the state took notice.

By 1874 Ware was called the unofficial poet laureate of Kansas. He was elected to the Kansas Senate in the early 1880s. In 1885 he published a popular book, _Rhymes of Ironquill._ (Ware used "Ironquill" as a pen name, although most Kansans knew his real identity.) As his book was reprinted in fifteen editions, he became Kansas' best-known poet of the period. Readers especially enjoyed his humorous political rhymes.

Ware practiced law in Topeka in the 1890s. From 1902 to 1904 he was President Theodore Roosevelt's commissioner of pensions. He was later a lawyer in Kansas City. ∎

Draws for sport

253 Ted Watts

**Artist. Anthony, Lyons, Winfield, Harper, Leavenworth and Oswego. (Born 1943)** Watts' father transferred from town to town as a railroad express agent, and the young artist-to-be saw much of Kansas before he finished high school.

Ted graduated from Pittsburg State University in the mid 1960s and later worked as an artist at an advertising agency in Oswego. When the agency closed, Watts received a contract from KSU to paint artwork for the cover of a football program. As word of his work spread, he was soon able to open his own studio.

Some of Watts' art has a Western theme, but his specialty is sports artwork. His work is always in demand and he sells over 200 paintings and drawings a year. He has done work for the U.S. Olympic Committee, the NCAA, and many colleges and universities across the country. Watts' artwork

hangs in the Baseball Hall of Fame, as well as in the halls of fame for basketball, pro football, college football and wrestling. ∎

Spins history into stories

254 Paul Wellman

Author. Cimarron and Wichita. (1898-1966) Wellman was best known for writing historical novels with realistic Old West settings, but he spent the first ten years of his life on the other side of the world. He and his missionary parents lived in West Africa, Spain and England.

Paul was introduced to the American West when his parents sent him to the United States to attend school in Utah, Washington, D.C., and Kansas. He graduated from high school in Wichita in 1914 and Fair-mount College (later WSU) in 1918. During summer vacations he worked on ranches in western Kansas and Oklahoma.

After serving in the U.S. Army during World War I, Wellman returned to Kansas and was a reporter for the *Wichita Beacon*. Ten years later he joined the rival *Wichita Eagle* as a news editor. In 1936 he became an editorial writer at the *Kansas City Star*. By that time Wellman had completed three novels. The books grew out of his research for several historical news articles.

In the mid 1940s Wellman moved to California and spent a few years as a screenwriter. He left the film industry to concentrate on writing novels, but interestingly, several of his bestselling books—including *The Comancheros, Broncho Apache* and *The Iron Mistress*—were later made into movies. Over seven million copies of Wellman's nearly 30 historical novels and nonfiction history titles have been sold.

Manley Wade Wellman, Wellman's younger brother, was also an author. He, too, went to school in Wichita and worked for the *Beacon* and *Eagle*. Manley wrote a variety of books for adult and juvenile readers. His *Candle of the Wicked* was a historical novel set in eastern Kansas. It included the "Bloody Benders" [**338**]. ∎

His artwork fights fires

255 Rudolph Wendelin

Artist. Herndon and Ludell. (Born 1910) Wendelin was born in Herndon and grew up in Ludell. He attended architecture classes at KU until the Depression forced him to quit school.

Back home in Rawlins County Rudolph drew maps for a government lake project until he got a draftsman's job in Wisconsin with the U.S. Forest Service. There he had a chance to attend art school. Within a few years he was promoted to an illustrator's job at the agency's Washington, D.C., office. When Wendelin returned from duty in the U.S. Navy during World War II, he

got a new assignment. In 1946 USFS officials asked him to design a friendly bear to advertise the dangers of forest fires. The bear's name? Smokey.

For nearly 30 years the Kansan supervised all of the artwork for the popular bear—posters, cartoons, publications, exhibits and other materials. He even produced some of Smokey's art after he retired in 1973. He has also illustrated books, designed several U.S. postage stamps, and painted a mural in the Rawlins County Historical Society Museum in Atwood.

Wendelin's Smokey came to life, by the way, in 1950 when firefighters rescued a real bear cub from a New Mexico forest fire. The bear was flown to the Washington National Zoo where he lived until his death in 1976. Since then, other New Mexico "Smokeys" have taken his place at the zoo. ∎

Dateline: Emporia

Newspaper journalist and author. Emporia and El Dorado. (1868-1944) The globe-trotting Amelia Earhart [*13*] and soldier-politician Dwight D. Eisenhower [*44*] achieved world fame after leaving their home state.

Another Kansan, the editor of a small-town newspaper, never lived more than a hundred miles from his birthplace. Yet he and his *Emporia Gazette* became famous around the world. From the turn of the century into the 1940s, millions read and respected the hometown opinions of William Allen White.

Almost history

White was born in Emporia, February 10, 1868. When his parents moved to El Dorado a year later, baby Will, according to family stories, almost became history. As their wagon forded a stream, he bounced off into the swiftly moving current. Wrapped in a big shawl, he floated in the water a few seconds before his anxious parents rescued him.

Allen White, his famous son later wrote, was "somebody"— doctor, druggist, storekeeper, politican, leading citizen. He was sentimental and easy-

going, and gave his son a love of nature, politics and people. *Mary Ann Hatton White*, on the other hand, was serious, practical and strong-willed. She taught her son to follow his beliefs, and gave him an appreciation of books and music.

The devil to pay

Thanks to his father, White's journalism career began when he was only eleven. Dr. White was a great believer in the value of work, so one summer he made Will into a "printer's devil."

The young man had to trade his place at the Walnut River swimming hole for a job at a local printing office. There he hauled buckets of water, inked the presses, swept floors, delivered newspapers and did other tasks. Then he discovered the truth behind his "job"—his father had paid the editor to hire him. He abruptly quit and went home in embarrassment.

Dr. White died when his son was fourteen. Will and his mother remained in El Dorado where he graduated from high school in 1884.

He spent a year at College of Emporia before returning to El Dorado to work for the *Butler County Democrat*. There he wrote his first news stories while learning how to set type by hand. Next he worked at the *Emporia News* and the *Emporia Democrat*.

White enrolled at the University of Kansas in 1886, and was joined in Lawrence by his mother, who rented a cottage and provided a home for him. With no other living children, Mrs. White always stayed near her son. (After his marriage, in fact, she moved next door to Will and his new bride in Emporia and lived there until her death at age 94.)

Will was not a strong student. He failed freshman geometry and struggled to pass other mathematics courses. Much of his time was spent outside the classroom. He was active in student politics, worked for a Lawrence newspaper and wrote for the campus literary magazine, as well as newspapers in Kansas City and St. Louis.

Foster father help

White left KU in 1890 when **Thomas Murdock**, the editor of the El Dorado *Republican*, offered him a job. Murdock was a close friend of Allen White before he died, and afterward he treated Will like his own son.

Beginning at a monthly salary of $18, White worked his way up the ladder at Murdock's paper.

In the process, he learned most of the jobs on a newspaper—printer, circulation manager, reporter, advertising salesman and office manager.

He eventually left El Dorado and became a political reporter for the *Kansas City Journal*. Things went fine until one day in June 1892. Will turned in what he felt was a front-page story about the nomination of Populist Lorenzo Lewelling [**70**] for governor—but the editor buried White's article on an inside page. The angry reporter walked out, went to the offices of the *Kansas City Star*, and was hired on the spot as an editorial writer.

A lifelong partner

A year later White married a Kansas City schoolteacher, **Sallie Lindsay**. She became a full partner in all of his activities, including checking most of his manuscripts. Their partnership, however, began with very little. During their honeymoon in Colorado, all their savings disappeared in a bank failure.

The couple lived in Kansas City until 1895. By then, Will knew big-city journalism was not for him. When he heard the *Emporia Gazette* was for sale, he decided to become his own boss. With just $1.25 in his pocket, he and Sallie rode the Santa Fe to Emporia, stepped

off the train, borrowed $3,000, and bought themselves a newspaper.

In their first issue of the *Gazette* he wrote, "The new editor hopes to live here until he is the old editor. . . . He hopes always to sign 'from Emporia' after his name. . .and he trusts that he may endear himself to the people." His wishes, obviously, came true.

What's the matter?

Just over a year later a White editorial—"What's the Matter with Kansas?"—brought national attention to himself, the *Gazette*, Emporia and his home state.

It was the hot summer of 1896. Politicians, the public and newspaper editors were choosing up sides for the fall elections. In an editorial, White spoke out in favor of Republicans, and against the growing Populist movement. His comments angered local Populists, many of them farmers. One Saturday a short time later, a group of them surrounded him on the street.

As the men "hooted" and jeered at the 28-year-old editor, he broke out of their circle, stamped back to his office and began writing. White worked quickly, for he was anxious to catch a train and join Sallie on vacation in Colorado. ✑

"What's the matter with Kansas?" he asked. Then he went on to attack Populism, the Democrats and their presidential candidate, William Jennings Bryan. The editorial was funny, effective and—as White later admitted—it was also unfair and inaccurate.

Republicans, of course, loved it. Someone on William McKinley's presidential campaign staff saw the stinging article and made thousands of copies. Quickly, the Kansas editorial became ammunition that helped the Republicans defeat the Populists and Democrats.

Overnight fame

White was famous almost overnight. At the same time, his first book was published. *The Real Issue*, a collection of short stories, sold out and was reprinted three times. It showed readers a side of White they had not seen in his editorials. Soon the literary and political attention he received brought the Kansas editor in contact with nationally known figures.

In Chicago and New York he met author Hamlin Garland, lawyer Clarence Darrow and muckraking journalists Lincoln Steffen and Ida Tarbell. At a Republican victory banquet he met President McKinley and other politicians. And in Washington, D.C., the next summer, he met Theodore Roosevelt. Roosevelt admired White's book; the young journalist was charmed by T.R.'s personality and politics. Quickly the two became friends.

By the time Roosevelt became president after McKinley's assassination in 1901, White's political beliefs were changing. He was shifting his support from Republicans and big corporations to laborers, farmers and small business owners.

In 1905 he admitted the Populists he had made fun of in the 1890s had perhaps been right. In 1910 Will followed Roosevelt out of the Republican ranks and into the progressive Bull Moose party.

For the next six years, White worked hard for the Progressives and the political reforms, or changes, they pushed. When his friend T.R. refused to run for president on the Bull Moose ticket in 1916, Will was heartbroken. He then rejoined the Republican party.

When World War I broke out in Europe, White, like many Kansans, felt the United States should stay out of the trouble. After he began to support the war, he reminded his readers that the fight was with the German government, not with the German people. In 1917 he was sent to France with fellow Kansan Henry J. Allen [**31**] to inspect Red Cross facilities. At the end of the war he returned with his teenaged son Bill [**257**] to report on the peace talks. Back home again, he pushed hard for the League of Nations.

Mary White

In the spring of 1921 Will and Sallie lost their sixteen-year-old daughter **Mary**. One afternoon after school, as she had done countless times, the energetic girl went riding. Tragically, she turned to wave at a friend just as her horse veered near a tree. Mary hit her head on a low-hanging branch and later died of a fractured skull.

The day after her funeral, White wrote about his free-spirited "Peter Pan" in a special tribute titled "Mary White." The tender essay was reprinted in newspapers nationwide and is still considered a classic piece of writing. In 1977 ABC Televi-

sion produced *Mary White*, a movie about the Whites and their daughter in the period just before her death. It was filmed in and around Emporia.

A 1922 editorial—"To an Anxious Friend"—brought Will his first Pulitzer Prize. In all, he wrote 23 books; the last was his autobiography published after his death. It, too, won a Pulitzer award.

Klan crusader

Even with his life-long interest in politics, White ran for office just once—as an Independent candidate for governor in 1924. But he said he had no desire to win; his goal was to force the Ku Klux Klan out of Kansas. He called the racist group a bunch of "ridiculous, hooded hoodlums," "cowards" and "traitors."

Although he spent only six weeks and less than $500 on his crusade, he traveled 3,000 miles around the state and received nearly as many votes as the Democratic candidate, Jonathan Davis [**39**]. Partly because of his work, the Klan's power soon declined in Kansas.

He continued supporting various political causes and candidates. In 1930 he served on a presidential commission in Haiti and in 1940 he founded the Committee to Defend America by Aiding the Allies. He was also president of the American Society of Newspaper Editors.

Cartoonist Jerry Doyle,
Philadelphia Record, 1935

Sage of Emporia

Even with all his involvement in world and national affairs, White always managed to keep his small-town perspective. He once wrote, "The country newspaper is the incarnation of the town spirit."

His town, of course, was always Emporia, although big-city newspapers offered him large sums to join them. He continually boosted projects for his hometown and was himself something of a civic institution.

He was also Emporia's number-one tourist attraction. At Red Rocks, their spacious home built of sandstone from Colorado's Garden of the Gods, Will and Sallie entertained Presidents Theodore Roosevelt, Herbert Hoover, and a host of other noted personalities. White also corresponded with all the U.S. presidents from William McKinley through Franklin D. Roosevelt, plus FBI head J. Edgar Hoover and U.S. Supreme Court Justice Louis Brandeis.

He counted a long list of fellow authors among his friends: Edna Ferber, Walter Lippmann, James Whitcomb Riley, H.L. Mencken, Carl Sandburg, Upton Sinclair, Willa Cather, Dorothy Canfield Fisher and Sinclair Lewis.

White was one of the original judges for the influential Book-of-the-Month Club and for decades his choices helped shape what the rest of America read.

On his seventieth birthday, *Life* magazine featured him in a photo story. At that time Mr. White still appeared at his cluttered *Gazette* desk almost every day. No matter how busy he was, his office door was always open to anyone who worked for him.

A Kansan to the end

White developed cancer and died on Kansas Day 1944, at the age of 75. His funeral was attended by a "who's who" of important Kansans. Newspapers around the country mourned the loss of the Small Town Philosopher and the Voice of Main Street. He had neighbors, the *New York Times* said, "all along the great American street that runs from sea to sea."

The Sage of Emporia received countless awards in life; many more were given after his death. The William Allen White School of Journalism was established in his name at KU. In 1948, his likeness was put on a U.S. postage stamp—making him one of the few newspapermen ever recognized in that way. In 1952 Ruth Gagliardo [**105**], a former *Gazette* employee, established the William Allen White Children's Book Award. It honors a children's book each year selected by Kansas schoolchildren. ⇨

Turns off technology

Considering his progressive ideas, White had very little patience with new inventions. Radio was very popular in the 1930s and 1940s, but Will and Sallie hardly ever turned on their set. They made exceptions for important presidential speeches or reports by their son when he was a CBS newsman. White rarely attended movies, either.

He did replace the family's horse and buggy with an automobile—but he tried to drive it only once. After his son patiently explained the controls of the car, White started cautiously down the street. He twisted the steering wheel sharply at the first corner, but he apparently thought it didn't have to be turned back again. The auto kept turning, and the editor ran into a neighbor's elm tree! From that day on he was always chauffered.

In earlier times, White bragged that he could handle all jobs at the *Gazette*, including printer. But as his print shop and office were modernized, he had no desire to understand the new equipment. He later said of his paper's pressroom, "[There] I'm a stranger in a strange land."

Distinguished alumnus

William Allen White helped many authors in their careers. One of the best known was poet *Walt Mason*.

Born in Canada in 1862, Mason worked at a variety of jobs before he was hired by Ed Howe [*211*] at the Atchison *Globe* in 1884. He quickly advanced to larger newspapers in bigger cities until he was laid off by a Washington, D.C., paper in the depression of the 1890s.

Mason turned to alcohol and drifted about looking for work. In Emporia, White hired the luckless writer and encouraged him to write poems for the *Gazette*. Soon Mason's poetry was a daily feature. He eventually wrote a syndicated column, "Rippling Rhymes by Uncle Walt."

Once he had conquered his alcohol abuse, Mason was never at a loss for words.

At one point he was turning out twenty poems a week for various publications, six stories a week for a Chicago paper, a Sunday story for the *Kansas City Star*, a rhyme a month for *Judge* magazine—along with his daily poems for syndication. He built an impressive home in Emporia, completely paid for—as the walls went up—by his writing. The more money the contractor needed, the more Mason wrote.

Although Mason had readers nationwide, he never enjoyed being popular. He left Kansas in 1920 and moved to California where he died in 1939. ■

Lives in original 'Little House'

258 Laura Ingalls Wilder

Author. Montgomery County. (1867-1957) Wilder was born in Wisconsin and later lived in Iowa, Minnesota, South Dakota and Missouri. She is remembered as the author of the popular "Little House" books.

The second book in her series, *Little House on the Prairie*, tells of her family's stay in Kansas. *Charles* and *Caroline Ingalls*, with their daughters *Mary*, baby *Carrie*, and two-year-old Laura settled in Montgomery County in the fall of 1869.

Wilder's book describes life on the prairie—their cozy log cabin, a frontier Christmas, a raging prairie fire, and visits from a pack of wolves and "tall, thin, fierce-looking" Indians dressed in skunk skins. The Indians were Osages, and it was on part of their southern Kansas reservation that Laura's family—and thousands of others—had set-

Like father, like son

257 William L. White

Newspaper journalist and author. Emporia. (1900-1973) At fourteen, White first wrote for his famous father [*256*] at the *Emporia Gazette*. After completing high school, he spent a year at the University of Kansas. "Young Bill," as he was known, graduated from Harvard University in 1924. He returned to Emporia and was a reporter on the *Gazette* for nine years. Like his father, he was an active Republican. During the early 1930s he served a term in the Kansas Legislature.

In 1935 Bill left Kansas to see the world. He took a job at the *Washington Post*, and then two years later moved to New York City to work for *Fortune* magazine. At the beginning of World War II, White was a European correspondent for CBS Radio and a group of 40 newspapers. In 1940 he joined the *Reader's Digest* staff and worked in London and other foreign cities.

After his father died in 1944, the younger White returned to Kansas and became editor and publisher of the *Gazette*. He remained in Emporia until his own death. During his career he wrote over a dozen books, most about his experiences as a reporter in World War II and the Korean War. ■

tled. For a time, war threatened. Tension eased when the Osages signed a new treaty and moved to Oklahoma. At that time the Ingallses could have legally purchased Montgomery County land. Instead, they returned to Wisconsin and their first home in the "Big Woods."

Years later, as a young housewife in Missouri, Laura wrote newspaper columns, but she didn't begin writing books until she was nearly 65. She published her eighth volume in the "Little House" series in 1941; a ninth book was released in 1971.

Little House on the Prairie, like Laura's other books, is not considered an autobiography. She did base many of the characters and episodes on real people and events, but other parts are fiction. In the 1970s, an NBC television series used the *Little House on the Prairie*'s title and some of the book's characters, but almost none of its episodes were based on events in Kansas.

Today visitors may tour a reconstructed cabin on the Ingalls family's land near Independence. The site is owned by **Bill** and **Wilma Kurtis**, the parents of television journalist Bill Kurtis [**219**]. ■

Writes of Western women

259 Jeanne Williams

Author. Elkhart and Stafford. (Born 1930) Williams was born as Jeanne Kreie on a farm near Elkhart. Hard times during the Great Depression and the Dust Bowl sent her family to Stafford where her father worked in a grocery store.

Jeanne taught herself to read before she started to school. She read almost anything she could find, including the Oz [**362**] books and volume after volume of historical fiction.

After her mother died of cancer, Jeanne lived with her grandparents in Missouri. There, as a fifth grader, she tackled her first writing project—a retelling of the Bible. Although she only got as far as the Tower of Babel, she knew she wanted to be an author. When a Sunday school paper printed one of her poems, her career was officially on its way.

After graduating from high school, she moved to Oklahoma City and worked in a bookstore until her marriage in 1949. In 1952, while her husband was serving in the Korean War, she enrolled in Oklahoma University. She took courses in writing and history, thinking she could teach if her writing didn't sell. That same year, a magazine printed one of her short stories. Soon she was writing full time. In 1957 her first book, *Tame the Wild Stallion*, was published. Although it was her first of several award-winning children's novels, editors convinced her to use the pen name J.R. Williams. They felt young boys wouldn't read a novel about a boy written by a woman.

By that time Williams had already written her first adult novel, but because it was about a woman in the Old West, publishers rejected it. The story was "too Western to be historical, and too historical to be a Western," they said. In 1976—nearly 25 years later—she sold her first "Western-woman" novel. Then, in 1981, she became one of the first women to win the important Spur Award for Western fiction. She has since won three more Spurs. She also writes historical romances.

She has written under several pen names—Jeanne Crecy, Kristin Michaels (her two children), Deirdre Rowan, Megan Castell, Jeanne Foster, J.R. Williams and Jeanne Williams. Together her 54 titles have sold over ten million copies. She has traveled in South America, Europe, Asia and across the American West researching locations for her novels, but Kansas is one of her favorite settings. *Oh Susanna!*, *Coyote Winter*, *Freedom Trail*, *Daughter of the Sword*, *Lady of No Man's Land*, *No Roof But Heaven* and *Winter Wheat*, a novel about the Mennonites [**96**], are among her titles set in the Sunflower State.

Williams and her third husband live in Arizona where she is active in environmental and animal right's organizations. ■

Closes Capitol controversy

260 Lumen Winter

Artist and sculptor. Belpre and Larned. (1908-1982) Winter grew up near Belpre and Larned. He studied art in Ohio and got his first job as a cartoonist in Michigan. In the 1930s he illustrated magazine articles and science fiction books.

Lumen painted his first mural in the Hutchinson post office and then worked as a U.S. Army artist during World War II. Later he created murals for the National Wildlife Federation and the U.S. Air Force Academy. His *Titans* mural in the United Nations building is the only painting at the UN by an American. Winter's murals in the AFL-CIO offices were dedicated by President Dwight D. Eisenhower [44] and those designs were used on a U.S. postage stamp. He also created a medallion for the Apollo XIII moon mission.

In 1978 Winter hung eight impressive murals on the walls of the Kansas Capitol. For the internationally known artist, it was the end of eighteen months of painting—often twelve hours a day, seven days a week. For Kansans, it was the end of an 80-year controversy about what should decorate their statehouse's walls.

The trouble began in 1898 when Jerome Fedeli's [197] paintings of Greek women in the Capitol dome offended Republican legislators. In 1939—after arguing with the legislature, women's clubs and other self-chosen art critics— John Steuart Curry [192] abandoned his mural project on the Capitol's second floor.

Those walls remained bare until the 1976 Kansas Legislature voted to finish the project. Rather than copy Curry's original ideas, however, legislators said a new muralist should refer to Curry's sketches.

Forty artists entered the competition, including a man who had been Curry's apprentice in the 1930s. But Winter, then living in New York, was determined to win. He designed eight large panels on four themes: history, agriculture, industry and education. To help sell his ideas, he made miniature paintings and displayed them in a scale model of the Capitol.

When the legislature's committee selected him, it agreed to a commission of $40,000— making Winter's murals the most expensive of the statehouse art projects. The artist completed the paintings in his New York and New Mexico studios. Afterward, he returned $1,000 to the Kansas treasury as a donation to his home state.

Winter's only large sculpture in Kansas, *The Great White Buffalo*, sits outside the Kansas Museum of History in Topeka. Shortly before he died, he finished plans for the lifesize buffalo bull pursued by an Indian hunter on a pony. His son then supervised the carving of the statue from eight tons of Italian marble. It was dedicated in 1983.

Other artwork by Winter is in the collections of the Vatican in Rome, the Smithsonian Institution, the Library of Congress and the White House. ■

By Wolfe, he signs his work

261 Byron "By" Wolfe

Artist. Parsons, Topeka and Leawood. (1904-1973) Wolfe grew up in Parsons and worked as a ranch hand in his youth.

After he received an art degree from KU he got a job at a Topeka publishing company. He then moved to Kansas City to do freelance art work, and eventually became art director at a Kansas City advertising agency.

Byron opened his own studio in Leawood in 1964. By that time his accurate paintings of the Old West were recognized around the country. He worked in pen and ink, colored pencil and oil, but many agreed his best work was done in watercolor.

Some of Wolfe's paintings are displayed at the National Cowboy Hall of Fame, the Eisenhower Library and several state historical societies. ■

Draws fire for 'drouthy Kansas'

262 Henry Worrall

Artist, composer and musician. Topeka. (1825-1902) Worrall was born in England and came to the United States as a boy. He grew up in New York and then studied music in Ohio. For years, he worked there as a musician, playing the guitar, organ and piano. He also gave music lessons and wrote songs. He sold many of his compositions to local music publishers for $7.50 a page. One tune, "Svastopol," became quite popular, although Worrall never received more than $15 for his two-page song.

Henry moved to Kansas in 1868 after a doctor recommended he travel west for his health. At his new home in Topeka he continued to give music lessons and perform on the guitar. He also began spending more time with his hobby, art. In 1869 he sketched a rain-soaked Kansas prairie filled with giant fruits and vegetables. *Drouthy Kansas*, as he called it, was meant as a joke for some of his Ohio friends—they believed Kansas was a large desert. Others enjoyed the humorous drawing, too, and copies of *Drouthy Kansas* quickly circulated. The sketch appeared in magazines, newspapers and on railroad posters to advertise the state.

The publicity helped Henry find more jobs as an artist. Soon his illustrations appeared in magazines and books, including Joseph McCoy's [165] important book on the cattle trade. Worrall enjoyed his new fame as an artist—until 1874. That year, dry weather hit Kansas, followed by billions of hungry grasshoppers. New settlers expecting to enjoy a land of plenty lost nearly everything. Many remembered Worrall's drouthy drawing and claimed they had moved to Kansas because of it. For a time, he was "cussed and discussed"

across the state. When the complaints died down, Worrall was asked to help design Kansas' exhibit at the 1876 Philadelphia Centennial Exposition.

The next year his drawings began appearing in *Harper's Weekly* and *Frank Leslie's Illustrated Newspaper*. He also created artwork for the Atchison, Topeka and Santa Fe Railroad [158]. "Drouthy" Kansas or not, Worrall's art did much to promote the Sunflower State. ∎

Sacred songwriter

263 Glad Robinson Youse

Composer. Baxter Springs. (1898-1985) Youse was known for the sacred music she composed. Glad was born in Oklahoma, attended college in Missouri and New York, and later lived in Baxter Springs. For years she was a popular director at music conferences in the Midwest and Southwest.

Youse wrote over 200 works for choruses, making her one of America's leading female choral composers. At one time, she had music for sale through 21 different publishers. Her compositions are often performed at music festivals around the country. ∎

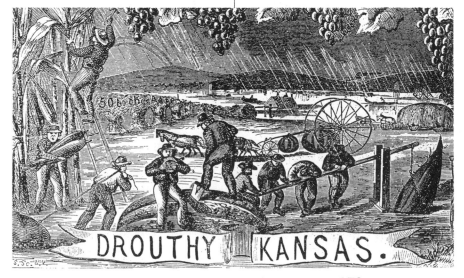

DROUTHY KANSAS.

Others who create

Ron Christie has been a commerical artist in Wichita for over twenty years. In the early 1980s he put his love of automobiles and his painting talents to work for the AMT model car company. Since that time hundreds of Ron's airbrush paintings of classic automobiles and "hot rods" have appeared on thousands of boxes of model car kits sold by AMT. ∎

Dorothy Canfield Fisher was born Lawrence in 1879 while her father was a professor at KU. After attending the University of Paris and Columbia University in New York City, she wrote a long list of books for children and adults; several of her novels were bestsellers. In 1957 the Dorothy Canfield Fisher Children's Book Award—much like the William Allen White [*256*] Children's Book Award created by Ruth Gagliardo [*105*]—was established in Vermont. Fisher died in that state in 1958. ∎

First Kansas writer

Louis Jolliet and Jacques Marquette led five other Frenchmen down the Mississippi River in the summer of 1673. Although the explorers did not actually visit Kansas, Jolliet later drew a map that included territory now part of the state. On it he labeled the Kansa Indians as the "Kamissi" or, according to some sources, the "Kausa." This label on Jolliet's map is believed to be the first time a word meaning *Kansas* was recorded on paper. ∎

Charlotte Hinger, born in Garnett in 1940, received praise for *Come Spring*, her 1986 historical novel about frontier life in western Kansas. Her interest in writing came from her work with local historical societies. Hinger now lives in Hoxie. She has written two other novels, but they are as yet unpublished. ∎

Earl J. Johnson was a reporter for his hometown newspaper, the *Winfield Daily Courier*, by the time he was seventeen. He also worked as a reporter while he attended college at KU. In 1921 he went to work at the Chicago office of United Press. Johnson was later vice president and editor of United Press International. During his 30 years with the worldwide newsgathering agency, he helped start the careers of several famous journalists, including CBS broadcaster Walter Cronkite. Johnson died in Arizona in 1974. ∎

Paul Jones was born in Lyons in 1882. During his junior year at DePauw University in Indiana, he left school to become a reporter. After roving between jobs for several years, Paul established the *Coffeyville Morning Sun* and later the *Pittsburg Morning Sun*. In 1918 he returned to Lyons and started the *Lyons Daily News*. He wrote so many editorials in favor of allowing liquor sales in Kansas that he was called the Admiral of the Kansas Navy. Before he died in 1954, Jones wrote several books about the Kansas visit of Francisco Vásquez de Coronado [*11*]—a subject that

always fascinated him. His brother, **Horace Jones**, was a partner in the Lyons newspaper and also wrote books about Kansas history. ∎

Bill Martin, Jr., was born in Hiawatha and attended Kansas State Teachers College (ESU) in Emporia—where he read his first book for pleasure at age twenty. After graduation he taught at St. John. Since 1945, he has written a long list of children's books and reading textbooks, twenty of them with the help of his artist brother **Bernard Martin**. With their imaginative arrangement of text and art, Bill's books take readers through new and unusual experiences on the printed page. He has also shared his ideas on several educational television projects. Martin lives in New York, but in 1991 the 75-year-old author returned to his hometown for the dedication of the Martin Children's Room in Hiawatha's Merrill Library. ∎

Kirke L. Mechem was born in Wichita in 1925 while his father, Kirke Mechem [*226*] was a reporter for the *Wichita Eagle*. Young Mechem grew up there and in Topeka. At an early age, he developed an interest in music, no doubt from his mother, **Katharine Lewis Mechem**. She studied piano in Germany and toured as a concert artist. Kirke has taught music at several California colleges. Orchestras throughout the Midwest and on the Pacific Coast have performed his musical compositions. His first well-known work, *First Symphony*, was introduced by the San Francisco Symphony in 1965. ∎

Melvin "Tubby" Millar grew up in Portis, where his family often found him doodling cartoon characters. His talent took him to Hollywood in the 1940s, and a job at Warner Brothers studio with world-famous cartoonist Friz Freleng. Although Millar had different assignments as an artist, he spent much of his time drawing Porky Pig, the star of *Looney Tunes* and *Merry Melodies* cartoons. ■

Bill Post, from Geuda Springs, has written music since he was seventeen. In the 1950s and 1960s recording stars like Connie Stevens, The Lettermen, Bobby Vee and Lawrence Welk recorded his songs. *Sixteen Reasons* made it to number two on the nation's top ten list. Another one of his songs, however, took years to gain any popularity. He first composed the marching tune while he was in Calcutta, India, during World War II. It was meant to be part of a Broadway play, but it was not. Over the years, he wrote several sets of words for his *We the People March Today*, but nothing came of it. Then in 1986 Post tried again. He put another set of words to his march and released it as *Here's Kansas*. After hearing a recording of the song, state Senator **Dick Rock** and his son, Representative **Rand Rock**, both of Arkansas City, introduced a bill to make *Here's Kansas* the official state march. The measure passed both houses of the legislature and Governor Joan Finney [45] signed it into law on April 23, 1992. In 1967 someone suggested another Post composition, *Where in the World but Kansas*, might make a better state song than *Home on the Range* [210, 217]. That idea didn't get very far. ■

Lester Raymer studied art at the Chicago Art Institute and moved to Lindsborg in the 1940s. Much of his art was in a primitive, or folk art, style. He was talented in many areas and produced a variety of artwork: paintings, prints, sculpture pieces, elaborate toys, and crucifixes and other art for churches. But Lester was also quiet and withdrawn. When the White House wanted to add one of his pieces to its permanent collection, he refused. And when New York City galleries wanted to sell his art, he said no. Raymer died in Lindsborg in 1991 at the age of 83. ■

Robert Richmond, a graduate of Washburn University in Topeka and the University of Nebraska, joined the staff of the Kansas State Historical Society as state archivist in 1952. He became assistant executive director in 1977 and also served as treasurer of the society for many years. Bob has written many articles on Kansas history, as well as numerous books. His *Kansas: A Land of Contrasts* has been reprinted many times in three different editions, and remains one of the standard works on Kansas history. A television course on Kansas history that he taught through Washburn was very popular and was the first such public television program in Kansas. Richmond retired in 1988 but he continues to write about the Sunflower State and its heritage. ■

Oscar Stauffer was born in Hope and attended high school at Emporia. His journalism career began under William Allen White [256] at the *Emporia Gazette*. After working at the *Kansas City Star* Oscar bought the *Peabody Gazette*. In 1924 he edited the *Arkansas City Traveler*, the first business in what became Stauffer Communications. His company grew to include the *Topeka State Journal* and *Topeka Daily Capital*, plus newspapers and radio and television stations in ten Plains and Southwestern states. Stauffer helped create the William Allen White School of Journalism at KU, supported it with scholarships, and gave it a donation of $1 million just before his death in 1982. ■

George M. Stone was born in 1859 and died in 1931. He studied art in Paris and later helped begin the art department at Washburn University in Topeka. Stone is best known for his portraits of Kansas governors and first ladies. Two of his murals decorate the governor's office. ■

Laurie Whitehawk is an Indian artist from Wichita. She enjoys creating paintings of Native American subjects. Laurie was the only American Indian artist whose work was displayed in the U.S. exhibit at Expo '92, the world's fair in Seville, Spain. ■

M. Wayne Willis was born in Galesburg. He earned a scholarship to the Kansas City Art Institute, but World War II interrupted his studies. In 1949 he began working as an illustrator at the Boeing aircraft plant in Wichita. In his spare time he produced wildlife paintings that appeared in many national publications, including *Field and Stream* magazine. When Willis died in 1991 he was called one of best outdoors artists in the world. ■

Fun & Games

Entertainers and Athletes

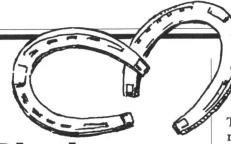

Wins, wins

264 Forrest "Phog" Allen

Basketball coach and doctor. Lawrence. (1885-1974) Allen, who was born in Missouri, was a student at the University of Kansas during the 1905-06 term. Although he had played basketball in high school, football was his sport at KU. When nearby Baker University offered him the chance to coach its basketball team, James Naismith [**305**], the game's inventor and KU coach, laughed and said, "You can't *coach* basketball, Forrest. You just *play* it." Years later, however, the Father of Basketball was the first to call Allen the Father of Basketball Coaching.

The next year Allen coached at Baker and was an unpaid assistant to Naismith. By the 1908-09 season he coached afternoons, evenings and nights—at Baker, the Haskell Indian Institute and KU—and he still won 116 out of 132 games. After completing medical school, he coached seven years in Missouri. When he returned to KU in 1919 he stayed 37 more seasons. Altogether, his Jayhawks won 24 conference titles, plus the national championship in 1952. When he retired in 1956, Dr. Allen had a career total of 771 wins—a record he held until one of his students, Adolph Rupp [**314**], topped it.

Thanks to Allen's efforts, basketball became an Olympic sport in 1936. Three years later he organized the first NCAA tournament. Allen was named to basketball's Naismith Hall of Fame in 1959. A sportswriter gave him the nickname "Phog" for his booming foghorn voice. ∎

Ringing up world titles

265 Ted Allen

Horseshoe pitcher. Natoma, Chapman, Abilene, Salina and Orion. (1908-1990) While Allen was a boy, his family farmed near several Kansas communities. For fun, he and his father often pitched horseshoes. Young Ted was good at scoring ringers—throwing the shoes around a stake 40 feet away—and he got even better as his father encouraged him to practice, practice, practice.

Teenaged Allen won his first tournament in Garden City in 1921. The next year the family moved to Colorado where he was crowned state champ—at age fourteen. By 1933 he had won a world championship. Between then and 1959 Ted set a record by winning nine more world titles. He was also crowned national champion numerous times.

Horseshoes became a way of life for the "barnyard golfer." Allen spent 24 years traveling across the United States, Canada and Cuba, throwing horseshoes for entertainment. In 1951 his accuracy earned him a spot in the *Guiness Book of World Records* when he threw 72 ringers—in a row. One of his favorite tricks was to hang a blanket between himself and and the stake, and then pitch ringer after ringer. He was a charter member of the Horseshoe Hall of Fame and also sold his own brand of horseshoes.

Kansas was the site of the first world championship of horseshoe pitching. **Frank Jackson**, who later lived in Blue Mound, sponsored the event at Bronson in 1909. Jackson, a top shoe tosser himself, won it. ∎

Acting is down her alley

266 Kirstie Alley

Actress. Wichita. (Born 1951) Alley, best known for her role as Rebecca Howe in the NBC television series *Cheers*, grew up in Wichita.

At age six Kirstie first appeared on the stage—starring as the sun in a class play. After she graduated from Southeast High School in 1969, she attended KU and KSU. She was interested in art at the time, and returned to Wichita in 1977 to become a freelance interior decorator. Soon, however, her life began to fall apart; she became addicted to cocaine. For over two years, she fought her problem, and then entered a drug rehabilitation program in Los Angeles. After her treatment she remained in California and got several small acting jobs in television and movies. In 1981 a big break came along—she landed the part of a Vulcan in *Star Trek II: The Wrath of Khan*.

Since then Alley has starred in movies with Tom Selleck, Sidney Poitier and John Travolta. She joined the cast of *Cheers* in 1987 and four years later won an Emmy Award for best comedy actress. Kirstie and her actor husband, Parker Stevenson, live in a 32-room estate in Beverly Hills. She has nearly 40 pets, and is helping zoologist Jane Goodall raise money for a chimpanzee refuge in Africa. Alley often travels the country as spokesperson for Narconon drug treatment centers. ■

Funny man in trouble

267 Roscoe "Fatty" Arbuckle

Actor and filmmaker. Smith Center. (1887-1933) Arbuckle was born in Smith Center and grew up in California. After he worked as a plumber's assistant he toured the country in carnivals and vaudeville shows. In 1908 he appeared in his first film as an extra. Soon he was one of the movies' first comedy stars—a nimble 320-pound comic everyone called "Fatty."

As a Keystone Cop in the 1913 film *A Noise From the Deep*, Arbuckle was hit with a pan full of paste, blackberries and whipped cream—perhaps the first pie-in-the-face in movie history.

He eventually wrote, directed and starred in many silent films, including *Fatty's Gift* and *Fatty's Faithful Fido*. In 1921 he was arrested after the acci-

dental death of an actress at a party. Almost immediately, theaters in Kansas and other states banned his films. Although he was found innocent, the scandal ended his acting career. Under the name William Goodrich he worked as a writer and director from 1925 until 1932. ■

Seven-time Emmy winner

268 Ed Asner

Actor. Kansas City. (Born 1929) Asner grew up in Kansas City where his father was a junk dealer. After graduating from Wyandotte High School, Asner enrolled at the University of Chicago. He took a few drama courses, but dropped out after two years and returned home. For a time he floated between

jobs—selling advertising, shoes and encyclopedias, and working on an auto assembly line. After serving in the Korean War Ed acted on stage in Chicago and New York. Television roles took him to Los Angeles in 1961.

Since then Asner has appeared in numerous movies and television shows, but he is often remembered as journalist Lou Grant from the *Mary Tyler Moore Show* of the 1970s. After the popular CBS comedy series ended, he starred in the drama *Lou Grant*. CBS dropped his show in 1982 after he made controversial statements about the United States' involvement in Central America. Three years later he resigned as president of the Screen Actors Guild after his outspoken comments angered the union. In 1992 he joined the cast of the CBS series *Hearts Afire*. With seven Emmy and five Golden Globe Awards, Asner is one of Kansas' most honored actors. ■

Wildcat plays with Tigers

269 Eldon "Big Six" Auker

Baseball player. Norcatur. (Born 1910) Auker grew up in Norcatur and attended Kansas State University. He won nine letters in basketball, football and baseball, and has been called the best athlete ever to compete for the Wildcats.

Eldon graduated in 1932 and gave up plans to teach and coach when the Detroit Tigers signed him to one of their minor league teams. By the middle of the 1933 season, he was in the major leagues, pitching for Detroit. Managers liked his underhanded throwing style, which he developed after he injured his shoulder playing football. Using his "submarine" pitches, Auker defeated the St. Louis Cardinals in the fourth game of the 1934 World Series. But when he faced the Cards' colorful pitcher "Dizzy" Dean in the crucial seventh game, he lost.

Auker's best season was 1935, when his winning percentage led all other American League pitchers. He spent 1939 with the Boston Red Sox and then finished his career with the St. Louis Browns. After he left baseball in 1942, he was a business executive in Detroit and Boston. He retired in 1975 and moved to Florida. Auker was elected to the Kansas All Sports Hall of Fame in 1969. ∎

Runs for the gold

270 Thane Baker

Runner. Elkhart. (Born 1931) As a youngster, Baker once joined in the cheering as Elkhart welcomed home its Olympic athlete Glenn Cunningham [*281*]. Thane dreamed of Olympic glory for himself—and then achieved it.

Ironically, like Cunningham, he first had to overcome a serious injury. After doctors removed a piece of steel imbedded in his left knee, Baker's left leg was shorter than his right. He trained hard in high school to overcome the problem and when he entered Kansas State University in 1949, a coach noticed his running ability. At the man's invitation Thane joined the track team.

At KSU Baker quickly began to run away with track records. He won ten Big Eight titles and an NCAA championship in the 220-yard dash. In 1952 he qualified for the Olympics and won a silver medal in the 200-meter dash at the summer games in Helsinki, Finland.

After graduating from KSU with a degree in economics, he joined the U.S. Air Force. Officers gave him time off from his training to participate in the 1956 Olympics at Melbourne, Australia. There Baker led the U.S. 100-meter relay team to a record-setting gold medal. He also won two medals of his own—a silver in the 100-meter dash and a bronze in the 200-meter. Later the Kansas All Sports Hall of Fame member was an executive for the Mobil Oil Corporation in Texas. ∎

Miss America, II

271 Debra Barnes

Miss America. Moran. (Born 1947) As a high school student in her hometown of Moran, Barnes was head cheerleader, drum majorette, football queen and class valedictorian. At Pittsburg State University she was a straight-A music major—but it took her two years to complete her senior year. The delay began when she won the Miss Pittsburg State beauty pageant. Then, at the state pageant in Pratt, she won again and became Miss Kansas. A few months later in Atlantic City, New Jersey, Barnes was crowned the 1968 Miss America—making her the second person from Kansas [*276*] to win the honor in just three years. After Debra's reign, she returned to Pittsburg State University, finished her senior year and graduated with a degree in music. She was later a minister in Missouri.

Marlene Cochran, a housewife from Shawnee, was crowned *Mrs.* America of 1967, the year between the reigns of the two Miss Americas from Kansas. ∎

Giant pitcher

272 Jesse Barnes

Baseball player. Circleville. (1892-1961) Barnes' talent in baseball took him from Circleville to the pitcher's mound of the Boston Braves in 1915. But after he led the National League with 21 losses in 1917, Boston traded him to the New York Giants. He spent most of the 1918 season in the U.S. Army, and then came home to win six out of the nine games he started. The next year Barnes was the league leader with 25 wins and nine losses. He won twenty games in 1920 and fifteen in 1921—plus two more in that year's World Series victory over the New York Yankees.

Early in the next season Jesse pitched a no-hitter against the Philadelphia Phillies. He was also on the mound in another World Series game against the Yankees that year, but it was called in the tenth inning because of darkness. Barnes was traded back to the Braves in 1923, led the league in losses in 1924 and then ended his major league career three years later with the Brooklyn Dodgers.

Virgil Barnes, his younger brother, was also a pitcher for the Giants. After Jesse was again with the Braves, they pitched against each other in ten games. ∎

Two-sport hall of famer

273 James "Jarring Jim" Bausch

Runner and football player. Garden Plain and Wichita. (1906-1974) Bausch was a football, basketball and track star at Kansas University during the late 1920s. He won positions on the college All-American football team two years in a row and turned down professional football offers to train for the Olympics.

Jim's training paid off, for at the 1932 summer games in Los Angeles he jarred the crowd by becoming only the second American to win a gold medal in the decathalon. Like other decathletes, Bausch tackled ten track and field events in a tough, two-day contest.

On day one he competed in the 100-meter dash, long jump, shot put, high jump and 400-meter run. Day two included the 110-meter hurdles, discus throw, pole vault, javelin throw and 1,500-meter run. Bausch's amazing point-total for the ten events—8,462—set a new world record. In fact, no one scored more Olympic decathlon points until American Bruce Jenner came along in 1976.

Bausch won the Sullivan Award as the outstanding amateur athlete in America in 1932. At the time, he also held ten individual records, in everything from dashes to field events.

He was inducted in the College Football Hall of Fame in 1954 and the National Track and Field Hall of Fame in 1979. His name is also included in the Kansas All Sports Hall of Fame. After his athletic career,

Bausch worked for the United States Department of Agriculture. He was living in Arkansas when he died. ∎

TV dad to Wally and the Beav

274 Hugh Beaumont

Actor and author. Lawrence. (1909-1982) Beaumont was featured in the popular ABC television comedy *Leave It to Beaver* from 1957 to 1963. As father Ward Cleaver, he was faced with all sorts of dilemmas and other "junk" caused by his sons, Wally and young Theodore—the "Beaver."

Hugh was born in Lawrence and became an actor after he was discovered in a Hollywood talent search. He appeared in numerous movies, including a series of private eye films where he starred as the tough detective Michael Shane.

He was also a successful writer and sold short stories, as well as several radio and television screenplays. After he retired from acting Beaumont moved to Minnesota and raised Christmas trees. He died while visiting one of his sons in West Germany. ∎

Silent beauty

275
Louise Brooks

Actress. Cherryvale and Wichita. (1906-1985) Brooks was born in Cherryvale and moved to Wichita with her fam-

ily in 1919. At age fourteen she left home and traveled with a dance troupe. After dancing in several Broadway shows, she appeared in a silent film in 1925. Audiences loved her large, expressive eyes framed by her short, dark hair. Within five years she had starred in thirteen American movies—plus two German films that became classics, *Pandora's Box* and *The Diary of a Lost Girl.*

Louise made her first sound movie in France in 1930 and then decided to return to Hollywood. But by that time, the screen beauty had such a reputation for being temperamental that few directors would hire her. Her last film appearance was in 1938, when she had a small part in a movie starring a new actor named John Wayne.

From 1940 to 1943 Brooks ran a dance studio in Wichita. She then moved to New York City and worked in radio soap operas and for a department store. In her later years she lived in

Rochester, New York, and wrote articles for several film journals. She has been called one of the most beautiful women ever to appear in movies. ∎

There she is

276
Deborah Bryant

Miss America. Overland Park. (Born 1947) When Bryant was crowned Miss America 1966, she was already an experienced beauty queen. Deborah was the 1966 winner of the Miss Kansas and Miss Kansas City pageants, as well as a finalist in the 1963 Miss USA contest. She was also *Teen* magazine's Most Beautiful Teenager of 1962 and the winner of several modeling contests in Kansas City. After her reign as Miss America, she transferred from a Missouri college to KU. Bryant graduated in 1969 with a degree in English. She later lived in Arizona. ∎

His voice takes him far

277 Harold Challiss

Opera singer. Atchison. (1876-19?) As a boy in Atchison Challiss raised chickens and sold his own brand of chicken lice remedy. In the mid 1890s he left home to study at the University of Chicago. After graduating, Harold sailed on a cattle ship for Europe.

There he found singing jobs with opera companies in Italy. In 1911 the young baritone sang for Spanish royalty in

Madrid. Three years later he starred in the important Bayreuth Festival in Germany. The Hamburg Opera offered him a three-year, $30,000 contract—but then World War I broke out.

In 1915 Challiss traveled to the United States to escape the war; afterward he worked for a Berlin exporter. By the 1930s he was back in America, singing and writing for music magazines. He performed under the name Bennett Challis. ∎

Thousands of buckets

278
Wilt "The Stilt" Chamberlain

Basketball player. Lawrence. (Born 1936) Chamberlain grew up in Philadelphia. There, as a six-foot, nine-inch seventh grader, he began playing basketball. Although he didn't like the game at first, that soon changed. In high school, his team lost only three times; twice he scored 90 points in a game. When a reporter called him a young man on stilts, he became Wilt "The Stilt." Chamberlain, however, preferred "The Dipper."

In 1955, he turned down offers from more than 200 colleges and universities and accepted Forrest "Phog" Allen's [*264*] invitation to attend the University of Kansas. During two years on KU's varsity team, Chamberlain averaged 30 points per game, led the Jayhawks to victory in 42 out of 50 games, and was twice named an All-American.

He left KU after his junior year and played a season for the Harlem Globetrotters before signing with the Philadelphia Warriors in 1959. The Dipper was by then seven feet, one inch tall. He set eight NBA records in his first season, and three years later scored 100 points in a game. He followed the Warriors to San Francisco, spent 1965 through 1968 with the Philadelphia 76ers and ended his career with the Los Angeles Lakers in 1973.

Although his amazing career total of 31,419 points has since

been topped, Wilt still holds nearly every other career, season and single-game scoring record in the NBA. He was the NBA's most valuable player four times and was named to the Naismith [*305*] Hall of Fame in 1978. ■

High-noter

279
Rebecca Copley

Opera singer. Lindsborg. (Born 1952) Copley has performed across the United States, in South America and in Europe. She has been a stand-in at the Metropolitan Opera in New York and is considered one of opera's most promising new sopranos. When she is not on tour or performing in New York, Rebecca and her husband live on their ranch near Lindsborg. Her first voice teacher was her father, *Elmer Copley*, who was for years the choral director of Bethany College and director of the Bethany Oratorio Society's nationally-known *Messiah*. ■

Ram-tough

280
Nolan Cromwell

Football player. Smith Center, Logan and Ransom. (Born 1955) Cromwell was born in Smith Center and grew up in Logan and Ransom. He was a high school football star and then set an NCAA rushing record as KU's quarterback. Nolan was also a world-class hurdler, and just missed a chance to participate in the 1976 Olympics. The next year he was drafted by the Los Angeles Rams. He played safety for the NFL team until 1988. Cromwell is now an assistant coach for the Green Bay Packers. ■

Runs from pain into fame

terrible sores had healed—but his legs were scarred, stiff and drawn up toward his body.

Although the doctor was sure he would never walk again, the young boy was determined not to be an invalid for the rest of his life. Month after month he exercised until he could stretch his legs and stand without help. At Christmastime in 1917 he surprised his family around their tumbleweed Christmas tree by taking his first steps since the accident. The next spring and summer, he walked and exercised outside, hanging onto the tails of his family's horse and milk cow to steady himself. Slowly and painfully, he learned to walk again, and then, to run.

Running over problems

By 1921 the family had moved to Elkhart—where they lived in a tent—then to Colorado, and back again.

The children didn't attend school in Colorado, and that, along with the time Glenn missed after the accident, made him a twelve-year-old fourth grader. But that same year he won his first foot race, battling not only pain in his legs, but teasing from those who called him "Scarlegs"—and his father's attitude that running in public was showing off.

At the county fair, he ran against several high school boys in the mile race and crossed the finish line ahead of them—twice! He ducked under the string on the final lap, then turned around and ran back, thinking he had to break the barrier to win.

Although his father was not happy, Cunningham joined the Elkhart track team in junior and senior high school. He had

Runner. Atlanta, Rolla, Elkhart, Emporia, Cedar Point and Augusta. (1909-1988) Cunningham was born August 4, 1909, at Atlanta. Five years later his family followed the wheat harvest west to the southwestern corner of the state.

Deadly fire

Outside of Rolla, his father rented a small farm. Nearby, in the winter of 1916, Cunning-

ham and his older brother were badly burned while they tried to light the stove in their country schoolhouse. With no hospital nearby, a local doctor cared for them at their home as best he could, but Cunningham's brother died several days later.

Seven-year-old Glenn faced a bleak future. His legs were so deeply burned the doctor wanted to amputate them. Enduring almost unbelievable pain, he successfully fought off infection. Six months later the had no formal training—and hadn't even been to a school sports event—but coaches quickly recognized his talent. He set so many local records that one coach took him to a national track meet in Chicago his junior and senior years. The first year he had to drop out at the last minute because of high fever and an infection. On his second trip, however, he set a new world record for the mile—four minutes, 24.7 seconds.

Elkhart townspeople welcomed him home with a ride down Main Street on the city fire truck. Several colleges telegraphed offers, but he had other obstacles to overcome. His father believed more schooling was a waste of time; the Great Depression had begun and Glenn, he said, should stay home and help support the family. At the same time, western Kansas was in the middle of the Dust Bowl and his mother was ill with dust pneumonia.

In hopes his success in athletics might lead to financial help for his ailing mother, Glenn accepted an offer to attend Kansas University. But to

Runs first four-minute mile?

Years later, Cunningham claimed he was actually the first to run a mile in less than four minutes. He said it happened during a high school track practice at Elkhart in 1930. According to Glenn, his coach told him not to tell anyone for fear they wouldn't believe it. Twenty-four years later, a British miler clocked the first official time under four minutes. Jim Ryun [316] was the first high school runner officially to break the four-minute barrier.

please his father, he spent his last year at home working at every job he could find. When he left, he turned all his savings over to his family—except for the price of a train ticket to Lawrence and $7.65 in spending money. At KU, to ease his father's pride, he refused a scholarship and worked to pay his own expenses. His first job was cleaning the football stadium and washing players' uniforms for 40 cents an hour.

Record-setting runs

During his freshman year he led the Jayhawks to the conference track championship. He qualified for the 1,500-meter dash in the 1932 Olympic games at Los Angeles the next year, but after he became sick during the finals, he finished only fourth.

In 1933 Cunningham became the second Kansan [273] in a row to win the Sullivan Award as outstanding amateur athlete in America. He led the U.S. track team on a tour of Europe and made a similar trip to the Orient in 1934. That year he set two world records for the mile, both indoors and outdoors, the fastest at four minutes, 6.7 seconds. Meanwhile, he had saved enough money to help his parents buy a small ranch in Idaho. There his mother's health improved.

In 1936 Cunningham again qualified for the Olympics, and at the summer games in Berlin, Germany, he won a silver medal in the 1,500-meter race. Two years later, the "Kansas Flyer" clocked his fastest official mile, 4:04.4.

At that time, there had been just 31 occasions when runners had beaten the four minute, ten second mark in the mile; twelve of those clockings were Cunningham's. He was

the most famous miler of the 1930s; one sportswriter called him the Babe Ruth of track.

Cunningham gave up running in 1940 and took a teaching position at a college in Iowa. It was there that a dentist discovered the source of his mysterious illnesses over the years—all eight of his front teeth were badly abscessed. The trouble apparently had begun in high school when he was hit in the mouth by a baseball. The infection was so severe doctors were amazed Glenn had been able to run, much less set world records.

During World War II he was a physical fitness instructor in the U.S. Navy. He spent part of his time working with burn victims in a San Diego hospital.

Helping others

After the war he moved to Emporia where he planned to teach. Instead, he married and moved to a ranch near Cedar Point. There, and later at Augusta, he and his wife operated a home for needy children. Although they later had financial and legal problems, the Cunninghams and their own ten children helped care for over 9,000 youths during the next 30 years. Glenn and his wife moved to a youth ranch in Arkansas in 1973.

The next year Cunningham was named to the National Track and Field Hall of Fame. He is also in the Kansas All Sports Hall of Fame. In 1979 New York City's Madison Square Garden honored him as its all-time outstanding track performer.

Cunningham died March 10, 1988, at his Arkansas ranch. Before his death, he and another Elkhart runner, Thane Baker [270], helped establish a scholarship fund for Morton County high school graduates. ■

Artist at the keyboard

282 James Dick

Concert pianist.
Hutchinson. (Born 1940)
Dick grew up on a farm near Hutchinson. He took his first piano lessons at the age of five. Twelve years and three music teachers later, he had won several state music contests.

As a high school senior his piano teacher urged him to enter the important Naftzger competition in Wichita, but James refused. He wanted to go into politics. He changed his mind, however, and became the youngest contestant ever to win the event. His victory led to a performance with the Wichita Symphony.

Dick studied piano at the University of Texas and received a Fulbright scholarship to study at the Royal Academy of Music in London in 1963 and 1964.

In 1966 he won fifth place in the important Tchaikovsky International Piano Competition in Moscow. Several years later he was the first American invited to judge the event.

Dick has performed throughout the Europe and the United States, including the famous Carnegie Hall in New York City. When he is not traveling between concerts, he lives in Texas. In 1986, he played for England's Prince Charles during a royal visit to America.

To encourage and instruct young musicians, Dick has established the Festival Hill Performing Arts Center in Round Top, Texas, near Austin. There he sponsors music festivals and annual summer institutes. Students and performers come from around the world to take part. ■

Acting for Kansas

Packers' top passer

283 Lynn Dickey

Football player.
Osawatomie and Lenexa.
(Born 1949) As a quarterback at Kansas State University, Dickey threw passes totaling 6,028 yards—a KSU record. Many fans still remember him leading the Wildcats to a 59 to 21 victory over Oklahoma University in 1969. It remains K-State's highest-scoring football game. After he graduated in 1971, Dickey joined the Houston Oilers and spent five years

with the NFL team. Next he played for the Green Bay Packers in Green Bay, Wisconsin. In 1983 he led the NFL in passes completed—nearly 60 percent. He was also the league leader in touchdown passes that year, with 32. In all, during his ten years with the Packers, he completed passes totaling over 19,000 yards. He now lives in Lenexa and owns Lynn Dickey's Sports Cafes in Westport and St. Louis, Missouri. ■

284 Marj Dusay

Actress. Russell. (Born 1938)
Dusay grew up in Russell as Marj Mahoney. Because of her fear of performing in front of others, she almost failed a freshman speech class at Kansas University. And, when she was crowned KU's 1956 homecoming queen, the shy Marj nearly fainted on the football field.

She left the university in 1958 and helped send her husband to medical school by modeling in Kansas City, Missouri, and then New York City. Although a talent scout offered her a chance to appear in movies, she politely refused. She didn't consider herself an actress.

Dusay's attitude changed when she moved to San Francisco in the 1960s. She made commericals and also worked at improvisational comedy clubs to improve her acting skills. After another move, to Los Angeles, she began appearing in television and in movies.

She has had roles in over 50 television series, including *Star Trek*, *Get Smart*, *Dallas* and *Facts of Life*. For several years

in the mid 1980s, she starred in the daytime drama *Capitol*—often memorizing 30 pages of script for each episode of the CBS soap opera.

In 1986 Dusay started her own video production company. That same year Governor John Carlin [**35**] asked her to chair the Kansas Film Commission, a committee that encourages motion picture studios to make films in Kansas. ∎

died in the disaster, but Evans' brave action helped save the lives of many others.

And he kept conducting after his retirement in 1969. Although he lived on the circus train much of the year and spent his free time in Florida, Evans always called Kansas his home. ∎

Big top bandleader

285 Merle Evans

Circus band conductor. Columbus. (1891-1987) As a boy Evans liked to sneak into the Columbus firehouse to hear the town band practice. By age ten he had his own cornet and was known as the loudest horn blower in Cherokee County. To help support his family he worked much of the time—shining shoes, peeling potatoes, carrying luggage and doing farmwork—but he also practiced music every chance he got.

He tried to leave home at thirteen and join a traveling band, but his parents had other ideas. Four years later, they gave in and young Merle began playing in a carnival band. For over a decade he worked with one traveling band after another—on a steamboat, in carnivals, with comedians, and in Wild West shows owned by William F. "Buffalo Bill" Cody [**349**] and the Miller Brothers' 101 Ranch.

When two of America's most famous circuses merged in 1919, John Ringling hired Evans as bandleader, replacing both shows' original directors.

For the next 50 years Evans crisscrossed the country with the "Greatest Show on Earth"—the Ringling Brothers and Barnum & Bailey Circus. In more than 22,000 performances, it was said the "Toscanini of the Big Top" was never late or missed a show.

Each performance required parts of at least 200 songs. In addition to accompanying the various acts, Evans had to be alert for problems and ready to mask any trouble with music.

To help keep order during a tent fire in 1944, he and his musicians played continuously, even as the smoke thickened and their uniforms began to scorch. Over 150 spectators

Takes his talent to Broadway

286 Lorenzo Dow Fuller, Jr.

Singer, actor and composer. Stockton. (Born 1919) Fuller's mother's family lived in the black colony of Nicodemus in Graham County. His father was ***Lorenzo Dow Fuller, Sr.***, a traveling musician who published an African-American newspaper in Coffeyville during the late 1890s. After Fuller moved to Stockton his wife and son traveled with him each summer, giving musical shows across the Great Plains. Young Lorenzo played the harp at the age of four, and later learned to play the piano and five other instruments.

He attended Kansas University in the early 1940s and received bachelor's and master's degrees in music. By the time Fuller left KU, he had starred in several university productions, written a musical, announced for the campus radio station and managed a quartet. In 1946 he enrolled at the famous Julliard School of Music in New York City. Soon he landed a part ⇨

in a Broadway musical, and when it closed, he took a role in *Finian's Rainbow.*

At the same time, he sang on two daily radio shows, one of which was broadcast coast-to-coast. In 1947 NBC offered him his own fifteen-minute variety program, making him the first African-American to host a national television show. He later performed on other television variety programs.

The tireless Fuller also appeared in the musical *Kiss Me Kate*, made a movie, worked as a writer and musical director for NBC, choreographed for Broadway productions, gave music lessons and wrote several compositions, including a ballet.

Ill health forced him to slow down and for a time in the 1960s he lived with his mother in Stockton. He later returned to New York City. ∎

Hale and hearty actor

287 Hale Hamilton

Actor. Topeka. (1883-1942)
Hamilton moved from Iowa to Topeka in 1899 when his father transferred to a new job with the Santa Fe Railway. Although he attended Kansas University in hopes of becoming a lawyer, he ended up an actor instead.

After traveling with a theater company, Hale starred in George M. Cohan's popular comedy *Get-Rich-Quick Wallingford* for two seasons in New York City. Then for nearly six years, he toured the world, playing stages in England, South Africa, Australia and New Zealand. During a visit to London in 1918, he gave a com-

mand performance at Windsor Castle for King George V. That same year he also entertained the emperor of Germany.

In 1918 the Keystone Comedy Corporation offered Hamilton a movie contract reportedly worth $500 a day. One of his first films was *Opportunity*, a comedy-drama based on a poem written by Senator John J. Ingalls [**63**]. Before 1940, Hale appeared in a dozen or more movies. His brother, **John D.M. Hamilton**, was Speaker of the Kansas House of Representatives. During Alf Landon's [**67**] campaign John was national chairman of the Republican party. ∎

Helps football off the ground

288 Jesse Harper

Football coach and rancher. Wichita and Sitka.
(1883-1961) Harper grew up in Illinois and Iowa, and graduated from the University of Chicago in 1906. After coaching at two other colleges, he became football coach at Notre Dame University in 1913.

At that time football was a running game, and Notre Dame's team was little known except in Indiana. That changed during Harper's first season when his team tried a little-used play—the forward pass—against the tough Army squad. Notre Dame captain Knute Rockne plucked

a string of passes out of the air, leading his team to a 35 to 13 upset over powerhouse Army. Sitting on the Cadets' bench during that contest, by the way, was young Dwight D. Eisenhower [**44**], sidelined with an injury.

Coach Harper scheduled contests around the country, and as his Fighting Irish demonstrated the effectiveness of passing, they also brought attention to college football teams outside the East. Jesse left coaching in 1918 and came to Kansas, his wife's home state. They lived in Wichita while he

helped his father-in-law run a 20,000-acre cattle ranch in Clark County. Rockne, by then a football legend, replaced Harper at Notre Dame.

When Rockne died in 1931—in a plane crash that happened, ironically, in the Kansas Flint Hills—the university offered Harper his old job. He spent another two seasons in Indiana, then returned to Kansas and lived on his ranch. ∎

Santa's number one helper

289 Henry Harvey

Radio and television personality. Baxter Springs and Wichita. (Born 1925)
Harvey grew up in Baxter Springs and spent time during World War II in noncombat service in the Phillipines and New Guinea.

When he returned home in 1946 he began broadcasting at Wichita radio station KFBI, now called KFDI. In the mid 1950s he joined the staff of television station KAKE. There he was an announcer, a news, weather and sports reporter, and the "pitchman" on countless commercials.

The robust Harvey is best known, however, as Santa Claus. He first put on a Santa costume at KFBI and distributed toys to needy children. Later, he appeared as Santa at a chain of Wichita bookstores. In 1954 his version of Santa Claus went on television with a children's show on KAKE.

When Harvey moved to another Wichita television station, KTVH (now KWCH), his annual Christmas show went along. For many years, he also appeared as Freddy Fudd on an afternoon children's program.

For over 35 consecutive Christmases, Harvey's Santa broadcasts on the Wichita television stations and their affiliated stations around the state made him recognizable to thousands of Kansans. In fact, some of Harvey's young viewers in the late 1980s were grandchildren of his original 1950s audience.

Henry retired from broadcasting in 1988, except for a few Santa appearances at Christmas. For a short time he managed a missionary radio station in Africa. Now he is a professional singer for a Wichita mortuary where he performs at nearly 200 funerals a year. ∎

Easy rider has tough time

290 Dennis Hopper

Actor and filmmaker. Dodge City. (Born 1936) Hopper was born in Dodge City and spent his early years on his grandparents' farm while his father was in the military.

His family moved to Kansas City, Missouri, after World War II, and then to California in 1950. There Hopper appeared in as many school plays as possible; he had decided while watching cowboy movies in Dodge City that he wanted to be an actor.

Fresh out of high school, Dennis worked as a stagehand at a Hollywood theater. After the owner helped him get a role as a young patient in a television medical show, he was offered other acting jobs. Soon the nineteen-year-old had signed a movie contract with Warner Brothers studio.

In some of his early films, including *Rebel Without a Cause* and *Giant*, Hopper was cast as an angry young rebel—a part he also played in real life. His addiction to alcohol made him difficult to work with. During the filming of one Western, he refused to follow the director's instructions. For eighteen hours, the man shot and reshot the same ten-line scene. Finally—after 86 times—the stubborn 21-year-old actor did it correctly.

Hopper's 1969 film *Easy Rider*. expressed some of his negative feelings toward society. He directed, co-wrote and starred in the box office hit, and then spent much of the profit on his alcohol and drug habits.

Although he continued making movies, his addictions deepened. By 1984 he was in a psychiatric hospital. After undergoing treatment in several institutions, he joined Alcoholics Anonymous and gave up drugs and alcohol. He returned to work in 1986, and was nominated for an Oscar in his role as a sober alcoholic coach in *Hoosiers*. Once again, his work and life paralleled.

In all, Hopper has appeared in or directed over 40 films. ∎

Singing sweet songs

Singer, actress, composer, choral director, author and poet. Coffeyville, Caney, Iola and Pittsburg. (Born 1895) Jessye had many roles in her talented career. And her performances took her from small Kansas towns to Broadway and around the world.

Hallelujah!

Jessye was born in Coffeyville, on Sunday morning, January 20, 1895. Across the street in a Baptist church, the choir sang "hallelujah." For that reason, family members said, Eva's life centered around music. That

interest was also influenced by her parents. All types of music were popular in their home. And her father was something of a local musical celebrity. By cleverly manipulating his vocal cords, he could sing two tones at the same time. Unfortunately, *Al Jesse* was also an outlaw.

For that reason Eva later changed the spelling of her last name. She didn't want to be known as "Al Jesse's daughter."

Eva's parents separated when she was three. Her mother moved to Seattle, and Eva stayed with relatives in Kansas. Much of the time she lived in Coffeyville with her grandmother or one of her aunts. When family members left each summer to pick cotton in Indian Territory, Eva spent time on a great-aunt's farm near Caney. After the day's chores were done, she enjoyed listening to her Aunt Harriet sing spirituals at night.

When she was seven, Eva joined her mother in Seattle and lived there for two years. During that time, she developed an interest in poetry. A friendly railroad porter often brought her poetry magazines to read. She enjoyed the poems and began copying verses to learn various styles.

'Little protegé'

After she returned from Seattle, Eva lived in Coffeyville, or with aunts in Iola and St. Louis. All the while, her interest in music continued to grow. At the age of twelve she organized her first singing ensemble, a girls' quartet. That same year, African-American musician Will Marion Cook and his musical troupe visited Coffeyville. Before their performance, someone lost the music scores for the orchestra, and Cook asked Eva to help recopy the missing pages. He called Jessye his "little protegé," and encouraged her to continue her musical studies.

A year later Eva's mother enrolled her in Western University near Kansas City since blacks were not allowed to attend high school in Coffey-ville. The thirteen-year-old was actually a year too young to enter the academy, but she quickly proved she had musical talent. Soon she was in charge of the school's chorus.

Musical heritage

During a campus visit of Booker T. Washington, the famous black educator told Eva's class never to forget the songs of their ancestors. It was a lesson she took to heart.

Eva graduated from Western in 1914 and spent three summers in Oklahoma at Langston University. In the fall of 1916 she began teaching elementary school music. After four years in the classroom Jessye moved to Baltimore where she became director of a college music department. She also worked for an African-American newspaper.

Doctor's orders

She left Maryland in 1926 to find a career in music in New York City. When she found that work was scarce, she applied for a job as a hospital dietician. A doctor came to interview her in her small apartment and noticed that she had been writing music. He asked why a musician such as herself was not following her profession. "Because I have to eat," she quickly replied. He insisted she stay with music and make it work, no matter what the price.

Following the doctor's advice, Eva continued to search for music jobs. To support herself, she ironed shirts for thirteen dollars a week and saved 25 cents a day for her meals. She also sang in the wings of movie theaters during silent films. Her first musical break came when she was hired as a singer in a Broadway movie theater to warm up audiences before the feature film. That led to her membership in the Dixie Jubilee Singers. The choir became popular for its regular appearances on the *Major Bowes Family Radio Hour* and other nationwide musical broadcasts.

Into show business

In 1923 her poetry first gained public attention when two of her poems appeared in a collection of works by black poets. At the same time, Eva earned commissions by organizing quartets and ensembles for radio. One of her groups, working at a Detroit station, performed one of radio's first singing commercials—a song advertising Van Heusen shirts.

In the late 1920s, Eva's musician friend Will Marion Cook urged her to publish a collection of African-American songs. She was desperate for money, and for nearly three weeks, she worked almost nonstop in her one-room New York ⇨

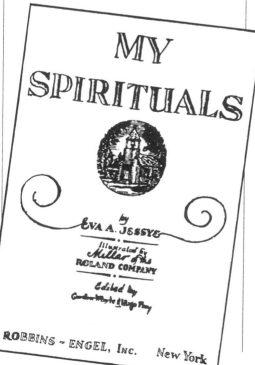

MY SPIRITUALS

by
EVA A. JESSYE

Illustrated by
Muller of the
ROLAND COMPANY

Edited by
Gardner Wright & Wright Play

ROBBINS ~ ENGEL, INC. New York

197

apartment—furnished with only a cot, a chair and a broken-down piano. She called that first book *My Spirituals*.

In 1929, Jessye was invited to Hollywood to direct the choir for the film *Hallelujah*, the first sound musical starring blacks. The temperamental Southern director fired Eva before the movie was finished, but a lawyer advised her to come to work anyway, so she wouldn't be accused of breaking her contract. Faithfully, she sat in front of the studio each morning, and when the stubborn director realized her replacement couldn't handle the job, he rehired her.

Four years later she was the choral director for Gertrude Stein's experimental opera, *Four Saints in Three Acts*.

A Florida college offered her a professorship, but Jessye chose to continue touring with her singers, the Eva Jessye Choir. The group was featured on Broadway and radio stations around the country as well as in England.

Porgy and Bess

Early in 1935, Jessye's singers auditioned in New York City for composer George Gershwin's new folk opera, *Porgy and Bess*. They were selected, and when this first true American opera opened on Broadway that October, Jessye was the choral director.

From 1938 to 1940 she was choral director at a South Carolina college. She returned to Broadway in 1942 when *Porgy and Bess* was brought back to the stage, and then directed World War II victory concerts.

After the war, Jessye's choir toured Europe, giving concerts in several foreign capitals. In a

bombed-out theater in Berlin they performed for refugees who had never seen American blacks. "They called us 'chocolate people,' and I said I hoped we were half as sweet," Eva recalled.

Honors from far and wide

Miss Jessye (she was twice married and divorced) also appeared in several movies, including *Black Like Me* and *Slaves*. Several universities gave her honorary doctor's degrees.

Her friends included musician Duke Ellington and first lady Eleanor Roosevelt. In 1963, she walked with Dr. Martin Luther King on his civil rights march in Washington, D.C. Her choral group was the official choir for the event.

In 1974 she established the Eva Jessye Collection of Afro-American Music at the University of Michigan in Ann Arbor, her home at the time.

In Kansas, Pittsburg State University selected Jessye to open its diamond jubilee celebration in 1978. During the festivities governor **Robert Bennett** led the state in celebrating Eva Jessye Day. Jessye was later honored as Kansas Musician of the Year.

She returned to Pittsburg in 1979 as an artist-in-residence, bringing along over four tons of memorabilia from her career to donate to the university's library. After living in Kansas several years, she returned to Michigan.

Even into her nineties, she was busy with a variety of projects—new musical productions, and books about *Porgy and Bess* and her own career. ∎

Wichita to Miami to fame

292 Don Johnson

Actor and singer. Wichita. (Born 1949) Johnson was born in Missouri but lived in Wichita two different times during his youth.

During his senior year at Wichita South High School, Don lacked enough credits to graduate until his counselor enrolled him in a theater class. He won not only the lead in the school play, but his diploma and a drama scholarship to the University of Kansas. He left KU after his sophomore year to study in California. There he was featured in a play, and then offered the lead in a movie.

The film was a failure, but it led him to other movie and television roles in the 1970s. At the same time, unfortunately, Johnson drifted into drug and alcohol abuse. In 1984, a year after he was treated for his addiction, he was cast in the lead of a new NBC series, *Miami Vice*. For several seasons, Johnson was recognized by millions as a tough, casually-dressed police detective. He also recorded an album during that time.

Between acting jobs, Johnson and his actress wife Melanie Griffith now live with their children on a Colorado ranch. ∎

Pitches by express

293 Walter "Big Train" Johnson

Baseball player. Humboldt and Coffeyville. (1887-1946) Johnson was born in Humboldt and lived there until 1904 when his family gave up farming and moved to California. There he played high school baseball and then joined a semi-pro league. In 1907 a scout for the Washington Senators discovered Walter pitching in Idaho. The major league team offered him a $100 bonus, a monthly salary of $350 and a train ticket east. He accepted.

Two years later his parents moved back to Kansas and lived in Coffeyville. Johnson spent his winters there until 1921.

In all, Johnson pitched 21 seasons for the Senators. Most of that time, the club was one of the league's weaker teams. Fans often said, "Washington: first in war, first in peace—and last in the American League."

That changed in 1924 when 37-year-old Walter led the Senators to victory in the World Series. In the decisive seventh game, he pitched four scoreless innings and won the twelve-inning contest with the New York Giants. Afterward he was named the league's most valuable player, an honor he had also received in 1913. When he retired from playing in 1927, Johnson had pitched in 802 games and won 416 of them. Two of his career records still stand: 110 shutouts and 38 one-to-nothing wins.

Although Johnson played before the era of electronic speed guns, he was thought to have thrown the fastest pitches in his time. As a result, he was called the "Coffeyville Express," "Big Train" and "Barney"—for mile-a-minute auto racer Barney Oldfield.

Fans, fellow players and sportswriters were also impressed with Walter's modest, mild and friendly personality. Some nicknamed him the "White Knight" and "Sir Walter," after the legendary chivalrous knight.

Johnson retired from baseball in 1935, after managing the Senators and the Cleveland Indians. The next year, he was one of the first five players elected to the Baseball Hall of Fame. ■

Jumps into acting

294 Gordon Jump

Actor and filmmaker. Fort Riley, Manhattan and Topeka. (Born 1932) Jump grew up in Ohio and wanted to be a doctor until he spent two years as a U.S. Army medic at Fort Riley. He decided laughter was his favorite medicine, and stayed in Kansas to get a communications degree at KSU.

After graduating, he spent two years in graduate school at Washburn University in Topeka. There he also worked at television station WIBW as a weatherman and the clown host of a children's show. Gordon left Kansas in 1963 and moved to Los Angeles a year later. He has appeared in numerous television shows, but is best known as the bumbling radio station manager Arthur Carlson from the comedy *WKRP in Cinncinati.* The series ran on CBS from 1978 to 1982, and was brought back to life in 1991 when new episodes were taped for syndication. Ironically, Jump worked at KMAN radio in Manhattan—but he was fired after two weeks.

For several years Jump has been the lonely repairman in Maytag appliance commercials. He has also directed, produced and acted in a number of movies. ■

Cinema and circus comedians

295 Joseph "Buster" Keaton

Actor and filmmaker. Piqua. (1895-1966) Keaton was born in Kansas—by chance—while his parents were acrobats in a traveling tent show with magician Harry Houdini.

As they spent the night in Piqua, their tent collapsed in a windstorm. The Keatons took shelter in a church, and a few hours later their son Joseph was born. (He earned his nickname as a toddler. When he fell down some stairs unhurt, Houdini remarked, "What a buster!") Keaton joined the family act as a three-year-old and by the time the group broke up in 1917, he was a talented acrobat.

The young man then signed a movie contract with Roscoe "Fatty" Arbuckle [**267**]. During the long career that followed, Buster made over 100 movies. In the silent films of the 1920s audiences loved his pantomimed stunts and deadpan stares at the camera. Known as "The Great Stone Face," he also helped direct and write movies. When "talkies" arrived in the 1930s, Keaton's popularity faded— although some of his early films were revived in the 1950s.

The famous comic once revisited Piqua—briefly. Keaton lowered the window in his chauffeur-driven car but had little to say about his Kansas birthplace. ∎

296 Emmett Kelly

Clown. Sedan. (1898-1979) Kelly was born in Sedan but while he was a small boy his father quit a railroad job and moved his family to a farm in Missouri. At school young Kelly

discovered he had a talent for drawing, and with encouragement from his mother, he took a correspondence course in cartooning. In 1917 he headed to Kansas City, Missouri, convinced that he was a cartoonist. But the only jobs he found were painting signs and working in a carnival.

Soon he was giving "chalk-talks," short stories he told as he drew chalk illustrations. Between art jobs he worked on farms, in an oil refinery and with a carnival trapeze act. Eventually he was a cartoonist at a Kansas City advertising company.

In the 1920s he joined a circus as a trapeze artist and clown. When that show closed during the Great Depression, he found work as a clown in another circus. But rather than appearing as the ordinary white-face clown in a colorful outfit, he decided to bring to life one of his early cartoons—a sad-faced hobo in tattered clothes and a battered hat.

From that first appearance in 1933, Weary Willie, as Kelly's character was known, became famous to millions of circus fans. As Willie, Kelly appeared in England during the late 1930s, and then toured nightclubs in the United States. In 1942 he joined the Ringling Brothers and Barnum & Bailey Circus. Two years later, he helped rescue circus-goers from a deadly tent fire in Hartford, Connecticut, while Merle Evans [**285**] and his band played to keep order.

After fifteen years, Kelly left the circus. He also appeared in movies, on television and as pregame entertainment for the Brooklyn Dodgers. Kelly's closing trademark was a scene in which Willie tried to sweep away all the light from a spotlight shining on a darkened stage. He has been called one of the greatest clowns of all time. ∎

Top musicians from jazz to opera

297 Stan Kenton

Jazz band conductor, pianist and composer. Wichita. (1912-1979) Kenton and his family moved to California when he was five years old. Although he enjoyed music, he refused to play for his piano-teacher mother. That changed when he was fourteen and he heard his musician cousins playing jazz.

From then on, Stan was "all music." He took lessons from an organist at a nearby theater, and practiced up to ten hours a day. In high school, he formed his first jazz group, the Belltones. After he graduated in 1930 he supported himself during the Great Depression by working as a $5-a-night musician.

In 1941 he formed his own jazz orchestra. After performing with entertainer Bob Hope, he signed a recording contract with Columbia Records in 1943. He composed many works for his band, including "Artistry in Rhythm" and "Eager Beaver."

In the early 1950s he toured with jazz all-star Charlie Parker [*306*]. Kenton helped launch the career of Maynard Ferguson and other jazz greats. He also pioneered Third Stream jazz—a combination of classical music and jazz. In 1965 and 1970 he formed new groups and again toured for several years. In all, he recorded over 50 albums. ∎

298 Kathleen Kersting

Opera singer. Wichita. (1908-1965) Kersting was born in Oklahoma. While she was a child, her parents moved to Wichita and opened a hotel. Kathleen showed musical talent at an early age, and she often entertained family and friends with her singing. At thirteen, she gave her first public concert at a Wichita theater.

On a visit to Kansas that same year, the famous French singer Madam Emma Calve heard Kathleen sing. She immediately insisted that the Kerstings allow their daughter to study with her. For two years, Kathleen took voice lessons in New York City—while her parents scraped together all their extra money to support her.

In the mid 1920s, the teenager returned to Wichita. She gave a concert to raise money for more study, and the Wichita Rotary Club agreed to help. Members soon raised $15,000 so she could study in France and Italy.

In 1928, she made her professional debut in an Italian opera company. Newspapers called her "the girl with the golden nightingale in her throat." Within two years, she was a star. Opera lovers in the United States and Europe packed theaters to hear her. On one of her European tours she sang under the direction of world-famous conductor Arturo Toscanini.

By the start of World War II Kersting had married a German army officer. For several tense months in 1939, no one heard from her. Officials would not let her leave the country or speak to her family in America. Then one of her friends in Italy contacted the Kerstings in Wichita. Their daughter was safe.

For part of the war, Kathleen was allowed to continue singing, but eventually she was forced to work in a German ammunition factory. After the war Kersting divorced her husband. She worked in cultural exchange programs, appeared in American opera companies—and sang at the White House for President Harry Truman.

She later taught in the United States and in Europe. Her last Wichita concert was in 1952. ∎

299 James King

Opera singer. Dodge City. (Born 1925) When King was born in Dodge City, his father was sheriff of Ford County.

James developed an interest in music at an early age and took violin, piano and vocal lessons through high school. After graduation, however, World War II interrupted his music studies.

Following service in the military, he received a bachelor's degree at Louisiana State University and a master's degree at Kentucky State. After more ↷

education at the University of Kentucky King spent nine years there teaching music. All that time, he developed his singing voice. He sang in operettas and with music companies, won tryouts with the American Opera, but was turned down— six times—when he auditioned at New York City's important Metropolitan Opera.

The impressive tenor went to Europe in 1962 and was offered a contract after his first tryout at the West Berlin Opera. Soon he had sung in leading operas across Germany and Austria. When officials at the Met then changed their minds, King was so busy in Europe he couldn't make it to the New York City stage until 1966.

King married a German actress and has lived in Germany for much of his career. He has appeared in operas around the world and has given recitals in his native Kansas. ■

Small town to big screens

300 Shirley Knight

Actress. Goessel, Mitchell and Lyons. (Born 1937)
Knight was born in Goessel and moved to the Mitchell area when she was in elementary school. She graduated from high school in Lyons. Before she left Kansas in 1957 she attended Wichita State University, wrote for the *Wichita Beacon*, worked at television station KAKE, sang with a dance band and attended modeling school.

Shirley planned to become an actress on Broadway, but her father convinced her to accept a scholarship to UCLA. In California she won a lead role in an NBC television drama, and turned down the scholarship. Within three years, she gave an

Academy-Award nominated performance in the movie version of William Inge's [*215*] *The Dark at the Top of the Stairs.*

In the next few years Knight made nearly twenty movies and appeared in over 200 television shows. But she became unhappy in Hollywood and went to the Broadway stage. Then, in the mid 1960s, she and her British husband moved to England. There she made several movies and raised their daughters. When they moved back to the United States in the 1970s Knight once again appeared in movies and television. She also received a Tony Award for her work in the Broadway play *Kennedy's Children.* ■

Fit to be Miss USA

301 Kelli McCarty

Miss USA. Liberal. (Born 1969) McCarty grew up in Liberal and won her first beauty pageant there in 1988. She continued competing in the Miss USA pageant at the local and state level for two more years. The third time was a charm, for in early 1991 she became Miss USA.

The news of Kelli's win came as no surprise to Kansas since she was crowned close to home—in Wichita—in front of a worldwide television audience of 350 million people in 30 countries.

During her year-long reign, she traveled the United States and met thousands of Americans— including President and Mrs. George Bush. And nearly every day, the ex-Miss Kansas USA said, someone told her a "Dorothy [*362*] joke."

Before her reign McCarty took communications classes at Wichita State University and was an aerobics instructor. After she gave up her crown she planned to continue her education in California and hoped to work in television or movies. ■

Oscar-winning acting

Actress and composer. Wichita. (1895-1952)
McDaniel, the youngest of thirteen children, was born in Wichita, June 10, 1895. Her father, **Henry McDaniel**, was an ex-slave who came to Kansas in the late 1870s. In Wichita he was a part-time Baptist minister, construction worker and entertainer. Her mother,

Susan Holbert McDaniel, was once a popular gospel singer in Tennessee. When Hattie was about five, the family moved to Colorado. They settled in Denver in 1901.

On the road

At an early age, Hattie enjoyed entertaining. She sang in church, at school and at home—until her mother offered her coins to keep quiet. When

she was thirteen she began appearing in a family minstrel show. Two years later, she won a speaking contest. Along with a gold medal, Hattie took home the desire to be an entertainer.

She left school after her sophomore year and joined her father and brother entertaining across Colorado in a minstrel show. Hattie sang and also wrote many of the songs they performed. Between engagements she worked as a cook and laundress. After her brother died in 1916 and the act broke up, she spent several years with show groups traveling through western states and into Canada.

She toured with another traveling theater company until 1929, but lost her job when the stock market crash left the group bankrupt. Hearing that there might be work in Milwaukee, she went there—but the only job she found was as a restroom attendant in a nightclub. One night the owner let her sing. The crowd loved her and she was once again performing.

Hello, Hollywood

In 1931 her sister and brother who had worked as movie extras convinced Hattie to move to Hollywood. With help from them she got a job on a weekly radio show. Soon audiences were calling it Hi-Hat Hattie and Her Boys.

Later that year, she landed several small movie jobs singing in choruses. But like her radio show, her movie work paid only $5 a performance. McDaniel later joked that in those days no one in Hollywood could count above five. To help pay her bills she worked as a maid.

Eight years later she came to the top with a part in the film of the decade, *Gone with the Wind*. And for her portrayal of ⇨

Scarlett O'Hara's mammy, Mac-Daniel received an Academy Award. Not only was she the first African-American to win an Oscar, but she was the first black star ever to attend the ceremonies.

Mammy criticized

Although the award brought her much attention and more work, it also brought criticism. As she was cast in more films as a servant, the NAACP criticized her—and other black performers—for playing stereotyped "happy slaves." Hattie, of course, didn't agree with the negative characterization of African-Americans. She had a simple answer for her critics: She would rather receive $700 a week for playing a maid than work as one for only $7 weekly.

By the time the controversy died down in the late 1940s, McDaniel's movie career was fading. She then made history in 1947 when she took the lead in the CBS radio series *Beulah.* Hattie became the first African-American to star in a sponsored radio program about a black character. Surprisingly, the Beulah character had been on radio since 1939—but white men had always done her voice! McDaniel refused to play the part in their stereotyped-sounding way. Within a year the show's audience doubled, to fifteen million listeners.

Beulah began on television in 1950 and after the original star quit, Hattie was offered the role. She was diagnosed with cancer, however, at about the same time. She died in a California hospital, October 26, 1952.

McDaniel's last two movies in 1948 brought her career total to over 300 films—although only about 85 of them included her name in the credits. ■

Miss Kansas in Hollywood

303 Vera Miles

Actress. Wichita. (Born 1929) Miles was born in Oklahoma as Vera Ralston. Later her family moved to Wichita where she graduated from North High School. She was crowned Miss Kansas of 1948 and was second runner-up in that year's Miss America pageant.

Vera's beauty contest wins took her to Hollywood where she worked in live television dramas.

She completed her first movie in 1951. Through the 1970s she was featured in a long list of television shows and movies.

Miles played in a wide variety of films—all the way from a Tarzan movie, Alfred Hitchcock's thriller *Psycho*, a Walt Disney picture with a tiger co-star, to numerous Westerns, including *Wichita*, the story of her Kansas hometown. ■

Comes from behind to win

304 Billy Mills

Runner. Lawrence. (Born 1938) Mills, a Sioux Indian, was born on the Pine Ridge Reservation in South Dakota. After he became an orphan at age thirteen he was sent to the Haskell Institute in Lawrence.

There he won two state championships in the mile and three state titles in the two-mile cross-country run. With a full athletic scholarship to the University of Kansas, Mills became the Big Eight cross country champion and led the Jayhawks to the NCAA championship. He also represented the United States in the 1959 Pan American Games at Sao Paulo, Brazil.

After he graduated in 1962 he entered the U.S. Marines. When an officer encouraged him to run again, he won a 10,000-meter race in Germany.

With the 1964 Olympics in sight he kept running—a total of 100 miles a week. He qualified for the U.S. team and at the summer games in Tokyo he ran one of the most exciting races in Olympic history.

In the last 300 meters of the 10,000-meter run, he was accidentally pushed by one of the other 36 runners. Twenty meters behind, he caught up to the rest—and won. His record time earned him a gold medal.

He was later in the insurance business and was then a public relations officer with the U.S. Bureau of Indian Affairs. He last lived in California. Mills was placed in the National Track and Field Hall of Fame in 1976 and the U.S. Olympic Hall of Fame in 1984. He is also in the Kansas All Sports Hall of Fame. ■

The father of basketball

Inventor, basketball coach, educator, minister and doctor. Lawrence. (1861-1939) Naismith was born on a farm near Almonte, Ontario, Canada, November 6, 1861.

Young orphan

When he was eight, the Naismith family moved to Quebec. His father died of typhoid fever that fall. Just two weeks later, on Jim's ninth birthday, the disease killed his mother. He and his sister and brother were sent to live with their grandmother in Ontario. Only two years passed before she, too, died, leaving the orphans in the care of their 26-year-old uncle.

At fifteen Jim quit school to help support his brother and sister. He worked as a lumber-jack during the winter and helped his uncle with farmwork in the summer.

Shortly before his twentieth birthday, he returned to high school. Within two years he completed his needed courses, and told his uncle he wanted to attend college. The uncle, who had expected his nephew to stay and help on the farm, said he would allow it only if Jim would become a minister.

Naismith agreed. In college at Montreal, he studied much harder than he had in high school, but he also got involved in athletics. Lacrosse and rugby football, a rough combination of rugby and soccer, were his favorites.

James graduated near the head of his class in 1887 and entered a Presbyterian seminary. While

he continued to do well in the classroom, his sports activities upset others. One Sunday, as a student minister, he faced his congregation with two black eyes left over from a Saturday rugby match! He wasn't embarrassed, but his teachers and friends prayed for his soul.

Minister of sports

In 1889 he began teaching evenings in a gymnasium. That experience, and a talk he heard by a young Christian athlete, changed his plans. When the speaker pointed out that being a good athlete and a good Christian took much in common—enthusiasm, perseverance and hard work—Naismith decided he wanted to spread religion through sports.

He left the seminary the next year and enrolled at a Young Men's Christian Association training school at Springfield, Massachusetts. One of the first students he met at the YMCA school was Amos Alonzo Stagg, the young speaker who had influenced him. Stagg was just beginning the training that would help make him a legend in football coaching.

A new game

In the 1891 fall semester, Naismith was given an assignment by one of his YMCA instructors: come up with a new indoor game for physical education classes. It needed to be simple, yet interesting enough for adults. As James put off the assignment, the teacher added an incentive to finish—a two-week time limit, and a gym class on which to experiment.

First the temporary teacher tried versions of children's games, but his young adult students weren't interested in new ⊃

ways to play tag and leapfrog. And when he adapted rough outdoor adult sports like soccer and rugby, both the gym and the players came out battered.

With one day left before his deadline, Naismith put together the basics for a brand-new game. A team of players would toss a ball back and forth, and try to score points by tossing it at a target. No tackling would be allowed and no one could run with the ball. (Dribbling was added a few years later.)

The December morning his students were to try the new game, Naismith asked the school janitor for a couple of wooden boxes to use as goals. The man rummaged in his storeroom and found two peach baskets. James nailed them to the edge of a balcony around the gym and went to his office. Quickly, he wrote out rules for his game. A secretary began typing them, and finished just before the 11:30 class started. Naismith thumbtacked the two pages on a bulletin board as his students entered the gym.

A class troublemaker saw the two peach baskets and grumbled, "Huh! Another new game!" Soon, he changed his mind. He and the other seventeen men on the nine-person teams enjoyed the new game.

When player **William Chase** made the first goal, the game was halted while the janitor climbed a stepladder to recover the soccer ball from the peach basket. At the end of the class period the score remained one to nothing.

Frank Mahan, the complaining player before the game, was the first to praise Naismith afterward. When classes resumed after Christmas, they continued playing the game with no name. Mahan suggested they call it Naismith ball. The creator said

no. A name like that would kill a game, he laughed. The young man then proposed "basket ball," and the game was named.

Mahan also swiped the rules from the bulletin board, but he later returned the souvenir to Naismith. In the years since, over 200 new rules have changed the game's scoring, number of players, court size and so forth. But twelve of Naismith's original thirteen rules are still followed.

Career in Kansas

In 1894 James married Maude Sherman. The next year, he accepted a job at the Denver YMCA, one of the largest in the United States. James was pleased, for there was a famous medical school nearby and he was anxious to study medicine. Somehow the 34-year-old college freshman kept up with a full load of medical courses while working at the YMCA.

Four years later he completed his medical degree and planned to use his training in medicine, religion and athletics to further the lives of young men at the YMCA. Then a boy in one of his classes broke his neck while tumbling.

The student's death put Naismith in a turmoil. With memories of the accident haunting him night and day, he prayed for help at the fatal spot in the gym.

A few days later, his old friend Stagg called and said he had recommended Naismith for the chaplain's job at Kansas University. Shortly, KU offered him the position. It also put him in charge of the physical education department and gave him some coaching duties. To the troubled Naismith, it was a prayer answered.

Ironically, although basketball was spreading around the country—largely through YMCAs—KU had no basketball team. A woman instructor had taught the game to a class of girls a year earlier, but it was then dropped. Naismith organized eight intramural teams and then assembled a varsity squad of the best players. At its first game in early 1899, the KU team beat a YMCA from Kansas City, Missouri, 17-14.

Naismith, the first KU basketball coach, retired from coaching after the turn of the century with a record of 55 wins and 60 losses—making him the university's only basketball coach with a losing record.

It should be pointed out, however, that his other duties often kept him at home while the team traveled—and two-thirds of KU's games were away in those early days. Dr. Naismith continued on the university's staff until the age of 75.

He did leave the campus for a time. In 1916, as a newly ordained Presbyterian minister, he served as a chaplain in the Kansas National Guard on the Mexican border. During World War I he traveled to France with the YMCA and helped run troop recreation centers. He also crusaded against the dangers of sexually-transmitted diseases. Afterward he was a substitute minister in churches around Lawrence for many years. In the 1930s he became an American citizen.

When basketball was made an Olympic sport in 1936, coaches across the country collected money to send Naismith to the games in Berlin. There he was honored for his achievement in the sport that grew from his game. He also enjoyed watching the performance of KU runner Glenn Cunningham [281].

Two years after the death of his wife he married a second time. He died in Lawrence five months later, on November 28, 1939.

The Naismith Memorial Basketball Hall of Fame in Springfield, Massachusetts, was named in his honor. His name was included in its first group of honorees in 1959. ∎

Gets an earful; pushes passes

The inventor of basketball also made contributions to football. A few months before the first basketball game, Naismith put together an important piece of football equipment—the helmet.

As a college player, his ears had been injured from the rough sport, leaving one a "cauliflower ear." While playing, he usually protected it with adhesive tape.

He tried something different before a game in the fall of 1891. Using several layers of flannel and a chamois skin, he made a bonnet and tied it under his chin. The other players laughed, but Naismith's headgear was later credited as being the first football helmet.

And, sports historians disagree about who developed the forward pass later made popular by coach Jesse Harper [288]. But most say Naismith was in part responsible for the effective football play, for it was based on his technique of passing a basketball.

Makes music with wings

306 Charlie "Bird" Parker

Jazz saxophonist and composer. Kansas City. (1920-1955) Parker's childhood in Kansas City was lonely. His father abandoned the boy and his mother, and was later murdered. To support her son, Mrs. Parker worked nights as a nurse. While she was gone, Charlie wandered in and out of local nightclubs, listening to jazz.

Band was the only class at school that appealed to him, but as much as he enjoyed the music, he was unhappy when the director assigned him to play the tuba. His mother understood and bought him an alto saxophone instead. But the predictable music Charlie was asked to play in the classroom had none of the excitement he heard at local jazz joints.

Parker practiced on his own and joined a group of high school students, The Deans of Swing. When he felt he knew something about jazz—he had learned two numbers—Charlie ⟳

tried to join adult musicians in their nightly jam sessions. At his first appearance, they laughed so hard he packed his horn in its paper-bag case and went home in tears. He refused to play again for three months. On his second try, a drummer interrupted his number by slamming a cymbal across the floor.

But by then, he was determined to prove himself. He spent the summer of 1937 with a band touring the Ozarks. Between performances, he played along with his collection of Count Basie records. When he returned to Kansas City, the seventeen-year-old sax player was hired by bandleader Buster Smith.

Parker looked to Smith as a foster father and when the bandleader went to New York City looking for work, Parker rode freight trains there following him. Smith helped him find dishwashing and janitor jobs. After hours, Charlie jammed with other jazz musicians.

Soon, he had joined the Jay McShann band back in Kansas City. As the group drove into Nebraska, Parker got his nickname. Their old touring car hit a chicken in the road and Charlie refused to continue without it. When they stopped for the night, he asked the boardinghouse owner to roast it. From then on he was "Bird."

After McShann's band performed in New York City's Savoy Ballroom, Parker came in contact with Earl Hines, Billy Eckstine and other influential jazz artists. In the 1940s he formed several small groups of his own. As he experimented with musical styles he helped develop a new form of jazz called bop, or bebop. In 1945, along with trumpeter Dizzy Gillespie, he made the first bop recordings. The music featured complicated chord patterns and complex rhythms.

In many numbers, he included long, dazzling phrases with many notes.

Although Parker had a promising future in music, he had used heroine since the age of twelve. He tried to fight the emotional and physical problems it brought, but he never overcame his drug addiction. He died in New York City at the age of 34. Jazz fans everywhere mourned his loss. *Bird*, a 1988 movie directed by Clint Eastwood, tells the story of Parker's life.

Today music experts agree his recordings and compositions like "Ornithology," "Confirmation" and "Yardbird Suite" make him one of the jazz greats. ∎

Entertaining producer

307 Brock Pemberton

Theater producer and newspaper journalist. Leavenworth and Emporia. (1885-1950) Pemberton was born in Leavenworth and graduated from high school in Emporia. He entered the College of Emporia but was thrown out for some of the pranks he pulled. Thanks to William Allen White [**256**], he then got a newspaper job in Philadelphia.

Pemberton returned to Kansas and graduated from Kansas University in 1908. For two years he wrote for White's *Emporia Gazette*, and then moved to New York City. There he was a reporter and drama critic on several newspapers, including the *New York Times*.

In 1917 he apprenticed himself to a Broadway producer. Three years later, Pemberton produced a play on his own. Soon afterward, his *Miss Lulu Bett* won a Pulitzer Prize. Through the 1940s, he staged scores of successful Broadway plays, including *Enter Madame* and *Harvey*. For years, he provided free tickets to his current shows for any Emporia residents visiting New York City.

During World War II, he helped set up canteens for American servicemen. He also helped organize the popular USO stage shows. ∎

Funny lady

308 ZaSu Pitts

Actress. Parsons. (1894-1963) Pitts was born in Parsons and moved to California as a child. She appeared in her first movie in 1917, and made over a hundred films in all, the last one completed just before she died. In silent movie days she played a variety of roles, but after sound films came along, she was most often a zany comedienne.

Through the 1950s she co-starred in the CBS and ABC television comedies *My Little Margie* and *The Gale Storm Show*. ZaSu's unusual first name came from combining parts of two aunts' names: Eliza and Susan. ∎

Sings as *primo basso*

Opera singer. Colby, Winona and Quinter. (Born 1942)
Ramey has appeared in operas around the world, but his solo singing career began at a Christmas program in a Winona church. After Sam was born in Colby on March 28, 1942, the Ramey family lived in Winona and then Quinter while he was in elementary school.

Opera? Yecch!

Sam first took voice lessons in Quinter and was often asked to sing solos as a high school student in Colby. Elvis Presley and Pat Boone were his favorite singers; the only opera he had heard was on Ed Sullivan's television show—and his reaction to that was "Yecch!" While he was a member of most of the school's musical groups, he also enjoyed journalism and drama as well as basketball and baseball.

After graduating in 1960, Ramey planned to become a music teacher. He enrolled at Kansas State University, but had to drop out when his father died. After working in a Colby clothing store for a year to help support his mother, he transferred to Wichita State University. To help pay his tuition, he worked part time at the *Wichita Eagle-Beacon*.

Arthur Newman, Ramey's WSU vocal instructor, had spent nearly twenty years with the New York City Opera, and helped introduce the young Kansan to opera. After Sam spent the sum-

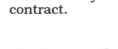

mer of 1963 singing with an opera company in Colorado, he was hooked on the musical form.

He devoted himself to his future career, taking ballet and working in dramatic productions along with studying music. But he couldn't afford to be a fulltime student, and drove a delivery truck and sold shoes to help support himself. In 1968 he was able to complete his bachelor's degree.

To the Big Apple

He spent the year after his graduation with a small North Carolina opera company as it toured the southeastern United States. In the summer of 1969 he headed for New York City. He soon found two singing jobs—in choirs at a church and a synagogue. While he waited for his chance to join an opera company he worked in the advertising department of a book publisher.

Sam also found a vocal teacher and a wife. His instructor had taught several basses who went on to the Metropolitan Opera; his wife was a friend of one of his Wichita friends.

His voice teacher ran a small opera in New Jersey, and there Sam had the chance to learn several different roles. As often as possible, he auditioned for different opera companies.

Fortunately, his boss at the publishing company was an opera buff and allowed Sam time off when necessary. In 1972 he attended the New York City Opera's open tryouts. The director liked what he heard, but it was a year before Ramey was offered a contract.

Makes *primo* appearance

At first, Sam sang only small parts, but in 1973 he premiered as the company's leading bass soloist, or *primo basso*. Within a year he was singing the lead in four different operas, and appearing in four others.

Music critics praised his voice, dramatic presence and musicianship. One wrote, "This is a voice with a future."

Ramey has lived up to their expectations. He made his foreign debut in 1976 and has performed with major opera companies in Europe—including those in Germany, ⟡

Italy, Spain, Austria, England, France and the Netherlands. Some of his appearances throughout the world have been booked five years in advance.

When his schedule became busier, he quit singing full time at New York City Opera, but he still tries to return there for a few performances each season.

Although he was a finalist in the Metropolitan Opera Company's national auditions in 1972, the prestigious Met didn't ask Ramey to make an appearance there until 1984—and then only after other opera stars insisted. He has since performed at the Met many times.

He tours the United States when possible, and has appeared in major cities. He has also given recitals in Kansas, including in his hometown, at WSU and at Bethany College in Lindsborg.

Ramey has a large audience through television and recordings. He has sung on several *Live from Lincoln Center* productions on PBS, as well as on British television. Recording companies in the United States and Europe have asked him to record, and he has albums on a variety of major labels, including RCA, Philips and Deutsche Grammophon. Ramey has been called the most recorded American-born bass in history. ∎

Hawk jets to Washington

310 John Riggins

Football player. Centralia and Lawrence. (Born 1949)
Riggins grew up in Centralia where his father was the local depot agent. Sports were always an important part of the family's recreation, and much of the time Riggins seemed to play in his older brother's athletic shadow. But John had his share of triumphs.

In junior high, he broke a record when he long-jumped over nineteen feet at a track meet. Unfortunately, he also broke his ankle—because he leaped past the end of the pit. He was also an excellent math student and was a member of the school band and orchestra.

As a high school trackster, Riggins won the state title in the 100-yard dash both his junior and senior years. After spending summers stacking hay bales, he was also a tough force to deal with in football each fall. He was ranked on a statewide all-star team his junior year. His senior year performance was amazing—1,456 yards rushing, 433 yards passing and 197 points. He was rated the top high school player in the nation.

Colleges around the country tried to recruit him, but he planned from the start to go to Kansas University. There he majored in journalism and joined his older brother in the football backfield.

The Jayhawks went to the Orange Bowl John's junior year; the next year he was the Big Eight's leading rusher and an All-American.

When the New York Jets chose Riggins as its first-round draft choice in 1971, he was frightened, he later admitted. The 22-year-old drove to the Jets training camp in an old Chevy, hoping he could leave unnoticed if he didn't make the cut.

He survived his rookie season and took $22,000 home to Lawrence. He injured his knee his second season and was sidelined for the rest of the year after surgery. That summer, he lived in New York City, shaved his head like a Mohawk Indian, and thought about leaving pro football while he could still walk. But when the Jets offered him $60,000 to return, he did.

After the Jets finished the next three seasons as losers, he signed a five-year, $1.5 million contract in 1976 with the Washington Redskins. Two years later the team called him the comeback player of the year when he rushed for over 1,000 yards.

John, who was a somewhat temperamental player, sat out the 1980 season in a contract dispute. But he returned for five more seasons, and helped the Redskins beat the Miami Dolphins in the 1982 Super Bowl. Riggins retired from the NFL in 1985. He and his family now live in Virginia. In 1992 he was inducted into the Pro Football Hall of Fame. ∎

Hollywood leads him back to Kansas

311 Mike Robe

Filmmaker. Arkansas City. (Born 1944) Robe grew up in Arkansas City and attended the University of Kansas in the 1960s. There he received a bachelor's degree in advertising, followed by a master's degree in radio and television broadcasting.

In the U.S. Air Force, Robe put his degrees to work by making informational films. He then moved to California where he and his wife spent seven years producing commercials.

Mike left the advertising business when a friend asked him to write an episode for a television series. Although writing paid less than making commercials, he enjoyed the chance to tell stories lasting longer than 30 seconds. He wrote episodes for several ABC series, including *Matt Houston* and *The Insiders*.

In recent years Robe has written and directed several television miniseries. In 1987 CBS broadcast his *Murder Ordained*, based on a real-life crime in Emporia. Robe's story followed Kansas Highway Patrolman *John Rule* as he investigated murders apparently planned by the Reverend *Thomas Bird* and *Lorna Anderson*, his secretary. To make the $6.7 million movie, Robe shot 60 hours of film in Emporia and Lawrence.

He also directed the 1991 ABC miniseries *Son of the Morning Star*, about George Armstrong Custer's [**351**] defeat at the Battle of the Little Big Horn [**384**]. The production won four Emmy Awards in technical categories. Later in 1991 Robe spent eight weeks in the Kansas City area producing and directing another miniseries for ABC.

Robe is a member of the Kansas Film Commission, a group that encourages filmmakers to work in Kansas. ∎

Bucks his way to the top

312 Gerald Roberts

Rodeo cowboy. Council Grove, Strong City and Abilene. (Born 1919) Roberts got started in his rodeo career early. To help break young colts to ride, his rodeo-producer father *Emmett Roberts* let Gerald and his older sister and brother *Marge* and *Ken* ride the half-wild horses to school. Sometimes the Roberts kids found themselves in a middle-of-the-road rodeo. They never lost interest in the sport.

Gerald joined the rodeo circuit in the 1930s, specializing in bull riding, bareback riding and saddle bronc riding. After fourteen years, he had won ten saddles, 40 gold and silver belt buckles —and two world championships. He was crowned All-Around World Champion Cowboy in 1942 and again in 1948. (The award is based on the total prize money won in official rodeos during the year.)

The champion cowboy was among the top three winners in bareback and bull riding several different years before 1950.

His brother Ken, a top contestant in the same events, was world champion bull rider from 1943 through 1945. He was called the best natural bull rider of all time.

As a teenager their sister Marge did trick roping and rode steers and bucking broncs in a Wild West Show. In 1941 she won the women's bronc riding at the world-famous Cheyenne, Wyoming, rodeo. After her death, she was inducted in the National Cowgirl Hall of Fame.

Emmett was named Rodeo Man of the Year in 1979. Gerald is now a member of the Kansas All Sports Hall of Fame. ∎

Sweet on 'America's Sweetheart'

313 Charles "Buddy" Rogers

Actor and filmmaker. Olathe. (Born 1904) While Rogers was growing up his father edited the *Olathe Mirror.* Buddy delivered copies of the newspaper, set type and helped at the printing press. When it came time to go to college he considered majoring in journalism, but studied music instead.

At the University of Kansas he organized a small band and often made $25 playing at weekend dances. Just before he graduated in 1925, a camera crew from Paramount studio came to Lawrence as part of a cross-country talent search. Although Rogers had been in only one play during high school, his father convinced him to make a screen test.

A short time later the studio invited him to New York City. After learning how to gesture and pantomime, he found himself in a silent film, *So's Your Old Man.* Not only was it Rogers' first movie, but it was the first made by its star, comic W.C. Fields.

Paramount then sent the young Kansan to California. He starred in the 1926 film *Wings,* the first movie to receive an Academy Award for best picture. The film about aviators and flying is now considered a classic.

Rogers was called America's Boy Friend when his career peaked in the 1930s. For a time, he traveled with an orchestra he organized. In 1937 he married popular actress Mary Pickford, known as "America's Sweetheart." A year earlier they had starred together in *My Best Girl.*

During World War II Rogers served in the U.S. Navy. After he returned to Pickfair, their glamorous Beverly Hills mansion, he produced and appeared in several more movies.

Rogers made his last film in 1957. ∎

His wins top the winner

314 Adolph "The Baron" Rupp

Basketball coach. Halstead. (1901-1977) In the sport of basketball, Rupp worked his way from the bottom to the top. On his family's farm near Halstead, he first played ball with a gunny sack full of rags. At a nearby country school he graduated to using a real basketball, but it barely held air. The playing surface was packed dirt, the basket was a barrel and his uniform was a pair of overalls.

During World War I he played his games for Halstead High— in the town hall. The ceiling was just a couple of feet above the goals. He and other players had to dodge around a furnace grate in the center of the court.

A few years later at Kansas University he played under legendary coach Forrest "Phog" Allen [**264**]. Rupp was a guard for KU and a member of the 1922 and 1923 teams declared unofficial national champions— in the days before national playoffs began in the late 1930s.

But all that was just a warm-up for Rupp's four decades of coaching at the University of Kentucky. Three years after his arrival in 1930, his Kentucky Wildcats were named national champs. Before he retired in 1972 they won the Southeastern Conference crown 27 times and the NCAA national championship four times, bringing his total career wins to as many as 880 games—depending on which "official" source one uses.

With win number 772 Rupp became the winningest college coach of all time—breaking the record set by his former coach Allen.

Since 1961, the Rupp Trophy has been presented to a top college player selected by sportswriters and coaches. The "Baron of Basketball" was inducted into the Naismith [305] Memorial Hall of Fame in 1968. His name is also included in the Kansas All Sports Hall of Fame.

Brown brings luck

For several years, the only suit Rupp owned was brown. When he bought a blue one and wore it to a game, the team lost. From that time on his coaching uniform was always the same: brown suit, white shirt and brown tie. In his lucky outfits he coached 25 All-Americans and 31 future NBA professionals. ■

A reel cowboy

315 Reb Russell

Actor, football player and rancher. Osawatomie and Coffeyville. (1905-1978) Russell and his family moved to Coffeyville when he was a child. As a college football All-American, he was invited to appear in a movie in 1932. After spending a season with the Philadelphia Eagles, he returned to Hollywood and made thirteen films in two years. Most were low-budget "B" Westerns —some churned out in ten days' time. Before he began ranching near Coffeyville he spent two years performing a cowboy act in circuses. In the 1960s he ran for the U.S. Congress, but lost. ■

Runs over 4-minute mark

316 Jim Ryun

Runner. Wichita and Lawrence. (Born 1947)
Ryun's record-breaking career as a runner got off to a slow start when he failed to make the track team in his freshman year at Wichita's East High School. Once he made the cross-country team the next year the coach recognized his talent. Under his direction Jim made a five-mile run each morning, followed by weight-lifting, swimming and calisthenics.

In his junior year, Ryun became the first high school athlete to run a mile in less than four minutes. He qualified for the 1964 Olympics that summer but became sick in Tokyo and failed to make the finals. In the spring of 1965 he won the mile at the state track meet with a 3:58.3 time. Jim lowered that mark by three seconds at the AAU championship in California that summer and set a new American record.

With offers from 40 colleges, Ryun entered KU that fall. As he ran in meets around the country, fans came to expect a new record each time. At the AAU championship in June 1966 he was booed for a time of "only" 3.58.6! A month later in Berkeley, California, he clocked his best time yet: 3.51.3—a new world record. The next summer he ran his all-time fastest mile: 3.51.1.

In the 1968 Olympics at Mexico City Ryun won a silver medal in the 1,500-meter. He fell during the same race in the 1972 games in Munich, Germany, but had nothing to be ashamed of. He had already been named *Sports Illustrated*'s Sportsman

of the Year and the Sullivan Award winner in 1966. He was inducted in the National Track and Field Hall of Fame in 1980 and is a member of the Kansas All Sports Hall of Fame. He and his wife live near Lawrence, where he is a youth minister. ■

317 Barry Sanders

In a big rush

Football player. Wichita. (Born 1968) Sanders was born in Wichita, July 16, 1968, the seventh in a family of eleven children. He and his two brothers spent summers helping their father in his roofing business. As he lugged loads of hot asphalt up ladders, Barry made up his mind to get a college education. His father agreed, and encouraged him to participate in sports in hopes of winning a scholarship.

Pigskin ticket to college

Barry preferred basketball, and in spite of being only five-foot-eight, he was talented on the court. But his father suggested he concentrate on football. There are more players and more chances for scholarships, he pointed out.

When Sanders went out for football at Wichita's North High School, however, he spent most of his time on the second team. He knew all the right moves, but his coaches felt he was afraid to get hit. After he graduated in 1986 and spent three years playing football at Oklahoma State University, he was hit all right—with a flood of national publicity.

After that record-shattering junior year, he was named the 1988 Heisman Trophy winner—the best college football player in the country. Among the thirteen NCAA records he set in that season were most rushing yardage (2,628) and most touchdowns scored (39).

When he returned home, Wichita proudly gave him his own Barry Sanders Day, complete with a key to the city and a salute from Governor Mike Hayden [*58*]. The young award-winner, in turn, shared his trophy by putting it on display at Georgio's, a popular neighborhood restaurant. He also shared the day's limelight with his brother ***Byron Sanders***, a standout college player at Chicago's Northwestern University.

Rushes into NFL

Although Sanders announced that he would return to Oklahoma State for his senior year, the pressure to join the NFL was too great. He was a first-round draft pick of the Detroit Lions in 1989 and signed a contract that included a $2.5 million bonus. One of Barry's first acts was to send $200,000 to the Paradise Baptist Church in Wichita. Before the start of the 1991 season he signed a new four-year contract worth perhaps $10.1 million. Sanders said he would continue to give ten percent of his earnings to his church; some of the rest of his money was invested in family businesses in Wichita.

During his first three seasons with the Lions he scored 47 touchdowns and gained 4,322 yards rushing. He was the NFL's leading rusher in 1990. In his rookie season he fell just ten yards shy of the title when he modestly gave up a chance to play at the end of the last game. He finished only fifteen yards behind the league leader in 1991. That same season he was named Pro Football Player of the Year.

In early 1992 Barry enrolled at Oakland University near his Detroit home. He planned to complete work on the bachelor's degree in business that he started at Oklahoma State. ■

Going the extra mile

318 Archie San Romani, Sr.

Runner. Frontenac and Wichita. (Born 1912) Like his teammate in the 1936 Olympics, Glenn Cunningham [***281***], San Romani began running after an accident.

As a boy in Frontenac, his right leg was crushed by a milk truck. The leg became infected and doctors wanted to amputate it, but San Romani refused. He started running to help regain his strength. As a track star at Kansas State Teachers College in Emporia (later ESU), San Romani beat world record-holder Cunningham in the 1937 and 1938 KU Relays.

His son, ***Archie San Romani, Jr.***, was a stand-out runner at Wichita East High School in the late 1950s and early 1960s. ■

319 Wes Santee

Runner. Ashland and Lawrence. (Born 1932) While in high school at Ashland in 1950 Santee set a state record for the mile run. He later attended KU and set several records in cross-country, the two-mile and mile events.

Santee was a member of the U.S. team at the 1952 Olympics in Helsinki, Finland, and at the 1955 Pan American Games. In 1953 he set a world record in the 1,500-meter run. He was named an All-American from 1951 through 1955. In 1956 Santee was suspended from competition for accepting more expense money than allowed by AAU and NCAA rules. Although many believed he would be the first runner to break the four-minute-mile barrier, the closest he ever came was 4:00.5—just one-half second above the magic mark. After serving in the U.S. Marines he went into the insurance business in Lawrence. ■

Kansas Comet

320 Gale Sayers

Football player. Wichita and Speed. (Born 1943) Sayers was born in Wichita and lived in Speed as a child. His family moved to Nebraska when he was nine. By the time he graduated from high school in Omaha, he had scholarship offers to play football at seventeen colleges.

He chose Kansas University where he was an All-American his junior and senior years. In 1965 Sayers was the first-round draft choice of the Chicago Bears and went on to become Rookie of the Year. He led the league with 132 points, 22 touchdowns and 2,272 yards gained. In a game against the San Francisco 49ers he tied an NFL record with six touchdowns.

Late in the 1968 season he injured his right knee and had to undergo surgery the next day. He came back in 1969 to win a trophy as the NFL's most courageous player. Injuries to his left knee in 1970 sidelined him for another season. Once again Sayers won the Most Courageous award, but he gave it to his Bears' roommate Brian Piccolo shortly before his friend died of cancer. Their friendship was later featured in an ABC television movie, *Brian's Song*.

Sayers retired in 1971. During his short career "The Kansas Comet" was considered pro football's best running back. When he was voted into the Pro Football Hall of Fame in 1977 the 33-year-old was the youngest player ever admitted. He is also a member of the College Football Hall of Fame and the Kansas All Sports Hall of Fame. ■

Learns his cue in Kansas

321 Jake "The Wizard" Schaefer, Sr.

Billiards player. Leavenworth and Dodge City. (1855-1910) Schaefer was born in Milwaukee and grew up in Leavenworth. There his father ran a billiard hall. At age fifteen Jake was an expert at the game.

In the 1870s, young Schaefer worked on Dodge City's Front Street as a bartender in the Beatty and Kelley saloon and restaurant. By that time he was so good with a cue that he could beat nearly any opponent. *James "Dog" Kelley*, one of the saloon's co-owners, sometimes called on his young employee to give unsuspecting strangers a "trimming" at the billiards table.

Schaefer won his first billiard championship in 1879 and was later declared world champion many times. For over twenty years, "The Wizard" was the most feared player in the game. His skill took him to tournaments and exhibitions around the world. To entertain audiences, he often played difficult variations of billiards. In fact, Schaefer—along with a handful of other billiards superstars—caused officials to change several rules in order to make the game more challenging.

Schaefer was living in Denver when he died of tuberculosis. In the 1920s his son was a world champion billiard star. ∎

In love with Popeye

322 Marilyn Schreffler

Comedienne and actress. Wichita and Topeka. (1945-1988) Schreffler was born in Wichita and graduated from Topeka West High School. After attending Washburn University she worked in comedy groups in Chicago and Cleveland.

Marilyn then moved to Los Angeles where she appeared in several television series and commercials for Alka-Selzer and Dole pineapple. Schreffler was best known for her behind-the-scenes work: She was the voice for Popeye the Sailor's cartoon girlfriend, Olive Oyl. ∎

His acting is something to sneeze at

323 Max Showalter

Actor and composer. Caldwell. (Born 1917) As a boy in Caldwell, Showalter decided he wanted to be an actor. He spent many pleasant hours watching movies in the local theater while his mother accompanied silent films on the piano. Mrs. Showalter, a former musician in a traveling Chautauqua show, also taught her son to play the piano and the organ.

One day, he got carried away while practicing on the pipe organ at the local Methodist Church. When members heard the fourteen-year-old's lively music up and down Main Street, they asked him to leave. From then on the young musician was a Presbyterian.

Later he took tap dancing lessons from a teacher in Wichita. Eventually he gave lessons himself, and invested his earnings in hogs. When he graduated from Caldwell High School in 1935 he sold his livestock and used the money to enroll at the Pasadena Playhouse in southern California.

Three years later he had a very small part in one of the theater's productions. When he delivered his five-word line, he giggled nervously. The actress

216

in front of him whirled around, causing her long costume to kick up a cloud of dust. Showalter began coughing and sneezing—sending the crowd into a fit of laughter.

Backstage after the show he expected to meet the angry director. Instead, a member of the audience—famous Broadway producer Oscar Hammerstein—invited him to New York City. One of Max's first performances was in a 1939 musical, broadcast in the earliest days of television. He also appeared in a Broadway play directed by Hammerstein.

During World War II, Showalter was in the U.S. Army's Special Services and made a world tour with songwriter Irving Berlin. Beginning in 1949 he worked in movies. After his first two films, Twentieth Century Fox changed his name to Casey Adams. A studio executive felt

Max Showalter sounded too German for post-war American audiences. As Adams he made more than 30 movies, playing supporting roles with the likes of Marilyn Monroe and Burt Lancaster. He also composed the music for several films. In 1956 he appeared in the movie version of William Inge's [215] *Bus Stop.* After making *The Music Man* in 1962, Showalter took back his real name.

During his career he appeared in over 50 films, in several Broadway plays, and in a wide variety of television shows—including *Gunsmoke* [326, 354], *The Lucy Show* and *M*A*S*H.*

Showalter never married, but after his parents died in an automobile accident, he raised his younger sister. He also supported a German war orphan. After living in Hollywood for many years he moved to Connecticut. ■

Rising star

324 Cynthia Sikes

Actress. Wichita. (Born 1954) Sikes was a journalism major at Wichita State University when she became the 1972 Miss Kansas. After her reign she studied drama at Southern Methodist University in Dallas. Cynthia went to California in 1974 and began acting in commercials and several NBC series.

She then spent time with a theater company in San Francisco. From 1982 to 1985 she was a cast member of NBC's *St. Elsewhere.* She has since had roles on *L.A. Law,* and in movies with Dudley Moore, Burt Reynolds and Jack Lemmon. ■

Stone Scarecrow was first

325 Fred Stone

Actor. Wellington and Topeka. (1873-1959) Stone was born in Colorado but his father was a traveling barber and the family lived in a string of Kansas towns. Fred's first performance was as an eleven-year-old tightrope walker in Topeka. Two years later he gave a show at a local opera house and took in $12.

Later he worked in circuses and medicine shows. At 21 he teamed with Dave Montgomery. Montgomery & Stone sang and danced in a vaudeville act, but they had little success until they

joined the Broadway cast of *The Wizard of Oz* [362] in 1902. Fred was the Scarecrow; his partner was the Tin Woodman. Soon they were earning $500 a week and were known nationwide.

After Stone was injured in a 1928 plane crash, doctors said he would never dance again, but by 1930 he was appearing in a new musical. Four years later he was praised for his role in *Jayhawker,* a Civil War drama by Sinclair Lewis. While most of his career was spent on stage, Stone also appeared in over a dozen movies. ■

Dodge City's doc

Actor. Burrton and Larned. (1904-1980) Stone was born near Burrton, July 5, 1904. He spent part of his childhood in Larned, but returned to Burrton after his father died. While still in high school he decided to be an actor, and he appeared in every school production that he could.

Puts on greasepaint

After graduation eighteen-year-old Milburn turned down an appointment to the U.S. Naval Academy to join a popular touring actor from McCracken, ***Arthur Names***. For $50 a week he traveled Kansas and Oklahoma in a little Willys Overland car, helping put on three-person shows in rented halls and tents. After six years with Names, Stone worked with the Wallace Bruce Players and two other acting companies.

At the beginning of the Great Depression, Stone and a partner did a song and dance act in Denver. They sang on a local radio station and performed at local theaters. But times were tough, and when a restaurant chain advertised it would give a free meal to anyone who found one of its 24-hour restaurants empty, the hungry Stone and his partner trudged from restaurant to restaurant night after night. They got a lot of exercise, but no free meals.

After working in Chicago "speakeasies"—illegal nightclubs during Prohibition days—Stone went to California. He planned to leave show business and settle down. For two years he did, pumping gas at a filling station. When he could no

longer resist the temptation to be on stage, he took a part in a play at the Pasadena Playhouse. Unfortunately his boss had no patience with part-time actors, and Stone was fired.

Movies galore

With help from his father's cousin Fred Stone [**325**] Milburn got a small part in *Jayhawker*, a Broadway drama. Although the play closed after a few weeks, the exposure helped him find acting jobs when he returned to Hollywood. In 1936 he appeared in a film, the first of over 150 he made before the mid 1950s.

Movie-goers often saw him as the villain on a black horse in "B" Westerns, but he also played supporting roles and leads in a wide variety of other films. His movie credits included everything from *Young Mr. Lincoln*, to *Sherlock Holmes*

Faces Death, Jungle Woman, The Spider Woman Strikes Back and *The Atomic City*. Several of his films were serials, a series of movies with the same characters and "cliff-hanger" endings designed to bring audiences back the next week.

Doc Adams

Stone's most familar role was on smaller screens. When CBS chose a cast for the television version of its *Gunsmoke* Western series in 1955, Milburn easily got a part. He became Dodge City's cranky, but loveable—and fictional—physician, ***Galen "Doc" Adams***.

At first he dyed his hair gray and wore a fake mustache, but as the popular show continued year after year, time took care of aging his character. Stone was also concerned with making Doc a believable medic as he treated other fictional Dodge City citizens—including Marshal Matt Dillon [**354**] and *Kitty Russell*, the owner of the Long Branch Saloon. Stone often said his ideas for the role were based on his grandfather.

Over the years, Stone and Doc Adams seemed to become one in the same. Even close friends called him Doc Stone. As he made numerous appearances around the country and in his home state, he was most popular with fans when he pretended to be Doc.

Before *Gunsmoke* was cancelled in 1975 Stone won an Emmy Award for a 1968 episode. He was one of the few non-doctors ever to receive an honorary membership in the Kansas Medical Society. In Dodge City

Stone and other cast members were made honorary city marshals. When St. Mary of the Plains College gave him an honorary doctorate degree in 1976, he happily announced, "Now I'm a real 'doc.' " Much of his career memorabilia was on display in the Milburn Stone Theater at the Dodge City college until its unexpected closing in 1992.

Although he lived on the West Coast for many years, Stone kept close ties to his native state. He proudly named his boat *The Jayhawk* and supported charitable and civic causes in several Kansas communities. One of his last projects was an attempt to produce a television series based on the life of pioneer Kansas doctor Arthur Hertzler [**108**].

Stone died in a California hospital, June 12, 1980. ∎

Top dancer

327
Clark Tippet

Dancer. Parsons. (1955-1992)
Tippet left his family in Parsons at age eleven and accepted a ballet scholarship in New York City. At seventeen he joined the important American Ballet Theater; by the time he was 24 Clark was one of its principal dancers. He then took a four-year leave of absence to treat a drug habit.

After returning to the ABT in 1983 he performed with the theater's famous Russian-born dancer-director, Mikhail Baryshnikov. Tippet died in Parsons of AIDS-related illnesses. ∎

Fills role of Charlie Chan

328 Sidney Toler

Actor. Anthony and Wichita. (1874-1947) Toler was born in Missouri and came to Kansas in the 1880s when his family opened a grocery store in Anthony.

In 1886 they moved to Wichita where young Sidney made his first stage appearance in *Tom Sawyer*. After graduation he attended the University of Kansas, but he left college to join a theater company.

For several years Toler toured as an actor and eventually made it to Broadway. After the stock market crashed in 1929 he moved to California. He found work in some early

sound movies and played character parts in a variety of films for nearly a decade.

When actor Warner Oland died in 1938, Toler replaced him in the role of movie detective Charlie Chan. Studio executives were anxious to continue the popular *Charlie Chan* film series, and—ironically—chose the Scottish Toler to follow the Swedish Oland in the Oriental role.

Beginning with *Charlie Chan in Honolulu*, Toler made 22 appearances as the clever Chan. After his death, other actors continued the role in movies and on television. ∎

Burns 'em over the plate

329 Mike Torrez

Baseball player. Topeka. (Born 1946) Torrez began tossing a baseball as a six-year-old. In Topeka High School, basketball was his favorite sport, but pro baseball scouts noticed him pitching in summer youth leagues. At sixteen Mike got an offer from the Philadelphia Phillies, but he chose to finish school. Just after his senior year, he signed with the St. Louis Cardinals. After three years with their farm clubs, he moved up into the majors in 1967. Before he retired from baseball in 1984, the six-foot-five Kansan pitched for six other major league teams: the Montreal Expos, Baltimore Orioles, Oakland A's, New York Yankees, Boston Red Sox and New York Mets. In the 1977 World Series he pitched two victories that helped the Yankees beat the Los Angeles Dodgers.

As he was traded back and forth, Torrez managed to beat every team in both the National and American Leagues—the first major league pitcher to do so. ■

Plays Lucy's best friend

330 Vivian Vance

Actress. Cherryvale and Independence. (1912-1979) Vance was born as Vivian Jones in Cherryvale. When she was two her father opened a grocery store in nearby Independence. Later, Vance toured as an actress and her family moved to New Mexico.

She eventually went to New York City to go to acting school. When she found the classes were full she auditioned and won a part in a Broadway musical. Vivian worked in other plays and several movies before she was asked to play the part of Ethel Mertz in a new television show starring Lucille Ball.

To make sure the glamorous Miss Ball was not outshone, Vance's original contract required her to wear "frowsy" housedresses and remain ten to twenty pounds overweight. But no matter what her size, Vance became famous as Lucy's zany sidekick in two CBS comedies, *I Love Lucy* (1951-59) and *The Lucy Show* (1962-68). After she retired to Connecticut in the 1970s Vance made a few guest appearances on a third Lucille Ball show, *Here's Lucy.* ■

On the road

331 George "Nash" Walker

Actor. Lawrence. (1873-1911) Before he began touring in a medicine show, Walker shined shoes on Lawrence's streets. In 1892 he paired with Bert Williams, a native of the West Indies. They became the vaudeville team of Williams & Walker.

The two later formed an all-black company of actors and performed plays and minstrel shows. Minstrel shows—white actors in black makeup telling jokes and singing—were a popular form of entertainment in those days, but Walker and his partner were the first to use black actors. Their company toured the United States and Europe. While one of their plays ran in London in 1903, they gave a command performance at Buckingham Palace.

After Walker died, Williams became one of the first blacks to star in silent movies. ■

E.T.'s mom

332
Dee Wallace

Actress. Kansas City. (Born 1948) Born as Deanna Bowers, Wallace's first role was as a young princess in a margarine commercial. After graduating from Wyandotte High School she turned down modeling offers and earned a teaching degree at KU. But after a year in a Kansas City classroom she decided to try modeling after all. In New York City she soon found work in commercials. One of her jobs—advertising Kraft peanut butter as a giant eye—took her to Los Angeles. There she did more commercials plus small roles in television dramas and movies.

Although she has made many movie and television appearances before and since, Wallace is still best known for one role—Elliott's mother in the enormously popular 1982 movie *E.T.* ∎

Speeds into first place

333 Rodger Ward

Race car driver. Beloit. (Born 1921) Ward was born in Beloit where his father ran an auto repair shop. When he was five, the family moved to California. Rodger built hot rods as a teenager, but it wasn't until he flew P-38 fighter planes during World War II that he learned the true meaning of speed.

Back on the ground, Ward took his love of speed to the racetrack. After making a name for himself driving midget racers on the West Coast, Ward entered larger cars in what is now the Championship Auto Racing Teams racing circuit, or CART. Each year's schedule includes races around the country, all leading up to the Indianapolis 500—racing's premier event.

For eight years, Ward entered cars in the Indy, only to suffer disappointment and disaster. His rookie race in 1951 ended after 34 laps with a broken oil

line. An accident in 1956 demolished his car and took the life of a driver just behind him. A year later, when other 35-year-old drivers had already retired, he came back to finish in eighth place. For the next two years, his cars again failed —in lap number 98 in 1958.

In 1959 Ward finally won the grueling 500-mile race with a record-setting average speed of just over 135 miles per hour. With one win under his belt, he placed no lower than fourth in the next five Indys—including a second victory in 1962. He retired with a total of 26 CART wins. Ward later owned several racing-related businesses in Indianapolis. ∎

His swings mean business

334
Tom Watson

Golfer. Mission Hills. (Born 1949) Watson was born in Kansas City, Missouri. His golfing career began when he caddied for his father at the Kansas City Country Club in Shawnee Mission.

Soon he graduated from carrying golf clubs to swinging them. At fifteen he was so accomplished he was invited to play an exhibition match with his idol, pro golfer Arnold Palmer.

Watson won the Missouri amateur championship four times and placed fifth in the United ⇨

States Amateur Tournament in 1969. He graduated from Stanford University in California with a bachelor's degree in psychology in 1971. That same year he turned pro.

His long career has included wins in many golf tournaments, plus eight major championships: the British Open five times, the Masters twice and the U.S. Open once. He has been voted the Professional Golfers' Association Player of the Year six times.

In 1980 Watson became the first professional golfer to earn more than $500,000 in a year. His career earnings now total just over $5.1 million, making him the all-time second-highest PGA money winner. ∎

Giant champ

335 Jess Willard

Boxer. St. Clere. (1881-1968)
Willard was a 29-year-old farmer from St. Clere—now a Pottawatomie County ghost town—when he first boxed professionally. Although he lost that first fight, he won his next eight contests. In 1912 he lost a twenty-round bout in San Francisco, and then won several matches in other cities. (One of his opponents in a 1913 bout died from a punch to the jaw.)

Willard's biggest fight came in 1915 when he went up against Jack Johnson, the defending world heavyweight champ. Johnson was the first African-American to become a world champion boxer. But in those days of open discrimination, many white fans didn't hide their prejudice. They called Willard "The Great White Hope," in hopes he would end Johnson's five-year reign as champion.

It was one of the most publicized prizefights ever held. Perhaps 25,000 spectators were at ringside in Havana, Cuba, when the opening bell sounded. Experts and odds-makers agreed Johnson had more skill,

but the six-foot-six, 235-pound Willard finally wore him down. After 26 rounds the Kansas Giant was declared the winner.

Many believed Willard was unbeatable. He was—until July 4, 1919. In another famous fight, he met Colorado boxer Jack Dempsey. Dempsey beat the Kansan in three rounds. Willard fought twice in the 1920s and then retired. He later lived in California. He remains the tallest man to hold a world boxing title—and the only world boxing champion from Kansas. ∎

Hurls smokers

336 "Smoky Joe" Howard Wood

Baseball player. Ness City and Hutchinson. (1889-1985)
Wood learned to play baseball while growing up in Ness City. His father, **John F. Wood**, was a pioneer lawyer who founded Ness County's first newspaper.

"Smoky Joe," nicknamed for his speedy fastball, broke into baseball at eighteen by pitching for a Hutchinson team. At nineteen he joined the Boston Red Sox. Four years later, in 1912, he had a remarkable season. He won 34 games, lost only five—and led the American League with ten shutouts. In that year's World Series he won three of the four games he pitched and helped Boston take the pennant over the New York Giants.

The next season Wood slipped on wet grass and broke his thumb. After it healed, pitching became so painful he had to leave baseball in 1916. He tried to pitch for the Cleveland Indians two years later, but his injury forced him off the mound. He played in the Cleveland outfield until he retired in 1922.

With one of the best fastballs in baseball, Wood was often compared to Walter "Big Train" Johnson [**293**]. The two Kansans faced each other on the mound in 27 games; Wood won eleven of them. One of his victories was part of a sixteen-game winning streak that tied a record then held by Johnson. ∎

First lady of basketball

Basketball player. Wichita and Lawrence. (Born 1959)
Woodard was born August 12, 1959, in Wichita. She began playing ball with her brother, using wadded up socks.

Choose her first

When she was ten, Lynette was a popular player on neighborhood choose-up-sides basketball teams. Even though most of the players were boys, the talented girl was chosen first—or was a captain choosing her own team.

She first played organized basketball as a ninth grader at Marshall Junior High. That year a coach at Wichita North High School asked her to join his junior varsity team, but she politely refused. Lynette felt she was good enough for the varsity.

As a sophomore at North High the next year, she proved it. The five-foot-eleven Woodard averaged just over 25 points a game, and took the school's Redskins from no wins and eight losses the previous year to thirteen wins and a single loss in 1974-75. In the season's last game, Lynette's assists and scoring in the final three minutes helped the North girls win their first 5A state championship.

By the end of her senior year, the Redskins had a 59-3 record and a second state championship—thanks to a last-second shot by Lynette. She was named the 1977 high school player of the year in class 5A, and was a starter on *Parade* magazine's all-America high school team.

Record-setting Hawk

With offers from over a hundred colleges, Woodard was undecided about which to attend. But, unlike prospective men players, she had to pay her own expenses to visit any campuses. In the end, she settled on KU.

There she led the Jayhawks to three straight Big Eight championships. She was named to the All-American team four years and scored a total of 3,649 points—the most by a woman in the history of the National Collegiate Athletic Association. During her amazing sophomore year she scored 1,177 points—an NCAA record that still stands. Along with many other honors, she won the Wade Trophy as the finest female player in America.

Olympian and Globetrotter

During her junior year at the University of Kansas Woodard was one of twelve women selected for the U.S. Olympic basketball team. Unfortunately, because of the Soviet invasion of Afganistan, the United States and many other nations boycotted the games in Moscow.

When she graduated from KU in 1981 Woodard left twenty school basketball records—and still had impressive enough grades to be a two-time Academic All-American. She was offered several coaching positions, but to keep playing she joined a league in Italy. Far from home, she averaged 31 points a game, but spent much of her time homesick. She then returned to KU and coached two seasons.

In 1984 Woodard again made the Olympic team. As its captain she led the squad in a successful drive for the gold medal at the Los Angeles games.

Following the Olympic victory, Woodard scored another victory—she became the first woman to play with the world-famous Harlem Globetrotters. Beginning in 1985 she spent two seasons touring with the popular exhibition team. The grinding schedule meant 200 games a year—sometimes two games a day in two different cities. Woodard has since played for professional teams in Italy, Spain and Japan. In 1990 she was a featured player on the U.S. team in the Goodwill Games. She has also coached again at KU.

Woodard has been honored by the NAACP and is also known for her work with charities. ■

More talented Kansans

Annette Bening was born in Topeka in 1958 and lived in Wichita until she was seven. Her family then moved to California where she attended San Francisco State University. After working on stage in California and New York, Annette got her first big break in the movies in 1988 when she landed a starring role with Dan Aykroyd. Bening made headlines in 1991 when she and actor Warren Beatty starred together in *Bugsy*—and were later married.

Bening is not the first Kansan to marry a Hollywood star. **Barbara Blakeley**, who moved to Wichita from Missouri at the age of ten, graduated from Wichita North High School and then moved to California. After working as a model and a Las Vegas showgirl, she met comedian Zeppo Marx in 1959. They were married three years later, and then divorced in the mid 1970s. In 1976 Barbara married another well-known celebrity, singer Frank Sinatra. In the early 1950s **Pat Wymore** from Salina married actor Errol Flynn. ■

Karla Burns, a singer, dancer and actress, graduated from Wichita West High School in 1972 and WSU in 1978. She has performed on stage in Los Angeles, New York City and London. In 1983 Karla was nominated for the Tony Award in the best featured actress category, based on her appearance as Queenie in the Broadway musical *Show Boat*. Burns has also appeared as Hattie McDaniel [**302**] in one-woman show about the Oscar-winning actress' life and career. ■

"Buck" Clayton was born in Parsons in 1911. The jazz trumpet player performed with jazz great Count Basie from 1936 to 1943, and then with Duke Ellington. Clayton led his own jazz bands in the 1950s. ■

Elwood "Bingo" DeMoss was born in Topeka in 1899. As a young man he played pro baseball in the Negro League. DeMoss led the Chicago American Giants to four championships. He was considered by many to be the greatest second baseman of his time. ■

Bill Farmer, a comedian who grew up in Pratt, began doing impressions of celebrity voices when he was fifteen. He first entertained his friends by ordering fast food at drive-up window speakers using the voices of movie stars. After graduating from the University of Kansas with a degree in broadcast journalism, he took his 100 voices on stage in Texas. In Los Angeles in 1986 he landed a job at Walt Disney Studios. Now he is the voice of Disney's loveable looser, Goofy. "Ya-ha-ha-hoooiiieee!" ■

Bill Koch, brother of Wichita oil company executives Charles [**162**] and **David Koch**, surprised many in 1992 when he won yachting's top prize, the America's Cup. Koch, who lived in Wichita as a child, graduated from a private military school in Indiana before enrolling in the Massachusetts Institute of Technology. He has since moved to California, where he spent several million dollars building yachts to compete in the race. After beating out Dennis Conner's *Stars & Stripes*, a past America's Cup winner, Koch and the crew of his *America*^{3} successfully defended the challenge by a yacht from Italy. ■

Pamela McKelvy, a reporter and news anchor for WIBW television in Topeka, was crowned Miss Kansas 1992. Pamela, a graduate of Grambling State University in Louisiana, is the first African-American to win the Miss Kansas title. In Atlantic City, the talented McKelvy finished third runner-up in the finals for Miss America 1993. ■

Danny Manning, who spent his senior year at Lawrence High School and graduated from KU in 1989, is one of several Kansas college graduates in professional basketball. Manning plays for the LA Clippers. **Antoine Carr**, a Wichita State graduate, was a first-round NBA pick in 1983, but chose to play in Italy during his rookie year. He then joined the Sacramento Kings. In 1991 he was traded to the San Antonio Spurs. **Xavier McDaniel**, another WSU graduate, has played with NBA teams in Seattle and Phoenix. He was traded to the New York Knicks in 1991. ■

Marilyn Maye, a recording artist and night club performer, is a native of Wichita. She was singing in a Kansas City, Missouri, night club in 1957 when entertainer Steve Allen invited her to perform on his late-night

ABC television program. She recorded her first album in 1965 and appeared on NBC's *Tonight Show starring Johnny Carson* nearly 80 times. Maye's recordings of "If My Friends Could See Me Now" and "Step to the Rear" were popular into the 1970s. ∎

Rick Mears, an auto racer, was born in Wichita in 1951 and now lives in Florida. He is a four-time winner of the Indianapolis 500 with champion performances in 1979, 1984, 1988 and 1991. Six times—a record —Rick's qualifying speed has placed him in the top "pole" position for the race. Mears qualified for the 1992 race at a speedy 224.594 miles per hour. ∎

Pete Mehringer grew up in Kinsley. After taking a correspondence course in wrestling, he started and coached the high school's wrestling team—while still a student. Although he had to hitchhike to Manhattan to compete, Pete became state heavyweight wrestling champion in 1928 and 1930. In 1932 Mehringer qualified for the U.S. Olympic wrestling team and won a gold medal at the Los Angeles games. He then went on to play professional football in Chicago and Los Angeles for thirteen years. At the same time, he was a stuntman in more than 40 movies. After retiring from sports, Pete remained in California and was an engineer with the City of Los Angeles. He died there in 1987. ∎

Steve Mills has worked in television since his graduation from KU in 1951, but viewers don't see him. He works behind the scenes. After directing and producing news and sports events, he approved television movies and miniseries at ABC from 1959 until 1973. He then had the same job at CBS until 1988. One of the 600 projects Steve helped promote was the *Murder Ordained* miniseries produced by fellow Kansan Mike Robe [*311*]. He is now an independent film producer in Los Angeles. In 1992 Kansas University honored Mills with its Buddy Award for his work in the entertainment industry and his service to the school. The award is named for KU graduate and actor Buddy Rogers [*313*]. ∎

Veryl Switzer, a native of Nicodemus, played football at nearby Bogue High School. He went on to become an All-American at KSU in 1953. Veryl then moved into professional football and spent five years with the Green Bay Packers. After serving in the U.S. Air Force and teaching in Chicago, he returned to Kansas in 1969. Since then he has held several positions at KSU, both in the academic and athletic departments. Switzer is currently associate athletic director in charge of academics.

Ronald "Ron" Kramer is another former Green Bay Packer from Kansas. Born in Girard in 1935, he played tight end and helped lead the Packers to NFL championships in 1961 and 1962. ∎

Fay Tincher grew up in Topeka and left Kansas in 1902 to study acting in Chicago. After appearing on stage in New York City she starred in silent movies directed by film pioneer D.W. Griffith. Most of her roles were in comedies; some called her "a feminine Charlie Chaplin." In 1917 she was earning nearly $1,500 a month. At the same time she started her own film company. By the mid 1930s she had married and given up her film career. ∎

Vada Watson became the Kansas Wheat Girl in 1925 when she won a contest sponsored by promoter F.W. "Woody" Hockaday [*109*]. During her reign she toured Kansas and the United States by train, greeting thousands of well-

wishers and promoting wheat. Along the way she met President Calvin Coolidge, silent film star Mary Pickford, and other celebrities of the day. After her tour, Vada returned to her studies at Sterling College. She then taught in Plains, Turon and Shawnee, before returning to her hometown of Turon to become Mrs. Vada Hoskinson. ∎

Alcott Zarn, an Ellsworth native, won the 1924 American Dog Derby—a tough dogsled race started in 1913 near Yellowstone National Park by two Kansans, *J.G. Ball* and *H.L. Woodburn*.

The rules of the contest said all dogs that started the race had to finish, so when one of Zarn's animals became dog-tired, he unhitched it from the rest of the team and held it on his lap in the sled. Thanks to the pulling power of his other dogs, the creative Kansan and his pooped pup won the derby. ∎

Wild & Woolly

Law Officers, Lawbreakers and Colorful Characters

Vanishes into history

338 Kate Bender

Prof. Miss KATIE BENDER

Can heal all sorts of Diseases; can cure Blindness, Fits, Deafness and all such diseases, also Deaf and Dumbness. Residence, 14 miles East of Independence, on the road from Independence to Osage Mission one and one half miles South East of Norahead Station.

June 18, 1872.   **KATIE BENDER.**

Murderess. Cherryvale. (About 1850-1873?) Bender and her family came to Kansas in late 1870 or early 1871. Near the Osage Mission Trail, a few miles northeast of Cherryvale and just inside Labette County, they built a small barn and house. A crude sign on their home advertised groceries. To travelers who stopped, they sold a few supplies, served meals— and sometimes delivered death.

John Bender and his wife, both around age 60, often kept to themselves, neighbors said. When they did attend church or neighborhood get-togethers, they had little to say. The same was true of ***John Bender, Jr.***, their son.

Kate, however, was different. Her outgoing personality, flashing brown eyes and reddish hair caught the attention of local young men. The attractive girl also seemed aggressive and domineering; some said she was the ruling force of the Bender family.

During the summer of 1872, Kate advertised herself as "Professor Miss Katie Bender." She claimed she could heal all sorts of diseases, and offered to give lectures on spiritualism.

At the same time, several strangers came into the area—and then disappeared. No one suspected the Benders were involved, except, perhaps, some neighbors. One local man said he had stopped at the Bender store to change a $100 bill. When the family learned he lived nearby, old man Bender stepped from behind the door holding a sledgehammer in his hands.

Another local resident, an elderly woman named Hesler, visited Kate one night. After dark, she said, the family began to act strangely. They drew pictures of people on the walls and stuck knives into them. Suddenly Kate's expression changed and she whispered in an odd voice: "The spirits command me to kill you—now!" Before the young woman could act, Mrs. Hesler jumped up and ran home.

It was the disappearance of a well-known Independence doctor, ***William H. York***, that finally uncovered the Benders' crimes.

When Dr. York didn't return from a visit to his brother in Fort Scott, relatives were concerned. A month later, his brother and a posse tracked the missing man to the Benders' store. Kate admitted that the doctor had indeed been

GOVERNOR'S PROCLAMATION.

$2,000 REWARD

State of Kansas, Executive Department.

WHEREAS, several atrocious murders have been recently committed in Labette County, Kansas, under circumstances which fasten, beyond doubt, the commissions of these crimes upon a family known as the "Bender family," consisting of

JOHN BENDER, about 60 years of age, five feet eight or nine inches in height, German, speaks but little English, dark complexion, no whiskers, and sparely built;

MRS. BENDER, about 50 years of age, rather heavy set, blue eyes, brown hair, German, speaks broken English;

JOHN BENDER, Jr., alias John Gebardt, five feet eight or nine inches in height, slightly built, gray eyes with brownish tint, brown hair, light moustache, no whiskers, about 27 years of age, speaks English with German accent;

KATE BENDER, about 24 years of age, dark hair and eyes, good looking, well formed, rather bold in appearance, fluent talker, speaks good English with very little German accent:

AND WHEREAS, said persons are at large and fugitives from justice, now therefore, I, Thomas A. Osborn, Governor of the State of Kansas, in pursuance of law, do hereby offer a REWARD OF FIVE HUNDRED DOLLARS for the apprehension and delivery to the Sheriff of Labette County, Kansas, of each of the persons above named.

In Testimony Whereof, I have hereunto subscribed my name, and caused the Great Seal of the State to be affixed. Done at Topeka, this 17th day of May, 1873.

[L. S.]

THOMAS A. OSBORN, Governor.

By the Governor,
W. H. SMALLWOOD, Secretary of State.

there, but she claimed he had watered his horse, made a purchase and ridden on. The men left and continued their search.

About two weeks later someone noticed the Bender place was deserted. When officials investigated, they discovered Dr. York's body in a shallow grave in the Benders' orchard. He had been robbed and his skull had been smashed. The searchers soon uncovered the bodies of seven other victims nearby. One grave held a father and his small daughter.

Curious spectators from miles around flocked to the scene. As for the Benders, they were nowhere to be found. The only real evidence in their disappearance was discovered several miles north, at Thayer. A wagon, team and dog believed to have been theirs were found on the edge of the small town. But Kate and her family were never seen again.

Over the years, many tales have been told to explain the Benders' fate—including one about a wild balloon ride that dumped them into the Gulf of Mexico. Historians suggest they were killed by local vigilantes, or were frightened away and took on new identities elsewhere. The truth may never be known.

Today, Bender Mounds—three round-topped hills in Labette County—are reminders of the mysterious murdering family. ∎

Shady sergeant

339 Ernie Bilko

Fictional U.S. Army sergeant. "Fort Baxter." (Created 1955) Bilko was the main character in the *Sergeant Bilko* television series during the 1950s.

As staff sergeant at a motor pool, Sergeant Ernest T. Bilko, serial number 15042699, was a likable con man with a big smile and a big mouth. He was supposed to be in charge of servicing and repairing motor vehicles. Instead, he spent most of each episode dreaming up get-rich-quick schemes and ways of getting around the authorities at his post. The show was set at Fort Baxter, Kansas, a "forgotten outpost" of the U.S. Army. In real life, Fort Baxter was more than forgotten —it never even existed.

The Bilko comedy ran on CBS from 1955 to 1959. It starred comedian Phil Silvers, and was also known as *You'll Never Get Rich* and *The Phil Silvers Show.* ∎

Builds for his people

340 Black Dog

Indian chief. Eastern Kansas. (About 1780-1848) Black Dog, an Osage Indian, was born near St. Louis. After his father died, the sixteen-year-old became chief of his band, the Upland-Forest People. Osages were often tall compared to other Plains Indians, and Black Dog was no exception. By age twenty the young chief stood nearly seven feet tall.

The name Black Dog, or *Zhin-gá-wa-ca* in the language of the Osages, may have come from a time when he was leading a war party against a group of Comanches. In the dark, it was said, Black Dog aimed an arrow toward the sound of a dog's warning bark—and killed the animal with one shot. Others stories say his name referred to a black wolf or a black horse.

Black Dog married an Osage girl named **Menanah** about 1800. Nearly 30 years later their only son, **Black Dog II**, was born. At that time their village was located along the Neosho River in present Labette or Cherokee County.

Black Dog was never the Osages' most important chief. He is remembered instead for his construction talents. A large underground storage room he helped build protected his people when Cherokees and Comanches raided the Osages in 1817. During the attack, members of Black Dog's band hid in the room and no one was hurt. Another of the chief's projects became one of Kansas' earliest roads. Under his leadership his band built a trail west from their village to their spring and fall hunting grounds. Using stone axes and hoes, they cleared small trees and bushes. When they finished, they had a route wide enough for 30 horsemen to ride side by side. The Black Dog Trail, or Osage Trail, ran west along what is now the southern border of Kansas to the mouth of the Ninnescah River near Oxford. It was marked with characters and signs carved into rocks and trees.

Black Dog, the Indian architect, died in 1848 while on a visit to one of his old village sites in Oklahoma. ∎

Peacemaker killed by war

Indian chief. Western Kansas. (About 1810-1868)
Black Kettle, a Southern Cheyenne, was born early in the nineteenth century, perhaps near the Black Hills of South Dakota. Some sources say he was the son of Swift Hawk Lying Down; others believe he was born several years later, the son of chief High-Backed Wolf.

Defends his people

As a young man Black Kettle was known as a good warrior. He led several raids against Kiowas, Comanches and Plains Apaches. In the summer of 1848 he led a war party against a Ute village. His group accidentally ran into the enemy camp without seeing it, and as the Cheyennes retreated, his first wife was captured. Black Kettle later married ***Medicine Woman***. According to Cheyenne custom, they joined her family's band.

In 1853 he carried the Cheyennes' sacred medicine arrows into battle against the Delaware Indians. ***George Bent***, son of trader William Bent and Owl Woman, a Cheyenne, was married to Black Kettle's niece and spent time with the chief's band. Bent said Black Kettle was present in 1857 when Cheyennes and the U.S. Army fought their first major battle on the Solomon River in modern Sheridan County.

Peacemaker

Black Kettle probably became a chief in the 1850s when the leader of his wife's band died. This group always had fine horses, large lodges and other well-made items. Other Cheyennes called them the "Stingies" because they were not generous with presents.

As Black Kettle grew older, he argued that peace was the best way to protect his people. In 1861 he and five followers signed a treaty at Fort Wise in what is now Colorado. From that time on, the U.S. government considered him the spokesman for the Southern Cheyennes. But because the tribe didn't recognize an overall chief, other bands of Cheyennes ignored the agreement. Dog Soldiers—the most militant band of warriors—were especially angered by Black Kettle's attempts at peacemaking.

Sadly, as he continued his efforts, circumstances always seemed to work against him. The trouble came to a head in 1864. That spring, several hundred Cheyenne warriors met troops north of Fort Larned. One of Black Kettle's friends, Lean Bear, rode peacefully toward the soldiers, displaying a medal he had received from President Abraham Lincoln.

The troops—under orders to "kill all Indians"—began firing. Lean Bear and another Cheyenne were killed almost immediately. When his warriors joined the fighting, Black Kettle rode among them shouting, "Stop the fighting! Do not make war!" When the shooting finally ended, several soldiers and one more Cheyenne lay dead. Within a few weeks troops and Cheyennes fought three more times—and the Army burned four Cheyenne villages.

The situation grew worse that summer. With many troops from forts in Kansas and the surrounding territory moved east to Civil War battlefields, war chiefs of the Sioux, Kiowas, Comanches and Cheyennes stepped up their raids on the Plains.

That fall, Black Kettle and other Cheyenne and Arapaho peace chiefs traveled to Denver. The Cheyenne leader told the governor of Colorado he had used his own ponies to buy freedom for several captured white children. He was trying to arrange the release of more prisoners, he said, but most of all, he wanted the fighting to stop.

The governor was angry that Denver had been held hostage by the summer fighting. He was in no mood to sign treaties.

After the meeting, Black Kettle visited Fort Lyon in eastern Colorado. He wanted to ask Major **Edward Wynkoop**, the fort's commander and his old friend, for rations. Wynkoop, however, had been suddenly transferred to Fort Riley. The new commander had no food to offer, but he assured the chief that his band would be safe at their new camp along Sand Creek, about 40 miles north of the fort.

Massacre on Sand Creek

That set the stage for an attack on Black Kettle's village by Colonel **John Chivington**. Chivington, a Methodist minister who had preached his way west from Ohio through Kansas, was known as the Fighting Parson. He had made a name for himself in 1862 as he helped drive Confederates out of New Mexico. In the fall of 1864 he commanded Colorado volunteers who had been called into service for one hundred days.

His regiment saw little action, however, and with just a short time left before their discharge, members of the "Bloodless Third" were anxious to fight Indians. Led by Chivington, they attacked Black Kettle's village at dawn on November 28.

At first, the trusting chief waved an American flag and a white cloth in front of his tipi; he believed the charge was meant only to frighten his people. But troops poured into the village, firing at everyone. Women and children ran for cover; men grabbed their weapons.

As Black Kettle tried to help his wife escape, she fell with a bullet wound. Before he could move her, soldiers rode up and shot her eight more times. Medicine Woman—miraculously—survived. Others were not as lucky.

An accurate count was not made, but perhaps 150 Indians were killed in the massacre—over half of them women and children. Many of the bodies were badly mutilated.

With their village destroyed and most of their horses captured, Black Kettle and his survivors joined the Dog Soldiers along the Smoky Hill River. Still, the chief believed in peace. A year later, he took part in a peace council with Christopher "Kit" Carson [**8**] and Army officials on the Little Arkansas River near present Wichita. After displaying the scars of Medicine Woman's nine bullet wounds, he and five other chiefs signed a treaty giving them land in northern Indian Territory.

In the fall of 1867 Black Kettle ignored threats by the Dog Soldiers and joined peace talks on Medicine Lodge Creek. And, after a tense four-day delay, he convinced the militant group to appear and sign the treaty.

Black Kettle's peacemaking came to an end a year later. After admitting some of his young men had taken part in summer raids in Kansas, he moved his

51 lodges along the Washita River in Indian Territory. Nearby were the camps of other tribes.

Death on the Washita

At Fort Cobb on November 20, 1868, officials told Black Kettle that Kansas troops were on the march, looking for hostile Indians. Back in camp, he and his headmen decided to move the village closer to the fort for protection. Although knee-deep snow covered the area, they planned their move for the next day—November 27.

At the same time, a Kiowa war party rode down the Washita. When Army scouts found the snowy trail, they mistakenly decided the raiders came from Black Kettle's camp. During the night of the twenty-sixth, Lieutenant Colonel George Armstrong Custer [**351**] and a large force surrounded the Cheyenne lodges. At dawn—just one day short of the Sand Creek anniversary—the troops attacked. The massacre that followed took the lives of over 100 of Black Kettle's people. The chief and Medicine Woman died in a hail of bullets as they tried to ride across the icy river.

A mobile way of life

Plains Indians are often called nomadic, giving the impression they wandered about aimlessly. Kansas historian Leo E. Oliva, however, points out that Plains tribes moved with a purpose, whether hunting, fighting or for protection. Dr. Oliva suggests the tribes should more correctly be called "mobile."

Black Kettle's movements illustrate this mobility. In the four years between the Sand Creek and Washita massa-cres, the chief located his village in Kansas, Indian Territory and possibly Texas. He camped along Lake, Wolf and two different Bluff creeks—plus the Smoky Hill, Pawnee Fork, Cimarron, Red, North Canadian and South Canadian rivers.

Black Kettle visited Forts Ellsworth, Hays, Larned and Zarah in Kansas, and Fort Cobb in the Territory. He also took part in peace talks along the Arkansas and Little Arkansas rivers, and Medicine Lodge Creek in Kansas. ▪

Gets the public's goat

"Doctor" and gubernatorial candidate. Hays, Axtell, Fulton and Milford.
(1885-1942) Brinkley was born on July 8, 1885—perhaps.

Fact or fiction?

At different times, Brinkley gave his birthplace as Tennessee, Kentucky or North Carolina. Historians believe he came from North Carolina, but the truth about this fraudulent—or "quack"—doctor is sometimes difficult to uncover. His mother—and there is some question about her identity—died when Johnny was about five. When his aging doctor father died several years later, he went to live with an aunt.

Brinkley taught himself telegraphy as a teenager. After his marriage in 1908, he took a job as a substitute depot agent for the Southern Railway. Later he worked for the Western Union telegraph company in Chicago. There he enrolled in a medical college, but he dropped out before graduating.

According to some accounts, Brinkley and his wife lived in several Southern and Midwestern states. Their stormy marriage included an incident during which he kidnapped their daughter and held her in Canada, trying to force Mrs. Brinkley to drop a lawsuit against him.

Doctor of fraud

Along the way he attended other medical schools, from Chicago's legitimate Loyola University to the not-so-legitimate "Midlandensis Universitatis Chicagoensis Seminarium Scientarium."

In the middle of his "schooling" —and just after his wife left him for the last time—Brinkley and another "Electro Medic Doctor" set up a fake clinic in South Carolina. For $25, their male patient-victims received an injection—colored water—that promised to bring back their "youthful vigor."

In the spring of 1915 Brinkley earned a degree from a questionable Missouri medical school, the Eclectic Medical University of Kansas City. For one hundred dollars and a few weeks of study, the "university" added its credits to those he had earned in Chicago.

Diplomas in hand, John and his classmates then went to Arkansas where professors helped them complete two and a half days of testing. After paying a $50 fee, Brinkley was given a license to practice medicine in Arkansas. With it, he was able to get medical licenses from a collection of other states, including Kansas.

By then Brinkley had married **Minnie Jones**, the daughter of a genuine doctor in Memphis. For a time the Brinkleys lived in Arkansas and then in Kansas City, Missouri. There he was a doctor at the Swift & Company packing plant. Although he spent most of his time bandaging workers' cuts, he later said that his position as "Plant Surgeon" gave him "an unparalleled opportunity for studying the diseases of animals." He claimed the Swift laboratory was where he first discovered the amazing powers of billy goat glands. He must have worked quickly, for his job at the plant actually lasted only one month.

According to his authorized biography, Brinkley then practiced medicine with a partner in an unnamed Kansas town. When he learned his partner performed abortions, he and Minnie moved, living briefly in Hays, Axtell and then Fulton. There he became the town's physician and mayor.

During World War I he spent a short time as a doctor in the U.S. Army. He was on duty just over a month when he told his superior officers he was too ill to work—he had a rapid heartbeat, he claimed. Years later he said his military career ended when he suffered a nervous breakdown—from "overwork."

After he returned to Fulton in the fall of 1917 he found that another doctor had moved into town. When he heard that the small community of Milford needed a physician, he opened an office there, just before the terrible influenza epidemic of 1918 swept through Kansas. Doc Brinkley quickly gained a medical reputation, for many of his patients survived the flu.

Goat glands galore

About the same time, Brinkley hit upon a new scheme. Based perhaps on the research of European scientists, the Kansan began transplanting portions of young billy goats' sex glands into men who believed they weren't able to father children.

According to Brinkley's version of the story, he got the transplant idea from a local farmer. The doctor reluctantly did as the man asked, and transplanted goat glands into him. Later the patient claimed his surgery was the reason his wife had a baby boy—named Billy, of course. Real doctors recognized the "compound operation" as a fraud, but as stories from Brinkley's satisfied customers began to spread, he had lines of men waiting for the surgery.

In the summer of 1918 he built his own sixteen-bed hospital in Milford. A pen of Toggenberg goats was nearby. (Toggenbergs were "practically odorless." He supposedly used Angora goat parts in a few early transplants, but his human recipients complained of the smell.)

No one, surprisingly, was hurt by Brinkley's antics. Neither was his bank account. At $750 or more per patient—and 50 patients a month—the money rolled in. To assist him, Minnie got her own "medical degree" in 1919 from her husband's Kansas City alma mater. (He also continued his "education," and eventually tacked a bizarre list of degrees after his name: M.D., Ph.D., M.C., LL.D., D.P.H., Sc.D.)

In 1922 Brinkley was invited to Los Angeles to perform his surgery on several influential businessmen. A few weeks later he had collected $40,000, free publicity in the *Los Angeles Times*, as well as the idea of building a radio station.

Just a year later, Brinkley's own KFKB was broadcasting in Kansas. As early as 5 a.m. or as late as 11 p.m., the good doctor could be heard preaching the benefits of his operation. In between, he filled the airwaves with musical programs, weather and agricultural reports, prayer meetings, fortunetellers and the popular "Medical Question Box."

Ask Dr. Brinkley

During those segments, the enterprising Brinkley read letters from listening patients. Based on their symptoms, he then prescribed medications over the air. Mildred in Manhattan, for example, might have been told to buy numbers 7, 28 and 59. The "prescriptions"—naturally—were his own concoctions, available at many local drugstores.

Most of his medicines were useless mixtures, but for a time he sold $55,000 worth a week. Expressmen at the Union Pacific depot in Milford handled impressive shipments of Brinkley's medicine going out to druggists in the region. At the same time, the railroaders unloaded barrels of medicinal syrup, box after box of bottles and corks, and crateloads of goats—all headed to the doctor.

When the mail-order medicine business became too great to handle, Brinkley sent his ⮕

No truth in broadcasting

Although Brinkley said the call letters of his radio station KFKB stood for "Kansas First Kansas Best," his was not the first commercial radio station in Kansas. Wichita station WAAP went on the air over a year before KFKB. Topeka's WJAQ, owned by Capper [34] Publications, also began broadcasting before Brinkley's station.

formulas to several hundred "affiliated" druggists. As each sold one of the numbered prescriptions, he returned a dollar to the doctor. One source estimated the income at $2,000 a day.

John "Johnny Boy" Brinkley, John and Minnie's son, was born in 1927. As soon as the youngster could talk, he was added to the radio schedule, first singing "Happy Birthday" and later reading letters from his father's satisfied patients.

Wizard of Milford

Through the 1920s, Brinkley collected an estimated twelve million dollars from his schemes! The Wizard of Milford used part of his fortune to build his own drugstore and bank. He also put in a water system for the town and constructed an electric power plant. When he needed to leave his growing empire, the doctor traveled in a fleet of vehicles that included a "block-long" Cadillac, a specially-built Lincoln and his own Travel Air [**134-135**] plane.

Brinkley's popularity reached a peak in the early 1930s. At the same time, the Kansas Medical Society, the American Medical Association, the *Kansas City Star* and William Allen White's [**256**] *Emporia Gazette* attacked him as a fraud. Investigations by the AMA's Dr. Morris Fishbein and reporters from the *Star* uncovered the doctor's questionable practices. In June 1930 the Federal Radio Commission voted not to renew

KFKB's broadcasting permit. That September the state medical board took away Brinkely's Kansas medical license.

Instead of quitting, however, Brinkley went on the offensive: he ran for governor. With KFKB still on the air after a court appeal, the Independent candidate broadcast a string of campaign promises. His list included something for everyone: lower taxes, free schoolbooks, free medical treatment for the needy, lakes across the state, support for Kansas manufacturers and workers, opposition to big corporate farms, and regulations for shorter trains to keep more railroaders employed.

'Brinkleyism'

His campaign included perhaps the largest political rally in Kansas history, an estimated 20,000 "Brinkleyites" who gathered in a pasture east of Wichita. Most of his campaigning was done over KFKB, however. It was too late for his name to be included on the ballot, so he reminded his radio listeners countless times to write in his name—J.R. Brinkley.

On Election Day, thousands of Kansans did so. "Brinkleyism" had hit the mark. The problem

was, supporters listed his name in various ways: Dr. Brinkley, Doctor Brinkley, John R. Brinkley, just plain Doc, and so on.

The election was November 4, but results weren't announced until November 16. It took that long to count the votes because the state attorney general ruled that each Brinkley spelling had to be tallied separately. (Under Kansas law, the doctor should have been given credit for all identifiable write-in ballots.) The 183,278 official votes he received as J.R. Brinkley—not including 20,000 more he got in Oklahoma!—made him third. Unofficially, according to some historians and politicians, Brinkley was the winner. Second-place Republican challenger ***Frank Haucke*** polled 216,920 votes—just 251 behind Governor Harry Woodring [**95**]. But neither the Republicans nor the Democrats wanted a recount. They feared Brinkley might win.

Without a license to practice in Kansas, Brinkley hired other surgeons to work in his Milford clinic. When the government forced him to sell KFKB, he leased a telephone line and broadcast by remote control from Kansas to a powerful station in Mexico, XER. (The new KFKB owner gave him airtime, too.)

He also kept his interest in politics, and ran for governor again in 1932. He campaigned in a Chevrolet sound truck—"Ammunition Train No. 1"—with a horn that could be heard five miles away. A cowboy musician and a

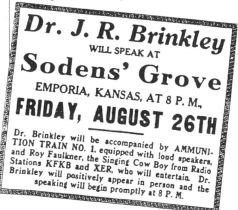

Dr. J. R. Brinkley WILL SPEAK AT Sodens' Grove EMPORIA, KANSAS, AT 8 P. M. FRIDAY, AUGUST 26TH

Dr. Brinkley will be accompanied by AMMUNITION TRAIN NO. 1, equipped with loud speakers, and Roy Faulkner, the Singing Cow Boy from Radio Stations KFKB and XER, who will entertain. Dr. Brinkley will positively appear in person and the speaking will begin promptly at 8 P. M.

Methodist preacher began each performance of his traveling road show, during which he promised voters anything and everything. With his name on the ballot, Brinkley received more official votes than in 1930, but he lost to Republican Alf Landon [**67**]. In 1934 he ran one last time, as a Republican. Landon easily beat him in the primary election.

South of the border

By that time, Brinkley had moved his medical and radio operations south. In Del Rio, Texas, he purchased a mansion and built a new clinic that specialized in prostate surgery and "rejuvenation" injections. But he faced competition from other quacks who set up shop nearby and offered cut-rate prices.

He also continued his radio crusade. XER could easily be heard in Kansas—and across the continent, for it often broadcast at illegal levels. He continued advertising his miraculous sur-

Fooled you, too

Among the Kansans taken in by Dr. Brinkley's brand of medicine was publisher Emanuel Haldeman-Julius [205]. In the 1920s he ran ads from the doctor in his weekly newspaper. He also wrote a magazine article about Brinkley's surgery and reprinted it as one of his Little Blue Books.

When Brinkley's tricks were exposed, Haldeman-Julius apologized publicly for his mistake. He took the Brinkley Little Blue Book off the market and replaced it with one about quack doctors.

gical procedures and cure-all products. Other broadcasters complained, and the Mexican government tried to shut him down in 1933. The doctor got a two-year reprieve after former vice president Charles Curtis [**38**] met with the Mexican president to plead his case.

When he finally lost his broadcast license, the clever Brinkley sold his station to friends and reopened it as XERA. He went off the air for good in 1941 when his

unhappy host country closed XERA and had its army tear it down. About the same time the U.S. government sued him for back taxes. Even though he had set up two successful clinics in Arkansas, he went bankrupt.

The Wizard of Milford died at his large San Antonio home on May 26, 1942. Surprisingly, he left an important legacy—tough government regulations against quack medicine, false advertising and illegal broadcasting. ∎

Top Communist

343
Earl Browder

Secretary-general of the U.S. Communist party, presidential candidate and author. Wichita. (1891-1973)
Browder was born in Wichita. He quit school there before he was ten to help support his family by delivering messages. As a teenager Earl read the writings of Karl Marx. He joined the Socialist party and sold *Appeal to Reason*, a party paper published in Kansas [**205-206**]. Several years later young Browder moved to Kansas City, Missouri. When he refused to serve in the military during World War I he spent a year in jail.

After moving to New York City in 1921 he gave up his Socialist membership and joined the newly-formed American Communist party. As he worked his way up, he wrote for one of the organization's newspapers and other publications. He also wrote several books about com-

munism. In 1930 he was named head of the party in America, a job he held until 1945. During that time he made several visits to Communist countries but was arrested by U.S. officials for using his passport illegally. He eventually served a prison sentence for the violations.

Twice Browder was the Communist party's nominee for president. Each time he faced a Republican candidate with Kansas connections: Governor Alf M. Landon [**67**] in 1936 and Wendell Willkie [**93**] in 1940. Democrat Franklin D. Roosevelt beat them all. Browder polled about 80,000 votes in 1936 and just over half that many in 1940. Few of the votes, however, came from Kansans.

In both campaigns Browder warned about dangerous Fascist governments in Germany, Italy and Japan. He also urged America to cooperate with the Soviet Union. When he continued to support the idea of peaceful coexistence, Soviet dictator Joseph Stalin expelled him from the party in 1946. At that time Browder was editor of the party's American newspaper, the *Daily Worker*. In his later years he gave up his communist beliefs. He was living in New Jersey when he died. ∎

Lives on in legend

Radical antislavery supporter. Osawatomie. (1800-1859) Brown was born in Connecticut. His family drifted from place to place, but he spent much of his unhappy childhood in Ohio. John received little schooling as his family moved about, and his stern father gave him little affection. His mother died when he was eight and after his father remarried, John couldn't accept his stepmother.

Hatred of slavery

During the War of 1812 he helped his father drive cattle to Detroit. On that trip, the twelve-year-old saw a master beat a young slave boy with a shovel. The more he saw of slavery, the more he learned to hate it. Like his father, John became a strong abolitionist.

While he was a teenager he spent a short time attending school in New England. He hoped to go on to college and become a minister; money problems and trouble with his eyes forced him to return to Ohio. There he worked in his father's leather tannery.

As an adult, Brown drifted from one unsuccessful job to another. He tried farming, selling land, raising livestock, grading wool and running a tannery. By his early fifties he had lived in four states and was a broken man—financially and physically. Fifteen times his businesses had failed. He had been accused of dishonesty and had been involved in several lawsuits. His first wife had died, along with nine of his twenty children.

In 1852 he moved to New York and helped freed slaves settle in a black community. He had already worked as an agent for the Underground Railroad, helping escaped slaves reach freedom in the North.

In late 1854 or early 1855 five of Brown's sons came to Kansas and settled south of Lawrence. Kansas Territory was brand new—and a showdown over slavery was fast approaching. Missourians and other Southerners wanted Kansas to enter the Union as a slave state; Northerners stood firmly on the opposite side. The residents of Kansas Territory would decide for themselves.

Bleeding Kansas

The new territory was already full of proslavery settlers. When Brown heard his boys' stories about Missouri Border Ruffians harassing Kansas Free State settlers, he was convinced there was a conspiracy to make Kansas a slave state. In the fall of 1855—and with a wagonload of guns and swords—he left New York and headed west. In doing so, some say, John Brown turned the slavery arguments into the battle of Bleeding Kansas. He wasn't the only one, however, involved in the fight.

Men on both sides of the issue had already formed military-type organizations. A group known as the Pottawatomie Rifles was headed by one of Brown's sons, ***John Brown, Jr.*** As proslavery men tried to force Free Staters to follow the laws of the proslavery territorial legislature, the antislavery forces refused, calling the laws "bogus." Tension built up and then exploded in a series of events: A Free State farmer died in a land squabble with a proslavery neighbor. Antislavery men burned the killer's home. The proslavery sheriff of Douglas County—using Border Ruffian help—tried to arrest Free Staters. Someone wounded the sheriff. Border Ruffians swept into Lawrence, destroyed two antislavery newspaper offices and bombarded the Free State Hotel with cannon fire.

All this was too much for John Brown. According to one of his sons, he went "crazy." Vowing that God was on his side, he and four followers went into action on May 24, 1856. In cold blood —and in front of their victims' families—they murdered five proslavery men along Pottawatomie Creek in Franklin County.

Persons on both sides of the slavery issue were shocked. Brown laid low for a time, but that summer he continued his guerrilla warfare—harassing and raiding proslavery forces.

He left Kansas that fall and spent time in the Northeast, trying to raise money for his cause. In late 1858 he freed eleven slaves in Missouri and led them out of Kansas in 1859. By that time he had a radical plan.

Brown hoped to steal weapons and distribute them to slaves who he would then lead to freedom in the North. That October he, along with 21 men, tried to take control of the U.S. government's large arsenal at Harpers Ferry, Virginia. During the attack, ten in his group were killed—including two of his sons. Five others in the band fled. Brown and six survivors were captured.

Brown was charged with conspiracy, treason and murder. After a three-day trial, he was found guilty and sentenced to hang. Although many people considered him insane, his execution on December 2, 1859, made him a martyr in the North. ∎

'John Brown's Body'

During the Civil War, "John Brown's Body" was perhaps the Union's most popular song. Ironically, its first version was *not* written about the abolitionist from Kansas.

The song originated in 1861 in Boston, where one member of a soldiers' glee club received a lot of teasing about his famous name— John Brown. That spring, the young tenor's friends wrote song lyrics poking fun at him. Their words were sung to the tune of an old Methodist hymn, "Say, Brothers, Will You Meet Us?"

As the "John Brown" song circulated, listeners assumed it was about the martyred abolitionist. Others added new verses. Within a few months Northern troops and citizens were singing about the real John Brown's attempts to end slavery—while his body "lies a' mouldrin' in the grave."

Verses that Julia Ward Howe wrote for the song are now the most familiar: "Mine eyes have seen the glory of the coming of the Lord."

King-sized chief

345 Abram Burnett

Indian chief. Topeka. (About 1811-1870) Burnett, a Potawatomi known as *Kah-he-ga-wa-ti-an-gah*, was born in Michigan. At the mission school he attended in

Indiana, he was given the name Abram Burnett—sometimes listed as Abraham. There he met *Isaac McCoy*, a Baptist minister who later helped start Indian missions in early-day Kansas.

The Reverend McCoy took an interest in ten-year-old Abram and asked him to serve as his Potawatomi interpreter. As he grew older Burnett continued to speak for the tribe. In the 1830s and 1840s he signed treaties that moved the Potawatomis to Missouri and then to Kansas. Beginning in the early 1840s the tribe lived along the Osage River west of the Missouri border.

In 1843, Burnett married *Marie Knofloch* and joined the Catholic church. By about 1848 he and his German wife had moved near present Topeka. There the chief farmed, traded horses and bought cattle.

The hefty Burnett was often seen in a suit and tie, with a dress hat and a fancy ➪

237

cane. Once in a Topeka store, he sat down on a keg of nails—not realizing there was a container of putty on top. His 500-pound frame was glued to the barrel until the storekeeper cut the seat out of his pants!

Although he spent little money, some people believed the chief was quite wealthy. Years after his death, treasure hunters dug up the land around the site of his cabin looking for gold. They found nothing. Today Burnett's Mound, a bluff just southwest of Topeka, is named for him.

Burnett's great-grandson, *Abram Burnett IV*, is an announcer at KFRM, a central Kansas radio station. ■

Tree-top hermit

346 Hugh Cameron

Hermit. Lawrence. (1826-1908) Cameron grew up on his family's farm in New York. Hugh didn't attend school, but he educated himself and was accepted into a teacher training school at age eighteen. Within five years he was a mathematics professor at a Washington, D.C., academy. Later he worked at the Treasury Department. His friends in Washington included important politicians like Daniel Webster, Stephen Douglas and Henry Clay.

After he suffered a lung hemorrhage doctors told Cameron to exercise—and he did: He walked to St. Louis! There he met members of the Emigrant Aid Society bound for Kansas Territory. He joined the anti-slavery group and took a claim near Lawrence.

During the Bleeding Kansas period, Cameron belonged to the Free State party, but he spoke out against both sides. He called Free Staters stubborn and self-righteous; proslavery men, he said, were murdering plunderers. When territorial governor *Wilson Shannon* made him a justice of the peace, Cameron issued an arrest warrant for a Free State outlaw. In turn, James H. Lane [*68*] and Charles Robinson [*82*] angrily ordered him to resign. He refused, and then had to escape after a mob kidnapped him.

Beginning about 1857 Cameron apparently operated a ferry across the Kansas River. During the Civil War he joined the Union Army. After leading cavalry units he returned to his Kansas homestead.

By 1868, he was again in Washington, D.C., where he watched with interest the impeachment trial of President Andrew Johnson. When Kansas senator Edmund G. Ross [*85*] voted in support of Johnson, Cameron was impressed with Ross' courage. The two became friends.

After editing a small newspaper and watching his friend Horace Greeley lose the 1872 presidential election, Cameron returned to Kansas. About the same time, his romance with a Missouri woman ended. Those disappointments apparently caused him to begin living as a hermit. He stopped shaving, quit cutting his hair, and moved into a simple log hut along the Kansas River. For years, he frightened visitors away with a gun; by the late 1890s he was friendlier. Guests then enjoyed hearing his stories and philosophy of life.

In 1896 he journeyed to New Mexico—much of the way on foot—to deliver a "message of forgiveness" from the people of Kansas to ex-senator Ross. He is also said to have walked to Washington, D.C.,—and back—

to attend the inauguration of every president from Zachary Taylor to William McKinley!

When he was nearly 80, the Kansas Hermit moved into Lawrence. He built a platform in a tree and dug a room out of a nearby creek bank. The tree was his open-air bedroom; the cave was his kitchen and dining room. His unusual home even included electric lights and a telephone. He continued living there until his death. ■

Queen of Boot Hill

347 Alice Chambers

Dance hall girl. Dodge City. (18?-1878) Chambers is believed to be the last person—and the only woman—to be buried on Dodge City's notorious Boot Hill. Little is known of her life, except that for a time she operated a dance hall in partnership with another woman. She also worked in other saloons.

In the year before her death, Alice seemed to have her share of troubles with the law. In early 1877 a Dodge City doctor sued her, claiming she owed him $15.75. Several months later she was arrested for fighting with a dance hall girl.

Soon after she died in May 1878, the city closed Boot Hill and opened a new cemetery. Her body was moved to the new site six months later. Of all those buried in the infamous graveyard, Alice had the shortest stay. ■

First Mrs. Sheriff totes a tommy-gun

348 Mabel Chase

Sheriff. Haviland and Greensburg. (1876-1962) Chase moved with her family from Indiana to Haviland in 1896. Three years later she married *Frank Chase*. He eventually became a veterinarian and also worked in law enforcement.

For several years before World War I, Frank was Haviland's city marshal. In 1922 and 1924 he was elected sheriff of Kiowa County. Because Kansas sheriffs could not serve more than two terms in a row, Mabel ran in his place in 1926.

When she won a close race against her male Republican opponent that November, the 52-year-old mother of four was the first woman in the United States to be elected sheriff. (Several women in different states had already been sheriff, but each had been appointed to fill an unexpired term.)

Once in office, Mabel's first action was to appoint Frank her undersheriff. During her two-year term, he did most of the actual law enforcement while she handled the bookwork. Sheriff Chase did, however, keep up with the latest in crime-fighting equipment. She bought a Thompson submachine gun and drove an armor-plated Hudson "Super Six" patrol car with bulletproof glass. When law officers were on the trail of the Fleagle [*360-361*] gang in the spring of 1928, Mabel sent Frank to join in the search. He came home empty-handed.

The Chases retired from law enforcement in 1930. They later moved to Arkansas. ■

Scout, buffalo hunter and entertainer. Leavenworth. (1846-1917) Cody was born in LeClaire, Iowa, February 26, 1846. He came to Kansas Territory with his family in 1854.

His father, *Isaac Cody*, was stabbed during an antislavery rally, but he lived to become a member of the "Topeka Legislature"—one of the unsuccessful attempts to organize Kansas Territory into a state. After the elder Cody died in 1857 from the effects of his injury, eleven-year-old Bill helped support his family. He worked for the Russell, Majors & Waddell company, hauling hay and delivering messages near Leavenworth. (Contrary to many sources, it is now believed Cody did *not* ride for Russell, Majors & Waddell's Pony Express as a teenager. This story is only one of several legends that come from fictional accounts he wove into his autobiography.)

Into the West

Cody's first trip west was probably at age twelve. After he argued with a schoolmate and wounded him with a knife, Bill headed to Fort Laramie with a friend. He soon returned home.

Mr. Wild West

Near the beginning of the Civil War he first met James Butler "Wild Bill" Hickok [**364**]. The two remained friends until Hickok's death. In early 1864 Cody joined the war conflict— by accident. After a night of drinking, he woke up to find he had enlisted in the 7th Kansas Volunteer Cavalry.

After his discharge, Bill married in 1866 and tried running a hotel near Leavenworth. When the business went broke after only six months, he left his bride with his sister and headed west. In Junction City, Cody met Hickok, who got him a job as a government scout.

In 1867 he joined a grading crew for the Union Pacific Railroad, Eastern Division. A year later he was hired to furnish buffaloes to feed the railroaders in western Kansas. During that period he became "Buffalo Bill"—although he was not the first to use the nickname [**369**].

From 1868 to 1872 he was a scout for the 5th U.S. Cavalry. During one Indian uprising, young Cody delivered dispatches in a wide circle through Forts Larned, Hays, Dodge and back again—riding an estimated 350 miles in under 60 hours. Soon Bill's adventures received public attention when author Ned Buntline made him the hero of a "dime novel."

Although the first story was so fictionalized

Cody didn't recognize himself, readers loved it. He was eventually featured in over 1,700 tales. Unfortunately, those stories and Cody's own exaggerated accounts have taken away from some of the frontiersman's genuine adventures. He took part in sixteen battles with Indians, including several in Kansas. He guided celebrities to the West, the most famous being the Grand Duke Alexis of Russia on a hunting expedition in 1872. He also took the West to the East—through entertainment.

Showman

Buntline first asked Cody to appear on stage in 1872. The next year Bill put together "Cody's Combination," a touring production starring himself and Will Bill Hickok. Hickok didn't last long as an actor, but Cody spent eleven years performing during the winter and scouting in the summer.

In 1883 he organized Buffalo Bill's Wild West. Although his outdoor spectacle often suffered financial problems, it traveled America and Europe in various forms for 30 years. Cody's show gave work to some Indians and, for one season, his staging of Custer's Last Stand [**351**] included the Sioux chief Sitting Bull. His cowboy exhibitions of roping and bronc riding led to modern rodeos. His traveling buffaloes [**382**] helped show the need to save the species.

Cody died in Denver, on January 10, 1917. Like the shows he produced in life, his funeral and burial were a spectacle. A crowd of 25,000 passed by his casket in the state capitol. Five months later, 3,000 automobiles chugged up to his burial in a specially-built steel tomb on Lookout Mountain, Colorado.

'Buffalo Bill'

At least two stories explain the background of Cody's nickname. Both are from the period Bill worked for the UPED Railroad in Kansas.

According to one version, Cody once spied several buffaloes while grading the railroad right-of-way. Unhitching his horse, he headed toward them. Along the way he met a party of officers from Fort Hays. Although they were chasing the same animals, the men agreed to let railroader Bill and his "work horse" tag along. Almost before the cavalrymen could react, Cody rode into the herd, fired a dozen shots—and killed all eleven animals. The amazed officers named him Buffalo Bill on the spot.

A more familiar story is told about Cody's $500-a-month job as a hunter for the railroad near Hays. For about a year, he furnished twelve buffaloes each day to feed 1,200 tracklayers—an estimated 4,280 animals. Tired of the same menu, one of the workers sang: "Buffalo Bill, Buffalo Bill, never missed and never will; always aims and shoots to kill—and the company pays his buffalo bill." ∎

Lincoln's avenger?

350 Boston Corbett

U.S. Army sergeant. Concordia and Topeka. (1832-?) Corbett was born in England and grew up in New York. As a young man he made hats in Connecticut. After his wife died in the 1850s he wandered about, a drunken vagrant. Then, at a religious revival, Corbett was baptized. In honor of the city where it happened, he changed his first name from Thomas to Boston. He also began preaching from street corners—claiming his messages came from heavenly voices—but listeners weren't impressed. Neither were his fellow soldiers when he joined the U.S. Army during the Civil War. They complained about the loud, endless prayers coming from his tent.

After President Abraham Lincoln was assassinated by John Wilkes Booth on April 14, 1865, Corbett was in a group of volunteers from the 16th New York Cavalry sent to capture Booth. Led by four detectives, they tracked the assassin to a barn in Virginia.

Early on the morning of April 26, the soldiers surrounded the building. Booth and an accomplice, David Herold, were ordered to surrender. Herold soon came out with his hands raised; Booth refused to leave without a fight. The troops, however, were under orders to capture him alive. Government officials wanted to settle the assassination in court.

Thinking he would end the standoff, the commander set the barn on fire. As everyone waited for Booth to emerge, a shot was heard. They opened the door and discovered the assassin dying with a wound in his neck.

In the fiery confusion, witnesses first assumed that Booth had killed himself. Sergeant Corbett, however, stepped forward and claimed that he had fired the fatal shot. When asked why, he answered, "Providence directed me."

Many of those at the scene argued that Corbett couldn't have killed Booth. No one saw him fire and or heard shots from outside the barn. According to the autopsy report, Booth was killed by a pistol ball; Corbett carried a rifle. The evidence is not clear, but some historians also doubt that Corbett did the shooting.

At the time, he was arrested for disobeying orders, but was later set free by Edwin Stanton, the secretary of war. After Corbett was discharged from the Army, he returned to his work as a hatmaker. He also tried preaching again and led a Methodist congregation in New Jersey. About 1878 he moved to Kansas, perhaps to escape his reputation as Lincoln's avenger.

For several years he lived on a homestead near Concordia where residents remembered him as an eccentric loner. Boston did little work and seemed frightened of strangers. In 1886 a local politician got him a job as a doorkeeper at the Kansas House of Representatives. While at work there a few months later, he threatened two Capitol employees with a pistol. A judge declared him insane and sent him to the state mental hospital in Topeka. (Some have suggested his mental illness was caused by mercury poisoning. The dangerous chemical was used by hatmakers at that time.)

Corbett escaped from the institution in the spring of 1888. He appeared briefly at a friend's home in Neodesha—and then vanished. What finally became of him is still a mystery. ∎

His luck runs out

U.S. Army colonel. Fort Riley, Fort Hays and Fort Leavenworth. (1839-1876) Custer, best known for his defeat at the Battle of the Little Big Horn in Montana, first fought—or tried to fight—Indians in Kansas.

Young Autie

Custer was born December 5, 1839, at New Rumley, Ohio. Both his father and mother had older children from their first marriages, but Armstrong, as they called him, was the first child of their own to live past infancy. When, as a small boy, he tried to pronounce his name, it came out "Autie." The nickname lasted for years.

Young Autie enjoyed playing soldier—and practical jokes. From an early age he was known as a mischievous and fun-loving boy. Before he was twelve, he went to Monroe, Michigan, to live with his half sister. For several years he divided his time between her home and his parents' in Ohio.

In Monroe he did odd jobs and errands for a local judge. Teen-aged Custer admired the man's attractive young daughter, **Elizabeth "Libbie" Bacon**, but a romance at that time was out of the question. She was a member of "society"; he was not.

Autie graduated from a local academy at age sixteen and returned to Ohio. There he was a teacher in a country school for a time. He boarded at a nearby farm and soon found himself in love with the farmer's daughter. About the same time that Custer decided a military academy would be a place to earn a free education, the wealthy farmer decided that Custer would make a better soldier than a son-in-law. Hoping to send him on his way, the man convinced an Ohio congressman to appoint the young teacher to the U.S. Military Academy at West Point, New York. The appointment came through in 1857. Autie graduated in 1861—with an impressive number of demerits and the lowest grade average in his class.

Up through the ranks

As Custer left West Point, the outbreak of the Civil War thrust the young lieutenant into battle almost immediately. His reckless bravery in several cavalry fights soon brought him to the attention of his superiors. By the summer of 1863 he was a 23-year-old brigadier general. At the end of the war he was a brevet, or honorary, major general and veteran of Bull Run, Gettysburg and other important battles. The dashing six-foot hero with his blue eyes and long golden hair was known across the North. What some called the "Custer luck" seemed to be in full force.

To reward his performance in the war, General Philip Sheridan presented the Boy General and Libbie (his bride of one year) with the table on which Generals Robert E. Lee and Ulysses S. Grant had signed the articles of surrender.

Custer in Kansas

After the war Custer spent a short time in Texas. Although he lost his honorary high rank and was a captain, by mid 1866 he was made a lieutenant colonel in the 7th Cavalry, a new unit that was being organized at Fort Riley.

In western Kansas during the spring and summer of 1867, Custer and the 7th got their first experience in dealing with Indians. Hoping to scare the Plains tribes into peace, General Winfield Scott Hancock led 1,400 troops toward a large Cheyenne and Sioux village on the Pawnee Fork near Fort Larned. Remembering the Sand Creek Massacre at Black Kettle's [**341**] camp three years earlier, the frightened villagers fled. Hancock, angry that the Indians refused to talk, eventually burned their 251 tipis and all their belongings.

Custer, meanwhile, took to the trail to find the missing Indians. All he found were stagecoach stations recently raided by angry warriors. With eight companies of troops and a group of scouts that included James Butler "Wild Bill" Hickok [**364**], he headed to Fort Hays. As he impatiently waited there for supplies, he sent for Libbie to join him. Upon her arrival, she helped care for the zoo he had collected—"wolves, coyotes, prairie dogs, jack rabbits, raccoons, porcupines, wildcats, badgers, rattlesnakes, owls, eagles, hawks, young antelope, deer, buffalo calves, . . .hounds and horses," according to one source. He had also adopted a baby beaver.

When supplies arrived several weeks later, Autie left to pursue Indians. Libbie stayed in camp near Fort Hays, nearly drowning in a flash flood on Big Creek. She soon returned to Fort Riley.

Except for a few minor clashes, Custer spent the next few weeks on a wild goose chase after Indians in northwestern Kansas and parts of Nebraska and Colorado. When he shot several deserters and then abandoned his command to visit Libbie, his summer on the Plains came to an end. He was arrested, court-martialed and found guilty. But his sentence was minor: a year's suspension without pay.

Autie and Libbie moved into General Sheridan's quarters at Fort Leavenworth for several months and then went to Michigan. Before a year had passed, however, Sheridan called Custer back to Kansas. His sentence had been lifted. Army officials had decided it was useless to chase Indians all summer; instead they wanted Custer to lead a campaign against the Plains tribes in their winter camps.

Trail to tragedy

Soon Custer was on the march to Indian Territory. At dawn on the day after Thanksgiving 1868, he and over 800 troops attacked Black Kettle's village on the Washita River. The massacre that followed took the lives of Chief Black Kettle, his wife *Medicine Woman* and over 100 of the chief's followers. To make sure surviving Indians wouldn't mount an attack, Custer ordered his men to destroy the camp's tipis and their contents, and to slaughter 800 Indian ponies.

Although he had recklessly charged into the Indian camp without knowing its size, he was lucky once again. The attack was a success from the Army's standpoint. It demonstrated to the Plains tribes that they could not expect to raid in Kansas during the spring and summer and then camp peacefully on their reservations during the winter. Unfortunately, Custer chose to destroy the village of a chief who had worked tirelessly for peace.

His performance also turned many of his own officers and men against him. During the attack, he ignored reports about a party of twenty soldiers under heavy fire several miles from the village. They were later found, dead and mutilated.

Custer and the 7th marched the Washita survivors to Fort Hays where they were held in an "Indian pen" for six months. The troops camped nearby along Big Creek, helping guard the railroad. They spent the next winter at Fort Leavenworth and returned to the area around Fort Hays in the spring and summer of 1870.

Two years of service in Kentucky and South Carolina followed, before Custer and his ⇨

His aim is deadly

Kansas was not only the place where Custer first chased Indians, it was where he first hunted buffaloes.

Early in the 7th Cavalry's pursuit of the Indians from the Pawnee Fork village, the column of soldiers came upon a small herd of antelopes. With his dogs and a bugler, Custer dashed off after them. The bugler soon dropped back, but Autie continued behind his dogs. He eventually lost the antelopes, but sighted a large, shaggy beast ahead. Custer was excited; it was his first chance to hunt a buffalo. He pursued the animal for several miles, but just as he took aim, the old bull turned and Custer's mount reared. The gun went off, and, to his amazement, the daring hunter discovered he had killed his own horse!

Alone, on foot, and in hostile territory, he was lucky once again. By following his dogs, he eventually sighted the dust from his moving regiment and returned to safety.

men were transferred to the Dakota Territory in 1873. There they protected survey crews of the Northern Pacific Railway and gold-seekers in the Black Hills.

As Indians on the northern Plains resisted white settlement, the 7th Cavalry was part of what the Army hoped would be the final campaign against tribes in the region. For Custer and five companies of cavalrymen, it was. On Sunday, June 25, 1876, he led an attack on a huge Sioux and Cheyenne camp along the Little Bighorn River.

Thousands of warriors poured into the battle. In fighting that lasted about an hour, Custer, two of his brothers, a nephew, brother-in-law, and over 200 7th Cavalry troops were killed.

The Custer Massacre, Battle of the Little Bighorn or Custer's Last Stand, as it has been called, remains one of the most closely studied military conflicts in American history. Thousands of pages have been written to explain its tragic ending, but perhaps the answer is simple: Custer's luck ran out. ∎

DALTONS!

The Robber Gang Meet Their Waterloo in Coffeyville.

LITERALLY WIPED OUT

A Desperate Attempt to Rob Two Banks

In a brotherhood of crime

352 Emmett Dalton

Outlaw. Coffeyville and Lansing. (1871-1937) Dalton was one of a flock of fifteen children. Between the 1860s and 1880s, his large family lived in several locations in eastern Missouri, northern Indian Territory and Kansas. They were living near Lawrence when his older brother **Gratton** was born in 1861. In 1886 they moved to a farm near Coffeyville for a time.

Although they were cousins of Cole Younger—a participant in William Quantrill's [**373**] Civil War raid on Lawrence and leader of a Missouri outlaw gang that included three Younger brothers—most of the Dalton brothers and sisters were respectable, law-abiding citizens. **Frank Dalton** was a deputy U.S. marshal in Arkansas beginning in 1884. When he was killed in the line of duty three years later, Gratton was hired to take his place. Soon **Bob** and Emmett were riding in

Grat's posse. But even before they lost their badges in 1890 for two questionable shootings, the brothers had begun to work on the wrong side of the law.

They stole horses in Indian Territory and then sold them across the Kansas border. They also hid bottles of whiskey in settlers' wagons, and then fined their victims for entering the Territory with illegal liquor. The fines, of course, went into the Daltons' pockets. When the brothers were nearly arrested at Baxter Springs with a herd of stolen Indian ponies, they fled as wanted men.

They formed a gang and soon graduated from horse-stealing to train and bank robbery. When part of the gang robbed a gambling hall in New Mexico, Emmett was wounded and went into hiding. The rest of the bunch went on to California where, in 1891, they pulled their first successful train rob-

bery. Grat was captured, but escaped and rejoined his brothers in Oklahoma. There they committed several bank robberies, but their reputation was growing faster than the loot they were taking in.

The Daltons' crime career ended in the fall of 1892 when they tried to pull holdups in two Coffeyville banks at the same time. Alert citizens recognized the former residents as they rode into town and surprised them as they tried to escape.

In the gunfight that broke out, four townspeople and four of the gang, including Grat and Bob, were killed. Emmett was wounded—21 times, some say. He was then put in the Kansas State Penitentiary at Lansing.

After serving over fourteen years of a life sentence, he was pardoned by Governor Edward Hoch [**60**] in 1907. Dalton married and moved to Oklahoma where he worked as a police officer. About ten years later he headed to California with an idea for a movie about his brothers' gang. He starred in the film—it was a flop—but he remained in California and sold real estate. ∎

Hero in a sad true story

353 Alvin Dewey

Highway patrolman, sheriff and KBI agent. Kingman County and Garden City. (1912-1987) Dewey moved from Kingman County to Garden City in 1931. After graduating from high school and junior college there, he attended San Jose State University in California and majored in police administration. That was the beginning of a 40-year career in law enforcement.

Al first worked as a dispatcher for the Garden City Police Department. He then became a trooper for the Kansas Highway Patrol. Next he spent five years as a special agent with the FBI. In the late 1940s he returned to Kansas and was elected to the first of three terms as Finney County sheriff and one term as undersheriff.

In 1955 he joined the Kansas Bureau of Investigation as its agent in Garden City. Several years later, that position put him in charge of solving one of the state's most publicized crimes. Late one November night in 1959, Finney County farmer **Herbert Clutter**, his wife, and two of their children were brutally murdered during a robbery at their home near Holcomb.

In the intensive investigation that followed, Dewey and local law officers pieced together clues that led them to the Clutter killers: **Richard Hickock**, a native of Edgerton, and **Perry Smith**. After both were found guilty in trials at Garden City, they awaited execution at the Kansas State Penitentiary. In 1965 Dewey witnessed the hanging of the two killers at Lansing.

That same year the quiet Kansas lawman received worldwide attention when author Truman Capote featured him in a factual novel about the crime, *In Cold Blood*. When the book became a bestseller and was made into a movie (filmed in Kansas), Al and his wife found themselves guests at celebrity parties in New York City, Washington, D.C., and Los Angeles.

Dewey retired from the KBI in 1975, but remained on part-time duty for several years. ■

Tames Dodge City— but never lives there

354 Matt Dillon

Fictional U.S. marshal. Dodge City. (Created 1952) Dillon, who is perhaps Dodge City's most famous resident, never lived there. In fact, he never even existed.

Fans of the long-running CBS series *Gunsmoke* often assumed the show's main character Matt Dillon was once a real-life U.S. marshal. In reality, the man who tamed the "Wickedest City in the West" was created by the producers of the popular series.

Dillon first came to life on the CBS radio network in April 1952. He was portrayed by veteran actor William Conrad, known to viewers in the 1990s as J.L. McCabe on the CBS crime-drama, *Jake and the Fat Man*. ⇨

Within two years, *Gunsmoke* was a hit. It aired two days a week, Sunday night and the next Saturday morning. Kansas Governor **Edward Arn** spoke for proud state citizens when he called the program "splendid," although he was quick to point out that modern Dodge City was much more civilized than the wild cowtown portrayed in the series.

For nearly six years, Matt Dillon had a split personality. As television became popular in the 1950s, many radio programs made the change to video. *Gunsmoke* was one of them, with its first television appearance in the fall of 1955. The radio version, however, continued with its separate cast until it went off the air in 1961. A total of 413 radio stories were produced.

Television producers offered the Dillon role to movie star John Wayne; he turned them down and suggested his friend James Arness instead. (William Conrad wasn't right for the video Matt, producers said. His voice was great, but they felt he was too short—and too "wide.") Although both Arness and Conrad influenced the Dillon character, Matt always remained tough, honest, upright and strong. Above all, he was loyal to his fictional Dodge City friends: **Chester Goode**, his faithful deputy and sidekick; **Galen "Doc" Adams**, the loveable but cranky town medic; and **Kitty Russell**, the glamorous yet down-to-earth owner of the Long Branch Saloon. After Chester moved out of Dodge, colorful **Festus Haggen** took his place alongside Matt in the marshal's office.

Of the principal actors and actresses who worked on *Gunsmoke*, only Milburn Stone [*326*], who played Doc on television, was a Kansan. (Ken Curtis, who appeared as Festus beginning in 1962, grew up

just across the state line in southeastern Colorado.) Most of the television cast did, however, visit the real Dodge City over the years. In 1958 several stars were on hand when the city changed the name of Walnut Street to Gunsmoke. They also helped dedicate a replica of the buildings on old Front Street.

After twenty years of being suspended in the Dodge City of the 1870s, Dillon and his friends left the air in September 1975.

The final *Gunsmoke* telecast was the last of 635 television episodes—over 500 hours in all. In 1987, Matt and Kitty appeared in a CBS television movie, *Return to Dodge*. Two sequels followed, both featuring James Arness as Matt Dillon.

Thanks to reruns on cable television, Dillon is still visible around the world. Visitors at Dodge City's popular Boot Hill Museum continue to ask about the lawman from Kansas.

Jeff, Mark and other aliases

Listeners weren't aware of it, but before the first *Gunsmoke* episode was broadcast on radio, Matt Dillon's name changed—twice.

Creators Norman Macdonnell and John Meston first proposed a radio Western featuring Jeff Spain, a character from an earlier CBS series. As their planning continued, Spain's name was changed to Mark Dillon. It was Meston who finally suggested the name Matt— Mark sounded too modern.

Other characters had name changes, too. Chester Wesley Proudfoot from the radio version became Chester B. Goode on television. Proudfoot, producers felt, was an Indian name.

Doc Adams' first name was Charles on radio and Galen on television. Star William Conrad suggested the original name in honor of Charles Addams, a popular cartoonist in *The New Yorker* magazine [*202*]. It's not clear why the name was changed. ∎

East of Eden

355 Samuel Dinsmoor

***Sculptor. Lucas.
(1843-1932)*** Dinsmoor was born in Ohio and served in the Civil War. After teaching school for five years in Illinois he began farming. In 1888 Samuel and his wife moved to Kansas and farmed near Lucas. He remained in the area the rest of

his long life, except for a one-year stay in Nebraska in the early 1890s.

Dinsmoor's journey into the unusual apparently began about age 64. At that time he decided to build a new log cabin—using twenty-foot "logs" cut from

limestone. When completed, the eleven-room house was, in his words, "the most unique home, for living or dead, on earth." On the inside, no two doors were the same size. Three thousand feet of fancy wood molding trimmed the windows, doors and baseboards. Outside, he added a cement balcony and porch with row upon row of cement spindles formed in beer-bottle molds.

And that was only the beginning. Surrounding his house, he soon began constructing what he called the *Garden of Eden*. Today the huge, rambling sculpture covers much of his yard. It includes over 150 statues perched in 29 trees—some of which reach 40 feet into the air. The entire intertwined piece is made of cement, supported by steel reinforcements and chicken wire.

Working on scaffolds, sculptor Dinsmoor used over 2,000 sacks of cement—about 113 tons—in his creation. He worked alone, except for an assistant who helped him mix his unusual medium. And because his "recipe" included a secret formula, they prepared new batches at night.

Dinsmoor's work includes figures of Adam and Eve, Cain and Abel, the devil, angels and other Bible characters. He also touched on politics with representations of the Goddess of Liberty, voters and workers. To top it off, a cement American flag, four by seven feet, flies overhead. He even installed his own generator—the first electrical system in the town—and strung nearly 50 electric lights to make sure the display would be visible night and day.

Samuel worked on his project for over twenty years, with part of his building funds coming from an extra pension check he mistakenly received each month. When he told the government about the error, an angry bookkeeper refused to correct it, saying his office didn't make mistakes.

When local officials heard of his plan to bury his first wife under his own tomb, they refused to allow it. Samuel first buried her elsewhere, and later moved her to his chosen spot in the Dinsmoor mausoleum—in the middle of the night.

To insure that his creation would have income in the future, he left instructions to open it to visitors, and to charge them at least one dollar to view his remains.

Before he died at age 87, he conveniently built his own cement coffin—complete with a glass window! Years after his death, Dinsmoor's fascinating sculpture continues to draw tourists. It is now owned by a group of artists, including Pete Felten, Jr. [**198**].

Great-grandfather to his own children

After his first wife died in 1917, Dinsmoor hired a young housekeeper from Czechoslovakia, *Emilie Brozek*. Several years later—when she was 20 and he was 81—they were married.

One of their two children, *John W. Dinsmoor*, spent 30 years in the U.S. Air Force, part of that time as an officer in the Strategic Air Command. Born when his father was 85, Colonel Dinsmoor had the distinction for many years of being the youngest child of a Civil War veteran. He now lives in the Denver area. ∎

Legend with a badge

356 Wyatt Earp

Policeman, deputy marshal and gambler. Wichita and Dodge City. (1848-1929)
Earp managed to zigzag across much of the West during his eventful life. He may have also zigzagged across the line of the law. Wyatt was born in Illinois and lived in Iowa, California, Wyoming and Missouri before he arrived in Kansas. Along the way he was a stagecoach driver, railroad section hand, buffalo hunter, gambler and city constable.

By some accounts Earp came to Kansas after he had been arrested for stealing horses in Indian Territory. In 1875 he was hired as a policeman in Wichita. There he spent a fairly quiet year—although he narrowly escaped death when his revolver fell out of its holster and discharged. He lost his job after he was arrested for fighting. He also couldn't account for some fines he had collected.

Earp moved west to Dodge City in 1876 and became deputy city marshal. There Wyatt renewed his friendship with William "Bat" Masterson [*368*], with whom he had hunted buffaloes four years earlier. Earp apparently remained in Dodge City until early 1877. He then drifted to Texas, but was back on the local police force in mid 1878.

The *Dodge City Times* mentioned Earp's return and noted,"We predict that his services as an officer will again be required this summer." The paper was correct, for although Dodge City's wild reputation has been exaggerated in movies and on television, 1878 was a year full of real excitement. On top of train robberies, street fights and an Indian scare, there were several killings. Within six months' time, two lawmen and ***Dora Hand***, a popular dance hall singer, died in shootings. Also killed was a Texas cowboy, wounded in gunplay with Earp and policeman ***Jim Masterson***.

At the same time, Earp boosted his monthly salary of $75 by working as a card dealer. His gambling friends included characters like dentist-gunslinger ***John "Doc" Holliday*** and gambler ***Luke Short***.

In 1879 Earp left Kansas for a job in New Mexico. Later he moved to Tombstone, Arizona, where he worked for the Wells Fargo express company and as a gambler. When his brother Virgil was hired as a deputy U.S. marshal, Wyatt became a deputy sheriff. ***Morgan Earp***, another brother who had been a lawman in Dodge City, helped them both.

The Earps became Western legends after a gunfight at Tombstone's OK Corral in 1881. They forced the Clanton-McLaury gang into a showdown, and when the shooting ended, three of the outlaws were dead and the other two were on their way out of town.

In the months following, Virgil was ambushed, Morgan was murdered, and Wyatt and Doc Holliday were accused of shooting Morgan's killer. With public opinion against him, Earp left Arizona and moved to Colorado.

In 1883 he appeared briefly in Dodge City to support his gambler friend Short who was in a dispute with city officials.

Wyatt then headed to Idaho where he owned gold mining claims and a saloon. He later prospected in other western states and Alaska, and also worked as a private detective and a boxing referee.

Earp last lived in California where he was an advisor to Western movie producers. Ironically, his own character appeared on film from 1955 to 1960 in *The Life and Legend of Wyatt Earp*, an ABC television series. The show starred Hugh O'Brian and was set in Dodge City. But—like its title suggests—it was largely fiction. ∎

A job no one envies

357 William Eckert

Forensic pathologist. Wichita. (Born 1926) Eckert attended medical school in New York and worked at hospitals in Florida and Louisiana before coming to Kansas in 1967.

He is now the deputy district coroner of Sedgwick County, and the only active forensic pathologist living in the state. William's work—a job few Kansans would envy—is to determine the cause of deaths through autopsies.

In all, Dr. Eckert has performed over 20,000 autopsies—about ten percent of them on crime victims. By combining his knowledge of medicine and criminology, he has discovered evidence that has helped solve thousands of cases. And, his reputation is worldwide. Eckert often assists criminal investigators and other pathologists

around the country. In 1968 he was asked to examine evidence in the assassination of Robert F. Kennedy.

In 1975 Eckert established the Milton Helpern International Center for the Forensic Sciences at Wichita State University. Named after a New York City medical examiner and a friend of Eckert's, the center is an information base that is available to pathologists around the world. ∎

Broken bonds

358-359 *Warren & Ronald Finney*

Bankers and thieves.
Neosho Falls and Emporia.
(1874-1935) (1898-1961)
Fresh out of Washburn College, 22-year-old Warren Finney was elected to the Kansas House of Representatives as a Republican. At the same time he organized the first telephone company in Neosho Falls. Over the years, he gained control of several phone systems in southeastern Kansas. He also invested in land, cattle and stocks. By the mid 1930s—when many Kansans were tightening their belts to survive the Great Depression—Finney owned banks in Emporia and his hometown, and was worth an estimated $800,000.

His son Ronald—a "born salesman"—ran their bank in Neosho Falls until the late 1920s. He then moved to Emporia and opened a Topeka office to handle his business deals.

Unfortunately, some of those deals involved the selling of fake state bonds. (When used

legally, bonds are sold by governments as a way of borrowing money. Bond buyers receive certificates that represent the government's promise to pay back the amount of the bonds, plus interest.) Ronald Finney, with the help of his friend, State Treasurer **Tom Boyd, Jr.**, stole state bonds from the vault in Boyd's office, had them counterfeited, and then sold the copies to unsuspecting buyers in Chicago and other cities.

The scheme came to light in the summer of 1933. Bank examiners discovered fake bonds worth hundreds of thousands of dollars in various places— including the three Finney banks and the

state treasurer's office. The scandal proved embarrassing for some of Kansas' top Republicans. Governor Alf Landon [**67**], just beginning his first term, was a personal friend and political ally of Warren Finney. In Emporia, the William Allen White family [**256, 257**] had been close to the Finney family for years.

Friends or not, Landon acted quickly. He ordered an investigation of the Finneys' business dealings and sealed off the treasurer's office with troops from the state militia and Kansas National Guard. When Boyd later resigned, the governor appointed respected William Jardine [**64**] as the new treasurer. Landon's response helped calm the public's fears.

Before long, investigators turned up evidence of other Finney crimes. Warren was eventually found guilty of embezzling over $50,000 from one of his banks. He received a prison sentence of 36 to 600 years. His several appeals were denied, and on the day the sheriff came to escort him to the state penitentiary in 1935, he committed suicide. By that time, his son was already in prison at Lansing.
Ronald ⇨

was serving 31 to 635 years for forging $1.35 million worth of state bonds. The sentence was the largest ever handed down in a Kansas court. Treasurer Boyd was given a ten-year sentence and served six years before he was paroled.

After spending eleven years in prison Ronald was paroled by Governor **Andrew Schoeppel** in 1945. William Allen White and his son had campaigned for the release. They also urged that he be pardoned. After Governor Frank Carlson [36] did so in 1949, Finney left Kansas. He spent the rest of his life in Florida and Oregon.

Relatively speaking

Although the Emporia Finneys were not related to Governor Joan Finney's [45] husband Spencer [46], they did have a relative with political connections.

Warren's father and Ronald's grandfather was *David W. Finney*, lieutenant governor in the 1880s under Republican John P. St. John [87] and Democrat George Glick [55]. Finney County was named for him in 1883. Fifty years later, embarrassed Finney County Democrats tried to change the name. ■

Dighton and kidnapped a local doctor, **William Wineinger**. After Wineinger had treated the man, they shot him and rolled his car into a ravine.

For over a year, nothing was heard from the Fleagles. They might never have been caught, but a Garden City policeman found a single, unidentified fingerprint on Dr. Wineinger's abandoned car. A year later it was matched to the prints of a suspected train robber in California. Although the man had been released for lack of evidence, the FBI identified the two sets of fingerprints as Jake's, based on records from Oklahoma where he had once been a prisoner.

Police then searched the Fleagles' parents' home in Finney County and discovered a letter written by the thieves in Illinois. Ralph was soon captured there and was flown to Colorado—the first time a prisoner was sent from one state to another by air. He was tried, convicted and hanged—along with two other gang members he identified.

Before his execution, Ralph admitted Jake had killed the bank clerk and the doctor, but he denied knowing where his brother was hiding.

Jake, however, gave himself away with a letter he wrote to the governor of Colorado asking for mercy for Ralph. The FBI sent samples of his handwriting across the country, and several more of his letters were traced from post offices in Missouri and Arkansas. Police tricked Fleagle out of hiding with a fake newspaper ad from an old friend. Jake took the bait. As he boarded a train in Missouri to meet his friend, FBI agents were waiting for him. He turned, guns in hand, but was killed before he could shoot. ■

Wanted brothers

360-361 Jake & Ralph Fleagle

Thieves and murderers. Finney County. (1890-1930) (1880-1930) The Fleagles were a pair of brothers from Finney County who led a gang of bank robbers and murderers in the 1920s. In Kansas they robbed banks in Ottawa, Marysville, Larned and perhaps other towns. On the West Coast they held up several trains.

Between robberies, they used a hideout north of Garden City—complete with an arsenal of weapons and a granary large enough to hide an automobile behind a secret door.

Their crime spree came to an end after they robbed a bank in Lamar, Colorado, in the spring of 1928. Dressed as farmers, they walked into the bank shortly after the lunch hour.

With guns drawn, they demanded money. In reply, the bank's elderly president shot at them with a revolver hidden in his desk. He wounded one gang member in the jaw, but he was killed when the bandits fired back. As the banker's son reached for a rifle in a closet, he was shot through the heart.

Scooping up $10,000 in cash and taking two clerks as hostages, the Fleagles headed west, then back east toward Kansas. One hostage was thrown out along the road; the other's body was later found near Liberal. To tend their wounded gang member, Jake and Ralph drove to

There's no place like home

Fictional farmgirl. Rural Kansas, Liberal and Sedan. (Created 1900) Gale is perhaps the best-known female from Kansas. She was created in the imagination of L. Frank Baum, who tried a variety of jobs—actor, newspaper journalist, merchant and traveling salesman—before he found success as an author of children's books.

The storybook land of Oz

Dorothy came to life one evening as Baum told his four sons a story in their Chicago home. The tale flowed easily, for Frank had enjoyed dreaming up fantasies since his childhood. The author later wrote that the characters in this particular story—a little farm girl, a living scarecrow, a man made of tin and a cowardly lion—"surprised even me. It was as though they were living people."

As Baum continued his tale, one of the boys asked where Dorothy's unusual friends lived. The storyteller glanced around and noticed his small file cabinet nearby. The bottom drawer was labeled *O-Z.* "In the land of Oz!" he exclaimed.

Dorothy, Baum said, was from Kansas—a state, ironically, that he probably never visited. (Baum was no doubt describing his former home of South Dakota, but he called it Kansas in order not to offend his Dakota friends.)

He had already published two other children's books, but when Baum took his ideas for the Oz story to publishers around Chicago, he was turned down time after time. Finally, one company agreed to publish 5,000 copies. Thus Dorothy and her friends first appeared in print on August 1, 1900.

Within three months, the book's sales had topped 60,000. Now almost a century old, *The Wonderful Wizard of Oz* has become one of the great bestsellers of all time. Readers around the world have purchased over five million copies.

Dorothy, as Baum describes her, is an orphan who lives with her **Aunt Em** and **Uncle Henry** on their Kansas farm. Times are tough for the little family, for the sun has baked the earth, the prairie grass, the crops, the house—even Aunt Em and Uncle Henry—to the same dull, sober gray. The only bright spot in Dorothy's life is her little black dog, **Toto**. It is a Kansas cyclone, or tornado, that takes the little girl and her dog to the enchanted land of Oz. There she meets Scarecrow, Tin

Woodman and Cowardly Lion. As their group is faced with one problem after another, Dorothy and her friends find they have the strength and power to solve each dilemma.

Colorful Oz is obviously much different from the drab, dreary Kansas that Dorothy comes from. But she is determined to return home to her aunt and uncle—and she does.

Series of sequels

And that was only the first of Dorothy's Oz adventures. Much to Baum's dismay, his readers would not let the story end after one book. Although he published five other fairy tales in the next four years, none sold as well as the *Wizard*.

Finally, after a flood of letters from fans—and some financial problems—he wrote *The Marvelous Land of Oz* in 1904. The next year Baum bought a California island where hoped to build an amusement park, "Oz Island." His plan failed.

Much more successful was a Broadway musical based on his *Wizard* book. Although the producer changed Baum's script in several interesting ways, the play ran nearly ten years after it opened in 1902. Almost overnight, it made the comedy team of Montgomery & Stone [*325*] into stars. (Baum dedicated his second Oz book to the popular pair.)

After more encouragement from readers, Baum continued the Oz series in 1907. For a time, he wrote a book a year, most of them published in time for Christmas. ✿

The girl from Kansas

Although Dorothy appeared in all but one of the sequels, her creator added little information about her background. He did reveal that she came to live with Aunt Em and Uncle Henry as a baby and that her last name was Gale; Em and Henry remained nameless. One Dorothy fan, Kansas author and Washburn University professor **Thomas Fox Averill**, points out that while her physical build and hair color varied as different artists illustrated the books, for twenty years she remained a young girl—perhaps age ten or twelve.

Some literary critics have called Dorothy the American version of Alice—the British heroine in Lewis Carroll's classic *Alice's Adventures in Wonderland*. Others point out that Dorothy is more of a leader than the shy Alice. They say through her strength and determination she represents the pioneer women who helped settle the Plains.

One critic, Henry M. Littlefield, claims Dorothy and her friends are actually part of a clever parable about Populism [**70, 78, 89, 102, 112**]. Littlefield says Baum's experiences as a struggling newspaper publisher in South Dakota during the early 1890s gave him firsthand knowledge of the problems that caused farmers to join the Populist movement.

Littlefield believes Baum's allegory, or story-within-a-story, contains meanings for nearly everyone and everything: Dorothy is "Miss Everyman," out to help little people (Munchkins) ruled by big government. The Scarecrow stands for farmers who are actually smarter than they think. The Tin Woodman represents workers oppressed by big business. The Cowardly Lion is William Jennings Bryan, the three-time Populist nominee for president. The Wizard is one of several U.S. presidents from that period.

The Yellow Brick Road and its dangers represent the problems caused by using gold as a standard for America's paper money. Dorothy is protected by her silver slippers because the Populists wanted silver to replace gold as the currency standard.

The saga continues

Whether or not Baum filled his first *Wizard* book with hidden meanings, he tried to end the Oz series once and for all in 1910. In *The Emerald City of Oz*, Glinda the Good Sorceress makes the enchanted land permanently invisible. The book closes with a letter from Dorothy. "You will never hear anything more about Oz," she writes.

But thousands of children and parents eventually proved her wrong. As Baum received their

The WIZARD OF Oz

USA 25

Dorothy on film

To moviegoers around the globe, Dorothy will always be sixteen-year-old Judy Garland in the 1939 MGM film classic *The Wizard of Oz*. (20th Century Fox studios had hoped to film the story with its child star Shirley Temple.) In its first release, *Wizard* was nearly overshadowed by another 1939 movie, *Gone With the Wind*. But since its annual television showings began in 1956 the Oz film has been a family favorite.

Years earlier, in 1914, L. Frank Baum tried to cash in on the popularity of his Oz books by producing several movies about the enchanted land. None of his silent films were very successful, however. One of them, *His Majesty, the Scarecrow of Oz*, featured the first film Dorothy, actress Violet Macmillan. A few years earlier, Baum had organized touring Oz shows using hand-colored lantern slides and film clips. These "radio plays" were also financial failures.

Over the years there have been other movies with Baum's characters, including *The Wiz*, a splashy 1978 musical starring Diana Ross as Dorothy. The 1939 *Wizard*, however, is still the most popular. Over the years it has remained in the hearts of Kansans—and Kansas. Some original footage from the MGM film is stored in the abandoned salt mines deep under Hutchinson.

requests, he resisted and wrote two books about a California girl named Trot. Again, readers wanted only Dorothy and Oz.

After declaring bankruptcy in 1911, he had no choice but to resume the Oz books. He wrote eight more, starting with *The Patchwork Girl of Oz* in 1913. His last, *Glinda of Oz*, was published in 1920, a year after his death. It was number fourteen in the series. Over the years, six authors, including Baum's son, published 27 more Oz books.

At home in Kansas

Baum never never revealed the exact location of Dorothy's Kansas home, but Liberal has claimed her as a resident since 1981. The city decided to adopt her at the suggestion of businessman **Max Zimmerman**. While at a San Francisco meeting, a waiter noticed his Kansas nametag and exclaimed, "That's where Dorothy lives!" Back home, Zimmerman proposed that the Seward County Historical Society provide a home for

Miss Gale. Governor John Carlin [**35**] helped by proclaiming nearby U.S. highway 54 as Kansas' Yellow Brick Road. Every year, thousands now visit Dorothy's House and its *Wizard of Oz* memorabilia. The town celebrates "Ozfest" each spring.

At the other end of the state, Sedan residents began building their own Yellow Brick Road in the mid 1980s. They hope to bring Oz tourists to their town, too. A Kansas City group has plans for a large Oz amusement park to be built in the future. Dorothy and her friends will be featured residents of the theme park.

Regardless of the claims made by these Kansas communities, most would agree that Dorothy also lives in the hearts of *Wizard of Oz* fans everywhere.

Toto the cow

Whether on stage, film or in books, producers of Oz stories have made changes in Baum's original ideas. In MGM's *The Wizard of Oz*, Dorothy's silver slippers became ruby red—silver didn't show up well on the movie screen. Several characters were more evil on film, including the flying monkeys who in the book were Dorothy's friendly guides.

When another illustrator took over the Oz books in 1904, Toto turned into a Boston terrier. In the Broadway version of *The Wonderful Wizard of Oz*, Dorothy was a young woman who fell in love with a "poet prince." Toto was transformed into Imogene—a comic cow. ∎

Preaches up a storm

363 Elmer Gantry

Fictional minister. "Paris" and "Gritzmacher Springs." (Created 1927) Gantry is the main character in Sinclair Lewis' 1927 novel *Elmer Gantry*. The story follows Elmer's rise to glory as a handsome evangelist with thousands of enthusiastic followers. But his methods in reaching the top are anything but Christian. On page after page, Lewis paints his Kansas preacher as ruthless, selfish, hypocritical and totally unethical.

The novel's setting includes the fictional Kansas town of Gritzmacher Springs. It is the site of Elmer's alma mater, Terwil-linger College, a Baptist school with "a standard of scholarship equal to the best high schools." Lewis also writes of Gantry's hometown of Paris, a Kansas village of 900 "plodding yokels" from Vermont and Germany.

Although Lewis wrote the book to make fun of organized religion, Kansans of the time didn't appreciate his descriptions of their state and the suggestion that it could produce such a "golden-tongued" hypocrite. Obviously, the novel received a lot of publicity. William Allen White's [**256**] review of it was on the front page of the *Kansas City Times*, and thousands of ⇨

legitimate preachers condemned it—but 200,000 copies were sold in just over two months. (A surprising number of those copies were bought by Kansans.)

Lewis, the first American to win the Nobel Prize for Literature, was at the height of his success when he wrote the novel. Before it was published, he spent time gathering "research" with ministers in Kansas City, Missouri. Like many of their Kansas neighbors, the preachers were also unhappy with the finished book.

A movie version of *Elmer Gantry* starring Burt Lancaster was filmed in 1960. The screenplay is different from the novel in several ways, but Kansas is still mentioned as the home state of the unscrupulous Gantry. ∎

Dealt a deadly hand

364 *James Butler "Wild Bill" Hickok*

Scout, soldier and lawman. Johnson County, Leavenworth, Hays and Abilene. (1837-1876) Hickok came to Kansas from Illinois as a teenager in 1856. He intended to claim land for his family to farm, but the Bleeding Kansas struggle led him into James H. Lane's [*68*] Free State Army. In early 1858 twenty-year-old James was elected constable of a township in Johnson County. A year later he was hired by Russell, Majors & Waddell as a teamster on the Santa Fe Trail.

About that time, Hickok first met William F. Cody [*349*], or "Buffalo Bill." By 1862 Hickok had his own nickname—"Wild Bill." (His older brother *Lorenzo Hickok*, with whom he had come to Kansas, was called "Tame Bill.")

Some say James was called Wild Bill after he survived a bear attack on the Santa Fe Trail. Others believe it came from a shooting incident at a Russell, Majors & Waddell relay station in Nebraska where Hickok was working in 1861. Three men

died there in what was called the McCanles Massacre, but they were probably not all killed by Hickok. By the time the story appeared in several magazines, however, Wild Bill had single-handedly gunned down a gang of ten, or even 30. Soon, like his friend Cody, more and more of Hickok's adventures—real and imaginary—began to appear in "dime novels."

Hickok spent part of the Civil War as a teamster and scout for the Union Army in Missouri and Arkansas. He may also have been a spy, working with the Missouri state militia behind Confederate lines. He did not, as some stories say, ride with a band of Kansas guerillas known as the Red Legs.

At the end of the war Bill killed a companion in a gun duel in Springfield, Missouri. In early 1866 he returned to Kansas as an Army scout and guide. In early 1867 he

hired on with the 7th U.S. Cavalry as a wagonmaster. That spring he was promoted to scout and received $100 per month. Hickok helped guide Lieutenant Colonel George Armstrong Custer [*351*] and the 7th as they searched for Indians in western Kansas.

By the fall of 1867 he was a deputy U.S. marshal, a job he held off and on for three years. A year later he scouted for the Army again as part of the campaign against Plains Indians. (He was with a cavalry unit in the Texas panhandle when Custer attacked Black Kettle's [*341*] village on the Washita River in 1868.) The next spring Bill visited his mother back in Illinois and rested for several weeks while his leg healed, probably from a wound caused by a Cheyenne lance.

Back in Kansas in the spring of 1869, Bill returned to his duties as deputy U.S. marshal. By that summer, he was the acting sheriff of Ellis County. Although he and his pair of Colt revolvers soon earned respect in Hays—a community known for its lawlessness—Hickok lost an election that fall that would have made him sheriff. His duties as deputy U.S. marshal, however, kept him busy. He made arrests near Hays, as well as in Junction City and Abilene.

Several months after the murder of Tom Smith [*375*], Wild Bill was offered the marshal's job in Abilene. The cattle drive season of 1871 was beginning when Hickok took office,

but he and his deputies managed to keep most of the violence under control in "McCoy's [*165*] Addition"—the part of Abilene where gamblers and cowboys hung out.

One night near the end of his eight months in Abilene, Marshal Hickok shot a gambler in a gunfight. Before the smoke cleared, another man ran from the darkness, waving a pistol. Hickok killed him, too, without realizing he was a special policeman working for a local dance hall. Two months later, Abilene residents decided they had had enough cowtown rowdiness and they banned any more cattle trade. Gamblers and other shady characters followed the cattlemen to other Kansas towns. Hickok was let go, his services no longer needed.

In 1872, Wild Bill appeared with a Wild West show in New York. The next year he toured with Buffalo Bill and his "Combination" show. But Hickok's theater career was short. He complained in front of audiences about having to drink "stage whiskey" (cold tea) and was unhappy when the spotlight shone more on Cody than himself. By the spring of 1874 he had given up acting and gone back to the West.

He spent time in Cheyenne, Wyoming, before marrying an Ohio woman early in 1876. Later that year he headed north to join the Black Hills gold rush. During a poker game in a saloon at Deadwood, Dakota Territory, he was shot in the back of the head by Jack McCall. (McCall claimed he was avenging the death of his brother, who was killed by Wild Bill in Kansas. The murderer was hanged several months later.) The cards Hickok was holding when he died—pairs of aces and eights—have since been called the "Dead Man's Hand." ∎

Number one on the wrong list

365 Alvin "Creepy" Karpis

Robber and kidnapper. Topeka, Hutchinson and Lansing. (1908-1979) Karpis was a 1930s gangster who was born in Canada and grew up in Topeka. There he began his life of crime by robbing a grocery store—at the age of ten! He continued his burglaries as a teenager. When his parents moved to Chicago, Karpis briefly worked there as a shipping clerk and a baker, the only two honest jobs he ever held. He came back to Kansas at age seventeen and sold liquor illegally during the days of prohibition.

A year later Karpis was arrested when he tried to rob a warehouse in Jackson County. He was sentenced to the Kansas State Reformatory, but his stay in Hutchinson did not end his life of crime. Another prisoner taught him all he knew about burglary, and the two escaped in 1929 by sawing their way out.

Karpis soon committed more crimes, was rearrested and was returned to Hutchinson. When he volunteered to work in the state penitentiary's coal mine near Lansing, his sentence was shortened and he was released.

By that time, Karpis had made friends with Freddie Barker, a member of "Ma" Barker's notorious gang of the 1930s. For the next four years Karpis and the Barkers committed kidnappings and robberies in towns across the Midwest—including Fort Scott and Concordia. According to stories, it was the

Barkers who nicknamed Karpis. His partners in crime called him "Old Creepy" because of the grumpy expression he always carried on his face.

By 1935, Karpis was at the top of the FBI's most-wanted list. After he robbed a mail truck and a train in Ohio, J. Edgar Hoover, the director of the FBI, promised to arrest this "Public Enemy Number One" himself. A year later Hoover kept his promise. He personally took charge of Karpis' arrest in New Orleans.

Creepy pleaded guilty and was sentenced to life imprisonment. He spent more than 30 years in federal prisons before he was paroled. After he was released in 1969, the U.S. government deported him to Canada. He died while living in Spain. ∎

Chief of peace

366 Little Raven

Indian chief. Western Kansas. (About 1817-1889)
Little Raven was a Southern Arapaho chief who ranged over the Plains, including western Kansas, during his lifetime. He was born as *Hosa*, or Young Crow, near the Platte River in central Nebraska. His father was a major tribal chief, and as a young man Little Raven took his first leadership role in the tribe. He was known especially for his intelligence and speaking ability.

By 1840 he had married a Kiowa-Apache woman, probably the first of his seven wives. (An Arapaho man often married the younger sisters of his wife, or the wives of a brother who died.) About the same time, he helped arrange a council at which the Southern Arapahoes and their Southern Cheyenne allies made peace with the Kiowas, Kiowa-Apaches and Comanches. When they stopped making war against each other, most tribes turned their attention to raids on Santa Fe Trail traders and other travelers in the region. Throughout the violence, Little Raven often spoke in favor of peace.

When his father died in 1855, he became the principal chief of the Southern Arapahoes. During a visit to Denver he enjoyed his hosts' food and cigars, and explained that he liked white men. He was glad to see them getting gold, he said, but he hoped they would soon leave his people in peace.

The chief was far-sighted. In 1857, two decades before buffaloes [*382*] were hunted almost to extinction, he told the agent for the Southern Arapahoes, "The buffalo are disappearing, and our people will starve unless we learn to cultivate the soil."

Little Raven signed the Treaty of Fort Wise in 1861, but he later joined Southern Cheyenne war parties when he became unhappy with the white men's broken promises. In 1864 he was reported killed in the Sand Creek Massacre, but he was in his own camp several miles away. Even though some of his band were indeed in Black Kettle's [*341*] camp at that time—as they were four years later when George Armstrong Custer [*351*] destroyed the unlucky chief's village along the Washita River—Little Raven returned to his peace arguments. On one occasion he even struck down two of his own braves with a war club rather than let them brawl with whites.

During treaty negotiations at Medicine Lodge Creek in 1867 he was described as "fat and good-natured." He greeted some of the peace commissioners with such big hugs that they were smeared with his face paint. He asked that they treat his tribe separately from the Cheyennes who he said had misbehaved and had gotten the Arapahoes into trouble. His speeches impressed many listeners.

During those peace talks he invited reporters and other whites to a tribal dance. When a gun was stolen from a scout during the festivities, Little Raven offered one of his own Colt revolvers to replace it.

Robert Wright, who worked on the Santa Fe Trail and was later a merchant and leading citizen of Dodge City, remembered another example of Little Raven's helpful nature. Wright, a stagecoach driver in the 1860s, had to leave a large Concord coach stuck in the mud west of Fort Larned. As he was riding on to the fort, he met Little Raven and some of his band headed in the same direction. Wright asked them to haul the heavy coach to the fort, and the chief agreed.

Sometime later Little Raven appeared at the fort—but without the stagecoach. He had left it twenty miles up the trail, he told Wright, and "blessed if he could get it any farther." With no harnesses, the Indians had tied the heavy coach to their ponies' tails—and had pulled the hair out of nearly every animal's tail in their herd!

In 1871, along with a group of Cheyenne, Wichita and other Arapaho chiefs, Little Raven visited several eastern cities. There he made speeches and met with government officials. When the chief returned to his people—who were then on a reservation in Indian Territory—he promised that the White Father in Washington would take care of them. Following his advice, the Arapahoes kept out of the Indian wars of the 1870s.

Little Raven died at Cantonment, Oklahoma, after many years as a respected leader of his tribe. ∎

Photogenic pioneer lady

367 Ada McColl

Pioneer. Medicine Lodge and Lakin. (1870-1956)
McColl, or the "Cow Chip Lady, as she is sometimes called, is the subject of one of Kansas' most recognized pioneer-day photographs.

Ada was born in Iowa and moved near Medicine Lodge with her parents as a small girl. The family left Kansas in 1884 and went to Florida, but they returned two years later and settled near Lakin.

In 1892 Ada bought a camera and learned to operate it with the help of Garden City photographer **H.L. Wolf**. A year later she and her mother took turns photographing each other standing by a wheelbarrow full of "cow chips." (Like other settlers, the McColls probably gathered the dried manure to use as cheap fuel.)

Ada developed her glass negatives and took them to photographer Wolf to be printed. He apparently kept the glass plates, for at some point he made dozens of photo postcards from the cow chip negative of Ada. It was circulated widely under the title "Independence on the Plains."

Ada, meanwhile, continued her interest in photography at least two more years. It isn't known if she sold copies of her cow chip picture, but she did sell other photographs marked "Miss Ada McColl, View Photographer, Lakin, Kansas." In 1895 she returned to Iowa where she got married and remained the rest of her life.

Over the years, the photo of Ada and the wheelbarrow became part of several museum and historical society photograph collections —but no one in Kansas remembered her name. For a time the photo was labeled "unidentified pioneer woman." Then someone said the picture was of a Mrs. Pickering. Next, several Garden City residents claimed the prairie woman was **Ella Sly**. The photograph remained under that identification for about 30 years—and became the basis of the Finney County Historical Society's logo in 1981.

The mystery was solved in the mid 1980s. For years, several of Ada McColl's descendants had recognized her photo in documentary films, magazine articles and in books. When the cow chip photograph appeared on the cover of a popular Kansas book, *Pioneer Women*, one of Ada's great-granddaughters decided to set the record straight. Using family letters and other sources, she visited the Kansas State Historical Society in Topeka and proved the identity of the "Cow Chip Lady." Family records showed the child who appears at the right edge of some copies of the photo is Ada's three-year-old brother. (Many thought it was the mystery woman's young daughter.)

A century after it was taken, McColl's photograph still graphically illustrates the hardy pioneer women of Kansas.

A real pioneer, too

Although she was not actually the pioneer woman in the famous photo, *Ella Sly* was indeed a pioneer woman.

Born in Indiana in the 1840s, she settled in Finney County in the 1880s. In 1892 she homesteaded 160 acres north of Garden City. Several years later she sold her land and moved closer to town. There she raised cows and poultry, and made a living selling milk, eggs and chickens. Ella also sold subscriptions to Capper [34] publications.

In her later years she worked as a maid at a local hotel and did housework in several homes. She died in 1934 at the county "poor farm"—a place to stay for people who had no money. ■

Hunts buffaloes, criminals

Sheriff, gambler and newspaper journalist. Sedgwick and Dodge City. (1853-1921) Masterson was born November 26, 1853, in Quebec, Canada. His family named him Bartholomew, which they soon shortened to "Bat." Although he went by that nickname most of his life, as a young man he adopted a new formal name—William Barclay.

Bat spent his earliest years on a farm in Canada. In 1861 his parents and their growing family moved across the border into New York. Later they farmed in Illinois. In the summer of 1871 the Mastersons settled on land in Sedgwick County north of Wichita.

Hide hunter

After helping their father build a sod house, Bat, then almost eighteen, and his nineteen-year-old brother **Ed** announced they were headed west to hunt buffaloes [**382**]. The pair spent that fall and winter with hunters working near the Salt Fork River in present Comanche and Barber counties.

Seven days a week, the hunters' big Sharps buffalo guns rang out, felling the shaggy animals by the hundreds. Bat, Ed and other beginners had the hard, dirty—and bloody—work of skinning the carcasses. They pegged the hides to the ground to dry, and then left the meat, except for the valuable tongues, to rot on the prairie.

During visits to neighboring hunting camps, Bat met frontiersmen and Indian fighters like **Billy Dixon**, along with future law officers, including **Tom Nixon**, **"Prairie Dog" Dave Morrow** and Wyatt Earp

[**356**]. The friendship that developed between Masterson and Earp that winter lasted a lifetime.

During the spring and summer of 1872, Bat and his brother worked on a crew building the Atchison, Topeka and Santa Fe Railroad [**158**]. They helped grade five miles of roadbed from near Fort Dodge to a tent town called Buffalo City. (By the time the first train arrived that September, the place was known as Dodge City.) After the job was done, their boss disappeared without paying them, leaving the Mastersons broke and discouraged.

Once again, they decided to hunt buffaloes. With several others, including their younger brother **Jim Masterson**, they set up a camp southeast of Dodge City along Kiowa Creek. But when buffaloes became scarce that January—an estimated 75,000 were killed near Dodge that winter—Ed and Jim returned home to Sedgwick. Bat stayed in Ford County.

The next spring he began to earn a reputation for being tough. When he learned that the contractor who had cheated him and his brother out of their wages was passing through town on a train, he met him at the depot. Bat cocked a gun in his face and told him to pay up, or else. The man didn't argue.

Until 1874, Masterson continued buffalo hunting. With the herds fast disappearing in southwestern Kansas, Bat and other hide hunters moved into Texas. But they ran into trouble at Adobe Walls, a small settlement about 150 miles south of Dodge City. Comanches, Kiowas and Southern Cheyennes, angry because the hunters had invaded their buffalo range, attacked them early one spring morning.

The fight should have been one-sided. There were 28 men and one woman at Adobe Walls; Indians with Comanche chief Quanah Parker numbered in the hundreds. But holed up inside the thick sod walls of three crude buildings, Bat and the others held out. When the siege ended after nearly a week, two hunters and an untold number of Indians were dead. Bat headed back to Kansas.

At Fort Dodge he hired on as a scout with several companies of the U.S. Army's 6th Cavalry and 5th Infantry. The troops traveled on a campaign into Texas where Bat stayed when the expedition ended.

In early 1876, he was wounded in a gunfight. A soldier, upset that Masterson was with a dance hall girl, found them in a saloon. He fired at Bat, but he hit the woman instead, killing her. In the shooting that followed, the soldier received a fatal wound, and Bat ended up with a bullet in his hip.

When he arrived back in Dodge City that spring, he was still walking with a cane. The town was preparing for the arrival of Texas cattle drives, and Bat joined his friend Wyatt Earp on the city police force for a time. Before the cattle season was over, Masterson had left Kansas to join in the Black Hills gold rush. He got as far as Cheyenne, Wyoming Territory, where he stopped to gamble.

Busy sheriff

Back in Dodge City in 1877, he was appointed undersheriff of Ford County. That fall, the 22-year-old was elected sheriff by just three votes.

Bat's two-year term was busy. He rounded up two train robbers in a blizzard, and then rode into Indian Territory and back after two more. Several months later his brother Ed, who was then city marshal of Dodge, was killed in a gunfight.

That fall, Northern Cheyennes under Chief **Dull Knife** raided parts of Ford County on a wild dash out of Indian Territory north toward their homeland. A month later, popular dance hall singer **Dora Hand** was murdered. Bat led the posse that captured her killer.

Before Election Day 1879 rolled around Sheriff Masterson had also helped arrange the trial of seven members of Dull Knife's band, chased a horse thief into Colorado, and then returned to that state to help the AT&SF railroad fight the Denver, Rio Grande and Western for a route through the Royal Gorge.

Surprisingly, voters didn't reelect the busy sheriff. He was criticized for spending too much money while in office. Others were unhappy because he was part of "the Gang," a group of local politicians headed by Mayor **James "Dog" Kelley**.

Traveling gambler and gunfighter

Soon after the election Bat left Dodge. He gambled in Leadville, Colorado, and then rescued a friend from trouble in Nebraska. In 1881 he traveled to Tombstone, Arizona, to join Wyatt Earp at the gambling tables. That spring he reappeared in Dodge City to help his brother Jim. Almost as soon as Bat stepped off the noonday train, he was involved in a gunfight with two men who had threatened to kill his brother. One of the shooters was injured, but he eventually recovered. Bat paid a $10 fine and left town that same day on the evening train.

Through the 1880s and 1890s he lived in various Colorado communities, as a law officer and gambling hall owner. He also made appearances in Dodge City, and spent enough time there in 1884 to publish a one-edition-only newspaper, the *Vox Populi.*

New York journalist

After managing a Denver saloon and theater, Bat tried promoting boxing matches. But he lost much of his money gambling and began drinking heavily. In 1902 he left Colorado and moved to New York City. There President Theodore Roosevelt, who he had met earlier while traveling in the Dakotas, appointed him a deputy U.S. marshal. About the same time, he was asked to write a series of articles about the colorful characters he had known in the West.

Masterson's writing eventually led to a job as sports editor of the New York *Morning Telegraph.* His sports column became popular and he was respected as an authority on boxing. He died at his desk, pen in hand, on October 25, 1921.

From 1958 to 1961, Gene Barry starred in the NBC television series *Bat Masterson.* It was the third television Western to feature Dodge City and its colorful lawmen—but like *Gunsmoke* [**326, 354**] and *The Life and Legend of Wyatt Earp,* it was largely fiction. ∎

A genuine plainsman

Scout, trader, buffalo hunter and banker. Present Rice and Barton counties, and Wichita. (1830-1916) Mathewson was born in Triangle, New York, on New Years Day—probably in 1830. (His Wichita tombstone says 1829.) William was one of eight children; when his father died the boy quit school and worked in lumber camps to help support his family.

Westward bound

Mathewson left New York at age eighteen and traveled west where he eventually worked for a Rocky Mountain fur company. In 1852 he joined Christopher "Kit" Carson [8] and others as they hunted in Colorado and New Mexico. For the next few years Bill traveled the Plains and Rocky Mountain region trading with Indians and trapping. He also spent time as a trader for Bent, St. Vrain & Company.

The first 'Buffalo Bill'

In 1858 he helped a father and son, **Asahel** and **Abijah Beach**, establish a trading post on the Santa Fe Trail at the Cow Creek crossing west of present Lyons. It was there that Mathewson got his nickname "Buffalo Bill."

During the dry year of 1860, hundreds of farm families in eastern Kansas lost their crops to drought. With no money to buy food, many of the needy settlers headed west to hunt buffaloes [382]. Few of them, however, had any experience in hunting the shaggy beasts. Mathewson led them to the herds, and then did most of the killing—as many as 80 buffaloes a day according to some stories. The grateful farmers butchered the animals and hauled the meat home to their hungry families. Mathewson refused any payment for his services, and when news of his generosity spread, hundreds of settlers asked for help from the man they called Buffalo Killer, and then later, Buffalo Bill.

'Dangerous man'

Among Indians, Mathewson had another nickname—*Sinpah Zilbah*, or the "long-bearded, dangerous man." The name came from a fight he had in 1861 with the colorful Kiowa leader Satanta [374].

The trouble began during one of the chief's trips to Bill's Cow Creek store. A young brave traveling with Satanta tried to steal a horse and the trader caught him in the act. Mathewson lectured Satanta about allowing that kind of behavior, but the Kiowas attempted another raid on the horse corral just a few days later. That time the trader shot at the would-be thieves. Even though he missed, the chief was angry that Mathewson would dare to resist him. Soon Satanta sent word that he intended to kill the trader.

True to his promise, the chief and a party of about twenty men again visited the trading post. Waiting until no other customers were around, they entered the storeroom and pointed their rifles at Mathewson. As the six-foot trader stood his ground, the equally tall Satanta delivered a long lecture—ending with the fact that Bill must die.

Before the situation could turn deadly, however, Mathewson started a conversation with the angry Indian. And—to punctuate his remarks—he smacked the chief with the butt of his revolver! As Satanta fell to the floor, the astonished warriors moved outside. Alone, the two men slugged it out. When the fight was over, Bill had won—leaving Satanta to limp back to his camp carrying a newfound respect for *Sinpah Zilbah*.

The chief stayed away from the trading post for quite some time. When he finally returned, he brought Mathewson a gift of twenty ponies. The trader accepted the peace offering and later returned the animals as a sign of good faith. Bill's action cemented a friendship between the two men that lasted for years.

In 1862 Mathewson moved farther west on the trail and built a trading post east of modern Great Bend. After a year he sold that store and joined trader **Charles Rath** at the nearby Walnut Creek crossing. (In the 1870s, Rath earned his own reputation as a buffalo hunter. He was also one of the first merchants in Dodge City.)

Trouble on the trail

Mathewson returned to the Cow Creek location in 1864, one of the bloodiest years on the Santa Fe Trail. Indians attacked wagon trains, burned bridges and ran off livestock at numerous trail locations—including Buffalo Bill's trading post.

For two days that July, perhaps 500 Kiowas, Arapahoes and Comanches kept Mathewson and a handful of men under siege at his headquarters. (Legend has it that Bill was warned of the raid by his friend Satanta.) While the Indians made off with cattle and other livestock, Bill and his crew protected themselves from behind a barrier of corn sacks. On the third day, the raiders—covered with war paint, waving lances, and yelling war cries—rode toward the traders in what appeared to be a final attack.

Bill loaded a small cannon with several handfuls of mini shot balls and whatever scrap iron he could find. As the line of attackers began crossing the bridge over Cow Creek, he fired. Several Indians fell—some dead, others wounded. Mathewson and his men then opened fire with their rifles. Although they were outnumbered nearly one hundred to one, the traders soon sent the warriors off in retreat. But for Mathewson, the fight wasn't over.

When he discovered a nearby wagon train was also under attack, he grabbed a rifle, stuffed six revolvers into his belt, and climbed on his mare **Bess**. Riding unseen through a ravine filled with tall grass, he approached the circled wagons.

Then, in a daring dash, he and Bess charged through the Indian lines and over the sides of the train's temporary corral. He was greeted by frightened teamsters who were somehow unaware that their train included several wagonloads of weapons headed for Fort Union. Mathewson, however, had been notified of the shipment ahead of time. Quickly, he helped the men and boys unpack crates of rifles and ammunition. With their new arms, they soon sent the Indians on their way.

A month later—after the excitement had died down—Bill married **Elizabeth "Lizzie" Inman**, a native of England. It is said that he didn't bring her to his Cow Creek ranch until she became an expert with a rifle and revolver. When he had to be away, she then bravely managed their operation.

Peacemaker

In 1865 Mathewson traveled among the Plains tribes, helping Jesse Leavenworth [**69**] arrange peace talks that led to the Little Arkansas treaty. The next year Bill was appointed postmaster at Fort Zarah. He and his wife apparently left Cow Creek at that time. (The well is all that remains of their Santa Fe Trail ranch today.)

Mathewson again rode across the territory in 1867, helping gather tribes for a giant peace ⇨

What's in a name

Throughout his long life, the original Buffalo Bill modestly avoided talking about his experiences on the Plains. (He once refused an offer of $10,000 from a New York City firm that wanted to publish his biography.) As a result, more Buffalo Bill stories—some real, many fictional—have been told about the scout, hunter and entertainer William F. Cody [349] than about Mathewson.

But Mathewson was indeed the first to hold the famous nickname. Some accounts say young Cody worked for Mathewson at one of his Santa Fe Trail locations in the 1860s—about a decade before the future showman earned his buffalo-hunter nickname. Years later,

when most people assumed Cody was the original Buffalo Bill, Mathewson quietly told a reporter, "The name of Buffalo Bill was tacked onto me before Bill Cody knew the difference between a buffalo and a jack rabbit. . .[but] if he has been successful in commercializing my reputation, I can only say, 'He is welcome.' "

As dime novelists and press agents pumped air into the legend of Buffalo Bill Cody, Mathewson held no hard feelings. He even agreed to pose for "twin Bill" photographs in 1913 when Cody's Wild West show performed in his pasture near Wichita.

The original Buffalo Bill's opinion of Cody's traveling extravaganza? Mathewson said he "despised" it.

council near Medicine Lodge Creek. Although Plains Indians considered him honest and generous, the trader found it was dangerous to approach their camps unrecognized. As he moved from village to village, he made a habit of creeping up as close as possible before he revealed himself. Once Indians saw who he was, they always greeted him warmly.

His reputation among the tribes also helped him arrange the release of several captive white women and children. The fact that he rarely talked about his adventures makes it difficult to prove, but he may have helped free as many as 54 prisoners.

On a trip to Texas in 1867 to return two boys rescued from Comanches, Bill followed the Chisholm Trail [**10, 165**]. Part of the way on his return north, he guided one of the first herds of Texas cattle to travel the trail. That same year Lizzie Mathewson and a friend from Missouri became the first women to travel the Chisholm Trail when they accompanied Bill to a trading post near Fort Sill in Indian Territory. At the Indians' request, he was a government trader there until 1873. At the same time he operated a store in the new town of Wichita.

Pioneer Wichitan

Mathewson took a claim near Wichita in 1868. He and Lizzie built one of the first houses in the future city, and for a time she was the only woman in town.

There Bill was a respected community leader. He ran a brick factory, established the Wichita Savings Bank and was the city police commissioner. The old plainsman died at his Wichita home, March 21, 1916. ■

Forever a five-year-old

370 Dennis "The Menace" Mitchell

Cartoon character. Wichita. (Created 1950) Dennis Mitchell—better known as Dennis "The Menace"—is a Kansan, according to Hank Ketcham, the popular comic strip character's creator.

For over four decades readers assumed the naughty but lovable five-year-old lived in "Anytown, U.S.A." But as Ketcham explained in his 1990 autobiography, Dennis, his patient parents **Henry** and **Alice Mitchell**, dog **Ruff** and cat **Hot Dog**, actually live in Wichita. The family owns a small two-story house in a quiet neighborhood along the city's Elm Street.

Henry works at a local aeronautical engineering company. Just next door, of course, are

Dennis' grouchy neighbor **George Wilson**, a retired postal worker, and his kindly, cookie-baking wife **Martha**. Dennis' young friends **Joey McDonald**, **Margaret Wade** and **Gina Gillotti** live nearby.

Since the beginning of the comic strip, Dennis has been age five, going on six. (Immediately after each sixth birthday he reverts to being a five-year-old.) To help celebrate Dennis' "fortieth" birthday, Ketcham came to Wichita in 1991 for the first time. Although the California cartoonist has never lived in Kansas himself, he said during his visit that he liked Dennis' hometown, and hoped to use scenes from the city in the comic.

Dennis was named after the artist's own son, who was a source of ideas when Ketcham began the strip. The famous youngster appears daily in more than 1,200 newspapers, and is a veteran of a long list of *Dennis* books, toys, other products, and advertising campaigns.

In addition to the comic pages, he has appeared on television. Young actor Jay North portrayed him in the CBS series *Dennis the Menace* from 1959 to 1963. (The Mitchells had apparently not yet moved to Wichita; at that time Dennis lived in the "television-land" town of Hillsdale.) The popular five-year-old has also been suggested as the featured character in a future movie or a Broadway musical. ■

Courtesy
Hank Ketcham

Unforgettable face

371 "Painless Romine"

Fictional dental model. Topeka. (Created about 1910) The face nicknamed "Painless Romine" was probably introduced to Kansans as part of an advertising campaign by **William Romine**, a dentist with an office in Topeka.

Dr. Romine, a native of Indiana, traveled across Kansas, Nebraska and parts of South Dakota practicing dentistry in a covered wagon. He called himself Painless Romine—sometimes misspelled as *Romaine*.

In the early 1900s Dr. Romine established a clinic in Wichita. In 1909 he set up a branch office in Topeka, manned by young dentists who operated under the Painless Romine trade name. To fill his new clinic with customers, Romine advertised in local newspapers, on posters tacked to telegraph and telephone poles, and through color lantern slides at Topeka theaters. His model for the ads was a happy-go-lucky red-headed patient with floppy ears—and a grin minus one tooth.

Where dentist Romine found the artwork for his "Painless" face is unknown, but evidence suggests he was not the first to use the silly-looking caricature. A 1909 German calendar featured a similar smiling face; a patent medicine company used a face much like Romine's about the same time. In the 1930s the character was "Happy Jack," the smiling logo on bottles of beverages made in California. In the 1940s he appeared on a postcard with the slogan, "Who me? I voted for Roosevelt." At other times he was called Little Herman or Hooey McManus.

Some have said that Painless is the father of a famous look-alike, Alfred E. Neuman—the mascot and cover model for *Mad* magazine. But that is not the case. Painless and Neuman might best be described as cousins. The confusion over their relationship dates to an article in *American Heritage* magazine in 1959, three years after Alfred first appeared in *Mad*. The *American Heritage* article, written by Topeka historian **John W. Ripley**, included a reproduction of a Painless Romine lantern slide. Reporters for CBS television and *Newsweek* magazine saw it, noticed the family resemblance, and announced that Alfred E. Neuman was a direct descendant of Painless Romine—and was, therefore, a Kansan.

In reality, *Mad* artists based their artwork on a 1950s postcard of a similar face. Research by the magazine has shown that their goofy-looking redhead—and probably Painless Romine and his other lookalike cousins—actually date back to a nineteenth century English caricature. The face with the tooth-missing grin was commonplace in the United States a decade or more before Painless first appeared in Topeka.

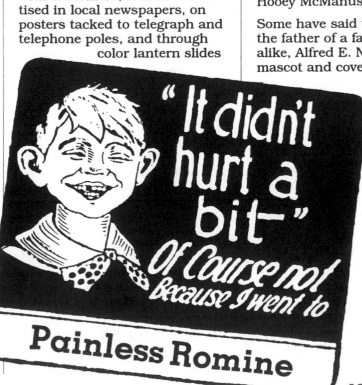

"It didn't hurt a bit—" *Of course not Because I went to* **Painless Romine**

Alfred's Kansas connection

Although *Mad* magazine's Alfred E. Neuman is not a direct descendant of Kansan Painless Romine, Neuman does have a Kansas connection. Over the years, he has been drawn by various *Mad* artists, including **Paul Coker,** a Lawrence cartoonist. Coker, who has worked in New York and California, is now back in his native Lawrence. He regularly contributes to *Mad* and does freelance work for other companies, including Hallmark Cards [153] and Rankin-Bass Television Productions. ∎

263

Ghostly lady

372 Elizabeth Polly

**"Ghost." Fort Hays.
(18?-1867)** According to legend, Elizabeth came to Kansas in the spring of 1867 as the new bride of U.S. Army soldier **Ephraim Polly**. He was a hospital steward at Fort Hays.

That summer an epidemic of cholera struck the area. (The deadly disease, which comes from drinking infected water, can cause vomiting, diarrhea and kidney failure. Victims often die from rapid dehydration, or loss of body fluids.) In just a few weeks, 36 soldiers and perhaps as many as 150 civilians died in the epidemic.

Some claim Elizabeth helped care for cholera patients at the fort before she, too, became a victim. According to their stories, Ephraim had her buried on a hill near the post. She requested the location just before she died, for she had often spent time there enjoying the view overlooking Big Creek Valley.

In the following years, the Army closed Fort Hays and eventually moved the bodies from the post cemetery to Fort Leavenworth. By 1905, the lonely burial site on the hill was the only known grave left at the abandoned fort.

Fifty years after her death—legend says—Elizabeth appeared on the hill. One morning in 1917 farmer **John Schmidt** reported seeing a woman in an old-fashioned blue dress and bonnet walking near his cattle herd. As Schmidt rode toward her, his horse shied and his dog whined and ran home.

The woman ignored him and disappeared into an abandoned cabin on the hillside. Schmidt's wife and children also witnessed the scene, but when the family examined the old shack, they found the door padlocked—and no trace of a human visitor inside. When Schmidt shared his story, older Hays residents said the mystery woman's description matched that of Elizabeth. She was buried, they said, in a blue dress and sunbonnet.

By that time the exact location of her grave was lost. In 1968 local women's clubs marked the hill with a monument created by Hays sculptor Pete Felten, Jr. [**198**]. In 1982 Felten did a statue that was placed in Elizabeth Polly Park in Hays.

Since John Schmidt's 1917 sighting, a police officer in 1954, a man harvesting wheat in the 1970s, and three FHSU students in 1987 have reported encounters with the mysterious blue lady of old Fort Hays. Interestingly, modern historians can find no record that Ephraim Polly ever married a woman named Elizabeth. They say the lonely Fort Hays grave may belong to one of Polly's young sons by another wife or to someone from Mexico who died in 1862. ∎

Bloodthirsty bushwhacker

373 William Quantrill

**Confederate soldier and outlaw. Franklin or Miami County and Lawrence.
(1837-1865)** Quantrill grew up in Ohio and graduated from the school where his father was principal. As a seventeen-year-old William taught school in Illinois for a year, and then returned home. In 1857 he headed to Kansas Territory to join three Ohio friends. The young men had taken land along the Marais des Cygnes River in present Franklin or Miami County.

Quantrill tried farming for a time, but in the spring of 1859 he went west on a wagon train. Some say he left the area using the name Charley Hart because he had been accused of stealing horses. He returned to Kansas that summer, however, and taught school south of Lawrence.

Like most Lawrence residents, Quantrill seemed to be an anti-slavery supporter. But secretly he joined Missouri Border Ruffians on raids to capture runaway slaves hiding in the area. Several months later he posed as an antislavery worker and joined abolitionists who wanted to free slaves in Missouri. He warned the slaveowner's son of the plan, however, and the Missourians were armed and ready when the Kansans arrived. In the gunfire that followed, one abolitionist was killed and two were wounded. Quantrill was arrested, but after he was released he moved to Missouri.

When the Civil War began, he headed south and fought with a Confederate force. Later in 1861 he returned to Missouri and formed his own group of guerillas to counteract Kansas jayhawkers [**387**]. Shortly after

Charles "Doc" Jennison
raided two Missouri towns in 1862, Quantrill and his men attacked Aubrey, Kansas.

Although Quantrill's Raiders joined the Confederate Army, to Kansans, "Captain" Quantrill and his guerillas were still nothing but outlaws. (The gang eventually included Frank and Jesse James, plus Cole and Jim Younger.) Olathe, Shawnee, and other Kansas towns felt the sting of their hit-and-run attacks.

By the time they raided Lawrence on August 21, 1863, Quantrill's followers numbered perhaps 450. He and his men swarmed into the city from the south, burning, looting and murdering. They hoped to capture or kill abolitionist James H. Lane [**68**], as well as retaliate for Lane's bloody attack on Osceola, Missouri in 1861.

Four hours later, 200 buildings were smouldering ruins, at least 143 Lawrence men and boys were dead, and many more were wounded. Jim Lane escaped the massacre by hiding—in his nightshirt—in a nearby cornfield.

Quantrill and his raiders continued their guerilla warfare. On their way to Texas that winter, they killed 79 Union troops in a surprise attack on Baxter Springs. They struck Union forces in Missouri in 1864, but suffered heavy losses. In 1865 Quantrill and his few remaining men headed to Kentucky. He was wounded there in an attack by Union guerillas and died a month later.

In the course of moving Quantrill's body to Ohio three years later, some of his bones were given to the Kansas State Historical Society. They remained there until 1992 when the Sons of Confederate Veterans reburied them in Missouri. His skull is in an Ohio museum.

A guerilla from the Kansas side

During the Bleeding Kansas fight over slavery, there were notorious characters on both sides. About the time William Quantrill was organizing his band in Missouri, *Charles "Doc" Jennison* was gathering his own group of guerilla fighters in Kansas. Jennison soon followed Senator James H. Lane [**68**], known as the Grim Chieftain, as the unofficial leader of the Kansas jayhawkers [**387**].

Jennison was born in New York. After training as a doctor in Wisconsin, he came to Kansas in 1858. In Mound City he practiced medicine and did other "odd jobs," including taking local residents—and a cannon—on a raid against a neighboring town in a county seat war.

Another time, he showed Indians on nearby reservations how to kill wolves with poisoned meat. He then sold them a high-priced barrel of what he said was strychnine—but the "poison" inside was actually flour.

By the summer of 1861, Jennison and his Mound City Sharp's Rifle Guard were part of the Kansas Militia. Their attacks against Missouri communities were so violent, however, that Governor Charles Robinson [**82**] was afraid Missourians would retaliate against Kansans.

In hopes of controlling the men, Robinson arranged their transfer into the U.S. Army as the 7th Kansas Volunteer Cavalry. But as often as possible, the jayhawkers continued raiding and robbing, leaving a trail of ruin. Early in 1862, frustrated Union commanders decided to move the 7th away from the troubled border.

Jennison gave a fiery farewell speech and then turned in his resignation, which Army officials quickly accepted. Jennison's Jayhawkers were transferred to Mississippi where their undisciplined behavior caused headaches for a new set of commanders. ∎

Determined warrior

Indian chief. Western Kansas. (About 1830-1878) Satanta was the best-known chief of the Kiowa tribe. The English spelling of his name came from *Set-t' aiñ-te*, meaning White Bear.

A life on the Plains

Little is known about Satanta's early life. He was born about 1830, somewhere in the Kiowas' territory on the Plains. Like other boys in his tribe, he probably had his own pony by the time he was five. Before he was ten, he was no doubt an expert rider. Young Kiowas and other Plains Indians were taught how to cling to their running mounts with their knees while they rapidly fired arrows. (Some Indian marksmen could shoot twenty arrows in the time it took a soldier to load and fire a musket once.) Satanta probably first joined Kiowa raiding parties into Texas and Mexico when he was fourteen or fifteen.

Flamboyant leader

When he began to show abilities as a leader, an old warrior named Black Horse gave Satanta a buffalo-hide shield. It was decorated with strips of red and yellow cloth, a whooping crane's head and the painted image of the sun. Like other Indian men, Satanta valued his shield for its protection from enemy weapons, as well as for its medicine—or magical powers.

He knew the shield's medicine was strong, for soon after Black Horse gave it to him, the old man was killed. From then on, Satanta carried the shield into every battle he fought. His battle outfit also included a buckskin shirt painted red on one side. He honored that color, it was said, out of respect for his father, Red Tipi. Satanta lived in a red tipi with long streamers of red cloth flying from the lodge poles. He often appeared at special ceremonies with his entire body painted flaming red.

Satanta was a large and powerfully built man, well over six feet tall. In the late 1870s—and after being held a prisoner for a time—he was still described as "proud," with "immense shoulders, broad back, deep chest, powerful hips" and muscles that "stood out on his gigantic frame like knots of whip cord."

Those who knew the flamboyant chief said he was a capable leader with a quick temper. Most of the time, however, he appeared happy and outgoing. He spoke several Indian languages, plus Spanish and a little English. He had at least one wife and nine children, including a son who later joined the 7th U.S. Cavalry.

Satanta had many contacts with Indian agents, traders and U.S. Army troops, but most of them didn't appreciate his brand of humor. In 1864, for example, a party of young Kiowas from his camp stole 172 horses and mules from the animal herd at Fort Larned. A few days later the chief sent word to the fort, saying he hoped the quartermaster would keep better horses in the future. The ones his men had taken were not of good quality!

War chief

As traffic increased on the Santa Fe Trail and other routes across Kansas, tension grew between Plains tribes and the outsiders who were entering Indian lands. Satanta took part in peace meetings called by the Army, but he represented the faction, or group, of Kiowas who wanted to fight for their territory. (Chiefs **Kicking Bird** and **Stumbling Bear** often spoke on the side of peace.)

Satanta did not trust the whites. "The good Indian, he that listens to the white man, gets nothing," he said. "The independent Indian is the only one rewarded."

That attitude kept Satanta from becoming a principal Kiowa chief in 1865. A majority of those on the tribal council supported peace and felt Satanta was too aggressive to replace a chief who had died.

In 1866 he led a raiding party into Texas and captured a woman and four children. Satanta took the prisoners to Fort Larned and offered to trade them for a large ransom. When the Indian agent refused, the chief took them to Fort Dodge where the commander paid for the captives' release.

During several meetings with officers at Fort Dodge that winter, Satanta demanded that the Army stop constructing new buildings there. He wanted that post and Fort Larned abandoned immediately. He also ordered that the Santa Fe Trail be closed and that construction of all railroads and telegraph lines in western Kansas be stopped. He angrily reminded his listeners that agent Jesse Leavenworth [**69**] had not delivered goods promised to the Kiowas at earlier meetings. He went on to warn that if his demands were not met, he and his braves would attack Fort Dodge in the spring. But because the horses and mules at the fort looked thin, he added, the Army should take better care of its livestock. He wanted to own only the best.

The next spring the Kiowas returned to Fort Dodge to attend another council. Satanta was chosen as the tribal spokesman. During his long speech, his attitude seemed more peaceful than before. He claimed that even though the Kiowas had lost grass, trees and buffaloes to the military, he was the Army's "true friend." It was at his request, he said, that the tribe had not gone to war against whites. He even promised to fight alongside soldiers against any tribe that tried to make war on the Plains.

Hearing the peace talk, General Winfield Scott Hancock was so convinced that he offered to hire 300 Kiowas as Army scouts. He then presented Satanta with a brigadier general's hat and full dress coat, complete with sash and shoulder trim.

Soon afterward, the unpredictable Satanta—wearing his new outfit—kept his earlier promise. He and about 200 braves raided Fort Dodge's livestock herd and captured all the horses belonging to a company of the 7th Cavalry. As a final gesture, he drove the stolen animals past the startled soldiers at the post and waved his plumed officer's hat in salute!

Orator of the Plains

Later in 1867, Satanta attended peace talks at Medicine Lodge Creek. When it was his turn to speak, he stood and shook hands with each commissioner. Hanging from his neck was a peace medallion with the profile of President James Buchanan.

"All the land south of the Arkansas River belongs to the Kiowas and the Comanches," he began, "and I don't want to give any of it away. I love the land and the buffalo and will not part with it. I don't want to settle [on a reservation]. I love to roam over the prairies. There I feel free and happy, but when we settle down, we grow pale and die."

Reporters who heard Satanta's speech were so impressed they called him the Orator of the Plains. But the peace commissioners couldn't be budged. They told him and the other Indian leaders to move to the south and give up their old ways. If they would accept their new homes on reservations in Indian Territory, they would be given annuities, or supplies. With few choices available, Satanta and many of the other chiefs signed the agreement.

Although the treaty said otherwise, the Kiowas were sometimes allowed to hunt in their old Kansas territory and trade with the sutler at Fort Dodge. On one such visit to the post, Satanta demanded that he be given food and whiskey. The major in charge gave each man in the chief's party ten days' rations—but no alcohol.

On his own, however, Satanta slipped into an officer's quarters and drank a full bottle of wine. He followed that with a bottle of sarsaparilla. By the time he entered the stables he was apparently not seeing very well. There he drained the contents of a third bottle—one full of medicine for a sick horse.

When he soon suffered violent stomach cramps and diarrhea, he was convinced the soldiers had tried to poison him. Leaving the post, the upset chief came upon a party of white hunters. In anger, he killed one of the men and took all the animals, clothing and bedding away from the others. ✧

Gracious host

In 1864, a government doctor who was vaccinating Plains tribes against smallpox spent several days in Satanta's village. He described the chief as "a fine-looking Indian, very energetic and sharp as a brief." The Kiowa leader put on "a great deal of style" for his guests. He seated them on a carpet and served them three meals a day on small decorated tables. To call them to eat, Satanta blew a brass French horn. (In battle, he was said to have imitated bugle calls with the same horn, trying to confuse Army troops.)

The end of freedom

In 1868 the government cracked down on hunting outside of reservations. Some Indian leaders asked tribe members to be patient, but Satanta and his allies called for war.

After Lieutenant Colonel George Armstrong Custer [*351*] attacked Cheyenne chief Black Kettle's [*341*] village that fall, the Kiowas, who were camped nearby, fled the reservation. Custer arranged a meeting with tribal leaders—where he then arrested chiefs Satanta and **Lone Wolf**. By holding them hostage, he believed, he could control the tribe. The plan backfired when the Kiowas became restless and angry. Custer released the pair early in 1869.

During the next two years, Satanta took part in several attacks on whites, mostly in Texas. He led more than 100 warriors on a raid that killed seven freight haulers near Fort Richardson in May 1871, and then bragged about it a week later when he picked up rations from the Indian agent at Fort Sill.

After his confession, Satanta and two other Kiowa chiefs— **Satank** and **Big Tree**—were arrested and ordered to stand trial. Satank was killed on his way to jail, but a jury of Texans found Satanta and Big Tree guilty of first-degree murder. They were sentenced to death by hanging, but the sentence was changed to life imprisonment when pro-Indian groups and a delegation of Kiowa chiefs protested. After two years in prison, the governor of Texas released the chiefs.

Satanta stayed on the reservation in Indian Territory until the summer of 1874. Then he and some followers joined in a Texas fight called the Red River War. When they later surrendered, Satanta was sent back to the Texas penitentiary. He committed suicide there by jumping from a second-story window in the prison hospital on October 11, 1878. The chief was buried in the prison cemetery, away from other inmates' graves. In 1963 the Texas Legislature allowed the Kiowa tribe to rebury Satanta's remains at Fort Sill, Oklahoma. The Haskell County town of Satanta honors his name.

White Bear and Sitting Bear

U.S. Army officials and others who had dealings with Indians sometimes confused Satanta and another Kiowa chief, *Satank*. The problem no doubt came from the similarities between their names. Satanta was *Set-t' aiñ-te*, or White Bear; Satank was *Set-angia*, meaning Sitting Bear. In person, there was no mistaking the two. Satank was one of the very few Plains Indians who wore a mustache.

One story sometimes told about Satanta actually involved Satank. The chief was a friend of *George Peacock*, owner of a Santa Fe Trail trading post near Walnut Creek. As they talked one day, Satank asked the trader to give him a letter of introduction that he could show to trail travelers. In fun, Peacock wrote, "This is Satank, the biggest liar, beggar and thief on the plains. What he can't beg of you he will steal. Kick him out of your camp, as he is a lazy, good-for-nothing Indian."

When the chief presented his letter to several passing wagon trains, he naturally received a cool welcome. After one wagonmaster popped him with a whip, the angry Satank asked a friend to interpret the letter. Once he heard its contents, the joke was over. He and some braves rode to Peacock's ranch. "Come out; the soldiers are coming!" he yelled. Peacock did so, climbing to the top of a lookout tower he had built. Without hesitating, Satank shot him dead. He and his men then killed Peacock's clerk and herder.

Satank was born in the Black Hills about 1810. He represented the Kiowas in the intertribal peace council that Little Raven [*366*] helped arrange in 1840. He signed a peace treaty at Fort Atkinson in 1853 as well as the Medicine Lodge treaty in 1867.

By that time, according to Satanta, Satank was no longer the Kiowas' leading chief and medicine man. When his son was killed in a raid in Texas, he joined Satanta and others in their attack on the wagon train near Fort Richardson, Texas, in the spring of 1871. When he bragged about his part in the raid, he was arrested with Satanta and Big Tree. But Satank couldn't face life in a prison cell. On his way to trial, the old chief sang a death song. He then pulled free of his chains, tearing the skin from his wrists. Sliding a knife out of his breechcloth, he slashed at a guard and jumped from the wagon—knowing he would be shot to death. ∎

Town-tamer

375 Tom Smith

City marshal and deputy U.S. marshal. Abilene. (About 1840-1870) Smith was marshal at Abilene during the town's heyday as a cattle shipping point on the Union Pacific Railroad. Although he is not as well known as James Butler "Wild Bill" Hickok [**364**]—who was Abilene's marshal a year later—most agree it was Smith, not Hickok, who first brought law and order to the wild town.

Few facts are known about Tom's early life. He was probably born in New York City about 1840 and was believed to have been a policeman there for a short time. After he left home, Smith may have worked for freighting companies in Iowa and Nebraska before he joined a construction crew that helped build the Union Pacific in 1868.

Some sources say he led railroad construction workers in a riot at the end-of-track town of Bear River, Wyoming. They

claim he was then nicknamed "Bear River" Smith. Other accounts say the riot involved a different Tom Smith who ended up in a Utah penitentiary. That version is more in keeping with the mild-mannered Tom Smith who arrived in Abilene in the spring of 1870.

At that time the wide-open Kansas cowtown needed law and order. Despite the efforts of local residents to control the situation, rowdy cowboys from Texas had all but taken over "McCoy's [**165**] Addition"—the south half of the city.

Tom had heard Abilene needed a lawman and he asked for the job. At first, the town trustees turned him down, saying they didn't know him well enough. Just a few days later, however, drunken cowboys destroyed Abilene's jail, helped an inmate escape and forced businesses to close as they rode up and down Texas Street filling buildings with bullets. Two other candidates for the marshal's job were in town at the time—but they took one look and headed back to St. Louis.

Smith, by then, was on his way to Denver. Abilene's mayor telegraphed him at Ellis and offered him the law enforcement job after all. Smith accepted. His pay, $150 a month plus $2 for each arrest he made. His first action was to announce that he would strictly enforce an ordinance against carrying firearms.

Unlike television and movie lawmen who marched up and down Western streets threatening offenders with pistols, easy-going Tom patroled the town on the back of his faithful iron gray horse, **Silverheels**. The marshal wore weapons, but he rarely drew them. When force was necessary, he used his fists, as Abilene's rough Texas guests soon found out.

The first cowboy to challenge Smith's ban on weapons was tough-talking "Big Hank." Proudly wearing his gun, he confronted the marshal on the street. When Smith told him quietly but firmly that he meant to enforce the law, the bully laughed and refused to cooperate. Suddenly, Smith pounced on him. A few punches later, Hank left town— without his pistol.

The next day "Wyoming Frank" tried to defy the marshal. Smith backed him into a nearby saloon. Minutes later, Frank was flat on the floor, nodding in agreement as the marshal ordered him out of town for good.

Time after time, Tom stood up to lawbreakers. While there were still rambunctious cowboys to be arrested, within a few weeks the marshal's brave actions helped the people of Abilene reclaim control of their city.

Unfortunately, the story of this town-tamer has a sad ending. Just six months after he came to Abilene, Smith was dead.

That fall Tom was made a deputy U.S. marshal. In November the Dickinson County sheriff sent him out to arrest a farmer accused of shooting a neighbor. As Smith and a deputy rode up to his dugout, the man stepped out with a rifle. Without warning, he fired, striking the marshal in the chest. As Smith tried to wrestle him to the ground, a friend of the farmer attacked him with an ax. The lawman died as his deputy ran for help.

Abilene buried its hero with honors, but his small tombstone soon disappeared and the grave became covered with weeds. Thirty-four years later, in 1904, the city reburied Smith in a new grave marked with a large Oklahoma boulder. ∎

Birdman

376 Robert Stroud

Murderer and "Birdman of Alcatraz." Leavenworth. (1890-1963) Stroud, the "Birdman of Alcatraz," actually spent more years behind bars in Kansas than on the famous prison island in California. Born in Seattle, he was sentenced to prison in 1909 for murdering a man in Alaska. After stabbing another prisoner in a Washington prison, Stroud was moved to the federal penitentiary in Leavenworth in 1912.

Within three years, he received —by extension—diplomas from Kansas State Agricultural College (KSU) in mechanical drawing, engineering, mathematics, music and theology. In the 1920s he began studying birds and bird diseases. By the time his 30 years in Kansas ended, he had published articles and a book on the subject. In 1942 he was transferred to Alcatraz prison in San Francisco. Seventeen years later he was sent to a prison hospital in Missouri. ∎

Superkansan

377 Superman

Fictional superhero. "Smallville" and Wellington. (Created 1938) Superman, under the name of his alter ego **Clark Kent**, grew up in Kansas. But like Dennis "The Menace" Mitchell [*370*], Superman's connection to the Sunflower State came to light only recently. For years, Smallville was somewhere in the heart of America. That changed in 1986 when the superhero remarked in a *Man of Steel* comic book, "At heart, I'm just a boy from a small town in Kansas." Based on clues in several stories, the fictional Smallville seems to be west of Kansas City, perhaps along or near U.S. Interstate 70.

Superman first appeared in June 1938 in a DC Comics series called *Action Comics*. He was born as *Kal-El*, or "Star Child," on the planet Krypton. When his space scientist father discovered their world was about to be destroyed by a cataclysmic explosion, he rocketed his one-year-old son to safety on earth. (**Krypto**, the boy's dog, had already arrived on earth on a test flight.) The boy's rocket landed just outside of Smallville, where he was rescued by **Jonathan** and **Martha Kent**. The childless Kents adopted the space traveler and named him Clark. When Clark started to school the family moved into Smallville and opened a store.

As a child he developed the ability to fly and other amazing superpowers. With the strength to do almost anything—except while under the influence of kryptonite—he began sharing his talents with the world as Superboy, and later, Superman.

After Clark graduated from Smallville High School, he moved to Metropolis, a fictional city—although citizens of Mctropolis, Illinois, claim it as their own. There he earned a degree at Metropolis University and then landed a job at the city's *Daily Planet* newspaper. As a reporter he was among the first to learn of crimes, disasters and other wrongs he could make right in his defense of "truth, justice, and the American way." He also worked as a journalist on WGBS television.

Off the comic pages, Superman also appeared in movies, on radio, television and the Broadway stage. Actor Bud Collyer was his voice on radio for many years, as well as in cartoons in the early 1940s. On television, George Reeves was "faster than a speeding bullet, more powerful than a locomotive" on a syndicated *Superman* series from 1951 to 1957. Modern audiences recognize Christopher Reeve as the Man of Steel from the four *Superman* films he made between 1978 and 1987.

Although Superman's Kansas connection wasn't official at that time, producers of the 1978 movie filled the big screen with images recognizable to Kansans: wide-open fields of waving wheat, grain elevators— even a *Kansas Star* passenger train for the teenaged Superman to outrun. (The movie, ironically, was filmed in Canada.)

In the early 1990s, Wellington residents decided their town should adopt Superman, much like Liberal adopted Dorothy Gale [*362*]. Visitors driving into Wellington now see a large sign reminding them they are entering the hometown of the superhero. Although DC Comics published an issue in late 1992 that included Superman's death, fans were assured the Man of Steel would return. ∎

New Yorker

378
Eustace Tilley

Magazine personality. Camp 50. (Created 1925) Tilley, also known as The New Yorker, came to life in February 1925 on the cover of the first issue of *The New Yorker* magazine.

With his monocle in hand, the unnamed "Regency dandy" was inspecting a butterfly. He was drawn by artist Rea Irvin, apparently to lend an air of class and sophistication to the new publication. Several months later editors referred to him by name—Eustace Tilley.

According to one legend, *The New Yorker*'s co-founder, Jane Grant [**202**], based the name on a fellow Kansan. The original Eustace Tilley is believed to have been a resident of Camp 50, a small mining community near Girard, where Grant grew up. The Kansas Mr. Tilley perhaps met Jane as a customer in her father's Girard store.

The cartoon Tilley still graces the pages of *The New Yorker*, and he makes a special appearance on the cover of each anniversary issue. ■

© 1925, 1953
The New Yorker Magazine, Inc.

Against almost everyone

379 Gerald Winrod

Minister and magazine publisher. Wichita. (1900-1957) Winrod was born in Wichita. His father was a bartender there—until Carry Nation [**121**] wrecked the saloon where he worked. When Mrs. Winrod was miraculously cured of cancer, Gerald's father converted to Christianity. The decision deeply affected young Winrod, too, and at age seventeen he joined a traveling evangelist. Four years later he began preaching himself.

Early in his ministry, he was concerned with modernism, or new ideas in religion. In 1925 he called a meeting in Salina of others who shared his conservative views. Those who attended founded an organization called the Defenders of the Christian Faith. Winrod was its executive secretary. A year later he established the group's publication, *The Defender Magazine*, which he edited until his death.

As he became even more conservative, Winrod spent more and more time speaking and writing about his "anti" beliefs. When Democrat Al Smith (who was in favor of liquor sales and was also a Catholic) ran for president in 1928, Winrod came out as anti-"wet" and anti-Catholic. By the mid 1930s he was anti-New Deal— he disagreed with President Franklin Roosevelt's plans to help the country through the Great Depression. He was also convinced that Jewish bankers and Communists were plotting to take over the world. His anti-list soon included members of the Masonic organization and even chain stores. He preached his warnings over KFH in Wichita, WIBW in Topeka and other early radio stations in Kansas. (Eventually he followed John R. Brinkley [**342**] and broadcast over XEAW, a "superstation" in Mexico.)

In 1935 Winrod traveled to Germany where he was impressed by Adolph Hitler and the Nazi party. Three years later he tried to run for a seat in the U.S. Senate. Using Dr. Brinkley's mailing list, he flooded the state with literature about his platform, "Fundamental Americanism." Although he was careful not to mention his anti-Catholic and anti-Jewish beliefs during campaign appearances and radio broadcasts, Kansans weren't impressed. He lost out in the primary election.

After he published pro-Nazi articles in the *Defender*, Winrod was indicted by a federal grand jury on charges that he had hurt the morale of America's armed forces. The charges were dropped in 1944. ■

Other colorful Kansans

Frank Bellamy, from Cherryvale, was a high school senior in 1895 when he wrote on his classroom's chalkboard: "I pledge allegiance to my Flag and to the Republic for which it stands—one nation indivisible—with liberty and justice for all."

His teacher was so impressed with the short composition that she encouraged him to enter it in a school essay contest. It won, and she saved a copy. Three years later, when Frank was serving in the Spanish-American War, the teacher entered his paragraph in a national patriotic contest. President William McKinley, according to some, declared it the winner.

When Frank returned home, he was quite surprised to learn of his honor, but said very little. Nothing more came of it until 1917, when the *Kansas City Star* published an article about a Kansas boy named Bellamy who had written the Pledge of Allegiance. Another Bellamy—Francis J.—saw the article in an Eastern newspaper. He wasn't happy, for he was the real author of the pledge, and he had proof. He had published it in a Boston magazine called *The Youth's Companion* in 1892—three years before Frank wrote it on the chalkboard. By that time it was too late to ask the Cherryvale resident about his "borrowed" essay; he had died in 1915. But although a Kansan didn't write the pledge, someone from the Sunflower State did help change it. In 1954, President Dwight D. Eisenhower [44] signed a law adding the words "under God" to Francis J. Bellamy's Pledge of Allegiance. Other changes were made in the 1960s. ∎

Dwight Chapin, born in Wichita in 1940, was a participant in the Watergate scandal that forced President Richard Nixon to resign in 1973. Chapin organized the "dirty tricks" unit that harassed Democrats in the 1972 presidential election. He was convicted of perjury, or lying under oath, in 1974 and was sentenced to prison. ∎

Dull Knife was a Northern Cheyenne Indian chief also known as Morning Star. In 1877 he and his people were forced to move south to a reservation in Indian Territory. After a year of sickness and hunger, Dull Knife and ***Little Wolf*** led over 300 followers on a desperate journey to return to their Montana homeland. They left the reservation near Fort Reno in mid September 1878. Once in Kansas, groups of warriors spread out, apparently taking their frustration and anger out on any whites they met. The Cheyennes' two-week flight across the state left a trail of death from Comanche to Decatur counties; an unknown number of Indians, and over 40 settlers and soldiers were killed. The incident has been called the last Indian raid in Kansas.

After their capture and escape from Fort Robinson, Nebraska, Dull Knife and only fourteen warriors made it to their former home. He died in the early 1880s on the Tongue River Reservation in Montana. ∎

Dora Hand was a singer who came to Dodge City from St. Louis in 1878. By that October she was dead—killed in her sleep by a bullet fired through the wall of a house owned by Mayor ***James "Dog" Kelley***. The colorful Kelley, whose nickname came from the greyhound dogs he raised, was gone at the time. It was assumed the bullet was meant for him. A posse of tough lawmen including ***William "Bill" Tilghman***, Wyatt Earp [356] and William "Bat" Masterson [368] soon arrested a Texas cowboy for the killing, but a Dodge City judge freed him for lack of evidence.

Those are the basic facts about Dora, also known as Fannie Keenan. This mystery woman appears in almost every book about Dodge City's wild and woolly history in the 1870s. She has been called everything from an opera star to a prostitute—but much of what has been written about her is false or can't be proven. Hand was not buried on Boot Hill [347]; she didn't have a love affair with Bat Masterson; and a dozen or more men probably didn't die fighting over her. Some of the Dora Hand fiction was included in the 1943 movie about her, *The Woman of the Town*, starring Claire Trevor. ∎

John "Doc" Holliday, born in Georgia in late 1851 or early 1852, moved West in the 1870s in hopes of curing his tuberculosis. He drifted from place to place, gambling, practicing dentistry and occasionally getting into gunfights. Holliday arrived in Dodge City in 1878 and became a friend of Wyatt Earp [356] when he disarmed a rowdy cowboy who had drawn a gun on Earp. Doc moved on to Arizona in 1880. He died seven years later in Colorado from the effects of his lung disease. ∎

George "Machine Gun" Kelly, the FBI's Public Enemy Number One in the 1930s, was convicted of kidnapping in 1933 and was sentenced to prison. Like other infamous criminals [**376**], Kelly served time in the Federal Penitentiary in Leavenworth. He died there in 1954.

Three years later, gangster **George C. "Bugs" Moran** also died at the Leavenworth penitentiary. In 1929 he took part in the Chicago gangland slaying known as the St. Valentine's Day Massacre. ∎

Elmer McCurdy, who also went by the name Frank Curtis, was born about 1880 in Maine, or so he said. In 1903 he moved to Iola and worked as a plumber. Before he joined the U.S. Army at Fort Leavenworth four years later, he also worked in Cherryvale. Once out of the military, Elmer took part in several train robberies in Oklahoma. In 1911 he was found dead in Oklahoma's Osage Hills, killed by some of his fellow train robbers or by a posse.

McCurdy's body was taken to a mortuary in Pawuska, Oklahoma. But because there was some confusion as to his identity, the sheriff ordered the undertaker to delay Elmer's burial until someone appeared to claim the body. For five years Elmer waited in the mortuary—a bizarre "conversation piece," propped in a corner with a gun in his hand. (Tests later showed the body was embalmed with huge amounts of arsenic, a chemical used by the ancient Egyptians to preserve mummies.)

In 1916 a carnival man whose show was playing in nearby Arkansas City apparently tricked the Oklahoma mortician into shipping Elmer to Kansas. By the time the undertaker realized the carnival owner wasn't a relative of McCurdy, the show—with Elmer's corpse on display—had left town.

After traveling the country for several decades, the dead outlaw ended up in a Los Angeles wax museum. Over time, his story was forgotten and people assumed he was just a strange dummy—"a crummy mummy," as someone described him.

By late 1976, poor Elmer was being used as a horror house prop in a Long Beach amusement park. During the filming of an episode of *The Six Million Dollar Man* television series at the park, one of his arms fell off. When stagehands noticed bones inside, the police were called. After weeks of investigation by the Los Angeles coroner, other government officials and historians, Elmer was identified. He was returned to Guthrie, Oklahoma, for burial in the spring of 1977—66 years after his death. ∎

"Mysterious Dave" Mather worked on both sides of the law during his colorful career. He was born in Connecticut in 1845, and was a direct descendant of the Puritan leader Cotton Mather. In the 1870s and 1880s Dave drifted in and out of Kansas at least three times. He was assistant marshal and deputy sheriff in Dodge City. At other times, he took part in two killings, and was reported to have been involved with horse thieves, train robbers and other shady characters. At one point, he and Wyatt Earp [**356**] were said to have been selling fake gold bricks to gullible cowboys in Texas.

During Mather's first stay in Dodge City, William "Bat" Masterson [**368**] and others persuaded him to attend a worship service led by a traveling evangelist. Playing along with their joke, Mysterious Dave listened earnestly as the evangelist appealed for his salvation.

When the preaching reached its peak, Mather jumped up with a hallelujah. Yes, indeed, he was saved! And, with a wave of his pistol, he added that he was ready to die—right then and there. Did the minister and deacons want to join him?

The churchmen's answer was lost in their mad scramble out the nearest windows and doors. Mather was later a lawman in Kiowa. He was last heard from in Nebraska in 1887. ∎

WU Shock, also called the Shocker, has been the mascot of Wichita State University since 1948. **Wilbur Elsea**, a junior art student at that time, created the tough-looking character as his entry in a contest sponsored by the Kappa Pi art fraternity. Elsea based his design on a shock, or bundle, of wheat because the crop had long been important to the school.

In its early years, Wichita University, as it was then called, had used a shock of wheat as a symbol. WU's earliest football games were played in the stubble of a nearby harvested wheatfield, and many farm students paid their tuition with income from the sale of wheat. ∎

Fur & Feathers

Mammals, Birds and other Animals

Rides high for the USA

380 Able

Chimpanzee space pioneer. Independence. (1957-1959) Able was a chimpanzee born at the Ralph Mitchell Zoo in Independence. Through a series of trades, she went to the National Aeronautics and Space Administration in Florida. There she joined the "animal astronauts."

In May 1959 Able helped test equipment for America's new space program. NASA launched her into space in a small capsule atop a Jupiter rocket. Her trip was short, for she traveled just 300 miles—at 10,000 mph!

Although she was not the first animal on a space mission, Miss Able was the first American animal to fly into space and survive. Her experience helped pave the way for human space travel. Sadly, she died four days after her flight when technicians tried to remove sensors from her heart. ∎

Oh, don't give me a home where the buffalo roam

381 Billie the Buffaloes

Pet buffaloes. Dodge City. (1880s) Billie the Buffaloes were a pair of buffaloes [382] owned by Dodge City stage line operator ***Philander Gillette "P.G." Reynolds***. He fed them from a bottle while they were calves, and later let them roam the streets of the town. Their searches for food got them into trouble more than once.

One day a housewife was startled when one of the Billies lifted her gate latch with his horns, strolled down the path and walked into her home. Quickly, the young mother grabbed her baby and dashed upstairs to safety. Hungry Billie headed for the kitchen and munched happily on a watermelon.

Another day, one of the buffaloes sniffed a barrel in someone's backyard and discovered a few cabbage leaves at the bottom. He rammed his head inside and when he tried to pull it out again, he was stuck. To add to the fun, a bystander threw a bucket of water on him.

Poor Billie took off, blinded by the barrel. He plowed through several fences, smashed against some houses and ended up downtown. There he hit a wagon, ran over a buggy and slid into a millinery shop.

The ladies inside had come to buy hats—but nothing as big as the barrel Billie was modeling. Customers and salesclerks screamed and dashed out the back door. Billie was close behind—but not before he and his barrel damaged showcases and merchandise.

In 1884 one of Reynolds' buffaloes tried to get a close look at a house fire. A volunteer fireman jumped off a ladder, grabbed the curious bison by the tail and pulled him out of danger.

Two years later one of the Billies spotted a marching band as it paraded down Dodge City's streets. The buffaloes were used to hearing Dodge City's famous Cowboy Band, but the music played by the visitors didn't charm the "savage" beast.

Billie charged into the band, scattering instruments, music and plumed hats everywhere. The drum major, waving his large baton, led the frightened musicians in a wild scramble over fences and onto the porches of nearby houses. ∎

Blankets Kansas in brown

State mammal. Statewide. (Designated 1955) Sculptor Bernard "Poco" Frazier [**199**] suggested the buffalo should be the state animal, and in 1955 the Kansas Legislature passed such a law. Because the ornate box turtle [**393**] became the state reptile in 1986, the buffalo is now more correctly called the state mammal.

Monarch of the Plains

The plains buffalo is also known by the scientific name *Bison bison bison*, or bison. It is the largest native animal on the Plains.

Full grown buffalo bulls stand five or six feet tall at their humps. They often weigh a ton or more. In the wild, buffalo bulls lived 20 to 30 years. Cows are shorter than bulls and weigh about 1,000 pounds or less. Their heads are less shaggy and their humps are not as large. Cows give birth to calves in the spring.

Most calves are yellowish or light brown when born. In a few months, their hair darkens to the adult brown and their humps begin to appear. Calves remain with their mothers for about a year. They are full grown after seven or eight years.

When buffaloes lived in the wild, herds were usually led by an old cow. Bulls stood outside the main group to act as guards. During the winter, bulls and cows often grazed in separate groups. As hundreds of buffaloes rolled in the dust to scratch away shedding hair and biting insects, large round holes were created.

When these "wallows" filled with rainwater, the buffaloes enjoyed them even more. The mud dried in the animals' hair and protected them from insect stings. Many buffalo wallows can still be seen in Kansas pastures.

In dry times, buffaloes may have traveled 50 or 100 miles to water. Several early Kansas settlers claimed to have seen thousands of thirsty buffaloes approach a flowing river—and drink until the stream ran dry. The herds did not, as some people have said, migrate north and south in the spring and fall. They drifted about during the year, probably a few hundred miles in any direction. ⇨

Indians' shopping center

Buffaloes' natural enemies were coyotes and wolves. For centuries, buffaloes and Indians lived together peacefully. Many Plains tribes relied on the shaggy beasts for almost everything—food, clothing, shelter, weapons, tools, medicine, religious items.

Early hunters killed buffaloes with spears or drove them off cliffs. Later Indians used bows and arrows, hunting close to the herds under the cover of old hides. When horses and guns arrived on the Plains, Indians increased their buffalo killing. For the most part, however,

Indian hunters "harvested" only the animals they needed for their band's survival.

The final hunt

Many white men didn't follow the Indians' example. Buffalo hunting became a business [*111, 349, 368, 369*], and the huge

herds quickly disappeared in the 1870s. Sometimes white hunters used the meat, but thousands of times, they took only the hides or tongues. Some hunters killed 100—even 200—buffaloes a day. An estimated four million buffaloes were slaughtered between 1872 and 1874 in western Kansas. In 1879, one of the last wild buffaloes killed in Kansas was shot near Dodge City.

Today there are several thousand buffaloes in the state. Except for those in zoos, all are owned by ranchers and Kansas Wildlife and Parks—over 70 herds in all. But seeing a small group of these animals in a pasture today is a far cry from witnessing the spectacle of the great buffalo herds in the past. ■

Millions and more millions

Some experts have estimated 30 million buffaloes may have once lived in North America. Others guess as high as 60 to 75 million.

Early visitors, too, had trouble finding numbers to describe the buffalo herds they saw on the Plains. Francisco Vásquez de Coronado [*11*] wrote, "I found such a quantity of cows [buffaloes] that it is impossible to number them."

One traveler said the buffalo-covered prairies were "black and appeared as if in motion." Others compared the number of buffaloes with "the locusts of Egypt" or "the fish in the sea." Another wrote, "The country was one robe."

Thomas Farnham, traveling on the Santa Fe Trail in 1839, witnessed a huge buffalo herd. For three days, he

moved through a mass of buffaloes that stretched fifteen miles on both sides of the trail. He estimated he saw 1,350 square miles of buffalo—an area a little larger than the state of Rhode Island.

In 1870, a Frenchman named *L.C. Fouquet* hunted buffalo in southwestern Kansas. In one area, he counted 63 separate herds, and estimated each had about 2,000 head, a total of perhaps 126,000 buffaloes.

Robert Wright came to Kansas in 1859. He later wrote, "I have indeed traveled through the buffaloes along the Arkansas River for 200 miles, almost one continuous herd. You might go north or south as far as you pleased and there would seem [to be no end] to their numbers."

Warts and all

383 Cloud's toad

Talented toad. Kingman. (1920s) A state legislator in the early 1920s claimed the same toad appeared at his home each spring for many years. Kingman County resident *Fred Cloud* said the intelligent amphibian recognized everyone in his family and followed them around like a puppy. It even performed acrobatic tricks when it was happy. As the family sat outside on summer evenings, the toad would sit nearby, contentedly eating insects. According to Cloud, when the creature had its fill, it asked for someone to turn out the light. ■

War-weary horse survives

384 Comanche

U.S. Army horse. Fort Hays, Fort Riley, Fort Leavenworth and Lawrence. (About 1862-1891) Comanche was captured by mustang hunters somewhere on the Plains. He was sold to the U.S. Army at St. Louis in the spring of 1868. Soon he joined the 7th Cavalry at Fort Hays. There he became one of Captain Myles Keogh's favorite mounts.

In September 1868 the animal was wounded as Keogh rode him in a fight with several Comanches. When a blacksmith pulled an arrow from his wound, according to stories, the horse cried like a Comanche. His cry became his name.

In the next seven years, Keogh and Comanche faced trouble in many forms: Indians near Fort Hays, "moonshiners" making illegal whiskey and the Ku Klux Klan in the South, plus trespassing miners and settlers in the Black Hills. During that time Comanche was wounded again.

In Montana they were part of the 7th Cavalry force that fought thousands of Sioux and Cheyenne warriors at the Little Big Horn River in June 1876. It was their last battle.

Captain Keogh, Lieutenant Colonel George Custer [351], and all the soldiers in their immediate command—over 200 men in all —died in the fight. When other troops discovered the scene two days later, Indians had already taken the few surviving horses. Comanche was the only living thing they found on the battlefield. The horse had seven wounds—including a bullet hole completely through his neck.

By wagon and riverboat, troopers carefully moved him to Fort Abraham Lincoln. After the animal was nursed back to health, the commander of the 7th Cavalry put out an order in his honor: The veteran horse was to receive a special stall. He was not do any work except being led in parades and, above all, Comanche was not to be ridden by anyone. From that time on, the privileged horse roamed freely around the post, and often begged soldiers for sugar lumps and buckets of beer.

Comanche and the 7th were transferred to Fort Meade in the Black Hills in 1879. In 1888 the outfit returned to Kansas and Fort Riley. The old horse died there in the fall of 1891. Cavalry officers then asked Professor Lewis Lindsay Dyche [12] of the University of Kansas' natural history department to mount Comanche's remains.

Today the famous horse is owned by KU and is the most popular exhibit at its Dyche Museum of Natural History. Except for a trip in 1893 to be displayed at the Chicago Exposition, Comanche has not left Lawrence. Although Montanans have tried several times to move him to the Little Big Horn Battlefield National Monument, the weary old survivor remains a Kansan. ■

Aced out

385 Deuce

Stunt bulldog. Wichita. (Born 1988) Deuce was raised by the **Louie Stumblingbear** family in Wichita. Due to a family illness, the Stumblingbears sent their bulldog to stay with relatives in Washington in 1990.

Deuce's adopted family raise registered bulldogs. When Paramount Pictures asked them for a bulldog to appear in an episode of the ABC television series *MacGyver*, Deuce beat out sixteen others for the part. Actually, the Kansas bulldog came in second —he was hired as a stunt double for Winston, an older bulldog.

After the episode was shot, there was talk it might lead to a new series featuring Winston and his double, Deuce. Hollywood, however, disappointed Deuce and his owners. A special program pre-empted Deuce's *MacGyver* appearance, and the new series idea was dropped. ■

A honey of a state insect

State insect. Statewide. (Designated 1976) Kansas gained an official state insect March 29, 1976, when Governor **Robert Bennett** signed the "honeybee" bill into law. The insect received the honor after a Coffeyville fifth grade student, **Larry Wood**, campaigned with the help of his classmates and teacher, **Becky Gillette**. Over 2,000 Kansas school children signed their petitions supporting the honeybee.

There are about 10,000 kinds of bees, but only honeybees make honey and wax that man can use. In fact, honeybees are the only insects that produce a food eaten by humans. Of all the bee species, honeybees have the most highly developed societies. Over 50,000 of them can live in one colony. A single honeybee may live only a few weeks or months, but the colony can exist for many years.

Female worker bees build a hive of six-sided honeycomb cells. Drones, or male honeybees, mate with a single queen bee. In each of the hive's cells the queen lays an egg—over 2,000 per day. Worker bees, flying up to twelve miles per hour, spend the summer collecting flower pollen and nectar. As they travel from blossom to blossom, the bees spread the pollen that allows fruits and vegetables to reproduce. They store pollen for food during the fall, winter and spring. They make nectar into honey that feeds the hive.

Honeybees live all across Kansas. In warm months, they can be seen in flower gardens, near wildflowers or in fields of alfalfa and other crops. They do not hibernate during the winter, but stay in the hive. The movement of workers' wings helps keep the temperature inside between 50 and 60 degrees. They build their hives in hollow trees, the walls of buildings or boxes provided by beekeepers.

About 36,000 hives in Kansas are shared between honeybees and beekeepers. The keepers remove part of the honey in the summer, but leave enough to support the hive during the rest of the year. Bees are big business, for Kansas apiaries, or commercial hives, produce over two million pounds of honey each year.

The honeybees' familiar buzz is caused by their wings beating the air 11,400 times a minute. But the sound is not meant as a warning to people, for only worker bees sting humans, and they do so only when frightened or hurt. They leave their stingers in their victims and die afterward.

Kansans should not fear their state insect, for as the honeybee law states, the creatures are usually "friendly bundles of energy." ■

Really imaginary

Mythical bird and university mascot. Statewide and Lawrence. (Created 1850s) Like the beginning of most myths, the origin of the Kansas jayhawk is difficult to trace.

Ancestors from Illinois or Ireland?

The word was perhaps borrowed from a group of Illinois men. The adventurers traveled to California in 1849 and called themselves "jayhawkers." A few years later, at the start of the Bleeding Kansas fight over slavery, some sources say both antislavery and proslavery forces used the jayhawker name.

Eventually, however, the name was given only to Free Staters who fought border ruffians. One early Kansan said the name originated with a group of Free State men from Linn County.

Others claim **Pat Devlin**, a Free Stater born in Ireland, started the name in 1856. As Devlin returned from a raid in Missouri he said he had been "jayhawking," just like the Irish jayhawk that lives off other birds. Ireland, of course, has no such bird.

A respected name

As the fight over slavery went on, the jayhawker name often had a negative meaning. This continued into the Civil War, when Governor Charles Robinson [82] tried to transfer guerilla leader **Charles Jennison** and his jayhawkers out of the Kansas Milita.

Jennison's Jayhawkers—minus Jennison—eventually moved to Mississippi but they did little to earn respect for the jayhawk name. Since that time, however, jayhawk troops have fought bravely in every American war.

KU mascot

A cartoon version of the Kansas jayhawk first appeared in the KU student newspaper in the fall of 1912. The artist was **Henry Maloy**, a sophomore cartoonist with the *Daily Kansan*. Maloy sketched his idea of a jayhawk after seeing a display of a stuffed chicken hawk with a KU pennant in its beak. At the time, a bulldog was the university's team mascot.

Maloy put long legs and shoes on his creature so it could get a "better kick" on KU's opponents. By the 1920s, it was the university's mascot. As others added their ideas to Maloy's cartoon bird over the years, it began to look more real than imaginary. This "bluejay" jayhawk was then changed to a duck-like version. In 1941, **Gene Williams** designed a jayhawk much like its modern cousin. The present KU Jayhawk was created by **Harold Sandy** in 1946. A year later the university copyrighted his design.

While the KU "Rock Chalk" Jayhawk is recognized around the country, other artists have drawn their own versions of this important bird, too. In 1954 "Pogo" cartoonist Walt Kelly featured his own Kansas jayhawk in his comic strip for several weeks. True Kansans, of course, have no difficulty recognizing a jayhawk, no matter how it is drawn. ⇨

Jayhawk mythology

Over the years, the jayhawk has become a part of Kansas mythology. In the 1940s, *Kirke Mechem* [226], a noted Kansas historian, gathered stories of the "mythical jayhawk." "But the jayhawk is very real," he wrote. "It is the spirit of the individualistic state of Kansas. A mythical cross between the mischievous bluejay and the soaring hunter-hawk, the jayhawk was hatched in the brooder-house of Bleeding Kansas." Mechem's tales help explain the state's most mysterious bird.

Some say the jayhawk was first attracted to Kansas because it needed a level runway to land at its great speed. Others claim the strong southwesterly winds in Kansas were created by the wings of millions of jayhawks as they flew to the Great Lakes for water. These jayhawk breezes then brought rain and vegetation to prehistoric Kansas.

Rock City, over 200 large sandstone spheres in Ottawa County, is actually a collection of petrified jayhawk eggs, according to some. Invisible jayhawks, Kansas farmers sometimes say, plant "volunteer" wheat that often sprouts in plowed wheatfields.

Old-timers said the 1874 grasshopper plague ended when jayhawks ate millions of the hungry insects.

Fighting hawk

During World War II, the pilot of a B-777 bomber nicknamed "The Flying Jayhawk" claimed a high-speed jayhawk came out of nowhere just as he and his crew were landing at a Wichita airbase.

They heard a swooshing sound above them, and then, through their plane's windshield they saw a shiny yellow foot. Its claws scraped into the aircraft's metal skin above their heads.

After they landed and taxied to a stop, the plane suddenly tumbled to one side. When the airmen climbed out to investigate, they found the left wheel missing from their landing gear.

The high-flying jayhawk had guided them to a safe landing! Sitting on a fence nearby, the pilot later told reporters with a grin, was a small blue bird with a big yellow beak. ∎

Picked chicken in the movies

388 Just Bill

Movie star chicken. Stafford. (1943-19?) Just Bill was hatched in Nebraska, but he became famous while living in Kansas. Champion chicken-raiser **Earl Kelly** of Stafford bought the rooster for $100 in 1946.

The next year Kelly took Just Bill to a national poultry show in Oklahoma City. There he won the first of many national titles. At the same event he also won a special crowing contest sponsored by the Warner-Pathe movie company. After years of beginning their newsreels with film footage of a crowing rooster, they wanted to update their trademark with younger, "fresher" talent. The handsome, twelve-pound Just Bill crowed on cue, and beat out several thousand chicken hopefuls from 40 other states.

After Just Bill was insured for $1,000, the Kellys took him to Hollywood. When the White Rock rooster went before the cameras, he performed like a trooper. Kelly waved his arms and Just Bill flapped his wings.

As his owner clucked like a hen, the champion rooster crowed proudly. Photographs of the filming were published in *Life* magazine. Just Bill's first film was released in 1948. ∎

High-stepper

389
Lemon Drop Kid

World champion horse. Scott City and Salina. (1948-1970)
The Lemon Drop Kid was a harness horse, trained to pull a cart with a high-stepping gait. Scott City farmer **R.B. Christy** bought the animal in St. Louis.

During the eight years Christy owned him, the Lemon Drop Kid won every major horse show in which he appeared. From 1956 through 1959 he was declared world champion at the finals in Kentucky. He also won several championships at the American Royal in Kansas City. Audiences loved the horse as much as he loved applause.

Lemon Drop's name no doubt came from his golden color. The magnificent animal was once featured on the cover of *Sports Illustrated* magazine. He was later owned by a Salina man. ∎

Moose on the loose

390 Morris the Moose

Wandering moose. Western Kansas. (Born about 1987)
Morris, as he was nicknamed, was a young male moose that kept Kansas Wildlife and Parks officials busy during the summer and fall of 1989. He drifted into the state from Nebraska, apparently looking for new territory. Morris probably began his odyssey in Montana.

Kansas game wardens tracked the lost moose from the Kirwin Reservoir, past Hays, Larned, and into the Oklahoma panhandle south of Ashland. When Morris reentered the state, a veterinarian caught him, treated him with antibiotics and hauled him into southeastern Colorado. The wandering moose has not been seen in Kansas since. ∎

of almost anything: cloth, clothing, canned goods, hardware, jewelry, machinery, mining equipment, military supplies.

On a return trip from Santa Fe in the fall of 1862, Old Dan was in the wagon train's "cavaydo," a herd of extra oxen that freighters used to replace sick or injured animals.

One morning, a young herder named **Robert Wright** was driving the cavaydo back into camp along the Arkansas River. As the weather warmed, Wright took off his coat. Instead of carrying it, he draped it over the tame ox's horns with the red and yellow lining flapping in the breeze. When they neared the caravan, the other animals were yoked and ready to roll. One young steer saw Old Dan's strange headdress and took off with a loud bawl. Quickly, other animals bellowed and ran —all except Old Dan.

When the dust settled, there was a fifteen-mile trail of wrecked wagons, damaged cargo and scattered cattle. Three steers and one man had broken legs. As they were cleaning up the mess, the wagonmaster asked Wright if he knew what had started the steer stampede. Probably a wolf, the young herder answered.

Old Dan said nothing. ∎

Steers wagons down trail

391 Old Dan

Santa Fe Trail ox. Leavenworth. (1860s) Old Dan was one of thousands of oxen that worked across Kansas on the Santa Fe Trail in the mid 1800s. Oxen, or steer cattle, were also used by travelers on the Oregon Trail and other routes in the state. Old Dan was owned by the freighting firm of Russell, Majors & Wad-

dell, based in Leavenworth. Like other animals in their herd, the steer probably made many freighting trips, perhaps covering 2,000 miles in a year.

Wearing a wooden yoke with a partner, he was hitched with at least five more pairs—called yokes—of oxen. The wagon they pulled carried two or three tons

Rarest turtle

392 Omar

Rare alligator snapping turtle. Montgomery County. (Born about 1940?) Omar is one of just a handful of alligator snapping turtles that have been seen in Kansas. The rare and secretive reptile first made news in 1986—24 years after the last alligator snapping turtle was sighted in the state.

KU zoologist **Joe Collins** named Omar when she was first caught, before he realized "he" was a "she." He took her to the university's Museum of Natural History for a short public display. Then, while the zoologists waited for special turtle-tracking equipment to arrive, Omar dined on carp in a private tank. Fitted with a radio transmitter, she was later returned to Onion Creek in Montgomery County.

However, her tracking gear soon failed and she wasn't seen again until fishermen accidentally caught her in 1991. She had traveled less than four miles. By that time, she weighed a hefty 59.4 pounds. Dr. Collins says Omar's large size means she is either very old, or extremely healthy. She probably eats smaller turtles as well as fish. Like all alligator snapping turtles she has a built-in fishing lure. On the end of her tongue is a piece of pink flesh she can wiggle like a worm.

In order to keep better track of this rare animal, zoologists equipped her with another transmitter—plus an extra as a backup. Before she was released, Omar met the public again, this time in Montgomery County.

One of Omar's relatives was the heaviest reptile ever discovered in Kansas. In 1938 a giant-sized alligator snapping turtle was caught in Labette County. The huge creature tipped the scales at 132.5 pounds! Unlike Omar, however, the heavy-duty turtle wasn't put on display. Zoologists couldn't find a tank large enough to hold it. ∎

At home in its shell

393 Ornate box turtle

State reptile. Statewide. (Designated 1986) The ornate box turtle was declared the state reptile as part of Kansas' 125th anniversary of statehood, thanks to a group of sixth graders in Caldwell.

The students and their teacher, **Larry Miller**, began the turtle's campaign for state reptile—after they decided against supporting the bullsnake. Class members helped push for passage of the "turtle" bill in the Kansas Legislature and then watched Governor John Carlin [**35**] sign it into law in Caldwell on April 14, 1986.

The ornate box turtle, or *Terrapene ornata ornata*, is found across the state. Its numbers are largest on the western prairies, but it is also at home in eastern Kansas fields and pastures. It may travel 200 to 300 feet a day, feeding on insects, worms and wild fruit. Each turtle ranges over an area of about five acres, and shares its territory with other turtles.

Female and male ornate box turtles may be distinguished by their eye color. Females have yellowish brown eyes; males' eyes are red. Both have shells that are dark brown or reddish brown with yellow or yellow-orange lines. Most ornate box turtles' shells are four to five inches long. However, some turtles with six-inch shells have been found.

When in danger, a turtle closes its shell after pulling its head and legs inside. Its natural ene-

mies are coyotes, skunks and other meat-eating mammals. Humans, unfortunately, often kill more turtles than their animal predators. Automobiles strike many of the reptiles as they rest on warm highway pavement during cool evenings.

The state reptile is quiet and secretive, but sharp-eyed Kansans may observe it between April and October. To protect itself during the coldest part of the year, the cold-blooded animal burrows six to eighteen inches into the ground. The ornate box turtle appears again in spring, after the weather has been warm and moist for a time.

Females nest from May to July, and lay two to eight leathery white eggs. Perhaps one-third of the females lay two nests of eggs per season. The eggs hatch in about two months, and the young turtles are fully grown in seven or eight years. Ornate box turtles may live 30 years or longer. ∎

Barely tame bear

394 Paddy the Bear

Pet bear. Dodge City. (About 1880-1883) Paddy was captured in Indian Territory and was taken to Dodge City in 1880. There the black bear cub was given to the town's mayor, *James "Dog" Kelley*.

Most of the time, Paddy stayed on a chain behind Kelley's restaurant. Children loved to play with her, but older pranksters liked to tease her with whiskey and practical jokes. Several times, the tormenting became too great, and the bear broke free.

Once, she ran into the Dodge House hotel and awakened an off-duty railroader. The bear chased him down the hall before a broom-waving maid shooed her outside. Another

day, Paddy slipped through an open window at the hotel and crawled under a bed. As she lay in her hiding place, the bed rose and fell with her breathing.

On the top side of the mattress, a half-drunk traveling salesman lay sleeping. When his "breathing" bed woke him, he threw a glass underneath it. The frightened Paddy suddenly stood up —bed, salesman and all. The terrified man took one look at the bear under his bed and ran screaming through the hotel's crowded dining room—wearing only his underwear. In his haste to escape, he plowed over a waiter, scattering an armload of dishes.

Unfortunately, as the tricks against Paddy became more cruel, she became meaner. To protect himself and others, Mayor Kelley had the bear butchered. Her last appearance was at the Kelleys' Christmas dinner in 1883. ∎

Everyone's city kitty

395 Sam

Town cat. Inman. (About 1976-1990) Sam was a lost kitten when he first appeared in Inman. He quickly got acquainted. At first the long-haired black cat lived at the local grain elevator; he later moved down the street to the appliance store.

For nearly fifteen years Sam seemed to own the town. He strolled along Main Street, greeting everyone with his

friendly purr. He even rode with city policemen as they made their rounds. Someone suggested the cat should be a candidate for mayor.

Sam was such an important part of the town's history that artist Stan Herd [*208*] included the familiar black cat in a mural he painted of early-day Inman. When the popular cat died in 1990, many area residents attended his burial services. ∎

Coon-dog goes the distance

396 Taylor's hound

Trail-walking dog. Scott City. (1880s) A Scott City dog no doubt set a canine distance record in the 1880s. The unnamed coon-hound belonged to a Mr. Taylor, who ran a stage line between Scott City and Dighton. For eight years Taylor's hound faithfully followed the stagecoach on its daily 45-mile round trip into Lane County and back.

In 1887, according to the estimate of the *Scott County News*, the hound had walked about 108,000 miles—a distance equal to over four times around the earth. By that time, however, the animal was dog-tired; he was making only three or four trips a week. It isn't known how long Taylor's hound lived. ■

Photogenic little lion

397 Tommy the Lion

Lovable lion. Garden City. (1951-1952) Tommy was abandoned by his mother soon after he was born at Garden City's Lee Richardson Zoo. Luckily for him, zookeeper **Claude Owens** and his wife **Mary** were willing to adopt the lonely lion cub.

He was a familiar sight in Garden City, walking on a leash with the Owenses or riding happily in their car. Tommy visited over 100 school classrooms in person and appeared in thousands more on film after an educational movie was made about him in 1952. He was also featured in a photo story in *Life* magazine. Other photos of Tommy were published in newspapers across the United States and in England.

Tommy died from a serious tooth infection at the age of eighteen months. He was the first of thirteen lion cubs, two bear cubs, a leopard, elk, mountain goat and wallaby that the Owenses cared for at home. ■

Cunning hunter

398 Two Toes

Notorious gray wolf. Meade County. (1880s) Two Toes terrorized cattle ranches in Meade County during the 1880s. The cunning gray wolf and his mate reportedly killed calves, full-grown cows and mules. His attacks on several bulls left them so seriously injured they had to be destroyed. In a few weeks, one ranch lost twenty head of livestock to the wolf and his mate.

Cattlemen could identify the predator from his distinctive tracks. One of the wolf's feet had been caught in a trap, leaving only two toes. As ranchers discovered more and more two-toed tracks near their dead cattle, they offered higher rewards for the wolf. But hunters always came back empty-handed.

That changed when an ex-slave named **Willis Peoples** took over the hunt. Day after day, Peoples patiently trailed the animal across the countryside. After the chase had gone on for two weeks, Two Toes' mate disappeared, leaving him to face the hunter alone. Ten days later, Peoples cornered the hungry wolf in a ravine and ended his life with one shot.

While Peoples displayed his trophy in Meade, someone borrowed a tape measure from a dry goods store. From the tip of the nose to the tip of the tail, Two Toes measured seven feet.

Grateful ranchers gave Peoples a sizeable reward. When they asked how he had found the wolf when no one else had, he answered, "One man with his mind made up is a majority." ■

Sings a song of Kansas

State bird. Statewide. (Designated 1937) The western meadowlark, or *Sturnella neglecta*, is the state bird of Kansas.

Lark that isn't a lark

Western meadowlarks, like their cousins the eastern meadowlarks, are not true larks, but they come from the same family as blackbirds and orioles. Meadowlarks are medium-sized birds, with brownish backs and wings marked with black and white. They have a bright yellow throat and underparts. A large black crescent stretches across their breasts and white outer tail feathers show when they fly.

Meadowlarks appear in all parts of the state, but not all of them stay year round. Like robins, some meadowlarks remain over the winter while others fly south. In the spring, male meadowlarks are some of the first birds to give a mating call. Their flutelike whistle may attract up to three females that nest near each other.

They build their nests in pastures, marshes and other grassy areas. When completed, each nest is difficult to find, hidden deep in tall grass and covered with a dome of woven grass. For added protection, the birds construct several "escape hatches"—tunnels leading out of the nest like spokes on a wheel.

Females lay three to seven white eggs, speckled with reddish brown. They sit on the eggs for two weeks while the male sings nearby. After hatching, the young leave their parents within two weeks. Because they have been raised in such deep grass, it often takes several more days for the chicks to exercise their wings and learn to fly. The birds eat insects and waste grain.

Meadowlarks' enemies include hawks and coyotes. In the early 1900s, meadowlarks were hunted. They were shipped east where their feathers were used to make hats. Today, like all Kansas songbirds, they are protected by law.

A popular choice

On Kansas Day 1925, over 120,000 Kansas school children voted for their choice of a state bird. After the ballots were counted, the meadowlark was the clear winner, with a total of 48,395 votes. It beat out the quail, cardinal and prairie chicken. The contest was sponsored by the Kansas Audubon Society.

It's official

After the 1925 voting, some claimed that Kansas was the first state to have a state bird. That may have been true, but the meadowlark didn't become the *official* Kansas state bird for another twelve years.

It was not until 1937 that the Kansas Legislature passed a bill naming the western meadowlark as the state bird (and the cottonwood as the state tree). The bill was introduced by **A.W. Relihan**, a legislator from Smith County. It was signed into law by Governor **Walter Huxman** on March 23, 1937.

Kansas shares its state bird with five other states: Nebraska, Wyoming, Montana, North Dakota and Oregon. ∎

Other Kansas creatures

Black Nell was the faithful horse of James Butler "Wild Bill" Hickok [*364*]. Like her famous owner, stories about her are legendary. Hickok, who said Black Nell "carried me along through many a tight place," is believed to have bought her from the U.S. Army while he served in the Civil War. To prove her training and obedience, according to one story, Wild Bill once ordered her to climb onto a billiard table in a Springfield, Missouri, saloon. She did. Some sources say the mare died in Kansas City in 1869. ■

Bull's elk was only one of several wild animals kept by General **Hiram C. Bull**, politician, postmaster and co-founder of Bull's City. All went well with Bull's menagerie until one day in 1879 the large male elk became unruly. When Bull tried to calm it, the elk rushed at him and gored him to death. Two of Bull's friends attempted to rescue the general, but they, too, met their doom under the elk's antlers. The murderous animal slammed a fourth man into a fence, but he escaped.

After the tragedy, Bull's City townspeople petitioned the post office department—with the help of some forged signatures—to change the name of their Osborne County town to Alton. **Sarah Bull** remained in Alton and took her husband's job at the post office. (Before his death Bull had often said his wife was the only female Bull in Kansas!)

For his crime, Bull's elk received the death sentence. His deadly antlers hung in an Alton store for many years. ■

Corky the Hornet has been the mascot of Emporia State University since the 1930s. Before that time, students at the school—then called Kansas State Teachers College—were the Yaps. Legend says the nickname referred to the fact that teachers did a lot of "yapping."

The unpopular name changed when *Emporia Gazette* [*256*] reporter **Cecil Carle** began calling the KSTC football team the Yellowjackets, and then the Hornets. (The "stinging" team wore yellow sweaters with black stripes on the sleeves.) KSTC used drawings of a real hornet to represent its mascot until a sophomore, **Paul Edwards**, created Corky the Hornet in 1934. In 1987, Edwards returned to the Emporia campus to dedicate a statue he sculpted of his cartoon character. ■

A western **cottonmouth** water moccasin discovered in Cherokee County in the fall of 1991 had the "honor" of being only the second member of its poisonous species to be found in Kansas. (The first cottonmouth was caught near Chetopa in 1937.) According to KU zoologist **Joe Collins**, the capture of this cottonmouth specimen means five—not four—species of venomous snakes officially live in Kansas: the **copperhead**, the **massasauga**, **prairie** and **timber rattlesnakes**, and now the cottonmouth. ■

Gus the Gorilla is the mascot of Pittsburg State University. The tradition began in 1920 when a group of PSU students organized themselves as the Gorillas. Basing their name on a slang term for "roughnecks," the group sponsored pep rallies. In 1923 the Gorillas asked art student **Helen Waskey** to draw the first artwork of their namesake animal. Two years later the PSU student body adopted the gorilla as the school's official mascot.

Over the years drawings of the creature became less ferocious; he eventually came to be called Gus. In 1952 his female counterpart, **Gussie**, was created by **Charles Galvin**. That same year, a cartoon Gus was drawn by **Lee Green**. The university presently uses stylized artwork of the primate. **Larry Wooster** sculpted a statue of Gus that stands on the PSU campus. ■

Hope, a German shepherd dog from Holcomb, saved her two-year-old friend **Gregory Garcia** from tragedy in 1991. Gregory, who is fascinated by trains, dashed away from his home one afternoon when he heard the whistle of an approaching train. Unfortunately, the boy's curiosity took him dangerously close to the railroad tracks.

As the warning lights flashed and the crossing arms dropped down, Hope went into action. Helpless motorists on the other side of the tracks watched as the dog pushed the toddler down and held him there—lying between him and the tracks—until the train passed. For her efforts, Hope was named National Hero Dog of the Year by the German Shepherd Dog Club of America. Before receiving her award, she and Gregory paraded proudly around an arena in the Houston Astrodome. ∎

Lawrin, a horse foaled in 1935 at Woolford Farm, Johnson County, won the Kentucky Derby in 1938. The thoroughbred was owned by breeder **Herbert M. Woolf**, and was ridden to victory in the Derby by the famous jockey Eddie Arcaro. ∎

Roger Rabbit, the cartoon character who starred in the 1988 animated and live action film, *Who Framed Roger Rabbit?*, grew up in Kansas. Steven Spielberg, Roger's creator, and Walt Disney Productions have plans for a movie "prequel" that will tell the story of the rabbit's rise from the Great Plains to the big screen. ∎

Tales of the **State Lake Snake**, a giant blacksnake of Kingman County, have been told for years. According to folklorists **Jim Hoy** and **Tom Isern**, witnesses claim the snake is about the size of a telephone pole. It supposedly has been seen sunning itself on U.S. highway 54 west of Kingman. The legendary creature has eluded capture by hundreds of searchers. ∎

The Fort Hays State University **Tiger** mascot has its origins out of state. The tiger and the FHSU school colors, black and gold, arrived on the Hays campus in 1913. That was the year **William A. Lewis** became president at the Kansas school. Lewis came from the University of Missouri, an institution that just happens to have school colors of black and gold—and a tiger mascot. Today FHSU uses two versions of their cat mascot, a friendly cartoon tiger dating back to the 1970s, and a fiercer tiger logo. ∎

Tom was a cat that lived at the Dodge City AT&SF Railway depot in 1930s. As he ate leftovers at the depot's Harvey House [**154**], Tom turned into a walking advertisement for the popular restaurant's good food. Between meals, the tubby tabby strolled up and down the platform, inspecting the tracks and greeting train travelers. ∎

Willie the Wildcat is the mascot of Kansas State University. His first appearance—in a papier-maché head and a K-State sweatshirt—came at a basketball game in 1964. He was nameless until a newspaper reporter called him Willie. The first cartoon Willie was drawn a few years later; he has since been changed from comical to fierce to friendly. The university also uses a stylized wildcat logo.

Willie isn't the first wildcat mascot to represent KSU. In 1920 a live wildcat named **Touchdown** made appearances with the football team. Touchdown grew up in Washington and was brought to Manhattan by a K-State quarterback. Over the years, he was followed by half a dozen other wildcats, both real and costumed. All carried the Touchdown name. ∎

Zak, a schnauzer dog belonging to the **Kirk Rufenacht** family of Ransom, was named 1992 Pet of the Year by the Kansas Veterinary Medicine Association. When the dog discovered a family member unconscious from a buildup of deadly carbon monoxide, he barked—just before he, too, passed out. Others in the house soon became ill, but thanks to the schnauzer's warning, they phoned for help and were rescued. All the Rufenachts, including Zak, survived the incident. ∎

Character Index

Names in boldface are the **399 numbered characters**. Numbers in brackets **[399]** are **guide numbers** used at the top of each page and with each character sketch. Numbers in plain type are page numbers.

Other characters with Kansas connections and their page numbers are listed in plain type, too.

This information became available after the main portion of the book was printed:

As a boy, the Reverend **Richard Taylor** [*129*] (page 95) lived in Dwight before he and his family moved to Enterprise. The Reverend Taylor retired as director of Kansans for Life at Its Best in late 1992. The Topeka organization is now headed by **Dave Schneider**, a graduate of Washburn University.

Race car driver **Rodger Ward** [*333*] (page 221) was born in 1922, not 1921. He and his family left Kansas and moved to California about a year later.

Professional basketball player **Xavier McDaniel** (page 224) bought out his contract with the New York Knicks before the end of the 1991-92 season. McDaniel now plays for the Boston Celtics. ∎

The characters behind this book

Dave Webb is a fourth-generation Kansan and assistant director of the Kansas Heritage Center, Dodge City. He graduated from Southwestern College, Winfield, and has taught in Scott City, Garden City and his hometown of Protection. He not only enjoys researching and writing about history, he lives in it. Dave's Comanche County home is a refurbished Santa Fe depot complete with a caboose in the backyard. He shares the 1887 railroad station with two cats, Atchison and Fe, and a computer named Mac. Since 1984 Webb has written learning materials for the Heritage Center, including *Indians in Kansas* and *Adventures with the Santa Fe Trail*. ∎

Phillip R. Buntin graduated from Olathe High School and Central Missouri State. After teaching art in Missouri, he returned to Kansas and taught outreach classes at Garden City Community College. Since 1979, Buntin has been a faculty member of Garden City High School. He is presently an art instructor and chairman of the school's art department. Besides donating his time and creative talents to various causes, Phil enjoys collecting antiques and doting over his bulldog Buckingham. *399 Kansas Characters* is the fourth publication Buntin has illustrated for the Kansas Heritage Center. ∎

Leo E. Oliva is a native of Rooks County and a graduate of Fort Hays State and Denver universities. Dr. Oliva has taught at FHSU, was chairman of the university's history department and has conducted numerous workshops on Kansas history topics. Leo and his wife Bonita live near Woodston where he divides his time between farming, writing, and supporting historical organizations. He is editor of the Santa Fe Trail Association's respected publication *Wagon Tracks*, and the author of *Soldiers on the Santa Fe Trail*, as well as histories of Kansas Forts Larned, Hays and Scott. Currently he is putting the finishing touches on a comprehensive history of Fort Union, New Mexico. ∎